Tchaikovsky

Pyotr Ilyich Tchaikovsky in 1893: from the portrait by N. D. Kuznetsov

Tchaikovsky

*A new study
of the man and his music*

by

LAWRENCE and ELISABETH HANSON

CASSELL · LONDON

CASSELL & COMPANY LTD
35 Red Lion Square, London WC1
Melbourne, Sydney, Toronto
Johannesburg, Cape Town, Auckland

Printed in Great Britain by
Cox & Wyman Ltd., London, Fakenham and Reading
F. 165

Contents

CONTENTS

PART IV FAME

Illustrations

* Tchaikovsky Museum, Klin

Preface

Some time ago David Lloyd-Jones broadcast a most interesting talk on Tchaikovsky. The substance of his talk was this—that Tchaikovsky was not the namby-pamby neurotic recent biographers have made him out to be and that a great deal of his unplayed music ought to be heard regularly. In short, as man and composer Tchaikovsky has been misunderstood and underrated. Mr. Lloyd-Jones called for a definitive biography which would establish the composer as he really was.

When this broadcast was made we were in fact hard at work on just such a biography, as we told Mr. Lloyd-Jones, with the exception that we did not aim at a definitive one. In the first place we have not the equipment for it, in the second place we doubt whether such a thing can exist unless the writer of the biography happens to be as great an artist as the man he is writing about.

We have written on Tchaikovsky because we admire him and his work, because we think it high time that he was looked at afresh, and because we believe the large amount of new material—letters and reminiscences chiefly—made available in the Soviet Union within the past few years helps the new biographer to present a more rounded and more accurate picture of him.

At the risk of boring those who know the past history of Tchaikovsky studies we give a brief résumé for those who do not know how the present widespread impression about him came into existence. It began with a large biography (only translated into English in part) by Modest, the composer's brother. Modest was the family black sheep, charming, silly and a poor writer. That he intended to do honour to his dead brother is certain but he fell into the trap awaiting all biographers—instead of identifying himself with his subject he identified the subject with himself. This biography, which has set the standard for all others, is in essence a biography of Modest Tchaikovsky as he would have been had he possessed his brother's gifts. In spite of its great length—three volumes—Modest was obliged to select from a mass of material (Tchaikovsky was a prodigious letter-writer) and his selection was, unconsciously no doubt, made to show the composer as Modest preferred to think of him, a man much like himself. The Tchaikovsky radically opposed to Modest—the vigorous, plainspoken lover of the good things of life—was soft-pedalled almost out of existence. The text of letters was tampered with to this end, and the biographer's commentary all pointed the one way.

Naturally such a book by a man who knew Tchaikovsky so well had an enormous effect on public opinion. More harm was done—again unconsciously—when Rosa Newmarch published a shortened version of the Modest book in English. She went even further than Modest and bowdlerized the long quotes from Tchaikovsky letters so as to make him appear the gentle, nervous creature, feminine to a degree, that, following Modest, she believed him to be.

Then came the era of 'freedom' in the West when discussion of sex was all the rage and it was scarcely possible for two young men or two young women to spend a weekend together without being accused of an abnormal relationship. The trend was expressed in biography too, and later biographers of Tchaikovsky drew the conclusion that he was a homosexual, and, in line with the tendency of the age, came out with it as a fact suppressed by Modest and the early biographers who followed him. What they did not do was to relate this surmise (at this time it was no more) to the man and his music, at once so introvert and so masculine. Admittedly they lacked much of the evidence now available, yet the most cursory study of his work must surely have indicated that he could not have been what can only be described as a normal homosexual.

Hence the popular view of Tchaikovsky as a moral and physical weakling and the bewilderment of those unable to reconcile this picture with the music. Our conclusions, based on a study of all known material, show him in a different light, as the kind of man who would have written the kind of music we all know. The misconception appears to have arisen from the nature of the emphasis placed on his sex life by certain modern writers and from the fact that he was both a deeply feeling man and a man of his age to whom the shedding of tears was as natural as our modern restraint is unnatural. Likewise with his music; to think of a man as neurotic and self-tortured is to find those elements predominating in his work. The vigour, liveliness, fun, elegance, and complete command of the grand manner just as typical of Tchaikovsky are not so much over-looked as put into the back of the mind because the picture of the man does not square with such music.

We have gone back to the sources and present as clearly and as fairly as we are able a picture of a great man as he reveals himself. Biographers are usually faced with incomplete material and this faces them in turn with a dilemma; if they attempt to use their imagina-tion, based on a study of what material exists, to fill in the gaps, they are liable to be written off as non-serious romancers; if they sit on the fence they are called dull and cowardly; if they simply state the bare facts as they know them they are called lazy. But with Tchai-kovsky the position is reversed. The Russians have surpassed them-selves in thoroughness. His letters and letters to him (thousands in all) have been printed. His diaries have been printed. All his writings, including many recently discovered letters, are being printed—as we write, eight out of ten volumes have appeared. A small host of reminiscences by his contemporaries has been printed—again, many recently—and a number of manuscripts have been collected in libraries, as shown in the Bibliography. And as if this were not enough the indefatigable Soviet authorities have printed a book in which Tchaikovsky's movements for almost every day of his adult life have been carefully noted.

The gratified but rather stunned biographer, faced with this plethora of material, is also puzzled. If a Western reader was pre-sented with all Tchaikovsky's letters (still mostly untranslated) he would have to struggle through many volumes—struggle is the operative word, Tchaikovsky not being a great letter-writer—and if he ever reached the end of them he would still know only Tchai-kovsky as Tchaikovsky saw him, which is not at all the Tchaikovsky seen by others, let alone the sum of Tchaikovsky which no one man saw. The reminiscences (also mostly untranslated) are very valuable, but they too, like all reminiscences, are written from the point of view of the author who had been presented with one side of Tchai-kovsky.

All this material, including hundreds of not very exhilarating reviews written by Tchaikovsky, has to be studied by the bio-grapher who really wants to get at the truth, and long before he has reached the end he is wondering whether it might not be a good idea to advise the reader simply to listen to Tchaikovsky's music. Not just the music usually played but all the music he wrote. Then he might get to the real man. But how is the man or woman in-

terested in Tchaikovsky to do this? Under the present dispensation
he cannot begin to do it. In default of this we offer the present study.
We do not include new material—that is, material formerly un-
printed or untranslated—just because it is new but only if in our
opinion it gives body to the picture of the man. The translations are
our own. We have also discussed in simple terms some of the many
neglected works of Tchaikovsky in the hope that readers may wish
to study them. Scores are often to be found and there are also
recordings of some of these works.

We ought perhaps to mention that the only quotations from
Modest Tchaikovsky in this book are taken from his unfinished
autobiography. This is by far his most satisfactory work because he
died before he could 'polish' it and remove what he would have
considered inartistic and damning references.

Our thanks for many and various favours must go to the staffs of
the Soviet Embassy in London and the British Embassy in Moscow
(in particular Mr. N. Kiasashvili and Mr. A. Brooke-Turner), to
the curator of the Klin Museum, the librarians of the CSALA,
Moscow and GCMMC, the Music Library, the Reid Library, and
the National Library in Edinburgh, the British Museum and the
Central Music Library, to Mr. Lloyd-Jones for his generous assistance, to Professor Dennis Ward of Edinburgh University for helping
to elucidate the text of a Tchaikovsky letter, to Dr. Kurt Eulenburg
of Ernst Eulenburg Ltd. for his interest and provision of scores, and
Miss B. Carpenter for her usual noble response to the call.

L.H.
E.H.

1965

Part One

Preliminary

CHAPTER ONE

The Tchaikovskys

1840-4

'I am Russian, Russian, Russian!' Tchaikovsky wrote in a fury when he heard that he and his music were being traced to Polish sources. He did not mean that he had no Polish blood in his veins, on the contrary he admitted ruefully that he probably was of Polish descent; he meant that he personally loved Russia with a passion and that his music expressed Russia.

This acknowledged, he did not care one rouble where he came from. When he became famous some members of his family busied themselves by cooking up equally famous ancestors. He laughed at them; it was much more likely, he said, that the Tchaikovsky advertising a corn cure in a Moscow newspaper was a distant relative; it was a fairly common name in Russia and even commoner in Poland.

It will be gathered from this that genealogies did not interest him; he was concerned wholly with his own sympathies. Yet as far as can be seen, which is admittedly not very far, his ancestors seem to have been as Russian as his music and in their inconspicuous way proved it.

The first definitely-placed Tchaikovsky proved it in his own way. This was Fyodor Afanasyevich, lieutenant in the Cossacks. He was mortally wounded in the service of Peter the Great in a battle which could be said to have led directly to the rise of Russia as a great European power (and, much more important, as a strong cultural influence in the world), the battle of Poltava against the Swedes. His father-in-law was wholly Russian too and spent his

3

adult life in a very Russian occupation; he was one of the deacons in a Petersburg church.

The son of Fyodor Afanasyevich, Pyotr Fyodorovich, entered government service and became Chief of Police, first at Slobodsk, then at Glazov, in the province of Vyatka. He seems to have been a versatile man, for he won a local reputation as a healer of the sick. It is a curious coincidence, when one considers the enormous size of Russia, that this grandfather of the composer held office within fifty miles of the town in which Tchaikovsky was to be born. Vyatka, half-way to Siberia, had no special connexion with the Tchaikovsky family and as certainly did not attract them—it was remote, primitive, unlovely; sheer chance was to bring Tchaikovsky's father back to it many years later.

On the maternal side the patriotic note is repeated as well as the connexion with the Cossacks. The woman Pyotr Fyodorovich married, Anastasia Posokhova, was a daughter of one of the many officers in the army of Catherine the Great who were slaughtered by the famous Cossack rebel Pugachev whilst trying to hold outlying frontier posts for the queen. The couple had many children and the youngest, Ilya Petrovich, born in 1795, was the father of the composer.

Ilya Petrovich Tchaikovsky was a brown-haired, blue-eyed man of medium height with a fine forehead and strong nose. His appearance was not remarkable—the most noteworthy thing about it was the quiff into which he brushed his hair. This gave him an aggressive air, misleadingly, for he was the mildest of men, good-natured and extremely sociable. He has been scurvily treated by the biographers of his famous son and for this, as for more serious errors of judgement, one has to look no further than the biography by Modest Tchaikovsky. In this book, on which succeeding writers have relied heavily and too often uncritically, Modest says his father worked hard and efficiently but sneers at his slow progress: 'It took him twenty years to attain the rank of lieutenant-colonel.' It only needed a reference to Ilya Petrovich's failure to master the flute in his youth to put the unfortunate man firmly into the category of unworthy sires of genius.

It is clear that he was no great shakes culturally; apart from the abortive attempt to learn the flute, he knew and relished a good tune and read the romantic novels of his day with great enjoyment, and that was about all he could claim in this particular line. However, to be weak in musical appreciation and to have a mediocre taste in books is not necessarily to be a nonentity, nor does it follow that Ilya Petrovich had nothing to hand on to his son. In the event, he passed on one of the greatest of gifts.

Apparently he did not distinguish himself as a student in the School of Mining, from which he emerged at twenty-two with a diploma in engineering. This was in 1815. Not until 1837—another twenty-two years—as we are told *ad nauseam* was he promoted to the rank of lieutenant-colonel and given an appointment as chief inspector of the government mines and factories at Votkinsk.

There is no dispute about these facts; what is in dispute is the conclusion drawn from them. To get your first important appointment at the age of forty-two is, in the eyes of Modest and his followers, to confess yourself a failure. But there is another interpretation of the facts which comes much closer to the truth. This is, that Ilya Petrovich's slow promotion demonstrated that he was one of the most remarkable civil servants in his country; his leisurely advancement was not because of inefficiency or laziness but because he laboured under the handicap of being an honest and incorruptible man. He did not curry favour, he would not lobby or smarm, he neither offered nor accepted bribes. He was that rarity, a sanguine and amiable man with strong principles. No wonder that he took twenty-two years to become a lieutenant-colonel; the wonder is, in the Russia of that time, that he ever arrived at such a rank.

It is doubtful whether anyone, least of all his own children, has done him justice; persistent amiability is a heavy burden to shoulder. But, as with his unheralded grandfather who gave his life for his country, this is also not nothing, and Tchaikovsky was to owe most of his considerable social success to his father. In his turn he was to be esteemed as a man of honour and, in his later years particularly, as a much-prized guest at any social gathering—and this not simply on account of his fame but of his invincible good-nature.

When Ilya was posted to Votkinsk in 1837 he at once came into his own. This town on the border of the provinces of Vyatka and Perm was just then developing fast. The iron from its mines was made on the spot into locomotives and wagons for the trans-Siberian railway which would pass within one hundred miles of Votkinsk and for ships for the Kama, the Volga, and the great Caspian canal. It was a busy and flourishing place, a typical product of the industrial revolution then beginning to show its first signs in backward Russia, and its new chief of mines took control of both the business and social life as to the manner born. He became the most important citizen of Votkinsk, having his special police powers, his seat on the bench, and his own Cossack guard.

He rose to the responsibility. The town flourished and so, in its admittedly limited way, did the social life which more and more centred on the Tchaikovsky house. There the latest music from Petersburg or Moscow was heard, there one found the best whist players, the best food, the best wine, and the liveliest conversation. It became a little haven of culture and good living with style in that far-flung manufacturing outpost of the Russian empire. People competed for the honour of an invitation.

Ilya Petrovich was the life and soul of the Tchaikovsky parties as he was the driving force of the state mines. By the time he arrived in Votkinsk his brown hair was greying and he had developed a heavy moustache, but his blue eyes were as gay as ever and his genius for entertainment had never been so masterly. Some people never expand until left on their own; he was in his element in this semi-barbarous mining town on the edge of nowhere, cheerful, sociable, a born good mixer. What he could not and did not attempt to provide was the cultural side of these gatherings of Votkinsk notables. This was left to Aleksandra Andreyevna.

Aleksandra Andreyevna was not his first wife. He had married in 1827, when he was thirty-two, a Russian of German descent, Maria Karlovna Keiser. She died two years later, soon after the birth of her only child, Zinaida, and Ilya Petrovich married again four years later. No doubt he wished to provide a home for his little daughter but he was, besides, a domesticated man and a lover of women. His second choice went to the other extreme; this time he chose a Russian of French descent.

Aleksandra Andreyevna could reasonably claim to be pre-dominantly French. Her father, the Marquis André d'Assier, had fled from France during the Revolution and, marrying a Russian, decided to make his home there despite the restoration in his own country. He was a man of taste and learning with a passion for the arts and brought up his two girls in this atmosphere of culture. His brother, who fled France with him, shared his tastes and was a gifted singer. D'Assier's sensibility seems to have run to excess at times—he was a victim of occasional attacks of epilepsy—but his children escaped the malady and one of them, at least, the sensibility too. Yekaterina Andreyevna had a real gift and as Madame Schobert had become very well known in Petersburg as an operatic singer; her sister, Aleksandra Andreyevna, showed her upbringing in more

conventional fashion, that is to say she sang and played the pianoforte adequately as every Petersburg society girl was honour bound
to do but without any sense of a vocation and, it appears, without
much feeling.

In the Tchaikovsky house at Votkinsk, however, she had next to
no competition and what she lacked in technique and fire she made
up for in grandeur. If Ilya Petrovich made his parties go, his wife
gave them the cachet which made the townsfolk eager to be invited.
She was an imposing woman of twenty-four when they settled at
Votkinsk in 1837, not so much good-looking as overwhelming—
tall, full-bosomed, with a regal carriage, dark hair piled high and
large dark eyes under heavy brows.

It is not surprising if the guests failed to notice that these eyes
lacked expressiveness, like their hostess's piano playing; she had a
distinguished manner, was gracious, and brought to the town an
appearance and clothes of a kind it rarely saw. Her performance at
the piano was commonly the crux of the evening's entertainment
and she was much sought after and much praised for it. Her real
beauty seems to have escaped everyone but her second son, and this
is not so surprising as it may sound, for though compliments on her
playing and singing abounded, no one but this son stared fascinated
at the keyboard the whole time she was playing. 'I couldn't even
begin to imagine hands which would compare with my mother's,'
he used to say years later.

It might reasonably be expected that children of the capable, kind,
and lively Ilya Petrovich and the majestically musical Aleksandra
Andreyevna, brought up in the midst of a whirl of musical and
literary gatherings, would show signs of distinction. The first living
child (a girl had died at birth) would have disappointed such expecta-
tions; Nikolai Ilyich, born the year after the arrival at Votkinsk, was
a stolid and rather lazy boy apparently without a spark of his father's
bonhomie or his mother's dignity and without any special gift. He
was also without malice and that is as much as can be said for him as
a child.

The second child, born two years later, on 7 May 1840, was quite
a different proposition. Pyotr Ilyich, his parents (and, indeed,
everybody in the house but one) thought, had altogether too much
sensibility, but there was no denying that he was gifted.

The exception was the third child, Aleksandra Ilyinishna, born
two years after Pyotr Ilyich. This, the only living daughter, worshipped Petya, and could see no wrong in him. The relationship

between this brother and sister was to last until death and is one of the most beautiful examples of its kind. Aleksandra Ilyinishna was, in fact, more level-headed than her brother, and was to spend much of her adult life trying to restrain and explain away the self-reproaches which he insisted on levelling at himself; their correspondence is always moving, even when the reader cannot suppress a smile at the brother's exaggerations, because it exposes complete love and faith on both sides, feelings which faltered once only in fifty years of intimacy.

At Votkinsk the relationship was in its infancy in every respect; little Sasha regarded Petya with awe as well as devotion and was too young to understand that her god could have weaknesses. What she did see clearly enough was that she had a rival (though she would not have put it in those terms) and that the rival was supreme; the greater part of Petya's love was given to his mother. True enough, he had plenty left for his father and brothers and sister—never was there a child with such a capacity for affection—but the human mainspring of his life from the very first moment he drew breath was his mother. Sasha was too young and too nice to perceive that her adored brother was worshipping before something approaching a graven image, but, love being what it is, perhaps neither he nor she would have acted otherwise even had they been gifted with adult insight. Aleksandra Andreyevna was a cold woman and accepted the devotion of everyone in the house with composure. To the impetuous, fiery Petya this composure could be chilling and often was; his mother did not care for warm hugs if a gown was in danger, and spent much of her limited time with the children repressing Petya's ardour. Fortunately for him, as for all warm-hearted people, to love was almost enough and the occasional response kept him happy for days.

He had, besides, another love—passion would be the more correct word—which was to govern his life, the love of music. Yet even this was in his early years to be connected indissolubly with his mother. It is a little ironic to reflect that the tepid performances of Aleksandra Andreyevna at the pianoforte and her correct but lifeless rendering of the sentimental ballads of the day could rouse a genuine musician to a frenzy of admiration. Wherever Petya got his genius it was certainly not from his mother, yet she, unknowingly and unwillingly (for she pooh-poohed his extravagance), fostered the genius in him. She was widely considered the leading musician in the town, a reputation which she accepted as her due. She was not averse to the praise she received every time she played or sang. Only little Petya's reactions displeased her. Whether this was because she knew in her heart that she was not what he thought, or, more likely, disliked his outbursts as smacking of the open-hearted plebs, we shall never know. Whatever her thoughts, destiny was too much for her; she could and did try to discourage him, but in vain; in her dull, stately way she was to be the harbinger of greatness.

She, of course, was chiefly concerned to see that he, like the rest of her children, behaved well—that is, did not bother or embarrass her—and fitted himself for the civilization of Moscow or Petersburg (return to which was one of her chief concerns) by mastering his lessons and learning the even more important rules governing the man who was *comme il faut* in the best society.

Her reactions could scarcely have differed more from her daughter's. Sasha was not particularly musical and considered Petya's feats on the piano with the almost indifference of the loyal subject who knows that her king will excel himself at anything he chooses to take up. What she loved about this brother was his loving kindness; his hatred of cruelty, his wish to see good in all, his immediate response to affection whether from her, his mother, his nanya, the cook, or any of the serfs who worked on the estate. In his small electric body he was, to her, love personified, and love was her god. That, too, would have been Ilya Petrovich's view, given with a genial laugh, for it was the father in the boy, a hundred times sensitized, that young Sasha worshipped.

The Tchaikovsky family at Votkinsk was completed by the birth of another boy, Ippolit Ilyich, in 1843, one year after Aleksandra, and not very long afterwards the whole family was photographed. The photograph is instructive, as so many were in those days of true artists behind the camera. On the right (the left facing the camera) is Ilya Petrovich, left hand on thigh, right hand pressing his latest born close to him. His quiff has turned grey, like the rest of his crinkled head, and a large greying moustache droops below his lower lip. Ippolit is little more than a pair of wondering eyes, but Nikolai, standing next to him, is seen in the round. His pleasant but rather blank face conveys next to nothing of the person, which was right enough, because then and for some time afterwards he was next to nothing. Beside him, five or six inches taller, stands the half-sister Zinaida with an arm round her stepmother's shoulder. Zinaida shows signs of self-possession (she was then well into her

9

teens) and a certain air of superciliousness. Her dark hair is parted in the centre in the fashion of that time. Her mouth is slightly alarming.

Sitting on a stool below her, with an elbow resting on her mother's knee, is Aleksandra Ilyinishna. As one hand is pressed against her cheek, Sasha's face is a little distorted. The widely spaced eyes are a feature of her face even then and she is looking at the photographer with some apprehension. Aleksandra Andreyevna, sitting in the seat of honour, has what is known as the Florence Nightingale hair style, her black hair pressed down over the ears under a lace cap. The fine eyes are there for all to see, as is the strong nose and somewhat discontented mouth. But the general impression of her face is of a placidity which owes nothing to the resolution of inward struggles and almost everything to self-satisfaction. Her large build is also clear, and the well-shaped hands.

The group is completed by the subject of this book. He stands on the right of his mother with one arm crooked round hers. His long hair looks darker than it really is and has been swept off the forehead comprehensively. The mouth is wide and, like the mouths of all painfully sensitive people, looks indeterminate and throws up the other features—the strong nose, the brilliant wide-spaced eyes, and, above all, the massive forehead. He was then only eight years old and anything but handsome, but one glance at the photograph is enough; of the seven faces his is the only outstanding one; the Tchaikovsky swan stands out from the geese. That he is pitifully vulnerable to all the assaults of feeling is plain enough; that he is exceptionally intelligent is as plain. The course of his life could almost be foretold from this one portrait. Rarely, perhaps, has genius shown itself so clearly and at so early an age.

CHAPTER TWO

Fanny Durbach

1844-8

It is now necessary to go back a year or two to introduce a young woman who is notable in the history of Tchaikovsky in two important directions: she was to influence the little boy profoundly in his formative years, and her reminiscences give a clear picture of the Tchaikovsky household at this time and specially of Petya. Apart from the occasional recollections of Nikolai Ilyich, Aleksandra Ilyinishna, Ilya Petrovich, and Tchaikovsky himself passed on in later years to Modest and 'brushed up' by him, these reminiscences are the only trustworthy record we have of the composer as a child.

In the late summer of 1844 Aleksandra Andreyevna went on a visit to Petersburg. This time she had another purpose besides the wish to stay with her sister and enjoy a few weeks of the civilized life she had been brought up in; she was looking for a governess. There was no school in Votkinsk to which she could send the children without loss of face, and as the birth of Ippolit Ilyich was only a few months away, Aleksandra Andreyevna dismissed the last vague thoughts of trying her hand at educating the six-year-old Nikolai.

The girl she found was, of course, French. Fanny Durbach came from Montbéliard, on the border of Alsace and Franche-Comté, she was twenty-two and was typical of her nation; that is to say, she was efficient, sensible, cool, and her romantic leanings were kept well under control. She needed all the sangfroid she could muster as the journey to Votkinsk spun out its dreary and uncomfortable weeks for the greater part of a thousand miles east of Petersburg.

During this apparently interminable procession of alarming ferries across huge rivers, of post-houses with their fleas and prolonged waits in smoky rooms for fresh horses, Aleksandra Andreyevna may well have told Fanny with a smile of the letter she had had from her husband informing her that Sasha and Petya had between them composed a song in her honour called 'Our Mama in Petersburg'. Petya was then four and a half and Sasha not quite two, so her contribution must have been on the slender side. The children were waiting feverishly to sing the composition to their mother as a kind of hymn of thanksgiving for her arrival home.

It is doubtful whether this significant feat—the first mention we have of Petya as composer—would have stirred Fanny Durbach. She was not musical and Petya was not supposed to be her pupil. In any case she must have been busy fighting her dismay as she found herself jerked inexorably mile by mile into what appeared to be a savage wilderness of forest, river, and plain. Votkinsk, when they at last came to the end of their 22-day journey, did not please her; it was noisy, dirty, and, as far as the workers went, drunken; there was scarcely a decent building in the town, the streets were rivers of mud, the shops pitiful.

The Tchaikovsky house reassured her somewhat. It was one of the few stone houses in Votkinsk, with an impressive pedimented first-floor gable and the then extraordinary luxury in the far provinces of second-floor rooms. The main apartments were large and very comfortably furnished—or overfurnished, as the habit then was in well-to-do families—and life lived in them was, in the eyes of the governess, absolute bliss, with an abundance of food and wine served by a large staff of serfs. The garden seems not to have been in any way extraordinary—Votkinsk was a comparatively treeless place and as flat as a board—but had its water and arbours and flower gardens bounded by vegetable gardens, orchards, and pastures. By Russian standards it was uninteresting, by Votkinsk standards almost paradisal.

Aleksandra Andreyevna was too lazy and too much of a fine lady to concern herself much with the running of the house or with the people living in it. She had her daily half-hours with the children dutifully grouped round her, she devoured novels and sweetmeats, she spent day after day like the squire's wife in Gogol's *The Barouche*, who would glance in the mirror for a moment and was still gazing a couple of hours later, having nothing better to do. Only in the evenings did she come to life. At the inevitable party she

would speak with calm authority on the work of the latest poets
and novelists to reach town and wind up the entertainment by com-
plying graciously with insistent requests for a song or pianoforte
piece.

Such a mistress gave the new arrival great scope, and the strong-
minded Fanny took her chance. She was soon mistress in most
practical senses of the word and earned Aleksandra Andreyevna's
gratitude by taking the children off her hands. She had been engaged
to teach Nikolai and a niece of Ilya Petrovich, Lydya Vladimirovna
Tchaikovskaya (who after the manner of those days had come to
visit and was staying more or less indefinitely), but soon attracted
Petya and even the tiny Sasha. These two competed for the honour
of being included with the older children—or, it would be truer to
say, whatever Petya did Sasha must copy—and it was not long
before Petya had wormed his way insidiously into the classes.

Fanny remained stern but was secretly very glad of him; Nikolai
was lazy and dull, Lydya 'difficult', but this younger child was quite
another matter. Indeed, Fanny's first reactions to Petya were those
of a dismay not far from horror, he was so sensitive. Yet he was
obviously gifted as the others were not, and all the pedagogue in her
rose up in determination to save these gifts from their almost certain
destruction by hypersensitiveness.

She gave way to his importunities, in themselves absurdly exag-
gerated, she thought, in the mood of a rescuer, and saw herself as
the saviour of high gifts, perhaps even of genius. At first she had
no idea what she was taking on, and for a short time tried to treat
him like the others. Only for a short time, as she herself reports.
'One day the two brothers failed to resolve a problem I had set them.
I reproached them vigorously, drawing a picture of their unhappy
father forced to sacrifice himself to make it possible for his sons to
have a good education, and so on. Nikolai heard me out to the end
with complete indifference, then went on with his games as if
nothing had happened. Petya remained sombre until supper. When
he was undressing for bed and I had forgotten all about the incident
he suddenly burst into tears, began to insist that he loved his father
deeply, that he was filled with gratitude towards both parents, and
reproached me for injustice. I had the greatest difficulty in calming
him, for his sensibility in everything passed all bounds of the
imagination . . . He was truly *un enfant de verre*.'

This judgement too she had to revise soon afterwards. Her porcelain child who needed protection from the world was missing one

day. He was not in the house, not in the garden. There was a hue and cry round the town. Eventually he was found smilingly returning from the poorer quarter of Votkinsk. Questioned angrily, he explained himself. In the kitchen where he liked to pass some part of each day (and where he was truly welcome as the rare 'little Master' who neither bullied nor tormented nor despised people who dared not answer back) he heard the servants talking about a cat who had just kittened. Every kitten but one had found a home. That one was to be destroyed. He went out, snatched up the kitten and, with it in his arms, toured the neighbourhood, calling at every house to beg the occupants to take it in. At last his pleas were successful and he came back triumphant.

This incident showed Fanny that she was dealing with that rare case, a sensitive child who had the courage of his convictions and would master even his paralysing shyness when need arose. And what a need! In the Russia of that day the lives of human beings were regarded by almost everyone with complaisance; floggings were a daily event, servants were freely beaten for the lightest offence, imprisonment and exile to the death in life in Siberia did not cause an eyebrow to rise. And here was a little boy who could not bear cruelty to anything and still less the taking of life, even the life of a kitten.

From that moment Fanny began to treat him with particular care. As she was the kind of logical woman, true to her nationality, who could not endure unreason, she looked for the cause of Petya's abnormal sensitiveness and soon found it. His ridiculous passion for music was at the bottom of the trouble. From the moment of her arrival, even before he became her pupil officially, she had watched, unwillingly fascinated, as the child displayed what she saw as an insane longing for music. He would stand by the piano absolutely silent and absorbed every time and all the time his mother played, and the moment she stopped he would beg to be lifted on to the stool. When his request was granted, he would at once begin to pick out the notes of the pieces his mother had been playing and would stay there, trying to perfect his recollection of the music for as long as his presence on the stool was suffered.

But to Fanny the greatest enemy to the development of the sensible in Petya was not his mother's playing but the orchestrion. As its name suggests, this was a superior type of musical-box, the superiority lying in the provision of stops which enabled varied orchestral effects to be obtained. The Tchaikovsky orchestrion spent most of its time in the children's play- and work-room and was rarely silent; an entranced Petya had to be dragged from manipulation of the instrument and Fanny was soon practically at screaming point. The repertoire was limited: airs from Bellini, Donizetti, and Rossini and from *Don Giovanni*—but to Petya they were all-sufficient. As after his mother's playing, he would dash from orchestrion to piano, trying to reproduce the tunes and something of the orchestral harmonies. He said long afterwards that the instrument drew him irrevocably to opera and that his overmastering devotion to Mozart began with it. To Fanny it was not only a bore but a threat to the mental stability of a promising child. She did what she could to discourage him, but he was stubborn, had always finished his lessons long before the elder couple, and was very quick to take advantage of the slightest opportunity to steal off to piano or orchestrion; she had only to turn a head or leave the room for a moment and he was off his chair and across the room, making music.

At last she forbade him absolutely to play during the hour, after supper, when he, Nikolai and Lydya and Sasha gathered round to tell her what they had done since lesson time and often to listen to some edifying tale. The ban at this time was particularly frustrating to him because darkness seemed to enlarge his ready imagination and he had begun to improvise on the piano, to invent new and gorgeous harmonies and tunes of every description. However, the governess was firm, watched him closely, and did not let him leave his chair.

The sequel might have suggested to a less determined young woman that she was wasting her time. Petya could not play the piano after supper but nothing on earth short of binding his hands would prevent him from playing music; he could not have the notes he struck out of the piano but at a pinch he could do without them, for they were in his head before the piano made a sound. Confined to his chair, he played with his fingers on any smooth surface near by; that, he thought, could annoy no one, since no one but him would hear a note.

But what notes he heard, what superb chords, what magnificent harmonies! He became intoxicated, he saw nothing, he was all sound, ravished away from the mundane play-room. When the smooth surface was a table, for instance, no harm could come of his disobedience except an occasional reproof for inattention when he failed to answer a question. But one day his chair happened to be next a window. No other smooth surface was within reach so he began to play on the window. At first he drummed lightly, then, as the imagined music swelled to a great climax, the drumming grew into a clatter, the clatter a ferocious pounding. Before Fanny could stop him the inevitable had happened, the glass broke, his hand plunged through, and in a second he was a badly frightened child holding out a hand streaming with blood.

For a time the shock kept him obedient. Then his parents staged a special musical evening in honour of a Polish pianist, Mashovsky, who was visiting the town. Mashovsky, of course, played Chopin, and Petya, carried away, imitated him in two mazurkas. He played the unknown pieces with such brio—his ability even so early to re-produce music on a first hearing was startling—that the honoured visitor embraced him publicly and hailed him as a musician of great promise.

The piano was scarcely silent all that evening until late but the boy went out long before the end. Fanny, seeing him go, thought with pleasure that he had more sense than she would have given him credit for; she had been prepared for strenuous pleas to be allowed to stay. Two hours later she herself went up to bed. Looking into Petya's room as usual she was amazed to find him still dressed. He was sitting on his bed weeping heartbrokenly.

'What is the matter, Petya?' she asked in alarm.

'Oh, the music, the music!' was all she could hear through the sobs.

She persevered, and at last he cried, clinging to her, 'Save me from it, Mademoiselle Fanny, save me! It won't leave me alone. It's here . . . here!' And he struck his forehead with one hand.

Fanny was not one to ignore an appeal of this kind. She herself went as far as to imagine her little favourite losing his mind because his head was filled with sound. But she had learned wisdom; she no longer forbade him to play or tried to belittle music. On the contrary, she encouraged his parents to regularize the passion for music by employing a local teacher—whether she was astute enough to realize that such a teacher could not compare with herself one does not know—and she tried to gain her way by flattery and tact.

Her ruse succeeded. The music teacher, Maria Markovna Palchi-kova, a freed serf who gave lessons as much out of gratitude to Ilya Petrovich as anything else, was a nice young woman and a hard worker, but her knowledge of music was slender and her ability even more restricted—Tchaikovsky afterwards said that he could not remember her being able to play anything from beginning to end. And when, inevitably, she was forced to sight-read she made such heavy weather of it that Petya used to take her place on the stool and read the piece for her.

Naturally, the lessons became rather farcical—more a case of Petya teaching Maria Markovna than the other way round—but though set hours for lessons and practice did not entirely stem his wish to play music all day long, they did have the reassuring effect Fanny had hoped for. To have what was virtually a grown-up pupil on his hands steadied him (for though he sometimes made fun of Maria Markovna he was too affectionate to go far) and the changed status of music calmed him too. It ceased to be a forbidden pleasure, frowned on by his beloved Mademoiselle Fanny, and by degrees the hysterical element went out of his regard for it and his true feeling took charge.

Rival studies had also appeared. For all her level-headedness Fanny had her weaknesses and one was for the romantic poets and novelists, the poets particularly. She soon cast Petya for the part of poet. Except for his very healthy appetite he looked and behaved like the popular idea of the poet; he was extremely untidy, not at all keen on washing himself, and had never been known to brush his hair; above all, he was incurably romantic. She did all she could to encourage an ambition to write.

Within a year or two of her arrival Petya was a middling French scholar and not a bad German one (she was bi-lingual), outdistancing the sluggish Nikolai, and had been introduced to all the romantics, whom he read and copied voraciously. Another year, and he was writing essays, mainly on French subjects though stubbornly refusing to acknowledge that the French could be in any way superior to the Russians, and eventually breaking into verse. Already his patriotism had reached a pitch of fervour. Fanny one day came across him with an atlas before him. It was open at the map of Europe and he was busy alternately kissing the large splash of colour denoting Russia and spitting on the other colours to the west of it.

She reproached him; knowing that he could always be led through the affections, was indeed wholly governed by them, she pretended to be hurt: if he spat on the map of France, she said, he was spitting on his Fanny; he ought to be ashamed of himself.

He had an answer: 'Don't scold me, Fanny. There's no need. Can't you see my left arm is covering France?'

His first efforts at verse were nevertheless on French subjects: on one of Fanny's goddesses, Saint Joan, and on the lost Dauphin of the Temple. Behind them came a string of romantic themes interspersed with intensely patriotic poems.

This outburst of literature at Votkinsk did not do more than tone down the passion for music. Music still held his heart; it was merely held in check, that was all. But when a young woman like Fanny drew tempting pictures of him as the poet Russia was waiting for, a modern Pushkin, or, if that failed, at least one of the great modern essayists and critics, no child, not even a Tchaikovsky, could pooh-pooh it.

One can scarcely doubt the result of this propaganda even if Fanny had been left to carry it to an end—she had met her match—but she was not given the chance. Soon after Petya's eighth birthday came a sudden, horrid parting.

Fanny had not taken his mother's place—there was room in this child's heart for innumerable loves—curiously enough, her coming had innocently elevated the passion for his mother. The more Aleksandra Andreyevna retired placidly from her children's affairs, the more Petya yearned after her. The cold always have the advantage over the warm, and Aleksandra Andreyevna proved it at Votkinsk by having less and less to do with Petya. Since the coming of Fanny she had become the great unattainable and her unearned reward was increased love.

But though forced to play second fiddle to his mother, Fanny had established her niche and a very powerful one it was, compounded of fear, respect, admiration, and the sheer animal love of a small boy for an attractive young woman. Life without her seemed inconceivable. Then, abruptly, she was gone, and his secure, ordered life dissolved into chaos.

CHAPTER THREE

Child
1848-50

Fanny Durbach had done Petya a great service; how great can be seen if the true meaning of her 'porcelain child' is understood. She did not mean that Petya was at all like the sensitive child found in so many modern autobiographies. He was, in fact, at the opposite pole from them, a child who loved his food, his walks, his games, his dirt. He loved nature, not with the kind of love shown by perpetually brooding in and over it but by using it for what it had to give a child. He was not a little tough nor was he precious, he planted flowers as well as liking the look and smell of them, he romped with animals as well as sitting quietly with them. He was, in short, in all external things what is known somewhat absurdly as the normal child.

Where he differed sharply from this hypothetical creature was in his reactions to art and specially to music. In this he was what the world calls unbalanced, and Fanny's alarm is comprehensible. Had he been left to himself during these vital years from four to eight, or to the not very tender mercies of an indifferent or stupid governess he might have echoed the history of the man he so obviously resembled, his maternal grandfather. Luckily for himself and the world he met Fanny. She could not change his nature but she could and did steady him, and the threat of epilepsy disappeared for ever.

As events turned out, the next four years seemed to have put him back where he started, but in spite of all their miseries he managed to come out of them sane and healthy, and livelier than ever. For this he had to thank the years with Fanny and correspondence with her afterwards.

The trouble began with his father. Ilya Petrovich had the faults of his virtues. The border line between trustfulness and credulity is hard to place, and his born optimism, which made him such a nice man, more than once landed him and his family in difficulties. Such an event took place in 1848. A Moscow friend urged him to retire from government service, promising him an excellent post in that city. Aleksandra Andreyevna and Zinaida Ilyinishna (who had joined the family at Votkinsk) were both more than anxious to get back to civilization again, so the good-natured Ilya Petrovich took his friend at his word, resigned his position with the rank of major-general and, in the autumn, packed up and left.

The entire family with its bulky belongings trapesed the six hundred miles or so to Moscow only to find that the friend had had second thoughts, had taken the job himself and would not budge from it.

To Petya by far the worst aspect of this calamity was what it led to—the loss of Fanny. It seems that the Tchaikovsky parents had intended to send their boys to a Moscow school rather than leave them in the care of a governess (though Sasha and Ippolit would still have needed one) but the false friend settled the matter; money immediately became precious and Fanny left to join a family of noble rank. Petya, of course, connected the one event with the other, knowing nothing about the school plan or refusing to believe it.

This serious blow—the loss of Fanny to Petya and the loss of an income to his parents—was followed almost immediately by a cholera scare. Because of the wretched hygiene or lack of it in the cities cholera was the most deadly of all diseases in Russia then and for long afterwards, the doctors being little more efficient than the hygiene. Tens of thousands died from it every year. When a servant went down with it in the apartment the Tchaikovskys had taken for the moment, Aleksandra Andreyevna panicked, not without reason, and insisted that they move on to Petersburg. Which they did. Ilya Petrovich rented a house on Vasilyevsky Ostrov and prepared cheerfully to find another post; the possibility of failure did not occur to him.

This search for work, added to the general chaos in the home after two rapid removals, had a further regrettable effect on Petya. His only powerful anodyne to the loss of Fanny and the only acceptable comfort when she had gone was his mother. But Aleksandra Andreyevna was preoccupied by one thing after another: the removals, the setting up of a new home in Petersburg and finally the use of her charm and social influence to help her husband meet men of consequence or, when he had brought them to the house, to entertain them attractively. It was not a work for which Ilya Petrovich had any aptitude. His wife, more worldly than he, possessed a fairly large acquaintance which she hurriedly took up again. She visited much and entertained much, understanding better than her husband that the secret of getting a good job is to appear not to be in need of it.

All this, together with a natural laziness and the effect of four years of freedom from intimate contact with her children, made her virtually unapproachable. She consigned them to the care of Zinaida.

This half-sister was no friend to Petya. She had joined the family at Votkinsk two years earlier, after she had graduated at the Yekaterinsk Institute at Petersburg. Like her stepmother and more than her, she took a very dim view of Votkinsk; for a seventeen-year-old girl just acclimatized to the bustle and parties of Petersburg and longing for more, it must have seemed the most savage of backwaters, without a presentable or at least marriageable man in it. Apparently she had not even the mediocre musical gifts of her stepmother to help her to shine in what society there was, or perhaps Aleksandra Andreyevna, only sixteen years older, made sure that she had no rival inside the family: the dress Zinaida is wearing in the family photograph of 1848 certainly suggests that she was being kept younger than her age.

There was no possibility that a disgruntled Zinaida would look kindly either on Fanny or Fanny's pride and joy. She would see him as a spoilt and boring little prig and his French and German and music triumphs as material for sarcasm. Her rejection of his instinctive offer of affection must have been a considerable shock to a child whose impulse was to love everyone, and who had never known unkindness other than the sort he could not recognize, his mother's calm refusal to allow the hugs that he would have longed to give her regardless of the dress she was wearing.

Little is known about Zinaida but, with every allowance made for the position she found herself in at Votkinsk and again at Petersburg, what she was can be deduced with fair assurance from the fact that Tchaikovsky never spoke or wrote of her or attempted to see her in later years. From a man so affectionate and with such a fanatically strong sense of family loyalty, this silent condemnation is inescapable; either Zinaida was not a very nice woman or she had treated him badly in his childhood.

Her method of caring for the children in Petersburg can be imagined. By the time Petya was sent to school with Nikolai late in 1848, the loss of Fanny, the absence of his mother for all practical purposes, and the nature of the few attentions Zinaida paid him, had reduced him to despair, as his letters to Fanny demonstrate alarmingly.

The Schmelling Boarding School proved immediately to the distraught child (still only eight and a half years old) that a worse fate than government by an unloving Zinaida existed only a few streets away. He was utterly wretched. He and Nikolai were comprehensively mocked by the other boys as country hicks—in clothing, manners, and attainments. Nikolai took the bullying with his accustomed stolidity, Petya collapsed as he was always to collapse in the face of motiveless hatred: boy or man, Tchaikovsky could never accept evil as original sin.

In certain directions he could normally have held his own with the boys; though younger than most, his French was reasonable, his knowledge of history and German good, and his gift for composition of essays considerable. But all these gifts vanished in the face of malice and he stood confessed as a dunce and a weakling. Bad marks led to homework—for the brothers attended as day boys—of fantastic length; often he (and Nikolai too, for different reasons) worked until after midnight, only to be on their way to school again at half past seven the next morning.

Petya had one substantial compensation for this run of misfortune; his parents engaged a music teacher for him. This man, Filippov, was a true professor of music, though of no particular eminence, and under his care Petya began to forge ahead. It was, after all, the first professional attention he had had in his life; a short life in years, admittedly, less than nine, but more than half of it had been devoted to music with an intensity and feeling so much stronger than most of us ever know that it is almost impossible for even the true music lover to imagine.

As a counterpoise to the savagery of school life in Russia at that time, contact with a civilized man was absolute heaven to Petya. Had he been allowed to continue his lessons with Filippov he could have fought all his troubles, school, Zinaida, and the withdrawal of

his mother. But it was not to be; bad luck pursued him; he and
Nikolai both caught measles and he could not throw it off. The
puzzled doctor, who had no conception of what his little patient had
been through since leaving Votkinsk, recommended a complete
break from work, and the Tchaikovsky parents took the advice so
literally that they stopped music lessons as well as school.

Petya's feelings are best not lingered on. His mother complained to Fanny, who was hearing her side of the question, that
nothing could be done with the child and blamed him for malinger-
ing. Stupidity could scarcely go further, nor could un-Russianness.
One Frenchwoman was writing to another and revealing the
limitations of their nation.

In May 1849, Ilya Petrovich managed to get a new post; it was a
good one, the management of an ironworks, but once again it took
him and his family into the wilds, this time to Alapayevsk in Perm
province. Alapayevsk was three hundred miles farther east than
Votkinsk and on the Asiatic side of the Urals, but to Petya the move
was a blessing; he could once more get into the country he loved, he
had books (Fanny was still propelling him enthusiastically by post
through French literature and he was exploring the Russians for
himself, Gogol especially) and he had a piano. He also had Zinaida,
a Zinaida furious that she had been dragged into a social desert for
the second time, but found an ally in that typically Russian phenomenon, a dependent relative. This was Anastasia Vasilyevna Popova,
daughter of Ilya Petrovich's sister, come to help Zinaida run the
house until Aleksandra Andreyevna, who was pregnant, felt able to
take charge again.

Anastasia Vasilyevna was an old ally of Petya though by no means
a blind one. 'When we received your letter, dear Fanny,' she wrote,
'Petyenka read it aloud and cried a lot. He loves you very much but
now that his health has improved his moods are a thing of the past.'
Aleksandra Andreyevna had withdrawn from all but the lightest of
contacts with duty but occasionally permitted Petya to accompany
her in songs. He remembered one of them, 'The Nightingale',
learned with Filippov, to the end of his life as marking moments
when he and his mother became as nearly as possible one person.
For the most part, however, she left him and the other two (Nikolai
had been put into the School of Mining in Petersburg) to the care
of Zinaida.

One feels sympathy with Zinaida—it was a dull life for a girl who
wanted parties and dances at which she could meet attractive and

eligible young men—but Petya, Sasha, and Polya suffered even more, for they had not the satisfaction of being treated as a grown-up with free entrée to such parties as Alapayevsk afforded. There were plenty of these, as at Votkinsk, but for the elders only.

Eventually what seems a fairly obvious solution to an onlooker occured to Aleksandra Andreyevna, but then only because of Zinaida's complaints. There was talk of a governess for the children. In the Tchaikovsky household things happened either at breathless speed—as when Ilya Petrovich decided to throw up his job—or at the pace of a snail. The governess question, which affected neither parent immediately, was in the latter category. Not until the last month of the year did Anastasia Petrovna Petrova arrive to free Zinaida.

Two vital facts about this new governess emerge from Petya's letters to Fanny: she was affectionate and she liked music. At once he cheered up. He did not forget Fanny or the rare sights of his mother, but instead of glooming in the garden or a chair when fits of melancholy came over him (Anastasia Vasilyevna was optimistic in thinking them 'a thing of the past') he played them off on the piano. It was a form of indulgence which Fanny would have put down firmly. The new governess had neither the will nor the wish; sooner or later the piano charmed her pupil from moodiness into the joy of making music, and he was then sunshine itself.

His devotion to the piano, and the efforts of Sasha and Polya to emulate him, at last moved the Tchaikovsky parents to another bout of action. They sent for Maria Markovna from Votkinsk. This diverted Petya but no more; this time there was not even a pretence that he would benefit. 'Sasha and Polya are to learn music,' Anastasia Vasilyevna told Fanny, 'but as Petyenka had lessons with the best teachers in Petersburg there is nothing she can teach him.'

It was perhaps as well for him that eight days before his tenth birthday his mother bore twins, Anatoly and Modest Ilyich. Their arrival threw up an aspect of him—his complete absence of envy or spite—which was to make the adult Tchaikovsky such a lovable man. There was every reason why he should resent the coming of the twins; he knew that he had seen so little of his mother during the previous months because of them. He knew that twins, even more than one baby, would draw her attention away from himself. Elder children more often than not are fiercely jealous of new babies in the home, and one would expect Petya, who yearned for the kind of love he offered his mother, to suffer more than most. Nothing of the kind happened. He begged to be allowed to see the twins, hung over their cradles with a kind of adoration, and wrote ecstatically to Fanny that the more he saw of them the more angelic they seemed to him to be. He could scarcely believe, he said, that they were not angels come down to earth.

He was not allowed to see much of them. In retrospect he seems pathetically young for the change, but his parents decided that he must follow Nikolai to Petersburg and school; not the School of Mining, in his case, but the Law School. They took no account of the difference in temperament between him and Nikolai; as the eldest boy was doing well at his school they assumed that Petya would do well at his.

In a sense they were right, as he was to prove; intellectually he remained far superior to his brother. But like most parents they wanted to toughen him up so that he became like all the other little savages; they thought of his extreme sensitiveness only as a blemish that contact with ordinary boys would rub off. The history of the Schmelling School went for nothing.

With a well-meant exertion of maternal feeling Aleksandra Andreyevna thought that she would help herself to recover from a severe lying-in and help Petya to make the break with the family by taking him to Petersburg. By September 1850 they were there and a few weeks later he matriculated brilliantly, spurred to great efforts by his mother's presence.

Aleksandra Andreyevna's praise was an oasis in a desert; this period in Petersburg was almost wholly an agony to Petya for he knew that she would go back to Alapayevsk and could neither bear to contemplate the break nor bear not to. There is nothing strange about the cold enthralling the warm-hearted—it happens every day —but it is sad and, in the case of Petya, is all the more wasteful because in little Sasha he had a true friend. He was to discover this later. In these autumn days of 1850 the poor child had not an easy moment—every thought blackened by the future—except for one unforgettable excursion. His mother took him to the Maryinsky to hear Glinka's *A Life for the Tsar*. Tchaikovsky was to say later 'We all come from Glinka' and the birth of this profound conviction was that final evening with his mother.

The next morning her carriage was ordered. They were staying with Ilya Petrovich's good friend Modest Alekseyevich Vakar, in whose honour one of the twins had been named. He and his wife promised to act as Petya's guardians and he was to spend every weekend at their house. Petya was very fond of them and of their little boy but nothing they could say or do saved him the anguish inseparable from deep feeling. As the minutes of that morning ticked away his grief alarmed everyone; he simply could not control himself.

At the last, when all farewells had been made, when his mother was sitting in the carriage and the door was closed, he refused to let go of the handle. He was dragged back to the door of the house. The coachman whipped up his horses, the carriage began to move. With a desperate effort Petya wrenched himself free, ran to the street and flung himself at the near hind wheel. He caught one of the spokes and clung to it, trying to hold the carriage back. Then he was shaken off and fell, muddy, bruised, half insensible on the pavement.

CHAPTER FOUR

Schoolboy
1850-4

It might reasonably be expected that this experience, which Tchaikovsky was to remember with such horror all his life that he felt ill at the very thought of it, would prostrate the young Petya. If he had been the hopelessly morbid creature so many biographers have made out, he would have collapsed then. But he did not; he delighted everyone by a determined effort to please his parents by doing well at school.

No doubt some part of this stand against loneliness and the rigours of school was due to the Vakars. Modest Alekseyevich was a very good man as he was soon to demonstrate nobly. But in less dramatic fashion he demonstrated it from the very beginning; he and his wife quickly became very fond of Petya, as almost everyone did who knew him, and this was quite enough to give him confidence and the wish to be worthy of their affection.

But when this is said there remains a Petersburg school of 1850 filled with young toughs contemptuous of the country boy and eager to teach the apparent softy to be virile. Petya had to spend six days out of every seven in this atmosphere, with his family more than a thousand miles away—so far as to be in another world. His sufferings, especially at night—for the dormitory ragging was savageness itself—defy the imagination.

It was then that he showed his spirit. He taught the boys that a child can be loving and devoted to art and yet take on the philistine at his own game. It is not every boy who can—or would dare to— fling himself at a moving carriage wheel and be up and about again the same day. His ten years of country air and good food and long walks had made him physically strong, stronger than many a weedy city boy. He had no wish to fight or even to oppose but when he did he held his own. After a few weeks the bullies began to respect him and leave him alone. His natural charm and liveliness did the rest.

By that time he had begun to show himself in another sphere more than the equal of most of his schoolmates; his natural intelligence and Fanny's teaching paid handsome dividends. He was soon high in his class and stayed there, but more by fits and starts than steady application. His letters home veer between triumph—'I have received full marks in the examinations in every subject but Latin and Scripture'—and frank admission that the old enemy has been at work: 'I haven't even tried to learn my lessons this week, so I have been given three black marks and shall have to stay in all next Sunday.' To which he appended the usual heartfelt 'Do please try to forgive me and I'll try not to learn so badly that I cause you pain. I know that I shall make you weep with this news. I have wept too but this won't help my dear angels of a mother and father—not at all.'

It is generally assumed that this period at school in which Petya distinguished himself so unexpectedly was a period in which for the first time he virtually dropped music, thus justifying all the arguments of Fanny at Votkinsk. Biographers have based this assumption on the fact that he rarely mentions music in his letters to Fanny—still his chief correspondent—and have puzzled innumerable students of Tchaikovsky, unable to understand how a boy so devoted to music could suddenly abandon it.

The truth is simple; he did not mention music to Fanny more often than he could help because he knew he would worry her. What she wanted to hear from him was talk of the books he had read and his own writings. There were no opportunities to use the piano at school so far as is known, but at weekends and on the many saints' days it was quite another matter; the Vakars were musical, and he not only heard music when they took him to opera or the rare concert but made it himself, alone and with them.

Nothing was easier for him than to become fond of people—they had only to behave decently—and he was soon like another son to the Vakars and an elder brother to the eldest Vakar child. He was too much a family boy and too much a Russian grandson of the Marquis d'Assier to be wholly at ease away from his own or to avoid fits of melancholy when he thought of them. But with these reservations he passed many good weeks in the winter of 1850. He was proud of his progress at school, not so much for himself as for his parents, who had been unwise and unkind enough a year earlier to reproach him by comparison with the steady Nikolai in the School of Mining. He was hearing music, not on the orchestrion but in the opera house. He was always hopeful that the family would move back to Petersburg—the comments of his mother and Zinaida suggested it.

It seems that whenever Tchaikovsky, man or boy, reached a tolerable state of peacefulness, he was destined to be jerked violently out of it. Lesser people know this apparent law of providence, but he was so much the more sensitive and his shocks so much the more brutal that one cannot be surprised at his preoccupation with the workings of fate in human lives. Almost at the end of the year, when he was looking forward to the breaking up of school and a Christmas period with the Vakars, fate intervened. An epidemic of scarletina ran through the school. Vakar at once brought him home to save him the rigours (and dangers) of school quarantine. Petya caught the infection but with home nursing quickly recovered. He had no sooner done so than the eldest Vakar child, a boy of five, went down with it. He died.

In spite of their grief the Vakars remembered Petya's extreme moral sensitiveness. They tried to pass off what their son had died from. In vain. Petya fell into a frightful fury of self-hatred, accused himself of a 'terrible breach of friendship' and went about the house half demented, demanding that he too die. He tried to avoid the parents, declaring that they must loathe the sight of him. He wrote letter after letter to his mother begging to be taken away from people he had treated so abominably.

He was in fact taken away later; Aleksandra Andreyevna was hard to persuade that he could be serious. But before then, as if to illustrate another side of fate, he had an experience that was all joy and which marked a crucial stage in his musical life. It came about through Vakar's perplexity. Neither he nor his wife could endure Petya's sufferings and one evening Vakar forcibly carried him off to the Maryinsky, believing that this was the only chance of turning his mind from the tragedy and his part in it.

They were playing *Don Giovanni* that night. Petya had almost to be dragged into the theatre but once the opera began he forgot everything but the music. The excerpts on the orchestrion had already given him a special love of Mozart; now, hearing the whole opera on stage, he was completely carried away.

The music of *Don Giovanni* was the first to conquer me completely [he wrote years later]. It awoke an ecstasy in me of which the consequences are known. It gave me the key to the spheres of pure beauty in which the greatest geniuses soar. Up to then I had known only Italian opera. That I vowed myself to music is due to *Don Giovanni*. . . . In this opera Mozart has put on stage an objectively tragic character, the most powerful and the most hallucinatory music ever created—Donna Anna. I simply cannot express what I felt when I saw this proud beauty appear, tragic and vengeful. When she at last discovers Don Juan, the murderer of her father and her seducer, when her anger flares out in a recitative of genius followed by a sublime aria, when her fury and pride are reflected in the slightest chord, the slightest whisper of the orchestra, I shiver with horror, I want to cry aloud, to weep, to throw myself about, overcome by the strength of the impression given by the Master.

In these last days of 1850 there seemed little chance of this hearing of the opera leading to anything constructive. Back Petya went to his school where he studied intensively for the next six months. He was the youngest boy in his class but easily kept abreast of most and ahead of many. Music, with the breaking of the link with the Vakars (he did not go back to them for the Easter holidays of 1851), was difficult to play but not at all difficult to think about, and he relieved his feelings slightly in letters to his mother. He did not forget it or his hopes for one instant, and when the summer vacations arrived he divided his time between the piano and lengthy walks in the country outside the city. There was no rivalry here; already he thought of expressing his love of nature by means of music, a music that would inevitably be wholly and distinctively Russian, just as the lakes and forests and gardens he saw could only have been found in his country. He loved them all passionately.

As if in reward for this prolonged and successful attempt to get the better of his temperament and of the latest blow of fate, Petya found his father waiting when he returned from one of his walks. Ilya Petrovich had good news; he was hoping to get a post in Petersburg and to bring the family back there. And sure enough, six months later, in May 1852, Petya had the happiest of twelfth birthdays, reunited with them all. He had proud news for them too; he was sure to graduate that summer from the preparatory school. As he did, his youth notwithstanding, and he went off for a summer holiday with the family knowing that he was now a fully-fledged student of the Law School.

ii

The next two years, from his twelfth to fourteenth birthdays, were by Petya's standards blissful ones. He forged ahead in school, he re-established contact with his family, coming closer in sympathy to the fast-growing-up Sasha, he made great strides in music and he finally got rid of Zinaida; she was married early in 1854 to Yevgeny Ivanovich Olkhovsky with a pomp which was to cripple Ilya Petrovich for some time afterwards. She was followed into matrimony by Nikolai's old reluctant companion in education, cousin Lydya (with a widowed aunt Lisa she had been a permanent member of the Tchaikovsky family for years) who to Petya's intense interest proved the adage that one marriage led to another: 'Lydya has married Colonel Olkhovsky, brother of Zina's husband, an admirable man who adores her.' The difficult girl of Votkinsk had disappeared. 'Lydya seems like another person,' he told Fanny. 'Now she is a splendid girl physically and morally.' Ilya Petrovich thought so too, it is to be hoped; he again paid up gaily for a wedding reception he could not afford and continued to live handsomely on credit.

Most important, in Petya's eyes only, was the music. These two years began, musically, with a prolonged treat, a summer holiday at Chornaya Ryechka at which his aunt, Yekaterina Andreyevna, set herself to tutor this obviously gifted boy. When he spoke of the performance of *Don Giovanni* and his feelings during and after it, she found a score and went through it with him, bar by bar, with illustrations on the piano. And when she discovered that he had quite a good voice she sang a duet from *Semiramide* with him and praised his command of the trills Rossini demanded so liberally.

From that moment he and she were virtually inseparable whilst the vacation lasted, and he came back to Petersburg and senior school in the curious but not unknown position (Stravinsky and Cherepnin, for instance, were to go the same way) that, outwardly vowed to the law, every instinct tied him to music. Had he lived in a different age or had his parents thought seriously of his obvious devotion to music, the Law School might have continued without him. As it was, neither mother nor father thought of music as anything but a spare-time pleasure and they were supported by the trend of the time. The professional musician was socially (and legally) beyond the pale—most of them were imported from Germany and Italy because Russians refused to take up a vocation which was not dignified with legal standing. Even the virtuoso career was not considered—that is to say, one would pay high prices to hear men and women opera singers, for example, but would never permit a child of one's own to follow such a profession, doubtful financially and damning socially. In the Russia of those days the good musician of good family remained an amateur, like Petya's aunt.

So to school he went and, after the usual painful readjustments (he was still younger than the average), discovered a considerable difference between preparatory school and school proper; in the latter, music had a strong hold, literature an even stronger, and the general atmosphere was civilized, as might be expected from boys in their middle and later teens preparing for a career in law. Petya was soon drafted into the school choir and, what was much more satisfactory, could talk music. He made friends, good ones, and his loneliness disappeared.

At home was the piano and his mother's playing and singing. There too was a governess who encouraged him to play and talk of music, Sasha a willing confidante, and the twins. His rapture in the little boys did not grow less; he developed a sort of proprietorial and protective attitude towards them. That this was a commentary on his parents he was never to see; his mind did not work in that way.

In every direction he was being fortified against the next severe blow; by new interests, new friends, a renewal of old interests, and, best of all for such a domesticated boy, the knowledge of a loving home near by even when he was not in it.

Then fate struck again; on 25 June 1854, Aleksandra Andreyevna died suddenly from cholera. The shock for everyone was the greater because she seemed to be recovering. Then came an abrupt relapse. She died in the bath of hot water reserved as a last desperate remedy. She was forty-one.

The death of Petya's mother has given the denigrators of Tchaikovsky a field-day and they have taken full advantage of it to establish and embellish the legend, first begun by Modest, of the composer as neurotic. His grief, they claim, was so excessive that it could only be explained by sexual abnormality.

Tchaikovsky's homosexuality will be considered in its place. It is only necessary here to look at the bases of assertions which have besmirched his reputation to the present day. These assertions boil down to two items. One is a highly coloured description by Modest (four years old at the time) who fancied himself as a romantic writer. His work—his opera libretti specially—is not merely bad in itself but reveals, as one might expect, that in his account of his brother he is in fact describing himself.

This is a common failing which the most conscientious biographer has to guard against constantly. Modest is a depressing example of the process at its worst, and the embroiderers of the legend have enlarged on him with gusto. But their *pièce de résistance*, which they trot out with a What-need-have-we-of-further-witnesses conclusiveness, is a single fact. This is, that Petya could not bring himself to announce the death of his mother to Fanny for two and a half years.

The fact is correct, the conclusions drawn from it wrong. What these biographers have overlooked is that there was another reason for the long gap of time between event and announcement. A very simple reason; the warm and confiding correspondence between the boy and his governess was coming to an end.

This decline had begun two years earlier, when the Tchaikovsky family returned to Petersburg. Not only was Petya reunited to his family then, but with another person who inevitably supplanted Fanny. This was the governess, Anastasia Petrovna. She was Russian and musical. She counteracted the French education and outlook of Fanny with startling effect—though French elegance was to be a hallmark of Tchaikovsky's music, the content was wholly and radiantly Russian, so that today he remains the Russian composer *par excellence*, expressing his country with grandeur and charm.

Petya did not forget Fanny but he was very young and very impressionable; all the signs point to the growth of a typical passion of a romantic boy in his early teens for the sympathetic Anastasia Petrovna, and he was soon to give open proof of it. So the correspondence with Fanny (herself increasingly occupied with other interests) began to dwindle from 1852 onwards until it almost came to a stop. The death of Aleksandra Andreyevna completed the process. Few boys would wish to write 'My mother is dead' if they could avoid it and Petya had the best of excuses, that Fanny was not particularly expecting to hear from him in any case.

If every boy who believed himself heartbroken when his mother died was written off as a neurotic homosexual, the masculine world would consist almost exclusively of them. Petya no doubt believed himself inconsolable, not because he had fallen into homosexual habits at school but because he was deeply feeling. For all the shock, what he was to remember with horror for the rest of his life was not his mother's death but the day, four years earlier, when she left him to the mercies of the preparatory school and the Vakars. It was then that he fought his fight with himself and began to grow up. After that nothing could be quite so terrible.

To a sensitive child there is not a great difference between absence and death; both mean the one thing, that the loved person is not present, cannot be touched or spoken to or heard. In Petya's day death was not a vague word to a child, it was a reality. Most children a hundred years or more ago had lost a brother or sister or both and had seen the loss accepted as inevitable, as the natural course of nature. The serfs in house and estate died like flies. Parents were considered long-lived if they reached fifty. To get cholera, for example, was virtually to die. On every side was death, early death, and resignation.

To say that Petya did not resign himself without a fight after his mother's death is to say the obvious. Certainly he never forgot her —why should he? But if we go by his actions, as we must, and by his later comments, it becomes obvious that he overcame this shattering loss courageously.

Take the after-comment first. It is 1891 and his sister has just died suddenly. He is worried about her son Vladimir, one of his great favourites. Then he recalls his own mother's death and his reaction to it and feels less worried. 'I know from my own experience,' he says, 'that one gets over such shocks with fair ease at his age.'

As for his actions in 1854, he continued his work at school without a long break and continued to do well in classes. His friendships deepened. At home his consolations were many—the love and faith of Sasha, the company and affection of the governess and the devotion of the twins specially. From the last he soon had what almost amounted to the trust and love given to a mother, and he vowed there and then to look after them as he imagined (perhaps not entirely correctly) she would have done.

Then, above all, there was music and his instinct to use it to express feeling. How he turned to it is shown by a simple but significant happening. His father caught cholera soon after the death of Aleksandra Andreyevna but was one of the few fortunate; he recovered. As soon as he was fit to travel he took the family off to Oranienbaum on the Gulf of Finland for a change of air and scene. At this holiday resort Petya wrote the first composition ('Our Mama in Petersburg' excepted) that has been recorded. It was not a lament for his mother, it was, prophetically, a cheerful waltz and was dedicated to Anastasia Petrovna.

CHAPTER FIVE

Government Clerk
1854-62

Pyotr Ilyich, as Petya must now become, spent five more years at the Law School and, against all the odds of the character that has been foisted on him since his death, this period was predominantly happy. It could, as a matter of fact, have been guessed with some confidence that a boy as sensitive as he who had weathered the hazards of the first two years would soar through the rest; and so it was.

The Director of the school was an ex-army martinet by the name of Yazykov. It pleased him to regard the students as yet another battalion to be licked into shape; military parades were the order of the day, the students were housed in barrack style and slept, if they were lucky, on the hardest of mattresses after the style of Nikolas I; discipline was ferocious, food plain, art was a word not acknowledged. It is difficult to imagine the Tchaikovsky boy surviving such a life, and still more so when it is remembered that his first year was spent under the eagle eye of one Alopeous, a master whose ideal was to reproduce in his class the precepts of the Director. Looked at from their point of view Pyotr Ilyich was not a promising pupil. He was not much more addicted to soap and water in his teens than in his childhood, he remained desperately untidy, his idea of time was hazy in the extreme.

Yet he survived and even flourished, thanks to the friendships he quickly struck up, thanks too to that in him which can scarcely be sufficiently emphasized, a physical toughness out of all proportion to his dreamy, lackadaisical air. And when, in his second year, the

35

unregretted Alopeous retired in favour of a Frenchman, Edgar
Prosper de Baccarat, he became quite at home and, in a year or two,
quite a distinguished member of the school.

It is a pity that more is not known about de Baccarat, for he had
a most beneficent effect on Pyotr Ilyich. There is no sign that he was
particularly interested in music but he was a civilized man and encouraged his pupils to develop their talents far beyond the rigid
schedule of the law classes. His forte was literature and, like Fanny,
the French romantics primarily, but any romantic writer in default
of none; poetry primarily but prose too on occasion. The little group
of which Pyotr Ilyich was not the least enthusiastic was soon de-
claiming de Musset, Byron, Lamartine and all the rest of them and,
naturally, trying their best to imitate them.

In this Pyotr Ilyich was far from being the most successful but in
some strange way—strange because he was the reverse of pushing—
he was chosen as editor of the school magazine *The School Messenger*, which de Baccarat founded. The little magazine is of no
importance; its young editor's success is; he was chosen over the
heads of many more gifted poets and writers than himself, but
justified the master completely. This provides a pointer to Tchaikovsky the man. The retiring, rather shy boy possessed, like the
man, an authority denied to many more obviously forceful characters. This authority was derived from breeding, from integrity,
from a personal charm which cannot be analysed and from an almost
invincible good humour—not the kind of good humour which
manifests itself in a perpetual smile but the more sterling kind, of the
person whose reactions to others were always positive, assuming the
best until the worst had been proved beyond doubt.

His main contributors were also his best friends, a fact which
owed nothing to favouritism. They were so because his friends were
naturally drawn from those interested in the arts. Less than half-way
through his schooldays—in 1855—Nikolas I died and was succeeded
by the liberal-minded Aleksandr II. The rigid censorship of the arts
was relaxed and amongst other benefits the law courts were reformed.
The reform encouraged some of the best minds in the country to
read for the bar and led to a sparkling era which has been called the
era of the Literary Lawyers. These men, coming from some of the
noblest families, were just beginning to go to the Law School in the
time of Pyotr Ilyich and were to enrich the literary and social scene
by brilliant speeches, first-rate literary criticism, some original
writing, and some rather less good poetry.

Four of these men, four of the earliest of the Literary Lawyers, were the boyhood friends of Pyotr Ilyich and his chief contributors in the school magazine. They were Apukhtin, Ertel, Gerard, and Maslov. Of the four only the first was to make more than an ephemeral name for himself in literature, and this one, A. N. Apukhtin, had considerable influence on Pyotr Ilyich. He was one year his junior, an aristocrat, a plump boy who rather incongruously went in for black cloaks and disordered hair and an attempt at a haggard face—all after Byron in particular and the romantic conception in general. He wrote poetry which was to make him a little later one of the most popular poets in Petersburg. It was highly romantic, yearning for past purity, soulful maidens, and lost dreams of knightly behaviour. After he left school Apukhtin lived a sufficiently dissipated life to justify the prevailing tone of his poems; at school his work was merely prophetic, echoing his romantic masters, but was already well done and promised a considerable gift.

It was largely because of Apukhtin, acting on very sympathetic material, that Pyotr Ilych expressed his contentment during these final years of school by writing letters which have misled so many later readers. Most of these letters were in the best romantic vein, almost a pastiche of his friend's poetry. It had never been and was never to be difficult for Pyotr Ilyich to see himself as a deplorable character, weak, sinful, self-indulgent. Actually this merely showed how nice he was, to try to take all the sins of the world on his shoulders. He began in earnest at school, in his poems as in his letters, and managed to enjoy himself thoroughly just as the would-be masochistic Apukhtin was doing. They were, in short, a happy band of friends though one and all would have spurned the attribute in horror.

Although literature occupied a considerable part of his spare time—he was meanwhile rising without undue effort or enthusiasm from class to class in school hours—it did not oust music, which soon had powerful supports. His best friend at school did not belong to the *littérateurs* but was a certain Adamov, a boy who was to represent the best element in the civilized lawyer class then being built up despite the ferociously militaristic Yazykov.

Vladimir Stepanovich Adamov was solemn, serious, and rather melancholy after the fashion of the time. He was, unlike most of his schoolfellows, devoted to law. He had a fine brain. But he believed that the man who was to practise law must be a leader in culture too as befitting one who interpreted the laws of his country and was looked up to far and wide. His interest outside law was given to music; he loved it, not with the instinctive passion of Pyotr Ilyich but with the joy of one who found in it a challenge and satisfaction to the keen and analytical legal mind. Like law it was highly civilized, intricate, unending in its intellectual satisfactions.

Obviously such a boy and the romantic Pyotr Ilyich would clash and make fast friends. Their arguments were endless and inconclusive but never fatal to friendship because each in his way truly loved music. The passionate Pyotr Ilyich leavened the calculating Adamov slightly, Adamov put a brake on Pyotr Ilyich's extravagances. They went very well together and lived music evening after evening, going to all the concerts and ballets and operas at weekends, discussing them, playing them over. Their taste was catholic but Pyotr Ilyich began to acquire the rudiments of an analytical sense.

In addition to the soberly encouraging enthusiasm of Adamov, Pyotr Ilyich was making his mark in the school choir, having private singing lessons from G. A. Lomakhin, and outstriding the school piano teacher, a man named Bekker, with whom he had begun lessons as soon as he entered the senior school and who was soon placed in something of the same position *vis-à-vis* the boy as the local instructress at Votkinsk. Becoming impatient with the man's incompetence, Pyotr Ilyich asked his father if he could not have private lessons from a teacher of repute.

By this time—it was the year of Aleksandr II's accession—a considerable change had taken place in the Tchaikovsky household. The retired Ilya Petrovich joined forces with his elder brother, Pyotr Petrovich, after whom Pyotr Ilyich had been named, and persuaded his sister-in-law Yekaterina Andreyevna and her family to move into his brother's house with him and his children. He did this, one suspects, because he loved gay company and his brother was anything but gay; Pyotr Petrovich had become seized with religious fervour after retiring from the army and was rarely seen in the house, keeping to his own apartments in which he wrote religious tracts destined to perish with him.

To a man like Ilya Petrovich this was sheer death, so he put his head together with his brother's wife, by no means of her husband's inclination, and enlarged the family. With very satisfactory results; one party after another and very much music. Yekaterina Andreyevna brought along with her a kind of ancient retainer in the form of an ex-opera singer from Naples (not a very good one, it seems) who had eked out a livelihood in Petersburg by giving singing lessons until taken up by the Schoberts. This man Piccioli was a character, a rouged and dyed dandy with very decided views and guaranteed to make every musical party hum with argument. He was naturally one hundred per cent in favour of Italian opera. He demolished the Germans and preached the virtues of the young Verdi, then almost unknown in Russia.

When Pyotr Ilyich arrived at this new home on the Kadetsky Line for his weekends he leapt straight into the general lively mood. Leapt is the *mot juste*. This supposedly morbid and brokenhearted boy (he was then in his mid-teens) showed himself a thorough madcap. The twins were ravished, two stout and fanatical worshippers; they waited all week for him and had eyes for none else when he was there. They were well rewarded: 'He radiated *joie de vivre*,' said Modest, looking back on those halcyon days, 'he was like a never-ending hymn of joy. Like the birds in spring who make senseless songs just for sheer joy of living so he made senseless jokes and made them so supremely well that he managed to colour them with a sort of fascination—how did he think it all up on the spur of the moment?'

He gives an example: 'Beckoning to me, he'd make me say "Pita, Pita, Pito, Piye, Pyetu, Petrushka!" before he allowed me to kiss him.' This declension of his name (which varied every time) never failed to create gales of laughter in the two small boys: 'Nothing could have seemed wittier or happier to us.'

As an inventor of games he was, in the twins' eyes, incomparable: 'I've never met anything like them. He didn't "condescend" to play with us, he became like one of us, improvised and created one game after another in the gayest of moods, all originating in his strange and magically charming nature.'

Sentimental exaggeration, one might think, from children overcome by such attention from a ten-years-older brother. Yet Modest's words were to be borne out through Pyotr Ilyich's life; men and women were to be almost literally bewitched by him, by the kind expression in his eyes, his natural grace, his beauty, his nice nature and, for the greater part of his life, by this spirit of original fun which enlivened party after party. Even in his last years he could reduce his friends to near hysterics and he was never to lose his rare gift with children.

In these middle fifties the boy carried his gaiety with him when he gave the twins their goodnight kiss and ran downstairs to the elders. Piccioli was a joy to him and he to Piccioli. He not only had all the music he could wish for but learned via this new friend to appreciate Verdi and was soon being driven to shift his defence of the beloved Mozart—he was, he came to agree, in every true sense of the word an Italian composer. His devotion to Rossini, Bellini, and Donizetti was encouraged by Piccoli who, finding eager talent on his doorstep, quickly monopolized the young student and paid him the considerable compliment of passing on his knowledge of opera. In later years Tchaikovsky was to recall these talks with gratitude, and placed them alongside the orchestrion of his childhood, the never-to-be-forgotten Glinka and Mozart operas at the Maryinsky and the summer holiday with his aunt as one of the seminal forces in his career.

Piccoli in fact continued that long-past summer's instruction of Yekaterina Andreyevna (which he had largely imparted to her in the first place) and left the young Pyotr Ilyich with a fairly strong grasp of the requirements for writing a singable opera—how the composer chose his libretto, how he built up an opera, how he wrote arias which made the most of the soloist's voice without asking for the impossible or the ludicrous, how to blend singer and orchestra to best effect.

The Italian also encouraged the boy—probably without much difficulty—to take up composition again. This time, naturally, the composition was a song, written strangely enough to the Italian translation of a poem by the Russian Fet, which shows how Italianate the impressionable Pyotr Ilyich had become. Not content with writing the song, 'Mezzanotte', he went to the length of having it privately printed. It was not a very good song but the event was a milestone and helped to put him still further out of sympathy with the idea of a legal career.

In view of this outburst of music in the new Tchaikovsky home it is no wonder that the diffident Pyotr Ilyich worked up enough self-interest to speak to his father about a good music teacher.

Ilya Petrovich agreed. It may be that he would have agreed in any case through sheer good humour, though this insistence on music by a law student must have struck him as odd. But events were in his son's favour; the nightly parties were making a drain on Ilya Petrovich's purse and his response to this was to begin to play the markets under the guidance of a friend with 'inside information'.

Ilya Petrovich was an optimist, as we have already seen, but he also had a conscience. He knew quite well that he was taking an unjustifiable risk when all his six children except Nikolai were far from earning a living and two of them were little boys. His response to the prick of conscience was in character; within reason he granted all that they wished. This cost still more money but eased his mind, which worked on the principle, if I throw my money about let them all have a share of it, and may even have dealt with the unimaginable possibility of disaster—that if disaster came, the children would at least have had a slight picking before everything disappeared.

However this may be, there was a rash of happenings in the Tchaikovsky family: Ippolit Ilyich went off to the Navy as a very well provided for midshipman in time to see the end of the scandalous war which England and France had forced on Russia; Aleksandra Ilyinishna was sent to the exclusive Smolny Institute for young ladies; Nikolai Ilyich was given enough financial backing to get him a good first appointment after graduating from his School of Mining; and Pyotr Ilyich was granted his much more modest request, to have a good piano teacher.

Rudolf Vasilyevich Kundinger has not gone down to history as a great teacher of the pianoforte and in fact he was not a great teacher. He has gone down to history all the same. His place in the memories of men is probably unique, for he is the only known example of a human being who taught genius and, in after years, did not claim to have recognized and fostered that genius from the word go. Kundinger, with superlative honesty, declared long afterwards that he found no genius in the young Tchaikovsky, none at all.

'If I could have dreamed what Pyotr Ilyich was to become I should have kept a record of our lessons,' he said. 'But I must admit, to my great confusion, that at no time did the idea enter my head that Tchaikovsky had the makings of a musician.' He continued, even more damningly, 'Of course he was gifted. He had a fine ear, a good memory, and splendid hands, but beyond this nothing, absolutely nothing which could foretell the rise of a composer or even of an outstanding instrumentalist—nothing special, nothing phenomenal.'

The years with Kundinger naturally did not convince his pupil that it was his bounden duty as well as desire to take up music. Kundinger's tepid praise banked down a fire ready at any moment to burst into a blaze. Pyotr Ilyich still regarded a career in law—even the reformed law—with a sort of incredulity, and waited hopefully for his father to make the expected millions before declaring himself quit of the farce.

What actually happened was, as might be expected, that, one year before his son was due to graduate, Ilya Petrovich lost every rouble and was forced to find another job. He did find one—he was appointed Director of the Institute of Technology after an agonizing search—but the harm had been done; Pyotr Ilyich could not be sure that his father, sixty-four by that time, could hold the position. His strong family sense prevailed against the distasteful thought of a government office. Nikolai was launched and was to follow his father, though with greater steadiness, Ippolit was obviously taking to naval life, Aleksandra had met Lyov Vasilyevich Davydov and a marriage was being talked about, but the twins were still some way from their teens. In the spirit of his self-imposed role as guardian, Pyotr Ilyich sacrificed music to ensure that they were given a fair chance to grow up educated and unworried. When he graduated, in May 1859, thirteenth in his class of more than fifty, he applied for a post in the First Division of the Ministry of Justice. He was appointed.

ii

The next three years or so, from the age of nineteen to twenty-two, consisted of almost nothingness. Pyotr Ilyich's career in the Ministry of Justice followed the course of any intelligent young man who took no interest in his work. Because he was intelligent and the work was simple he could scarcely avoid occasional demonstrations of ability: he received regular promotion and in less than a year had become senior assistant to the chief clerk. Because he was good-natured, charming, and well born, his frequent lapses of memory— he had a queer habit when in a day-dream of chewing documents to pieces—were overlooked. Like his father he was a good mixer. Interested he was not. His invariable politeness may have given the impression that he was, but as a government career was understood to be a social and financial necessity for most well-born Russians, too much interest or attention to duty would have been considered bad form. By four o'clock every afternoon he could be seen with a hundred other government clerks taking the air on the Nevsky Prospekt, preening himself in his uniform and taking note of the young women promenading by the river at the fashionable hour.

For he had become a dandy. In November 1860 Aleksandra Ilyinishna married the young Davydov and left for the Davydov estate in the Ukraine, and the withdrawal of her steadying influence caused this much-loved brother to lose hope. This has been held against him as appalling weakness of character. Such a judgement takes no account of the feelings of a highly gifted young man of twenty immured in a government office day by day when all he wanted to do was to make music, and of an extraordinarily affectionate young man who has lost his best companion, friend, sister, and mother all in one.

He knew what he was doing; his letters to Aleksandra Davydova, which were to continue for the rest of her life, were filled with self-reproaches. These were so violent that the reader who examines his life at this time is perplexed to find his sins so white. He became a dandy and led the life of one—that was his whole weakness. He joined the group of young officials in their life of pleasure, grew the *à la mode* little beard, was always faultlessly turned out, smoked furiously, drank more than was good for him, flirted madly and was usually to be found at one of the smart restaurants and cabarets or the musical soirées and dances where he was in great demand, not so much for his voice or his abilities as a dancing partner as for his willingness to pound out a waltz, gavotte, or minuet almost indefinitely so that his companions might dance their way through the night. He attended all the operas, operettes and ballets and duly fell in love with the reigning soprano and ballerina.

Indeed love was the motif of these years—how much because it was the fashion in his set to be enamoured of some society girl or other cannot be said—and his letters to Aleksandra Ilyinishna drew the picture of a would-be Lothario. He only told her of the girls. He did not mention the young men he was impartially flirting with—not because he was ashamed but as a matter of decorum and of slight importance. He would marry and the habit would die, that was his not unreasonable defence.

His old friends were little help, and the one he saw most of, Apukhtin, was no help at all. Apukhtin, now busily practising what he had preached at school, urged Pyotr Ilyich in one breath to devote his life to poetry and in the next breath carried him off to a brothel or a house or cabaret which was little better. He was leading a rakish life and making good poetry out of it; such a gift was beyond his friend.

Adamov, it seems, Pyotr Ilyich fought shy of. No doubt he was ashamed of himself, a state only too easy for him to fall into, and could not often face the earnest musician-lawyer his friend had become.

There were aspects of this lighthearted existence which were wholly good and display the dandy in a different light. Pyotr Ilyich at home was always at his best. The twins still found him quite marvellous and no wonder; he spent a lot of time with them and they always felt the better for it. One of their great joys was to sit him at the piano and join in the latest popular songs he played with immense abandon. Another and even greater joy was to watch him imitate the ballet dancers he was following so assiduously at the Maryinsky.

This second joy was a little marred for Modest, who already had similar aspirations and nursed a natural sense of injustice which the younger so often feel towards the elder.

Petya could always turn the blamable (for me) into the permissible (for him). He was passionately fond of imitating ballerinas and all their special mannerisms. I wanted to do this too. But when I tried it everyone mocked me and told me to stop clowning. Petya on the contrary fascinated everyone so much—children and grown-ups alike—that he used to give entire performances of this ballet-baiting in the evening, usually near the *dacha* in the broad ditch separating the New Place from the English Park. No one thought the performance unfitting; all applauded and youths of his own age used to jump into the ditch, fired with the wish to emulate him, and threw themselves into similar clever caricatures of the dance.

Ilya Petrovich first put the brake on this frivolous existence. Not for moral reasons but in a fit of conscience. He had settled into his post satisfactorily, his monetary affairs were as stable as they were ever likely to be, and he saw with distinct uneasiness his son wasting his time at the Ministry. He knew well enough why Pyotr Ilyich was there. Eventually he asked him whether he ought not to take up music seriously.

This was an epoch-making suggestion—the first time any member of the young man's family had so much as recognized the obvious—but by the time it was made Pyotr Ilyich had worked himself into such a state of self-disgust that he could not even begin to consider acceptance; he had lost faith in himself as a musician as well as a man.

The idea stuck, nevertheless, as it was bound to do, for not even a Tchaikovsky can escape his destiny. The crucial moment came a few months later, in the summer of 1861, when he went off with a friend for the time-honoured European tour. The tour itself produced no notable reactions from the 21-year-old traveller. He did not care for

44

Berlin, liked nothing about London, not even the singing of Patti, and only said of Paris (which entranced him nevertheless) that in most ways it was not a patch on Petersburg.

The value of the trip lay in his meditations when left to himself, free from the Petersburg enchantments. He returned to write a particularly extravagant letter to his sister, blaming himself for throwing money away the moment he had it, and very foolishly too. He was still doing it, he assured her, which proved his weakness to the hilt. And to make matters worse, without even the result vanity might hope for: 'I am having no luck at all in love.' This meant that the conventional remedy for sowing wild oats—which was to occur to him more than once in his life—to marry a pure girl, had failed.

Then, having spent himself, came the historic announcement which must have made the fond Aleksandra Davydova radiant with pleasure. This time he did not end with the usual flood of promises of amendment but with a piece of hard news. It was scribbled as a postscript. 'I am studying thoroughbass and am doing quite well.' Followed by an even more acceptable: 'Perhaps in three years or so you'll be hearing one of my operas, or, better still, singing the arias from it. Who can tell?'

iii

When Tchaikovsky cried, 'I am Russian, Russian, Russian!' he was, unknowingly, warning all non-Russians not to equate the Russian temperament with the Western and judge a Russian as if he were one of themselves. Anyone who knows the Russians will be familiar with two outstanding characteristics common to virtually the entire nation: they are a feeling people and they are subject to fits of sloth or what could be called paralysis of the will to action. These two characteristics merge time after time when the Russian, regarding this period of sloth, cries to heaven that he is the most contemptible of men, that he makes resolutions only to break them, that he is unworthy to exist, that his faculties rust and decay because of his appalling weakness. And so on, at length and in the most impassioned terms.

The Westerner, reading or hearing this, accepts it at its face value and pities or scorns according to his nature. What he rarely understands is that the difference between him and a Russian is not that the one is lazy and unrestrained and the other businesslike and sensible but that the one feels so deeply that he says exactly what he feels when he feels it whilst the other has been schooled to govern and conceal his feelings when he has them. In brief, the one tells the exact truth about himself, the other does not. The amount of work done by both is, in fact, very similar in the long run, for the Russian, spurred by his feeling of guilt, works at a rate and with a fury of concentration that the Westerner knows little of.

If this is born in mind when a reader studies the letters of Tchaikovsky he will understand the man very much better. Every living man has many moments of guilt, not to speak of the myriads of neurotic fancies which oppress humanity, and the fact that the Westerner keeps them to himself is not the merit he often pretends, for concealment is almost always much more unhealthy than the outspokenness he criticizes. If there is a difference between Tchaikovsky and most of his countrymen it is that, being a great artist, he is absolutely frank and even more devastatingly self-abusive. He meant what he said, every word of it, at the moment of writing, but half an hour after posting his letter he was as likely as not to be found furiously working. And how he worked! He was often to perform miracles—such as the writing of *The Sleeping Beauty* score in forty days—but even in his earliest years he threw himself into everything musical with a fervour quite foreign to the drawling, leisurely dandy.

Perhaps the best proof that the young Pyotr Ilyich must not be judged so harshly as he judged himself is the inactivity of his sister. Aleksandra Davydova loved him with a selfless passion rarely found in any man or woman, let alone brother and sister. She heard all his news and shared all his feelings. If she had been a Western woman she would have rushed up to Petersburg from Kamenka the moment she read almost any one of his youthful letters, they were so despairing, so denunciatory of all he was and was likely to be. But she did not move. She knew her Russians, she knew her brother.

When these facts are borne in mind the drastic nature of Pyotr Ilyich's decision to prepare himself for a career in music will be appreciated—for this was at the back of his mind when he began lessons in thoroughbass with Nikolai Ivanovich Zaremba in 1861. For Pyotr Ilyich was not only the most Russian of Russians, sharing their feelings to the highest degree, he was also a young man of twenty-one having a very good time in one of the gayest cities in the world. His charm and good nature and excellent manners made him a welcome addition to the ranks of bright young things who were dancing and drinking the nights away. Women liked him because he flirted with an air and made a most obliging cavalier; men like him because he was open-handed, a loyal friend and without a tinge of malice in his make-up. Even the boring hours in the Ministry were made more acceptable because of his widespread popularity in all ranks; he treated the old clerks with consideration instead of the customary insolence and his manner with his superiors was so delightfully easy as to excuse even the nibbling of documents and the occasional spells of forgetfulness when he went into a brown study for hours at a time.

In short, there was every reason why this young man with his fair share of native indolence should be spoilt and flattered out of all thought of music. He could so easily have relegated his part in it to the role of appreciative listener at the opera and performer of the latest ballads and gypsy dance tunes. And when, stirred by a wish to follow the opera libretti precisely, he took up the study of Italian, he might well have considered this as paying sufficient tribute to conscience after office hours.

In spite of all this, temperament, temptation, flattery, and the natural wish of the young to enjoy themselves in the company of the young, he voluntarily approached Zaremba and persuaded him to accept him as pupil. This shows not only the power of music but a strength of purpose with which he has never been credited outside his own country.

iv

He had to persuade Zaremba to take him on because Zaremba was a teacher of some distinction in the Petersburg musical world of the day. Zaremba had a greater distinction; he was the first musician of consequence to tutor the future great composer. His effect on Tchaikovsky's career cannot be over-estimated. He came into Pyotr Ilyich's life when the young man made his first serious effort to take up music as a profession. The counter-attractions to music being what they were, much responsibility devolved on the man he asked to teach him. Zaremba was equal to it. His theory was somewhat rigid—he had studied harmony under Marx—but in his inelastic way he loved music and had no serious thoughts of anything beyond music. To work under such a man was to live with a calm, unspoken acceptance of the superiority of the arts and of music especially which reinforced Pyotr Ilyich's decision at precisely the right moment; he felt that he had chosen rightly and inevitably. There were backslidings in the sense of doubts about his own gifts—Zaremba was a harsh critic—but they were not long lasting.

Zaremba, moreover, appeared to Pyotr Ilyich as much more than a solitary professor of repute, he represented a new spirit in Russian music, a spirit which had first shown itself publicly two years earlier, when Anton Rubinstein, powerfully supported by the Tsar's aunt, the Grand-Duchess Yelena Pavlovna, launched the Russian Musical Society with royal approval. That winter the society began to give its own concerts which Pyotr Ilyich attended enthusiastically and sadly too, for the formation of the society coincided with his entry into the Civil Service.

The society also held classes for students. It collected a notable staff including, besides Zaremba, two Poles, Henri Wieniawski and Theodor Leschetizky, the cellist-composer Karl U. Davydov, and an old friend of Pyotr Ilyich's, his singing teacher of schooldays, Lomakhin. The classes were held at the Grand-Duchess's Mikhailovsky Palace and Pyotr Ilyich went there when he first took harmony lessons from Zaremba in 1861.

Rubinstein and his supporters were not contented; they felt that the society was worthy of its own home and that not until it obtained one would its prestige force a change in the position of the musician in Russian life. They struggled hard against bureaucratic refusal to accept the obvious. Rubinstein often told the story of the registration which, being a baptized Jew, he had to carry out every three years. When asked his profession he replied, 'Musician'. The clerk refused the explanation, saying that there was no such thing according to Russian law. Not until Rubinstein mentioned his father was he allowed to go, being described in the register as son of a merchant of the second guild.

It was this attitude he was now fighting, and three years after the establishment of the society he succeeded; the Tsar agreed to finance him, and what came to be known as the Petersburg Conservatoire was opened in its own splendid quarters facing the Neva. This was one year after Pyotr Ilyich had begun lessons with Zaremba.

With what interest the young man followed Rubinstein's efforts is known by the sequel. His year with Zaremba had been unenlivened by a single motion of lightness—musical theory is a sobering subject at the best of times and when taught by a stiff-necked Russian who has learned this theory from a German it becomes fearsome to think of. But the supposed butterfly Pyotr Ilyich went diligently and methodically through it and his hours of practice at home raised protesting moans from the twins, accustomed to much lighter fare from him in the previous year or so. In vain; he stuck grimly—and happily—to it.

The Conservatoire opened its doors on 20 September 1862, and one of the first of its students—he had put himself down for the matriculation examination as soon as he heard the news—was Pyotr Ilyich.

Part Two

Apprenticeship

CHAPTER SIX

Musician
1862-6

Not for another six months did Pyotr Ilyich formally give up the farce of the Ministry, but his entry to the Conservatoire in the autumn of 1862 and not his resignation from the Civil Service almost on the dot of his twenty-third birthday marked the real decision to devote his life to music. With this decision comes the need for a summary of the state of Russian music at that time—music that the new recruit was to do so much, perhaps more than any other man, to make world-famous.

It would be more correct to say, a picture of the state of music in Russia in 1862 because there was virtually no Russian music. There had been a time, centuries earlier, when Russian church music was the finest and richest in the world and Russian folk songs (partly adopted by the peasants from the church music, partly pagan in origin) were incomparable in number and variety. That day had long passed by 1862. Folk music still existed but the only composer who had tried to make use of it was scarcely ever heard; church music had gone into decline owing mainly to the rise to power of zealots who abolished all but the simplest and oldest of Byzantine chants and even tried to proscribe the use of musical instruments throughout the country.

When this iron rule of the Church was at last relaxed there were practically no professional Russian musicians left and no recognized Russian music. Folk songs flourished in the villages but were despised in Moscow and Petersburg as crude and barbaric. These were the days which followed Peter the Great and his policy of westernizing Russia. One of his most effective methods was to invite foreign musicians, singers, and actors to his chief cities, and his successors, Anne, Elizabeth, and Catherine, improved on this; they established foreign opera and ballet companies in Moscow and Petersburg under resident composers and ballet masters—almost all Italian—and patronized them lavishly. This standard set by the court was followed by all the influential nobility until by the beginning of the nineteenth century it could be said that the only music admitted as music in the two capitals was Italian. When Aleksandr I came to the throne in 1801 he changed this trend slightly but, from the point of view of the Russian composer or musician, unhelpfully—he began to encourage French and German composers and artists rather than Italian.

By a curious mental quirk on the part of Russians in positions of authority, although they made much of foreign actors, artists, musicians, and composers—so much so that the capitals were filled with resident foreigners received in or at least patronized by the best society—they did not consider these careers suitable for Russians. Not only the capitals but all the great country houses of Russia had their orchestras and many their opera houses and theatres in miniature, but in all of them Russian performers were conspicuous by their absence. When Petya was born in 1840 Russian actors had not long been permitted an official existence; when he entered the Petersburg Conservatoire in 1862 Russian musicians remained pariahs, without official status, and with one notable exception Russian composers, what few there were, obtained a hearing only by diligently copying the Italians or French. It was necessary for a conductor to be able to speak Italian or German if he wanted to control his orchestra; for most of the men playing under him were foreigners who would not demean themselves by learning the despised Russian. In court and society circles French was *de rigueur*—the mother tongue was considered *outré*, barbaric, a language for peasants, coarse like Russian music.

The exception amongst Russian composers was, of course, Glinka. Unlike his few predecessors he had genius and, what goes with genius, moral courage. He had one aim, to produce music which could only have been written by a Russian, and for that purpose he chose Russian themes for his operas and went to the Russian folk song for his music, sometimes genuine folk songs, sometimes created by himself from folk song material.

Glinka was far from being a rabid nationalist; he was a travelled man who appreciated what other countries had to offer in art and understood that their experience of unfettered experiment through the centuries when Russia was artistically dead could not be neglected. His first opera, *A Life for the Tsar*, was Italianate in construction but is filled with melodies taken straight from Russian life—even to an echo of balalaikas—and introduces the *leitmotiv* which Wagner was to make German in a Germanic manner; in Glinka, the originator, the idea is carried out with characteristic deftness and lightness.

A Life for the Tsar was first performed in 1836, four years before the birth of Petya. It was received enthusiastically and remained in the repertory—that was how Petya was able to see it at the Maryinsky ten years later—but a great deal of its popularity was due to its exceedingly patriotic libretto, with the heroic Russian peasant knowingly giving his life for his country and Tsar. As far as Glinka's innovations went, he received no appreciation in the circles which counted. Most of his aristocratic audiences did not even notice them and the few intellectuals who did dismissed them with a sneer as 'cabmen's music'—this because Glinka had actually used a well-known cabman's song in the first act. The feeling that the making of public music in any form was beneath the dignity of the Russian and, going to the other extreme, that no existing Russian music was worthy of an opera stage, was still as powerful as ever.

In *A Life for the Tsar* Glinka wanted to write 'a Russian opera in which my beloved countrymen would feel at home ... a big work that is absolutely national, not only the subject but the music'. In Russian eyes he had succeeded—that is to say, he was at once recognized as the first great Russian composer. In his eyes, he was only half-way to his objective; the Italian framework had to be discarded and a purely Russian opera constructed. *Ruslan and Lyudmila* was this opera.

For a man starting virtually from scratch, this is an astounding piece of work. When analysed, it is found to consist of a medley of different influences, not all Russian, but blended with such genius that the simple and most satisfactory test, to ask the opinion of the man in the street, has always the same result: the man says 'Russian music'. At one stroke Glinka created the idiom which was more and more to conquer the world—that fresh, powerful, rhythmical, virile music that is known everywhere as standing for Russia at her greatest and best.

When he joined the Conservatoire at the age of twenty-two Pyotr Ilyich had not heard a performance of *Ruslan and Lyudmila*, then twenty years old, for the good—or rather, bad—reason that it was never repeated. There was nothing obviously patriotic about

Pushkin's fairytale, the libretto had been unhappily mangled and the Russianness merely struck its first hearers as barbaric and in bad taste. Particularly did the aristocratic first-night audience object to the oriental note in so much of the opera which was thought to be retrograde when all intelligent Russians were looking to the West for their culture. The Church objected to the story being set in pagan days.

The opera failed dismally and was hissed off the stage for many years. It broke the spirit and health of Glinka—only thirty-nine then—and he never wrote another opera. 'It may be recognized in a hundred years,' he said bitterly of *Ruslan and Lyudmila*; and to the shame of all concerned his estimate was not far wrong.

ii

Pyotr Ilyich's enthusiasm for Glinka—based on *A Life for the Tsar* and the composer's smaller works, especially his *Kamarinskaya*—had long since penetrated the Tchaikovsky family to such a degree that when he decided to throw up the Ministry in the spring of 1863 his elder brother Nikolai Ilyich, by that time an up-and-coming mining official in the provinces, protested at this waste of Civil Service talent in a sneer which has become notorious. 'I can't see you becoming another Glinka.'

His brother's reply has also gone down into history as a noble affirmation of faith: 'I may not become another Glinka but sooner or later you will be proud of me.' In fact he was to become another Glinka, doing for Russia in orchestral works what Glinka had done in opera. His family's pride goes without saying.

In the Conservatoire he heard nothing about Glinka or that other remarkable Russian composer, Dargomyzhsky, whose opera *Rusalka*, based on Pushkin, attempted to popularize Russian folk songs, and who was at that moment working on his staggeringly original *The Stone Guest*. Or to be exact, if Pyotr Ilyich heard Glinka or Dargomyzhsky mentioned in the Conservatoire, it would be in terms of disparagement. The official attitude precisely echoed that of Nikolai Ilyich.

Anton Rubinstein was no lover of Russian music. He was proud of being a Russian and would no doubt have described himself as a Russian composer—he was to leave a bewildering amount of music behind him, all moribund—but his sympathies were entirely with the Germans; his own work was a poor copy of German music and he followed the Germans in everything and the early Germans at that; he worshipped Beethoven, permitted occasional glances at the not too daring works of Mendelssohn and Schumann, and that was his limit.

His originality consisted in the one important battle he fought, for the right of Russian musicians to be acknowledged as following a calling worthy of respect and good salaries. What he expected these Russian musicians to play was quite another matter; his aim was to turn them into impeccable performers of music composed outside his own country. In this he was absolutely at one with men he despised, the clever aristocrats who had jeered at *Ruslan and Lyudmila*. He openly rejoiced at its failure, pointing to it as a lesson to his students to reject what he called 'barbaric theories'.

Pyotr Ilyich's enthusiasms therefore received rough handling in the Conservatoire, but there was a place in Petersburg where they would have been surpassed. This was the apartment of Mily Balakirev. Balakirev, three years older than Pyotr Ilyich, was a gifted pianist and musical thinker whose future was decided by a meeting with Glinka. A self-educated composer, he wrote at eighteen a fantasy on themes from *A Life for the Tsar* and, more important, already appreciated the originality of *Ruslan and Lyudmila*. When he met his hero that same year, 1855, Glinka praised his pianoforte playing, praised his Fantasy, paid him the honour of a gift of two themes from his notebook to form the basis of another fantasy, and agreed with his strictures on the study of counterpoint. Glinka, like this young admirer, had not studied very seriously, though for different reasons, and said, 'Who knows? Maybe it was for the best, after all. The strict German counterpoint isn't always good for the free imagination.'

In one way and another he was charmed and impressed, and wrote to his sister and chief supporter, Lyudmila Ivanovna Shestakova, 'He is the first man I have ever met whose views on music correspond to mine exactly . . . I believe that in time he'll become a second Glinka.'

He did not say this to Balakirev but the implication was plain in his attitude. From that moment the young man's task was clear, to support Glinka to the hilt and do all he could to see that his music was appreciated and played throughout Russia and the world. He thought of himself as an immature disciple—Glinka was only forty-six—but within a few months his hero was dead and his role abruptly changed to that of a leader.

He rose to the challenge. He settled in Petersburg and with the help of Vladimir Stasov, to whom Glinka had introduced him before he went off on his last journey abroad, he set about forming a nationalist school.

Stasov was another Adamov but a much cleverer one. Educated in the Law School, he became a brilliant speaker and writer, with a keen, incisive wit and a formidable power of analysis. He was deeply interested in all the arts, in music especially, and was no mean performer on the piano, but he had no wish to take up music as a career; his wish was to forward the nationalist cause of Glinka by propaganda and education.

The two men, Stasov and Balakirev, formed a whole, the one intellectually dominant, the other dominating by his deep feeling and instinctive artistry. All the worth-while intellectuals of Petersburg met at Stasov's house; he introduced the unknown Balakirev to them, provided him with pupils and recital engagements, and when they were together discussed and amplified their plans to carry on the nationalist movement. He, it was agreed, would take on the public exposition of these aims; Balakirev would look about for disciples.

He soon found them. In 1857, the year after Glinka's death, he met and fascinated Tsezar Kui, an officer in the Engineers who had leanings towards composition and journalism. Kui brought a second recruit in another young officer, Modest Musorgsy, already an excellent pianist, whom he met at Dargomyzhsky's house. In 1860 the three became four with the adhesion of Nikolai Rimsky-Korsakov, a midshipman. Two years later the fifth and last great name was added to the group in Aleksandr Borodin, who worked in the Academy of Medicine.

All the young men took lessons from Balakirev, played four-hand arrangements with him, and succumbed to the spell of his remarkable gifts—he could sight-read and improvise with startling ease—still more remarkable personality, and inspired love of Russian music. The lessons were unorthodox. There was no textbook instruction in harmony and counterpoint—Balakirev's grasp of music was purely instinctive—but an endless study of the work of the great masters and a relentless dissection of the work of lesser men. His invariable method was to play over a work, then criticize it, then improvise it as it ought to have been written. Everything his pupils wrote was subjected to this discipline—a discipline made palatable by the teacher's delightful sense of humour and his obvious belief that the criticized pupil loved music as much as he and would be satisfied with nothing short of perfection.

Like Glinka, Balakirev and Stasov were not crudely nationalist in the sense of rejecting all western forms of music. Their aim was to use the untapped wealth of Russian music embedded in the folk tunes of every province but on the basis of a study of the advanced Western composers, Schumann, Chopin, Liszt, Berlioz. They went farther than these in a criticism of eighteenth-century forms such as the sonata necessarily governing all composition, in their dislike of strict counterpoint, and in their wish to impart realism into operatic writing (after the manner of *The Stone Guest* which Dargomyzhsky was then beginning and of *Boris Godunov* which was yet to be conceived) instead of permitting opera to follow the Italian pattern of a vehicle for displays of vocal pyrotechnics. Their aims were summed up by Kui, who was often to speak for the group, as 'to exploit all the seductive elements in music—the charm of harmony, the richness of polyphony and orchestral colour'—to which was added, naturally, the popularization of music specifically Russian.

The first task, as Balakirev and Stasov saw it, was to fight the traitor within the gates. The traitor was Rubinstein. In their eyes the Society of Russian Music, which Rubinstein founded the year the Balakirev group gained its first adherents, was wholly bad, its noble aim of liberating the Russian musician proving worse in the long run than allowing him to stay in his present lowly position. They argued that if Rubinstein had his way the Russian opera houses and concert halls would be filled with Russian musicians who had been taught that music derived from Russian sources was barbaric, musicians who would for ever be playing the older German masters and despising the art of their own country. They jeered at the Conservatoire as 'a hive of professors' and a Germanic organization with 'not one Russian in the whole outfit'—a jibe near enough to the truth to hurt.

But to jeer was not enough. Balakirev was not a man to sit down and await events; he made them. Long before Borodin completed The Mighty Handful, as the group was to be nicknamed, its leader had acted. Supported financially by Glinka's sister and Stasov and his influential friends and given plenty of newspaper publicity by Stasov and Kui, he opened the Free Music School in opposition to the Russian Music Society. He offered free tuition to anyone, man or woman, interested in music, and introduced evening classes for day workers. Far from insisting on a grounding in musical theory, as in the Conservatoire, he and his associates based their teaching on analysis of major works. And though—as the response was great— he had to teach by class, he was careful to provide individual tuition whenever he thought the student worthy of it—again in contrast to the strict Conservatoire principle.

To popularize the school and bring in funds he organized concerts in opposition to the Musical Society concerts of Rubinstein. The programmes were advanced—Liszt, Schumann, Berlioz, Glinka, and Dargoymzhsky forming the bulk of the music played— and as soon as The Mighty Handful produced compositions of their own he killed two birds with one stone, giving his disciples a platform for public performance they could not have found elsewhere, and introducing his large audiences to up-to-date nationalist music by himself, Musorgsy, Rimsky-Korsakov, Kui, and Borodin.

iii

When Pyotr Ilyich entered the Conservatoire, therefore, he found two rival parties in the city, the nationalist and the Conservatoire, with both of which he felt considerable sympathy.

The question has often been posed—what would have happened to him if he had thrown in his lot with Balakirev? That he would have developed more quickly is certain, proved by the historical fact that he was not to write his first wholly individual work until he met Balakirev and had been guided and inspired by him on a theme chosen by the older man.

On the other hand he was to owe his greatest strength—as one of the world's greatest orchestrators—to the thorough grounding in counterpoint and harmony and the theory of music he received at the Conservatoire. Years later, when they knew one another, Balakirev wrote to him, 'The classics can never teach you independence of form. They give you what you learned from Zaremba when you listened respectfully to his profound lessons on "the correspondence between the form of the Rondo and the fall of the first man"!' It is easy to make fun of the traditionalists, but dangerous to ignore all they have to say, however pedantically they say it. It goes against the grain to criticize Balakirev, who did so much for Russian music and has been so scurvily treated ever since, but it must be said that had he been able to learn music from the bottom upwards he would have been a more resourceful orchestrator and his works would now be played everywhere. It is a question whether, if Tchaikovsky had come under his influence in 1862, he could have written the works which have made him loved all over the world.

As it was, Balakirev, unknowingly, had lost a disciple after his own heart—more so perhaps than any of the men who rallied to him —and Pyotr Ilyich followed Zaremba into the Conservatoire without a second thought—it was as simple as that. Balakirev attacked musical conservatism because it might stifle genius, but if the history of Tchaikovsky is any guide, the only thing the pedagogues can stifle is mediocrity; the genius sooner or later will assert itself. In 1862 Pyotr Ilyich did not know that he had declared for the conservatives and anti-Russians. When he did understand it he showed that not even a Conservatoire directed by Anton Rubinstein could hold him down indefinitely.

In 1862 nothing of this was within the bounds of his imagination; he was a student trying to nerve himself to the plunge of resignation from the Ministry. This had suddenly become an economic matter as well as a spiritual one; Ilya Petrovich, tiring of his post, resigned on a small pension and withdrew to a fairly humble apartment with the twins. He could support and educate them; he could not spare a rouble for Pyotr Ilyich, only a bedroom.

How to live on music? That was immediately the problem, but typically the student did not wait for it to be resolved; he resigned his post; six months at the Conservatoire had shown him clearly the way he had to go.

He was helped, generously helped, by Zaremba, Rubinstein, and the other professors he worked under. This shows better than any words the impression he had given in these six months. Pupils were put in his way, engagements as accompanist at concerts were found, he was employed as copyist, doing this dreary job into the early hours of the morning. He managed to live, though at a rate so beggarly that one wonders how a young man who had cut such a figure in society, took cabs everywhere, ate the best food and drank the best wines and put his hand in his pocket at the slightest hint of a loan, could endure the pinch without a moan. But there were no moans; he was doing what he wanted to do and that was worth every luxury he had been used to.

The change from the government clerk of 1862 to the dedicated musician of 1863 is best seen in photographs. In 1862 Pyotr Ilyich is still the dandy though he has shaved the beard; his morning coat is faultless, the hair carefully drawn back from the forehead, the gloves still in the hand, the cane ready for the careless swing as he strode the Nevsky Prospekt. The face is immature too. It is an enlargement of the photograph of the small boy leaning against his mother, the mouth so sensitive, the cheeks not yet free from puppy fat. Only the noble forehead and the dreamy, deep eyes were to be carried forward.

Towards the end of 1863 comes the fledged musician. The clothes are shabby, the hair lank and overlong, the whole impression rather seedy. But the face is taking on strength of purpose, the slightly puffy cheeks have begun to sink into hollows and the beard that has come back is no longer the neatly trimmed little matter demanded by young Petersburghers but a sprawling collection that could not care less what is thought of it—the beard of a man who is too busy with higher matters to be bothered with a razor.

Something of this, it must be said, was due to Apukhtin who supported the apparent change to bohemianism with approval. He preferred that his friend should be a bohemian in art rather than a self-consciously rakish government clerk. He was to be disappointed about the bohemianism which went no further than appearance; Pyotr Ilyich, he found with a shock, really intended to work and was neglecting his appearance rather than relapsing into sluttishness because he got more work done that way.

All other friends except the steady Adamov, quietly pleased, had dropped off. No more loans, no more wit, no more silliness: they became bored with the serious Pyotr Ilyich and gave him a wide berth. They did him a service; the last temptation disappeared.

He worked like a trooper. How hard, the one famous recollection of Rubinstein will prove. He had been taken into the great man's classes in composition. One day Rubinstein asked him to write a series of contrapuntal variations on a given theme. 'I expected that he would present me with about a dozen,' said Rubinstein; a dozen being regarded as a fair test of a student's ability. 'But Tchaikovsky turned up the next class day with more than two hundred!' Rubinstein soon thought so highly of him that he took the unheard-of step of excusing him from the compulsory pianoforte class so that he could concentrate on theory and composition, the compliment here being double-edged, to the excellence of his piano playing and to his prospects as a composer. Those two hundred variations were significant of much and the Director took the hint.

What Pyotr Ilyich thought of his Director could be gauged by the increasing length of his hair as the years passed. There were two massive heads of hair in the Conservatoire. The first was owned by Leschetizky, the professor in pianoforte, then in the first stages of a career as world-famed virtuoso, now remembered when at all by the curious fact that all his four wives were distinguished musicians. But Anton Rubinstein had set the fashion which the Pole merely followed; his hair approached the fantastic, a great bob to the neck, and Pyotr Ilyich did his best to emulate him.

His worship of Rubinstein was understandable. The entire Conservatoire worshipped him, these and a host of concertgoers. He remains to this day something of a mystery. His antics on the pianoforte stool have been rivalled many times, his antics on the conductor's podium remain unique. At concerts and rehearsals he was like a man possessed, throwing himself about, screaming, sweating; his rehearsals were one long fight, but he carried perfection into the performance proper too; he would stop a symphony in the middle of a bar if he did not think the orchestra was following his conception of the music to a hair's-breadth. He cared for nothing and nobody; the audience would have to hear the work again from the beginning, just as the orchestra would have to play it over again. Of course the audience loved it; what was much more remarkable was that the hard-boiled musicians (most of them Germans who loathed Russians, anyway) accepted it too; they rebelled, they declared themselves outraged, they swore they would not play for him, but they always did in the end and, what is more, when the concert was done they were the first to rise and applaud.

Then came the queer part of the man. After a performance—whether he had conducted or played as soloist—he would collapse on to a sofa and lie there like one dead. But he was not dead, he was very calm and collected. Looking at him or listening to him, one could not believe that this apparently cold man was the gesticulating creature of a few minutes earlier. In his exhausted way he was businesslike, every faculty keen and alive.

When he taught in the Conservatoire the concerts were repeated on a minor scale. Enormous emphasis, temperament flying, students dismissed from class on the slightest pretext—this was daily fare, and Pyotr Ilyich watched and listened, fascinated. He saw him as a genius who had given his life to music, and that was enough for him.

Among the students he soon found a particular friend who gave the key to the prevailing mood of the Conservatoire years. Disciple would be the better word, for the seventeen-year-old Herman Avgustovich Larosh, though something of a prodigy as linguist and composer, attached himself to Pyotr Ilyich from the moment of meeting. This clever boy of German descent was an unmitigated prig, like so many prodigies, and was to become a music critic of smug and often wildly inaccurate judgements. But he did see at once the possibilities of the student Tchaikovsky and his later reminiscences of the composer, though often suspect and with altogether too much Larosh about them, do make clear that the impressionable and self-depreciatory Pyotr Ilyich came to depend a great deal on his earnest encouragement—to the point of becoming a pretty comprehensive prig himself.

As a person, Pyotr Ilyich does not cut a very attractive figure in these years. What with the adulatory-monitor Larosh, his own excessive repentance for wasted years (he was in his early twenties), and his passionate regard for the self-righteous, self-worshipping Rubinstein, a young man of Pyotr Ilyich's pliant nature is apt to swing violently to extremes. As he did. Devotion to music is all very well but when the true self is sacrificed to it the result cannot be self-expression. If there was one thing he was decidedly never meant to be it was straitlaced. So, though working extremely hard and mastering his trade thoroughly, he remained a shadow of his true creative self; this was buried under the weight of idolization, remorse and the effort to live up to the impossible—and undesirable—figure set up by Larosh.

The other rare company he kept in his new mood could not release the real man. Adamov was a nice edition of Larosh, altogether too earnest when Pyotr Ilyich was not opposing him with laughter and lightheartedness. Apukhtin was fading out of the picture and one sympathizes with him, ass though he was making of himself in the low society of Petersburg. He was all for his friend's outward picture of the romantic musician, furrowed brow, funereal clothes, wild beard, and the rest of the rigmarole, but when Pyotr Ilyich abandoned drink and smoking and women and relaxations in general, he thought he was going altogether too far. He expected an artistic rake, he found a monk. They drifted apart.

One of the few gleams of humour in these grim and uncharacteristic years is seen in Pyotr Ilyich's begging letters. He was always short of ready money and devised a unique method of earning a meal or two or the price of a score he was made to buy and study. He did not crudely write and ask for money; he put the request in music; strung out through his letters were a few bars of melody set to the refrain of 'Don't deny, dear friend, this excessively reasonable plea' and so on. He evidently found the method effective for he kept going.

Unhappily for him, the antipathy of Conservatoire for Free Music School and vice versa was growing ever more intense; so much so that it would have amounted to treachery of the deepest hue for a member of one to converse with a member of the other. Balakirev remained as unapproachable and unthinkable as if he and his group were in Timbuktoo instead of a few streets away.

The one man he did meet outside the Conservatoire group was of doubtful value to him. Aleksandr Nikolayevich Serov, twenty years his senior, had been yet another student of the Law School fascinated by music. He went much further than Stasov, for long his friend, because he intended to be an opera composer. Having heard Wagner, he abandoned Stasov and Balakirev's nationalistic aims; he and his old friend fell out and began to write articles in the Press attacking each other's theories. Serov was as virulent about the old-fashioned Rubinstein as about the nationalists, and occupied a platform of his own consisting entirely of Wagner worship. At least he put his theories into practice, and in 1862, the year Pyotr Ilyich joined the Conservatoire, his first lyrical drama, as he called it, *Judith*, was produced in Petersburg. It was more Meyerbeer than Wagner but it had a smack of the grand manner and caught on. Tchaikovsky said later, in one of his pithy comments on contemporaries, 'Serov knew how to appeal to the masses. His work is weak in melodic inspiration and recitative, lacks organic sequence, and offers only crude harmonic effects with instrumentation which is no more than decorative, but he does manage to achieve dramatic effects.'

To the student Pyotr Ilyich he was naturally a figure to be reckoned with. In fact Serov merely succeeded in confusing the young man still further *vis-à-vis* nationalist and conservative and offended him greatly by his arrogance, but he performed one service, he emphasized what Pyotr Ilyich felt, Rubinstein notwithstanding, was essential to him as a composer of modern times—that was, to make use of a large orchestra and all the instruments available.

The next year, 1864, he made his first attempt to break loose from Rubinstein's narrow orchestral gospel. He was a great admirer of the playwright Ostrovsky and specially of his fine play *The Storm* and decided to write an overture for it. In his score he defied all Conservatoire precepts by including parts for harp, tuba, and English horn as well as writing for tremolo and divided violins, all of which were regarded by Rubinstein as inventons of the devil. The result was certain harmonic novelties long afterwards to be recognized as characteristic of Tchaikovsky, and more than a hint of themes whose origin was not an inch west of Moscow.

The score was duly castigated by the Director and not for another year did any sign of the known Tchaikovsky appear. In 1865 Ilya Petrovich, then aged seventy, married for the third time. Pyotr Ilyich knew his wife well. She was a widow, Yelizaveta Mikhailovna Aleksandrovna, a very homely and understanding woman liked by all the children. Had he been a victim of the Œdipus complex as so many have alleged, Pyotr Ilyich could never have accepted another woman in the place of his mother. As it was, he welcomed the marriage, discussed his music freely with his stepmother, and breathed a sigh of relief at the thought that the twins, now in their middle teens, would have motherly attention and a comfortable home to live in.

This event freed him from one anxiety, and when his father went off to present his new wife to the Davydov family in the summer of that year, he did what he had long wanted to do; he seized the excuse to join the travellers and spend a long holiday with his sister at Kamenka.

iv

The significance of this visit in the history of the composer has been strangely overlooked, for it provided the beginning of one of the most notable aspects of the mature Tchaikovsky and of Russian music as known today. His talks with Serov and the furore of Wagner's visit to Petersburg in 1862 to conduct excerpts from his operas put an idea in his head which appealed strongly, the use of a massive orchestra. His hearings of Berlioz, Liszt, and Meyerbeer in concerts and operas at Petersburg appealed to another but allied side of him, the use of instruments new to the Russians and the novel use of classical instruments. At once he grasped dimly the enormous possibilities of rich orchestral effects by including these new instruments and the new use of old instruments in a large orchestra. Kamenka, following on his passion for Glinka, provided a third outstanding strand in his work.

The Ukraine is famous for its beauty, the province of Kiev in the Ukraine contains the loveliest Ukrainian scenery and the finest architecture, and the estate of Kamenka in Kiev province was one of the most beautiful examples of a Russian country house set in an estate of surpassing loveliness. It had everything that the Russian novelists have made world-famous, the large balconied house with its suites for guests, its spacious reception-rooms and ballroom, its lake, river, forest, and extensive rich farmland bordering the flowered garden and orchard.

By 1865 Kamenka had become famous in another way, for it was there that Pushkin spent one of his many rustications by Nicolas I and there that he wrote *The Prisoner of the Caucasus*. The choice of Kamenka was perhaps a little curious since Lyov's father Vasily Davydov had been a notable Decembrist, one of the brave men exiled to Siberia for his resistance to the accession of Nicolas. By the time Pyotr Ilyich made this first stay at Kamenka, Vasily was dead, his wife Aleksandra Ivanovna who had shared his exile had moved to Petersburg with her daughters, the estate had passed to Nikolai Vasilyevich, the elder brother of Lyov, and the political atmosphere had become the reverse of the father's. All was conservative.

It may be doubted whether Pyotr Ilyich cared very much one way or the other; he was no politician. He spent hour after hour with Sasha. He went the rounds of the sugar beet factory with Lyov, a born estate manager. He played with his sister's two little girls on the lawn and in the nursery. He practised the piano in his suite every morning, and in the evenings entertained Aleksandra and her guests on the magnificent grand in the drawing-room. He fished, shot, gardened. He ate enormous meals—fresh country food—and walked them off. He walked for miles. The vast estate was not big enough for him; every afternoon he would take his stick and be off to the villages beyond it.

It would be hard to say what he loved most in these summer months, to be reunited with Sasha, to luxuriate in the domestic life he craved for, or to experience another kind of reunion, with the true and ancient Russia of field, steppe and village and forest and lake that he had not known since the days of Alapayevsk. He was to tell Aleksandra, 'I don't know what I should do without you, I can't be happy apart from you,' and he did not exaggerate; he leaned on her love, sought her advice, could scarcely bring himself to go out of her sight. Her family life was exactly the life he imagined for himself, with a devoted mate, lively children, and a home in which grandeur always gave way to homeliness; her calmness, her good sense, her faith in him soothed and encouraged him, it was so civilized and based on the only things that mattered in life.

But the solitary walks, when he stepped out briskly, strong and tireless, were a joy too. He could savour the country as one never could in company and he could begin to equate it with his music, the one thing suggesting the other. Like so many composers he worked on the move and at Kamenka in this summer of 1865 he was given his first hint of the rich source he was to find in the Russian countryside. Here Kamenka proved a rare boon, for it was in the centre of the province in which the finest of all Russian folk songs were to be found. During his walks Pyotr Ilyich heard the peasants singing and began to note down their songs.

Back in Petersburg late that summer he finished a set of dances based on the Kamenka songs. This little work *Character Dances* was played at one of the open-air concerts outside the city that autumn and was very well received. The work is not heard now but is historic not merely because it was the first performance of an orchestral work by him but because it pointed the way he was to go; it was wholly Russian and it was Tchaikovsky too, and several of the fascinating themes were to reappear in his mature compositions.

Almost immediately afterwards, in a matter of weeks, came an unexpected offer which was to change the course of his life. After a number of successful years managing the Moscow branch of the Russian Musical Society Rubinstein's younger brother Nikolai had just opened the Moscow Conservatoire. He invited Serov to be his Professor of Harmony. Serov accepted. Before the New Year term opened Serov's second opera *Rognyeda* had its premiere in Petersburg. To his surprise it was an immediate success. His reputation soared. He was a made man. He withdrew his acceptance of the post.

Nikolai Rubinstein, left in the lurch at short notice, asked his brother if he had anyone else in mind. Anton recommended Pyotr Ilyich, recommended him warmly as a hard worker and as a young man very well versed in the theory of composition. Perhaps he also said that this student could be had cheaply; at any rate Pyotr Ilyich was offered the post at a figure well below the salary Serov would have received, no more than fifty roubles a month.

Very much his father's son, Pyotr Ilyich did not give a second thought to the salary. Somewhat sadly, for he loved Petersburg and had only unhappy memories of Moscow, he accepted. In the early days of January 1866 he left for Moscow. He was in his twenty-sixth year.

CHAPTER SEVEN

Professor and Symphonist
1866-8

The Rubinstein brothers were small men, devoted to music and fine pianists, but when this is said the resemblance ends. Nikolai was the finer musician though overshadowed by his brother's reputation even to the present day. One reason for this is that he detested to look or act the musician as his brother and Liszt had established him in the public eye. When he met Pyotr Ilyich at the railway station in Moscow and saw a taller version of his brother, long-haired, unkempt, and haggard, he gave an inward whistle, took the young man to his rooms, insisted on a shave, a beard-clip, and haircut and borrowed a morning coat for him; he was not prepared to staff his Conservatoire with Anton Rubinsteins.

There was another substantial difference beside a sense of humour in the one brother and its absence in the other. Anton was a puritan, an austere, rigid-minded man, reserving all exuberance for the concert platform. Nikolai's dandified appearance suggested the fashionable roué. His carefully crinkled hair, moustache, and beard —a mere slip of a thing—his immaculate clothes, debonair manner, and witty speech all spoke of the gregarious man at home in higher society and its rather less high adjuncts. He was, superficially, the *bon viveur* in person, and within a day or two the astonished and somewhat apprehensive Pyotr Ilyich had been wined and dined expensively at the famous Var, whirled into the English Club where he consumed large quantities of liquor and through a haze watched Nikolai Rubinstein gamble away what would have been his harmony professor's year's salary, introduced to exclusive Moscow families where he learned from his Director how to flirt without committing oneself, and driven out of town to the gypsies where Rubinstein enjoyed himself without finesse of any kind.

All of this, the gambling excepted, was not new to Pyotr Ilyich, it seemed a sort of revival of the useless life he thought had gone for ever. What was new was the style with which Nikolai Rubinstein carried out his fast living, a style which made the government clerks of Petersburg seem as callow and crude as they were. Confusing the new arrival almost beyond endurance was the thought of one of Russia's famous musicians, a man whose devotion to musical education was a Moscow legend, making a public exhibition of himself.

Pyotr Ilyich, it must be admitted, showed himself provincial and dense too in his reaction to his new Director. He allowed appearances to guide him like any second-rate mind. Then and for a long time afterwards he looked up to Anton Rubinstein as the serious man, dedicated to his art and altogether admirable, and down to his brother as a frivol. This in spite of the fact, which also took his breath away, that Nikolai would get up after a couple of hours of sleep, trim and in businesslike mood, that he was on the dot of the hour in his classroom, that his students worshipped him and—most telling of all—that his comments to his latest professor about his method of teaching, his music, his outlook, and his compositions, were soberness itself and demonstrated a sound grasp of his subject and of men.

For all his equivocal reception of Nikolai Rubinstein, Pyotr Ilyich enjoyed himself well enough in Moscow after the first shock had passed. Nikolai was an admirable teacher, of staff as well as students, and once his new professor managed to subdue his nervousness in front of a class he began to make a quiet name for himself in the Conservatoire.

He found admirable foils to Rubinstein in the professor of singing, Karl Karlovich Albrecht, and the witty pianoforte professor, Nikolai Dmitrievich Kashkin, and his wife, a quiet couple who kept open house for him in their apartment where he had evening after evening of music and cards. If he wanted pretty girls and a luxurious home he had them in the Tarnovsky house where he and Rubinstein (only five years his senior) tried to outdo one another as gallants. If he wanted good talk and celebrities he could find them at another Rubinstein haunt, the mansion of the Superintendent of the Moscow Opera, Vladimir Petrovich Begichev, a strong supporter of the

Conservatoire and one of Moscow's big men in music. There Pyotr Ilyich met his future publisher, Pyotr Ivanovich Jurgenson, whose enthusiasm had made the founding of the Conservatoire possible, his literary hero Ostrovsky, and the ailing Dargomyzhsky, struggling to finish *The Stone Guest*.

If he wanted to meet these people all over again in less formidable surroundings he had only to drop into the Pukirev house on Tversky Avenue. There he could find on one evening or another members of the circle founded by Nikolai Rubinstein, Ostrovsky, and the old theatre and music patron Prince Odoyevsky. Anybody who was anybody in the arts in Moscow, with quite a few lesser fry, gathered there—Maly actors, Bolshoi singers, dancers, and choreographers, playwrights, poets, novelists, and musicians from every corner of the city. The talk was good, the drinks plentiful, and the music fascinating to a man who thought almost wholly in terms of his next composition. After the rigours of Petersburg where he had no entree into the only excitingly forward-looking music group, of Balakirev, and was too little known to be invited to important literary or theatrical soirées, the camaraderie at Pukirev's seemed like heaven to the young professor.

The difficulty was to fit it all in. He was soon living in four worlds, the hectic world of Rubinstein, the gay world of fashionable Moscow, the cultured quiet of the Kashkins, and the studious world of the Conservatoire classrooms. The world of his own music began to blossom too. He found a sharp critic in Rubinstein—he was to agree with him in almost every particular after the first automatic bitterness—but a loyal supporter too; when the Director thought he had written something worth playing he spared no effort to get it played.

The trouble was that Rubinstein was limited too. Pyotr Ilyich was not fortunate in his early leaders and supporters; Anton Rubinstein's crushing conservatism, the idiotic exaggerations of Larosh (who soon joined him in Moscow), and the conventional judgements of Nikolai Rubinstein all in their various ways put him off his true track. The first composition Nikolai Rubinstein approved and arranged to be played—the Overture in F Major—was little more original than the beginnings of an opera, the Andantes, the Adagios, the Agitatos, the Allegros, the Oratorios, the Variations, and the *Ode to Joy* Pyotr Ilyich had composed under the rule of Anton. The main result of the new influence was to encourage him to turn out too much music and to worry too much about it. What with the stony wrath of Anton at the slightest deviation from his norm and the bantering of Nikolai, who soon began to see in his new professor an irresistible subject for practical and verbal jokes, Pyotr Ilyich was well on the way to becoming a writing machine. His fine technical background actually proved a disadvantage—he found composition only too easy.

The dichotomy in his nature grew more marked under the Moscow régime. He learned to drink heavily—he was never wholly to unlearn it—he went regularly to the English Club with his Director, to the society salons, he flirted, he was flattered, he went to the gypsies with the same taskmaster. Then, home again, he repented with the gusto he gave to everything and set himself, nerves jangling, to hour after hour of composition—often spending the rest of the night at his bedroom table—and to walk down to the classrooms in the morning, heady, nervy, and dispirited.

From time to time he expressed himself humorous-despairingly on the subject of Moscow life, as when he told Anatoly, 'Our first concert takes place on Saturday and very glad I am of it for generally speaking they take their pleasures in Moscow more sensually than spiritually—they eat and drink enormously. The concerts will provide a musical pabulum I am greatly in need of. Without it I am like the bear in his den, I have to live on my own resources—that's to say my own compositions, and they won't always come out of my head. No matter how much I try to live quietly one can't get on in Moscow without guzzling and hard drinking. For example, for the past five days I've got back in the early hours with my belly filled to bursting point. But don't imagine I'm doing nothing, I keep at it every day from morning to late dinner.'

This war of apparent opposites—for he could not resist the big meals, the drink, the gambling—left him after a few months hopelessly in debt. Nor could he resist generous gestures that drew him closer to the looming money-lenders of Moscow's back streets. It was a firm principle with him that everyone connected with the family must be cared for, and in the letter to Anatoly already quoted he says, 'A week ago I sent 40 roubles in silver to Avdotya Yakovlevna [the twins' old governess-nurse] and 25 to Ditlova [an aged relative of his mother].' That was his month's salary given away in one day!

He was not only hopelessly in debt, he was in what often seemed to be a hopeless mental muddle: which world did he want, Anton's or Nikolai's? That he did not want either did not occur to him, so vividly did he incline towards the necessity of a guiding star, and he must be counted unlucky that both Rubinsteins insisted on the very need which Balakirev, in his group at Petersburg, was then demolishing, the need to follow rigorously the classical sonata form.

For, inevitably, he was soon at work on his first symphony, and at once came up against that in him which could not accept the Rubinsteins' immutable law, the teaching he had accepted without comment from Zaremba. To have a nice nature is to find oneself at a disadvantage, as he began to discover; he was grateful to all three men, admired Zaremba's rectitude, worshipped Anton without reservation, and was in a fair way to think very highly of Nikolai. To differ from them was painful and caused him suffering which only the warmhearted know; he felt a traitor, an ingrate, and, being naturally modest, felt sure that his instincts must be a form of original sin to be resisted and put down.

Later, he was to write, 'In certain compositions such as the symphony the form is fixed and I keep to it. But only in its broad outlines and in the order of movements. When it comes to the details I think it permissible to take every liberty, believing that these are dictated by the natural development of the musical idea.' But in the spring of 1866 he had not found himself, he had not met Balakirev, he was a grateful disciple, tried to bend his natural feelings into conformity with what he had been taught, and was in despair when he found his pen running away with him.

By April his feelings broke out in a cry of frustration:
'My nerves are completely wrecked:
1. My symphony is not getting on.
2. Rubinstein and Tarnovsky, having discovered the weak joints in my armour, spend their time infuriating me.
3. I know I shall die before I have finished my symphony. I look forward to a summer at Kamenka like the promised land. From yesterday I have given up vodka, wine and even strong tea. I hate everyone and want to live in a desert. I have already got my ticket for the coach on May 10.'

May 10th came and went and the promised land eluded him. The coach could not make the journey owing to bad roads. He had not enough money to pay for a private carriage for three (he had planned to go with the twins) and compromised in typical fashion; he paid for Anatoly to go to Kamenka and made with Modest the shorter journey to Peterhof, near the Oranienbaum of his childhood. Here they stayed for the summer with the Davydovs' mother, Aleksandra Ivanova Davydova, and her four daughters.

Pyotr Ilyich was in high spirits when he set off. His symphony had not advanced but Anton Rubinstein had played his Overture in F Major at one of the Petersburg Conservatoire's concerts, it had been vigorously applauded, and Apukhtin wrote to say how well he thought of it. This gesture by his old hero and the generous letter from his old friend lifted all depression and he opened the holiday in great form. The Davydovs were favourite companions—they had come to live in Petersburg some years earlier—and a special attachment had grown up between Pyotr Ilyich and the second daughter, Vera Vasilyevna. There is no sign that he thought of marriage—he was more taken that way by the prettiest of the Tarnovsky girls— but Vera was musical and intelligent as well as good-looking, they were often at the piano playing duets, they had long talks and walks together and he felt a soothing sense of minds akin.

All went swimmingly until he began to orchestrate the symphony he had brought with him. The old difficulties sprang up and the longer he worked the more formidable they appeared. The first care-free days with the Davydovs had glossed over not only the threat of the symphony but the conditions which made him unfit to finish it. For all his cheerfulness he had arrived a wreck after months of teaching—twenty-six hours of it every week—after the strain of living up to Nikolai Rubinstein who, sensing a boon companion in him, rarely gave him a day's peace, after night upon night of work on the symphony whenever he could elude his Director.

All his symptoms of the spring came back, redoubled. A great deal has been made of these symptoms which, we have been told, prove him once more to be the hopeless neurotic. If so, then most of us are neurotics, for his symptoms are well known to everyone who has overworked and is worried besides—insomnia, weird and alarming internal pains, violent headaches, palpitations.

The difference between Pyotr Ilyich and most men is not that one has certain symptoms and the other does not, it is that he frankly confesses them as he confessed everything. His reactions are more violent than most because he felt more deeply than most. Again he thought he was dying and—this was what mattered—that his symphony would die with him. Added to this, which is familiar to many creative people, he had the further frightful problem, what to do with material which would only go his way and not the way of the men he admired? The result was neurasthenia.

A doctor was called in. He advised him to stop composition and forbade all night work. Pyotr Ilyich tried to obey, but the effort went completely against the grain. As he was to explain, 'I live on music. Apart from this I am good for nothing. I must hurry because I am afraid of dying before being able to pass on to others what I have in me to give.'

Eventually he was persuaded to send the unfinished symphony to Anton Rubinstein and Zaremba. They were shocked by the liberties he was taking. They indicated at length what he must do to the score to make it acceptable—that is, to follow classical precepts exactly.

Crushed, he went back to Moscow and to months of revision. Early in the new year of 1867 he finished the symphony on the lines suggested by his old masters and resubmitted it. They damned it decisively.

This second blow did him a service, though he suffered severely; it loosened the musical ties still binding him to Petersburg. Only a few months earlier, when the Moscow Conservatoire was transferred to a fine new building, he had spoken at the celebration banquet, his chosen toast being Anton Rubinstein and the Petersburg Conservatoire. Now, Anton's attitude to the symphony which had been remodelled precisely according to his wishes was too unreasonable for even the fervent Pyotr Ilyich to defend. The vodka, the wine, and the strong tea were taken up again.

As Anton fell into the background, Nikolai advanced. In his tipsy moods he was still a sore trial, but his kindness and faith cheered Pyotr Ilyich through a bleak winter and spring. Nikolai had doubled Pyotr Ilyich's salary when he came back from the summer holiday, his suggestion that he should speak at the banquet was a compliment, as was his would-be scandalized face when Pyotr Ilyich sat down at the piano at the after-banquet concert and played from memory the overture to *Ruslan and Lyudmila* so that, as he said, Glinka's music should be heard first in the new headquarters of music in Moscow. More importantly, Nikolai, understanding the depression caused by his brother's treatment of the symphony, offered more than once to play it. His offers were only accepted in part by the stricken composer, who was in the state familiar to many, not knowing what to believe in, his own instincts or the advice of those supposed to know better than he did. The first performance of the entire symphony was still some way off.

In the midst of this indecision he was diverted by the first of his many ignes fatui. Taking his Glinka worship too literally, he felt that he must write an opera, that Russian music must advance in that form. He approached Ostrovsky. Ostrovsky suggested making an opera libretto from his play *Voivode*. Pyotr Ilyich was much too flattered by the agreement to question the subject; he would have set to music anything written by such a man. In early spring he was at work, with enthusiasm yet not with success. With the symphony he had allowed himself to be guided by traditionalists; he now encouraged himself to take on a subject he was temperamentally unfitted to portray satisfactorily.

What with this and the mutilated symphony, he was back once more in the toils of neurasthenia by the time summer came round. He had intended to go to Kamenka, so infuriatingly missed the summer before, but when the moment arrived he again changed his mind—this time for the characteristic reason that he would not present himself to Aleksandra in a condition which could pain and worry her and (such was his unconquerable modesty) make her think less of him.

Instead, he took one of the twins, Anatoly this time, for a holiday in Finland. Most typically—to his dying day he was hopeless (or splendidly careless, according to the way you look at it) with money—he soon found himself without funds, having miscalculated the cost of the trip. After a hazardous but amusing voyage across the Baltic, they found themselves in the arms of the Davydov mother and daughters who most opportunely were spending the summer in Estonia, at the little seaport of Hapsal.

In such company cheerfulness soon returned and it became extremely difficult for him to persuade himself that he was a born misanthrope. He had had the sense to leave the symphony behind or had forgotten to bring it—with him one can never be sure—and the work he did on the *Voivode* was one of the best things in that ill-fated opera; he reorchestrated the Kamenka *Character Dances*. This apart, the only writing he did during another holiday of walks and talks and piano duets was the composition of three little piano pieces dedicated to Vera Vasilyevna. All three are charmingly melancholy, the last was to become famous as Song without Words in F Major.

One could also say infamous, for this little piece has been castigated by great critics as cheap and saccharine and subjected to many other epithets. But these critics miss the point; the notable thing about this light work, thrown off quickly, was that it provided the first demonstration of another facet of Tchaikovsky the great composer. One thing all these great men have in common, the ability to write good tunes. Tchaikovsky, as all now know, was to prove the master of all in this essential deparment of genius, and here, in this much-berated piano piece, was the beginning of a fabulous gift.

By winter the opera was on its way and the symphony was returning by fits and starts to its pre-Anton Rubinstein content except for improvements which occurred in the act of scratching out the great man's instructions. In December Nikolai Rubinstein played the *Voivode* dances at a symphony concert—the first of three successful performances within a few months. A few weeks later came Berlioz, recently the honoured guest of Balakirev and Dargomyzhsky at Petersburg, to give a series of concerts of his own works.

All Pyotr Ilyich's generosity and wish to praise came to the fore. Berlioz was one of the gods of The Mighty Handful, whom Pyotr Ilyich had been taught to regard as vulgar deriders of his own heroes, but no matter, he was courageous, original, and shockingly ill-rewarded and the young harmony professor said so. Not only in his letters and in conversation but—a tremendous ordeal for such a shy man—in a speech in French at a banquet given in the old composer's honour by the music lovers of the city.

Both Stasov and Balakirev had followed Berlioz down from Petersburg and after the Master's departure for Paris each met Pyotr Ilyich. These meetings were momentous. It was not possible to be five minutes in the presence of these men without realizing that they were far from the crude and bad-mannered nationalists Pyotr Ilyich had been led to believe. He was not the man to hug a false conception for an instant in the face of such evidence. Stasov charmed and awed him, Balakirev exerted his usual mesmerism without apparent difficulty. Personalities were excluded, the future of Russian music was the one subject discussed. On such a subject both Petersburghers were irresistible.

Thinking over the meetings after Balakirev and Stasov had gone home, Pyotr Ilyich began to adjust his mind. One aspect of the man which has never been understood widely is his commonsense. It is easy to go astray in dealing with artists for they often appear to invite snap judgements. Pyotr Ilyich was nervous, for instance—so much so that when he found himself on the conductor's podium not long after this he went stiff with fright and felt 'that his head was going to tumble from his shoulders at any moment unless he held it absolutely rigid'. He was seemingly without self-confidence in everything, he was extravagant and knew nothing about the value of money, he drank too much, he had no idea of time, orderliness, discipline, as these things are understood by the crowd.

He was in short the artist personified as the philistine imagines him—hopeless apart from his art which is a thing apart. Yet never was there a falser judgement. He had a strong vein of commonsense in everything that mattered. He understood that art was a part of life— its finest part—and must not be divorced from it. He was the very opposite of that philistine Nikolai Ilyich, his elder brother. Nikolai, like all philistines, took with immense seriousness everything in life that was of no importance and treated with frivolous lightness everything that was truly important.

One example of Pyotr Ilyich's attitude will suffice. He had a very good appetite and never missed a meal but he did not eat largely just because he enjoyed his food, he did it because his commonsense told him that he could not work at his music satisfactorily on an empty stomach. Now this commonsense applied itself to Balakirev and the nationalist school. Having met Balakirev, all inhibitions dropped away but he did not succumb to his fascination as the members of the 'Five' had done; he saw that he was genuine, perhaps great, that much of what he said was true and vital to the future of Russian music, but there he stopped. His fund of commonsense was greater than that of the ebullient Balakirev. He saw the dangers of shutting oneself in a group and shouting abuse at the backward—the cramping, narrowing effect on one's music. He believed one could be truly nationalist without wasting time and energy on propaganda and labelling musicians as those one met and those one did not. He believed that if he wrote Russian music as he felt it, the music would do its own work.

So he sent his *Voivode* dances to Balakirev to play in Petersburg but reserved judgement about the offer to join the nationalist school. He began to think that one could be nationalist without flying any kind of flag. Balakirev finally released him from the Anton Rubinstein school but failed to lure him into another. He set him free to be himself.

At that moment Balakirev's influence was shown practically in the work on the symphony. Tchaikovsky was never to throw off wholly the feeling that his deviations from the classical mould were faults in himself. This effect of Mozart-worship was expressed years later when he said, 'I have always suffered from my inability to assimilate musical forms and handle them correctly. I have struggled hard against this defect and can claim, with legitimate pride, that I have made progress. But it is only too clear, nevertheless, that I shall never compose anything with a perfect form to the end of my days. In everything I write there are masses of faults which the most casual glance can discover easily.'

If he felt like that in his maturity, his feelings in 1868 can be imagined. He was still trying to erase the sensation of guilt every time he differed from Anton Rubinstein, and his replacement of original material criticized by Rubinstein still seemed little less than crimes of ingratitude and presumption. Balakirev arrived in his life at precisely the moment best calculated to encourage his natural gifts. As soon as the nationalist leader had gone back to Petersburg, Pyotr Ilyich flew at his score, wiped out the last remnants of Zaremba and Rubinstein and asked Nikolai Rubinstein to play it.

As he did in the middle of February with unquestionable success. How modest the composer was may be gathered from the fact that, sure of failure, he had not even troubled to dress himself for the occasion. The delighted audience, insisting on a personal appearance, were surprised to find, when Pyotr Ilyich had at last been routed out from his corner, that the young man who edged on to the platform looked rather like someone who had spent the night in his clothes.

From that day to this the First Symphony has been neglected in the most extraordinary fashion. Most music lovers have never heard it, critics seldom mention it. What has been said about it since Tchaikovsky's death is better not repeated, it is so biased, so inadequate. Naturally the symphonies written in his maturity are finer works, but in this First Symphony the Tchaikovsky of the future is plainly and often charmingly revealed. It deserves regular performance in its own right.

The work has a title, 'Winter Daydreams', as have all four movements, and the few critics who have dealt with it have not failed to exercise their wit: 'Lots of daydreams, little winter' is a typical example; it is not very funny and is wholly untrue.

The first movement title—Traveller's Dreams—can be read in more than one sense, for the work is a voyage of discovery into the mysteries of symphonic writing. Tchaikovsky uses his love of the Russian countryside—particularly the expanse of snowy steppe —symbolically and with the happiest of results. This first movement opens to the manner born, as if the composer had created the Tchaikovsky idiom many years earlier, flute and bassoon announcing a cheerful melody leading into the principal theme struck out by full orchestra. The way in which he manipulates his theme at once places him as a composer to be reckoned with; it runs the gamut of the emotions representing the changing moods of the traveller as he journeys on and is tossed from section to section of the orchestra with a technical skill nicely screened.

The link between first and second theme is just as representative of the established Tchaikovsky, a series of chromatic scales taken from a primitive Russian instrument, the *gusli*, chiefly famed for its rich arpeggios. It was to become a fetish with him to search for instruments which would add unusual colour to the orchestral tone and this was to reappear in all his symphonies.

The movement ends with another Tchaikovskyan device, a thrilling orchestral crescendo dying away to the suggestion of a tolling bell—not a bell itself, be it noted. This too provided a fore-taste of the future. Every lover of music knows how often Russian composers imitate or use bells in their orchestral works and for a very natural reason; church and town bells pealing far across forest and steppe are one of the Russian's most familiar memories and at once bring his countryside to life.

This is one of two outstanding points about the opening move-ment of the G Minor Symphony which will quickly strike the listener—the extraordinarily skilful recreation of atmosphere which reminds one of Pushkin's great poem *Byesy*, building up without one false touch the picture of a traveller passing through a snowy countryside. It is in fact a musical impression of the effect achieved in words by the poet. The other point is that the symphonist is ready made and offers the certain sign of supremacy in this form; besides giving fascinating proof of resourcefulness in orchestration he speaks throughout with one unmistakable voice and this voice is his alone.

Not until the transformation music in *The Nutcracker* was Tchaikovsky to rival this highly successful atmospheric score. It remains unique to this day in that, unlike most impressionistic music, it does not demand a certain mood in the listener, it creates it, because Tchaikovsky's music is vigorous and manly as well as poetical.

The Andante—Sad Country of Mists—opens with one of Tchai-kovsky's mellow themes and ends with a stroke of ingenuity, the bassoon used against a background of strings. The theme is given, as one would imagine with this composer, to the woodwinds, the instruments he perhaps loved best and certainly used with the most ravishing effect. In this First Symphony the theme is melancholy and wistful, a theme which could have come only from Russia.

It is notable that Pyotr Ilyich had already adopted a proceeding which the mature Tchaikovsky was to carry out automatically; unlike a Rimsky-Korsakov who takes folk themes and orchestrates them more or less as they stand, he transforms them. When one listens to this Andante one has the sense of a Russian theme which has been spiritualized to meet a certain mood required by the composer.

The Scherzo opens gaily with the piccolo—the traveller is approaching the village in which he will stay the night—and moves into a waltz, yet another precursor of the world-famous Tchaikovsky. This waltz is not one of his best but his use of the orchestra is not far from masterly, providing the kind of delicate embroidery at which Tchaikovsky was to excel, at once putting one in mind of the French elegance which was to pervade much of his work.

The last movement returns to the first theme of the opening movement, then—the traveller is watching a village fête—breaks into a fine rousing dance measure. This cheerful refrain, given to all sections of the orchestra with a fullblooded zest that reminds one of Glinka—of whom the composer was undoubtedly thinking—demonstrates not only that Pyotr Ilyich could be as lively as his hero but that he had already passed beyond him in the use of orchestral colour.

Perhaps the most impressive point about this movement is the contrapuntal treatment of the dance tune. The counterpoint is most felicitous, striking without subtlety, and the coda, though equally obvious, is always varied and always effective. Indeed, one of the most revealing things about this symphony is the composer's command of the orchestra. He also senses what was to be such a joy in the work of the mature man, that constant change of mood and tempo is essential to hold the listener and, a further refinement by which the great composer can always be distinguished from the lesser, that a returned theme must be varied slightly—not simply by giving it to another section of the orchestra, but by actual changes in the writing. There are beautiful themes which could only have come from a Tchaikovsky and there are even hints of the elegant sophistication for which he was to become famous.

This First Symphony is a young man's work in many respects; it is often emotional but never soul-searching, often clever but never profound, but in originality, in charm, in genuine feeling it stands squarely on its own feet as a work able to give pleasure without reference to anything the composer might have written in later years. The idea of playing such a work as a curiosity because it happens to be by Tchaikovsky is as ridiculous as the attitude sometimes adopted by musicologists when they write as though no early Tchaikovsky symphony can be taken seriously. The reason given is that they are so little subjective and do not deal with a theme of importance to mankind.

The absurdity of this argument—which is mere snobbism—does not need to be stressed. A man can write a symphony precisely as he pleases; all one dare demand is that the form expresses the content truthfully, the rest is up to the composer. And in this First Symphony, as in his next two, Tchaikovsky chooses to show himself pre-eminently the disciple of Balakirev the nationalist and as the man who was to give the world its greatest ballet scores. This Symphony in G Minor is not only the first truly Russian symphony and, as such, as important as *A Life for the Tsar*, it is far ahead of its time. When one remembers that Brahms was not to write his First Symphony for another ten years, one sees precisely how advanced Tchaikovsky was in this first attempt and how successful.

One further point of moment; this, his first large-scale orchestral work, offers the double drama that is found at its height only in Tchaikovsky and certain works of Stravinsky. As all concert-goers know, a Tchaikovsky symphony, concerto, or tone poem has the power to stir deeply for two reasons, that it provides both aural and visual excitement. This magic of the great composer who is also an inspired orchestrator can be seen as well as heard in the Tchaikovsky First Symphony.

CHAPTER EIGHT

Suitor and Opera Composer
1868-9

Tchaikovsky was much more than a very nice man, he was that rare creature, a noble-minded man. He was incapable of spite or meanness, and in fifty-three years not one nasty action or unkind word was recorded against him. To be with him was to feel the better and to act better. From the very beginning of his life his effect on people was shown to be wholly good, from his softening influence on the sharp Fanny to the conquest of the little brutes in the Petersburg preparatory school, and a list of his friends shows how every type of man felt drawn towards him, from the rake Apukhtin to the sedate Adamov, from the napoleonic Anton Rubinstein (who criticized his music but always spoke with unusual respect and even fondness about him) to the difficult Nikolai Rubinstein who began by laughing at him and ended by preferring him to any other man in Moscow.

The victory over Nikolai Rubinstein was a notable triumph of unassuming goodness. Pyotr Ilyich learned much from his Director —for instance, he became a man of the world in the best sense, transforming Nikolai's worldliness into a truly civilized approach to life and people—but he gave more than he received. By the time the 'Winter Daydreams' symphony had been performed Nikolai had quite changed his views. He did not change his manner of life but he began to understand in 1869 that the harmony professor who had amused him so much in 1866 might well become one of the hopes of Russian music and a particular advertisement for the Moscow Conservatoire, and was prepared, in theory at least, to give him every chance to compose, and in practice, to play what he did compose.

In his own way he too had been forced to respect the young man who had seemed at first little more than an admirable butt and an amiable drinking companion. And when one remembers that behind his apparently flighty manner Nikolai a mere three years earlier had held musical opinions as conservative as Anton, the feat achieved by the outwardly mild and gentle Pyotr Ilyich will be seen in its true impressive proportions; to widen the views of a man in Nikolai's position was to provide Russian music with a powerful striking base. So one saw the amusing but not uncommon spectacle of the moderate radical beginning in his quiet and commonsensical way a revolution just as important and rather more successful than the violent upheaval preached by the rebels—for the Balakirev group had not the power of an established Conservatoire behind it.

In the Moscow Conservatoire Tchaikovsky had become in these three years the most popular professor; his classes were jammed, his lectures were listened to in respectful silence, and after he had done he always found it difficult to escape to his room because of the crowd of eager young men and women besieging him with questions and invitations.

Some of his popularity with the young women was no doubt due to his looks and manner. At twenty-nine he had become a very handsome man, tall, upright, strong, his wonderful blue eyes contrasting with thick dark hair brushed back to show the full white expanse of forehead. The beard was taking the form it was to have for the rest of his life, he had beautiful hands—a legacy from his mother—and a melodious voice. And his manner was altogether charming, the manner of the well-bred man who expects—and gets —from others the polish and kindness he invariably offers them. The men students were just as taken with him; his approach was without favour, he simply and obviously loved music and wished to impart his love and knowledge in the clearest and most civilized way—the splendid Taneyev, for instance, afterwards admitted proudly that he owed everything to him. Tchaikovsky was not, in fact, a lover of teaching; his lectures caused him more pain than pleasure, but he evidently concealed his feelings or they were overborne by his devotion to music.

It was now the turn of the Balakirev group to fall under the spell of his charm and goodness. Balakirev and Stasov had carried back favourable reports of him but as he had refused to indulge in per-

above The Tchaikovsky
family in 1848 (see pages
9–10)

below Aleksandra and
Lyov Davydov, 1860

Tchaikovsky (*above*) in
1861, (*below*) in 1868

sonalities he was still regarded with suspicion in the group as an Anton Rubinstein man. His charm was obvious, what lay behind it not so obvious.

Then came a charity concert in Moscow at which he conducted his *Voivode* dances (this was one of the occasions when he felt that his head would leave his shoulders at any moment) and he and his music were received rapturously by the fashionable audience.

Not so another item on the same programme. This was one of the earliest orchestral works by the young Rimsky-Korsakov, *Fantasia on Serbian Themes*. It was received coolly and the next day reviewed very harshly in a Moscow newspaper.

Tchaikovsky had never met Rimsky-Korsakov and knew nothing about him except what Balakirev had told him; if he had had any feeling about him it could have been caution about a fervent nationalist group member. No such thought entered his head; he knew what most interested him, the young man's music, and that was enough. He thought the Fantasia was good, promising music. Putting himself in the composer's place, as he always did, he imagined the shock of this first Moscow review. He was not prepared to allow some anonymous reviewer, who could not have written a note of decent music to save his life, to discourage an obviously gifted musician at the very outset of his career.

Burning with indignation, he at once sat down and wrote his first piece of music criticism, a long and favourable notice of the Fantasia, and sent it off to a well-known Moscow journal. When it was printed he found himself hailed as a critic of power and discernment in his own city. More to the point—for he had no leanings that way —the notice dispelled the last remnant of suspicion in the Balakirev circle; what he had done was courageous and selfless, they all saw that. From that moment the name of Tchaikovsky occupied a unique position in the nationalist camp; he stood for a nationalist composer who preferred to go his own way, a man to be respected.

This attitude warmed into open admiration soon afterwards when Tchaikovsky spent that Easter of 1868 with his father in Petersburg and was introduced to the rest of the nationalist disciples. His easy and tactful manner pleased everyone, even the spiky Kui who had damned his *Ode to Joy* three years earlier. Some, notably Rimsky-Korsakov, admired the polish of the man and his work immensely, and his fiancée, the pianist Nadyezhda Purgold, could not praise him enough.

For his part, Tchaikovsky liked their wholehearted love of music and of Russia and concentrated on this rather than on the more controversial points, such as a lack of finesse in their work and a lack of charity in their general outlook. When he went back to Moscow he went in effect as their spokesman and sympathizer.

ii

He came back greatly cheered by the new friends he had made and their obvious belief in his talent. He threw himself into *Voivode* and by the time the Conservatoire classes ended in early summer had finished it and sent it to the Bolshoi.

That June he had a welcome break and a much-needed addition to his income when he accompanied Begichev and one of his step-sons to Berlin in the role of music teacher. The boy became ill and the whole party—Begichev never travelled without a large retinue —hurried to a chest specialist in Paris.

The boy, Vladimir Shilovsky, was one of his students at the Conservatoire and a very brilliant one too—at fourteen he had had his compositions publicly performed. Shilovsky (the Volodya one meets so often in Tchaikovsky's early letters) also possessed immense charm, for Pyotr Ilyich and for the whole family. A few months later he is found at one of his many spas, Baden-Baden, where, as Pyotr Ilyich reports, 'He spent the whole time with Aunt Katya [Aleksandra Andreyevna's sister] and became extremely inti-mate with her.'

Pyotr Ilyich had moved some way from the traveller of twenty-one who thought the Petersburg theatres mounted opera and stage plays so much better than the French. Possibly he had been jolted out of the last of his chauvinism by meeting so much of it in the Balakirev circle; at any rate in 1868 he looked at the Paris theatres with an unbiased eye and told Aleksandra frankly that the Russians had no conception of the care taken in production by the French.

He had become an assiduous correspondent, pouring out letters by the dozen. His friends heard regularly from him, his family oftener still and Aleksandra almost every other day. 'My future happiness is impossible without you,' he had told her only a few weeks earlier, and in June, in a Paris which thrilled and delighted him, he nevertheless found time to think with longing of Kamenka, to picture it, and to insist that his feelings were there. 'That smelly but beloved jasmine is now enjoying itself flowering by the side of the house that holds my nearest and dearest.'

When he wrote this, he had already met the woman who was to arouse the deepest feeling in him of anyone outside his family. A few weeks earlier a touring Italian opera company had arrived in Moscow after a triumphant visit to Warsaw. The triumph rested in their star artist, Désirée Artôt, who had performed the exceptional feat of singing the roles of Leonora and Azucena on alternate nights. Tchaikovsky did not go to the Moscow performances—he was then in the final stages of *Voivode*—but was introduced to Artôt at a supper given after her benefit night.

As his letters say nothing of her at this time, the meeting evidently made no impression on him. This is not surprising for Artôt was a plain woman who, like so many artists, only 'came alive' on the stage. He did, however, attend the opening night of the company's autumn season when he had come back to Moscow and the Conservatoire after a round of family visits. She played Desdemona, and Tchaikovsky, like the rest of the audience, fell in love with her.

It is significant that at that moment, in the midst of considering various plans for a second opera, he was writing a tone poem which he was to call *Fatum*. He explained the programme. 'Fate is a power of destiny which forbids us to be happy, watches jealously to see that our felicity and serenity is never unalloyed, holds itself over our heads like the sword of Damocles and instils a slow poison into the soul. It makes sure that our existence is a succession of painful realities, of ephemeral dreams and mirages of happiness. One has to submit to it and resign oneself to sadness without end.'

Nothing could have seemed more improbable a few weeks after he had begun work on this Byronic theme than that it could have bearing on his present life, for he was obsessed by Artôt and could think of nothing and no one else. Characteristically he could not bring himself to seek her out, thinking her far above the attentions of such an insignificant man as himself—and this even when, having met her again at a musical evening, she expressed hurt surprise that he had not tried to renew the acquaintance of the spring. The man to bring them together was, of all people, Anton Rubinstein. Visiting Moscow, he insisted that his old student accompany him to another reception for Artôt. This time Tchaikovsky, for all his diffidence, could not hide his feelings and Artôt was more than interested. She knew that he was rated as one of the most promising of young Russian composers and she could see for herself that he stood out of the ruck of men at the reception (and as he did at every gathering) with his distinguished face, fine carriage, and kind smile.

They talked. She was French and had been trained by Turgenyev's Pauline Viardot. Was not this an omen? Was not he destined to marry into the nation which had produced his mother?

They began to meet every day. Soon he was writing to everyone except, significantly, Aleksandra, in high emotion. 'Ah! If only you knew Artôt!' he told Modest. 'What a singer! What an actress! Nobody on the stage has ever produced such an effect on me. How I regret that you can't see and hear her! You would be in ecstasy with her gestures and the infinite grace of her poses.'

He added, 'I have become very friendly with her and she treats me in the most affectionate manner you can imagine. Rarely have I met a woman so kind, good, and intelligent.'

They were soon the talk of Moscow. Prince Odoyevsky, who flourished on theatre gossip, noted, 'Tchaikovsky seems to be courting Désirée Artôt prodigiously.' The autumn production of *Voivode* was postponed, *Fatum* advanced lethargically, everyone was waiting for the announcement of an engagement.

On the first day of the new year, 1869, Tchaikovsky broke the news to his father. 'If nothing prevents it, we shall get married in the summer.'

But he had not written to Ilya Petrovich simply to announce the engagement but to ask his advice. 'The worst of it is that there are obstacles to the marriage, several of them.' He detailed the obstacles, which arose on both sides. On Artôt's side there was the inevitable mother who went everywhere with her. 'She thinks me too young [Artôt was five years older] and is afraid that I should insist on her daughter living in Russia always.'

On his side, the objections came from his friends, led by Nikolai Rubinstein. 'They are doing all they can to prevent the marriage. They say that if I marry a famous singer I shall become a "wife's husband", live on her earnings, follow her round Europe and have no time to write music.'

On her side 'she insists that for all her great love for me she can't bring herself to give up her work which earns so much money for her and without which she would feel lost'.

He sums up. 'On the one hand I am heart and soul in love with her and feel that I can't live without her, on the other hand calm commonsense insists that I consider carefully whether my friends' objections have any weight.'

The mere fact that he thought it necessary to ask his father's advice—favourable though the advice was—showed how undecided he was. He and she were faced with the old and insoluble problem that neither wished to give up his art, that each feared that his art would be submerged by the art of the other. They agreed that he should come to her home near Paris that summer and settle the matter one way or the other, but there was little chance that a woman of Artôt's temperament would accept the arrangement for long; to her, a man who would agree to wait for six months to know his fate had declared in advance what his fate must be.

She did not hesitate for long. The company left for a return visit to Warsaw late that month. A week or so afterwards Nikolai Rubinstein came into the Bolshoi where Tchaikovsky was superintending final rehearsals of *Voivode* and broke the news: Artôt had married the company's leading baritone, Padilla y Ramos. Rubinstein, who could be cruel, cried cheerfully, 'Well, so I was right after all. You are needed by Russia. You were never meant to be a foreigner's valet.'

Tchaikovsky said nothing. As white as a sheet, he walked out of the theatre. Commonsense told him that Rubinstein was right, his heart told him that he was wrong. He mastered the shock. Only once did he lose his self-control, when he broke out against her, saying that after their intimacy a marriage to another man was farcical. For the rest, he controlled himself and behaved as though he had not been snubbed, as though the people of Moscow were not whispering about him behind his back. In the future he and Artôt were to become good friends and he never missed hearing her sing, but the first time he heard her again (it was the winter of that same year and she sang Marguerite) he stared at her without taking the opera glasses from his eyes throughout the entire time she was on stage, tears ran down his cheeks and he made no effort to check them because he did not know that they were there.

He felt, perhaps, what most people will think; that she had been right but that he would never again have the chance of a full life with a woman of his own. Suddenly and against all probability, his introduction to *Fatum* had been proved only too correct; he was the sport of destiny and destiny would not leave him in peace until he died. And though he lost the chance of a happy marriage because the woman sensed his inability to relegate art to second place, he can scarcely be blamed for feeling that fate had marked him out and that his symphonic poem had been fate's work too. He was doing no more than express in his Russian fashion the despair felt by most great creative artists when they suspect that domesticity and all its joys are not for them.

iii

Many biographies of Tchaikovsky, following contemporary reports, say that he reappeared at rehearsals calm and unmoved the day after Nikolai Rubinstein's dramatic news and the days following. They assume, rather naïvely, that his feeling for Artôt had somehow died in the night, that it was shallow and worthless.

This point needs comment because it is generally taken for granted that Tchaikovsky wore his heart on his sleeve, that impassioned (and morbid) self-revelation was the rule of his life. In truth, nothing could be further from the fact. In his music and in his letters to and conversations with intimates, Pyotr Ilyich was absolutely frank and, as has been seen, when he felt wretched or guilty (which like all nice men he often did) he said so with the utmost extravagance, in real Russian style. But with acquaintances and in his day-to-day life in Moscow he behaved as the aristocrats behaved with whom he had mixed for so much of his life, taking care not to worry others with his private sorrows.

Pride took a hand too; he knew that Moscow was buzzing with stories of the way in which its favourite young composer had been jilted by the French opera star, and would not for the world have given scandalmongers the satisfaction of seeing how hurt and mortified he was. So he appeared as the contemporary reports made out, calm, apparently unconcerned, possibly a little more silent than usual, but anxious to get on with the rehearsal. It was a notable victory for the last virtue with which Tchaikovsky is ever credited, self-restraint.

Work was, of course, the one answer, and he worked, leaving himself no time to think. He worked on the final stages of *Voivode* and *Fatum*, he worked at a new opera. And at first it seemed as though his decision to sacrifice married happiness for music was to be rewarded. The premiere of *Voivode* on 11 February was a considerable success—fifteen curtain calls for Tchaikovsky—and Prince Odoyevsky, who never missed a first night, was so taken with what he called a 'masterly work' that he decided to make the composer a gift. It was a curious gift, as Tchaikovsky reported home with a chuckle, nothing less than the replacement of the Bolshoi cymbals which the Prince did not think were fit for a man who had such talent for introducing them at the right moment. 'So the dear old fellow scoured Moscow for a good pair of "piatti" and sent them to me with a delightful letter.'

Two weeks later came the first performance of *Fatum* under Nikolai Rubinstein, and this too was sufficiently well received to give Tchaikovsky the illusion that at last he had written a symphonic work which would remain in the concert repertory.

Both ventures disappointed. Both were damned, politely and not so politely, by the critics. The opera did not last beyond its fifth performance and the disgusted composer destroyed the score. *Fatum* quietly died and this score too was destroyed by Tchaikovsky.

One of the most virulent critics was, of all people, Larosh, who had scarcely a good word to say of opera or symphonic work. Tchaikovsky was greatly offended—not so much at the tone of the reviews as of the secrecy with which his supposed friend had concealed his views when they met. He did not speak to Larosh for two years and never afterwards completely trusted him.

It must be said that Larosh for once had the rights of it, though his admiring attitude to Tchaikovsky while the works—which he knew quite well—were being written cannot be excused. Any hope of *Voivode* making a good opera was destroyed quite early on, when Ostrovsky withdrew from the collaboration after the first act. Pyotr Ilyich took over the writing of the libretto and the work was doomed from that moment. Tchaikovsky was singularly unlucky in his librettists and it is a question who was the worst, he or his brother Modest. It is almost always a mistake for opera composers to take any hand in their libretti, and Tchaikovsky was unfitted for the work in every way; he was no poet apart from his music and his taste in literature was generally unreliable. He could write a good, self-revealing though uninspired letter—he was to write thousands —and he wrote sensible music criticism, but a creative writer he was not.

Sagging under the weight of its untheatrical and banal libretto, the score presented a *mélange* of Italian and German operatic conventions leavened (or burdened) by writing which could only have come from one source, Anton Rubinstein. For the strange eclipse of the First Symphony after apparent success—it was not to be played again until he was well known—had thrust Tchaikovsky back to what he had been taught at the Conservatoire.

His destruction of the score was much less peevishness than self-knowledge. He kept what he still thought promising, and this was, specially, the dances and a song, the 'Romance of the Nightingale', which has been well described as an early effort in musical impressionism. Up to then soloist or chorus in opera had sung words which advanced the action, words accompanied by a tune which exploited the range of the voice but had little to do with the words sung. In *Voivode* Tchaikovsky tentatively changed the balance; he chose to make the music advance the story by conveying the emotion hitherto left to the words. It was a notable innovation which he was to develop in his later operas.

One further point about the opera; the ever-searching Tchaikovsky had with much joy—and secrecy—embodied in the score a part for yet another instrument not yet heard in a full orchestra. This was the celesta which he was to use to such effect in *The Nutcracker*.

Fatum, which was resurrected from orchestral parts and published after Tchaikovsky's death, is an unequal work, but whether it deserves the total oblivion it has been consigned to is questionable. Like the First Symphony it has a very beautiful and wholly characteristic Andante, and the other movements, though less successful, possess much interest. The trouble is that the movements are not properly integrated and that the form is unsatisfactory. For, veering away from his conservatism in *Voivode*, Tchaikovsky, uncertain which way to pursue, wrote the work in free form.

The best comment comes as so often from Balakirev. Tchaikovsky sent the score to him soon after the Moscow premiere, asking him to play it and to accept the dedication if he thought the work worthy of it—the usual disarming approach which made Pyotr Ilyich so beloved.

Balakirev played it and accepted the dedication, but this did not prevent him from forthright criticism. 'I don't really like the work,' he wrote bluntly, 'because I don't think you have thought enough about it. It shows signs of being composed in a tearing hurry—the joins are only too apparent—and the form just won't do. Larosh says this is because you haven't studied the classics enough. I beg to differ. I think the reason is that you don't know enough modern music.'

Tchaikovsky accepted this plain speech. He did not in fact dedicate the work to Balakirev because he never had it printed, but luckily for himself and the world he swallowed his chagrin and allowed the older man to guide him to his first authentically Tchaikovskian composition.

Before this happened he had finished his second opera. He took a little time to find a suitable subject. Ostrovsky suggested Alexander the Great but Pyotr Ilyich wisely rejected the compliment. Eventually he settled on his favourite story, of Undine. Here, for the first time, he followed his instincts. The subject, as the future was to show, suited him precisely.

At this point fate intervened, comically in one sense, disastrously in another. La Motte Fouqué's story had been splendidly done into Russian by Vasily Andreyevich Zhukovsky, the great translator of the *Odyssey*, but Tchaikovsky was led by his goddess to a bookshop where he discovered a libretto after Undine perpetrated by Vernoy de Saint-Georges, a charlatan who emulated Scribe only too faithfully. And as if this was not enough, he handed over the translation to Vladimir Aleksandrovich Sollugob. Sollugob was a count who moved in the Moscow social circles frequented by the composer. Possibly he had personal charm, certainly his literary ability was slight; he was a poet without promise, a dilettante. The translation was abominable, losing all the magic of the poetry.

With this heavy burden on his back, Tchaikovsky wrote freely and often well, inspired by the subject. He was particularly cheered on by the promise of Gedeonov, Director of the Imperial Theatres, to stage it. As none of the work was then in a state to be seen, the compliment was considerable. A date was even fixed; in November of that year. He wrote so rapidly that by August the score was in the Director's office.

And that, virtually, was the end of *Undine*. It took Tchaikovsky five years to get the score, or a firm comment, from the authorities. When it came, the comment was freezing: 'Your opera has been judged unworthy of inclusion in the repertoire of the Imperial Theatres.'

That score too was burned by the infuriated composer. But he kept some numbers and remembered others with the happiest of results; he had not been wrong, the subject suited him, and his music—or that of it which has been preserved—indicated for the first time where one great facet of his genius lay, in the portrayal of the fairy world as no other man has done. The music of *Undine* was to reappear in Ostrovsky's *Snyegurochka*, in the Second Symphony, and, most important, in *Swan Lake*.

When he went off to Kamenka for the summer of 1869, Tchaikovsky had no conception of the fate awaiting his newly completed opera. He found most of the family there—the newly married Ippolit, well established in the Navy from which he was to retire as an admiral, Anatoly graduated from the Law School and posted to Kiev, Modest, who had no clear idea what he would do when he left the Law School, Aleksandra, as great a joy as ever, the calm and affectionate Lyov Vasilyevich, and nieces, four of them, who would have commandeered him from morning to night if he had let them. He revelled in Kamenka as always, and when at last he had to return to the Conservatoire for the autumn term he did so with immense reluctance; he was no teacher, he told Aleksandra, and longed for his compositions to bring in money enough to free him from lecturing.

In general he looked on Moscow with a gloomy eye, comparing it very much to its disadvantage with the peace and beauty of the Ukraine estate and the warm love of Aleksandra and her family. Yet in Moscow, waiting for him, was Balakirev. This was the reverse side of the fate he thought of as always dogging him, for Balakirev was to open his true destiny to him.

Part Three

Fulfilment

CHAPTER NINE

Balakirev and *Romeo and Juliet*
1869-72

Balakirev was in great form; he had just composed his Overture to *King Lear*, was working on *Tamara* and trying to persuade Borodin, who was in Moscow with him, to follow up his promising First Symphony by getting to work on *Prince Igor*, which Stasov—who usually presented the disciples with subjects—had more or less commanded.

No one ever hurried Borodin. He was not so much lazy as suspended between two worlds—he was making valuable researches in organic chemistry at the Petersburg Academy of Medicine—and not even Balakirev could lure him from his interest in practical science. Tchaikovsky offered more hopeful material, and Balakirev was soon suggesting that he too wrote on a Shakespearean theme. He said quite firmly what the theme must be; for a Tchaikovsky *Romeo and Juliet* was obvious and inescapable.

It so happened that Tchaikovsky at last had a room into which he could invite a friend with some hope of an uninterrupted talk. He and Rubinstein had moved quarters. Ironically their old quarters had become less and less tolerable the more the Conservatoire flourished; they were next door to the practice rooms, the walls were thin and Tchaikovsky, trying to entertain or to write music, was distracted by students trying to make up for lost time with piano, harp, every kind of woodwind, and, worst, the violin or their own voices. Rubinstein survived the racket without blenching; he liked noise, made plenty himself and did not reckon to be at home in the evenings in any case. It was a very different matter with

Tchaikovsky; when he could avoid his Director's blandishments he made the motions of working but rarely managed to write a tolerable bar until late at night when the students had forsaken their instruments for bed.

The noise and the frustration put him off not only composition but his food and he had grown into the habit of dining with Albrecht and his wife every evening and staying on until he thought his room would be reasonably quiet. But this was frustrating too; he enjoyed Mme Albrecht's meals but grudged every moment away from the music which was at once the only thing he really wished to do and the only hope of eventual escape from the routine of teaching. He had never thought of himself as a teacher and his popularity in class (which was to prove temporary) did not move him in the least. 'My tortures have begun again,' he writes after the first day of the new term.

Now all was changed, at home if not in the Conservatoire, as he cheerfully told Anatoly: 'We dined at home for the first time yesterday and Agafon's wife prepared an excellent dinner. I shall not go to the Albrechts again for dinner but shall always dine at home. You will eat with us when you come here.' To which he added a very typical, 'Do excuse me, old chap, that I can't send you more than twenty silver roubles for the moment; at the first possible opportunity I'll send more.'

His spirits soared as quickly as they fell and Balakirev found him in excellent form in his new room. They discussed *Romeo and Juliet* there, in restaurants, cafés, and during long walks along the boulevards, the swarthy, broad-faced Balakirev doing most of the talking. The meetings were not always free from silent resentment, silent because it was Tchaikovsky who felt it. Balakirev remained blissfully ignorant that his companion sometimes seethed when treated like one of the disciples in Petersburg and would have been astounded to know that his musical views were being described in letters to the family as narrow and his tone as authoritarian.

But these unveiled tussles did not mar the general harmony nor his companion's view that he was a splendid man—for Tchaikovsky was fair to a fault and sensible too; he knew that the encounters with such a mind and such selfless enthusiasm could do him nothing but good. Whether he understood how much good is doubtful, but by the time Balakirev went back to Petersburg the farewells were very affectionate and the idea of *Romeo and Juliet* had stuck.

By November he had sketched it out and had told Balakirev so.

He was at once deluged with instructions, almost all pertinent. The most sound was Balakirev's advice how to encourage the right ideas. Nothing showed better how perceptive Balakirev was; he had come to the conclusion that, apart from his friend's deplorable introduction to the classics by way of Zaremba, Tchaikovsky's worst enemy was himself, his habit of striking out music too rapidly and without due preparatory thought. So: 'Put on your goloshes, take your stick in your hand and go for a long walk round the boulevards. Begin at the Nikitsky, let your mind soak in the theme and I don't mind wagering that by the time you reach the Sretensky you will have discovered something good in the way of an episode or motif.'

Tchaikovsky did as he was bid and wrote such warm-hearted letters to Petersburg that a much-cheered Balakirev 'ran out to the Nevsky Prospekt—not walking but dancing!—and composed Tamara on my way'.

The enforced thought away from piano and composing table did all that Balakirev had hoped. Reflection took the place of immediate emotional reaction. Within a few weeks Tchaikovsky sent a sketch of the main themes to Petersburg and received with commendable patience the master's criticisms, sugared with a genuine 'this is the first work you have written that I can unhesitatingly describe as thoroughly good in essence. It is full of wonderful things.'

The collaboration continued in fits and starts for the next eighteen months, long after, to Balakirev's dismay, the work had been published in Berlin on the intervention of Nikolai Rubinstein. For Balakirev was not the only man to perceive that Tchaikovsky had at last found his subject and with it his true style; though he was to blot his copybook more than once in the future, Rubinstein never seriously doubted after reading this score that in his harmony professor he had found one of the great hopes of Russian music; with exceptions, one of them wholly inexplicable, he was to back Tchaikovsky to the hilt.

The fruitful year of 1869 ended with the publication of a group of six Tchaikovsky songs. The best of these was a setting from Goethe's 'Nur wer die Sehnsucht'. 'None but the Lonely Heart' is perhaps Tchaikovsky's most famous song. This is not surprising since it provides a perfect vehicle for the poem but is unfortunate because it has obscured the greatness of other songs by the same hand just as Tchaikovsky the song writer has been obscured by his more obvious gifts. This is a pity because, as with the *Voivode* fragment already discussed, he added something all his own to vocal music as he was to add to almost every genre of the art.

He was to write many songs and to fail in many. Few men of high emotional range are free from occasional descents into sentimentality and Tchaikovsky's warm heart when linked to his uncertain literary taste often led him astray. Some of the lyrics he set to music are rubbishy and the music, faithfully expressing them, is rubbishy too.

But he was to succeed in many too, whenever the words struck real fire from him. For instance, 'During the Ball', 'Forgotten so Soon', 'Pimpinella', 'Greek Song', 'Corals', 'Mignon's Dream', and 'Don Juan's Serenade' are all in their widely differing styles marked with the stamp of the master—the peculiarly Tchaikovskian gift of conveying precisely, economically, and unforgettably the particular emotion roused by the lyric. Even in Schumann, his direct exemplar, the piano is often little more than an accompaniment to the words; with Tchaikovsky it is always a musical impression of the words; that is to say, if one could not hear the words (which is not as unusual as it ought to be) one would still receive the full sense of them because of the composer's complete identification of himself with them.

Some critics, anxious to point the 'morbid Tchaikovsky' legend, have commented on the fact that most of his songs are sad. This is true. But it is also true of all great song writers and natural, since only when they portray struggle and sorrow and loss can they feel and stir the most powerful emotions.

ii

The year 1869 had been a year of fruitfulness, the year 1870 was barren. The tone of 1870 was set by the failure of *Romeo and Juliet* when Nikolai Rubinstein first played it in March—a failure summed up in Tchaikovsky's comment on the would-be triumphant after-concert dinner at Gurin's, one of the smartest of the Moscow restaurants: 'Nobody said a single word to me about the Overture the entire evening—it wasn't mentioned.'

Such insensitiveness in the leading lights in Moscow music is difficult to imagine today; music lovers will find it hard to credit that an audience, let alone composers, musicians, and critics, did not instantly rise to this work which contains in essence everything that has made Tchaikovsky known and loved wherever his music is played. There was, for example, none of the obvious floutings of harmonic convention which were to make Prokofiev regarded forty years later as a young monster of modernism. On the contrary the score of *Romeo and Juliet* was melodious without difficulty, filled with themes which the man in the street could reasonably be expected to whistle, it was romantic, it was brief. No one has yet explained satisfactorily why Tchaikovsky was to have to wait more than ten years before this masterpiece of romantic writing became one of the most popular works in the concert repertory.

Romeo and Juliet is now too well known and is played too often (and too sloppily—a frequent fault with renderings of Tchaikovsky) to need analysis here, but one or two facts must be mentioned. The first is that the composer held strictly to his title; the work is a Fantasy Overture and not a symphonic poem. Tchaikovsky makes no attempt to tell the Romeo and Juliet story in order or in detail; what interests him and what he does is to portray a series of impressions of action and character just as he would have done if this had actually been the overture to an opera. *Romeo and Juliet* is, in short, an extension of his principle in song writing, to illustrate states of soul.

Behind this, guiding all, is his obsession with the victims of fate. Romeo and Juliet are the first of several to be dealt with by him, and his sense of a fate menacing human lives gives the story intense dramatic power. He conveys this in notable manner, for he chose to follow the pure sonata form. As has been seen, he was to complain all his life of deviations from classical form. Musicians know that he is a master of form in all his great works and in many of his lesser— the kind of instinctive marriage of form and personal expression— but in *Romeo and Juliet* even he could not castigate himself, it was a *tour de force*.

Romeo and Juliet presents for the first time virtually the whole range of the great composer. He revealed himself a born dramatist, moving from scene to scene and mood to mood with vivid contrasts of pace and feeling and always with the utmost economy. The speed never slackens, the listener is carried from one superb melody to another, from one climax to another. Such rich orchestral writing had not been heard in a concert hall in Russia; the composer was clearly in complete command of his forces from first note to last, never thickening the texture and making highly inventive use of the orchestra. The score is dominated by a controlled rapport between composer and subject; he understood the fate which would part the lovers but he felt the love too and recreates it with a touching blend of passion and compassion; never before had the fire and poetry of young love been communicated with such truth and charm.

He did not destroy the score of this unsuccessful work; his critical sense overbore the inevitable reaction and mood of hopelessness after failure; he knew that *Romeo and Juliet* would come into its own. But such a reflection is poor comfort to a man getting on for thirty who wants a home of his own and freedom from teaching so that he can write uninterruptedly. He remained desperately poor—his stipend inadequate, his optimism and generosity abnormal, his grasp of arithmetic negligible—and a week or two later he was writing urgently to Albrecht, 'For God's sake send me four roubles or I shall starve!'

Four roubles. Eight shillings! And this was not the only frantic note to Albrecht and Albrecht was not the only friend to receive them. A whole bunch of them dates from this year of failure. Sometimes they are lively—'You are a pig, you prefer Larosh to me. That will cost you five silver roubles. By messenger, please!' and 'Please send me ten roubles. If you don't, the next issue of *Sovremennaya Lyetopis* will carry a complete account of the man you really are!', for example—sometimes they are sombre, always they indicate bare pockets. He knew what poverty was and every time a work of his was damned he saw an extension of this poverty stretching ahead indefinitely. After *Romeo and Juliet* he reacted into melancholy, seeing no hope of a miracle.

He wrote the beginnings of another opera *Mandragora* (a fragment to become well known as the Insect Chorus) when Kashkin stepped in firmly with such devastating criticism of the libretto—by a professor of botany—that he threw it up. He began yet another opera, *The Oprichnik*, this time with an excellent libretto, but the repulse of *Romeo and Juliet* haunted him, the depression would not lift and he once again hated the streets of Moscow and longed for Kamenka. But it was to Paris and Germany that he went. Begichev told him that his stepson's life was despaired of in Paris and asked him to go and Tchaikovsky was off gladly, out of the Russia which refused to recognize his genius.

This was the first of many disgusted flights from his homeland, all of which ended with a rush back, as homesick as he had been home-hating a few weeks earlier. The Begichev boy recovered sufficiently to be moved to a German spa and there Tchaikovsky languished for a few weeks trying unsuccessfully to persuade himself that the waters were doing him good. His day was unvaried and unexciting, as he told A. Y. Bakireva, the twin's old governess. 'We get up at six, drink the waters, then stroll about till eight. Then we drink coffee and at one o'clock we dine. Afterwards we walk or drive until evening, drink tea at eight and go to bed at nine.'

The rest of the letter, and the cause of it, is much more interesting because it illustrates two unvarying facets of the writer, his moral courage and his true democracy at a time when governesses were household pariahs, too plebeian to associate with the family, too educated to mix with the servants. Of all this he was blissfully unaware; he took people as he found them, judging not by class but by heart.

The incident leading to the letter was obviously a derogatory reference by Avdotya Yakovlevna—not the most patient of women —to one of the many voluble non-workers in the Tchaikovsky household, a dependent relative.

I parted from you so unpleasantly [Pyotr Ilyich now writes] that I must write these few lines to tell you that I love you as always.

I very much regret that your morbid irritability led to a quarrel. I advise you to go to Papasha and apologize. He is a 75-year-old man and, what's much more important, one of the best people in the world. Consequently there will be no kind of humiliation for you in the act. Besides, you really did behave indelicately in abusing his kinswoman. What would you say if someone spoke so cuttingly about your sister?

He was to continue to supply the old woman till her death with money he could not afford, to swell out Ilya Petrovich's government pension. For the moment, in Soden, he felt increasingly bored and unhappy. The company of the loved and loving Shilovsky was not enough. Tchaikovsky's letters show him looking into the future. A few weeks earlier he had written to his sister, 'I feel a passionate wish to hear children's voices. I want to be able to take part in all the little things that make up a home. In short, I long for a family life.' The attractions of the German spa in no way compensated for the lack of a home and family of his own; the frivolity of the life there—aged rakes trying to prolong a useless existence—and the falsity of the friendships and flirtations struck up out of sheer ennui made this warm-hearted man detest every minute of it.

The most significant part of this depressing German visit with an invalid who rarely showed signs of real recovery was a trip to Wiesbaden where Nikolai Rubinstein was busily losing his last rouble at the roulette tables. Tchaikovsky reported that his Director was 'convinced that he will break the bank'. Of course the bank broke him, and for the rest of the year he and Tchaikovsky (who threw his money away just as effectively in loans that were never repaid) were on their beam ends.

Tchaikovsky's answer to all this—the effect of weeks in a stuffy German spa with an invalid, the prospect of interminable Conservatoire lectures and interminable rejections of his music by the public, the prospect of a life lived alone since he could find no woman comparable with an Artôt or an Aleksandra, added to, at that moment, bitter thoughts of the futile Franco-Prussian War in which his mother's country was being humiliated—was to drink even more heavily. This merely threw him into deeper misery, and a guilt complex was set up which he was never wholly able to throw off; his prolific imagination got to work and all the horrors unrolled before him. Chief of these was public disgrace, not so much for him as his family; he saw himself an outcast from society, perhaps even dismissed the Conservatoire, his brothers' careers fatally hampered, his sister's heart broken—nothing was too lurid. Homosexuality was an offence punishable by prison, insobriety could lose him his post.

Rubinstein was not the best of company for a man in a state he could not begin to comprehend; his remedy for low spirits was high living and forgetfulness until the next morning when, in any case, classes took one's mind off everything but music. He merely succeeded in further damaging Pyotr Ilyich's nervous system whilst systematically making sure that his salary could not possibly meet his expenses. Deep in debt himself, he could not think too seriously of his colleague's (to him) trifling embarrassments.

Tchaikovsky's ambivalent attitude to Nikolai began to turn definitely towards a separation; he admired him as much as ever, more than ever he appreciated his good nature and generosity, he wanted to work under him if he was destined to work under somebody, but he wanted to live with him no longer. Nerves on edge, he panted for an apartment or room of his own.

Typically, it was Rubinstein who helped him to it. He suggested at the beginning of 1871 that Tchaikovsky promote a concert of his works. This would make his music better known and, if he was lucky, bring in quite a sizeable sum at the box office. The idea of an all-Tchaikovsky concert had not occurred to the composer—giving some idea of his quite extraordinary modesty even at this late stage in his career—but he jumped at it.

At first he thought naturally in terms of a symphonic concert with Nikolai Rubinstein conducting but he had overlooked the considerable cost of arranging such a concert; he wrote for a large orchestra and his music needed a large hall at a large rent.

Foiled, he turned to the idea of a chamber concert. The difficulty here was that he had not sufficient items to make up even a short programme—merely his six songs and a number of little piano pieces. He decided to write a string quartet to give body to the programme. By March it was done and at the end of the month the concert was held. Nikolai Rubinstein played two pieces in the middle of the programme, a well-known soprano sang some songs, and the audience was highly titivated by the unexpected arrival of Turgenyev in the hall.

Modest claims that the presence of Turgenyev went some way to make the evening, but the real success of the concert was its first item which Turgenyev apparently did not hear—the First Quartet in D Major. This work at once established Tchaikovsky as masterly in yet another department of music. Like some later compositions of his—one thinks of the Trio and Serenade for Strings—this quartet has become famous for a single movement which is often, too often, played apart from the rest of the work. This Andante Cantabile is hauntingly and most misleadingly Tchaikovskian. The first theme he had taken from a peasant song he heard sung under his window at Kamenka two summers earlier, the second, almost equally luscious was his own invention; his handling of both demonstrated his supreme musicality in this sphere.

As he sat in the hall and listened, Tchaikovsky wept throughout this movement as Tolstoy was to do whenever he heard it and as many lesser listeners have done and may continue to do; it was the very essence of one kind of romantic music he was to write more effectively than any other man, just as he was to excel in vigorous romantic music too. This excessively Victorian movement has obscured the quartet as a whole and this is much to be regretted, for the work is first rate from beginning to end. The glittering first movement shows Tchaikovsky at his most elegant—French to his fingertips—as an adept at syncopation (as he was so dazzlingly to demonstrate in his Second Piano Concerto) and a master in counterpoint when he unites and develops the first and second themes. The Scherzo is wholly classical in construction and includes a fascinating Trio led by the cello, and the vigorous Finale, in rondo form, brings the quartet to a rousing finish.

On the whole the concert paid handsomely, with good reviews, an enthusiastic audience and a gratifying monetary return, and soon afterwards, partly as a result of it, Tchaikovsky was offered, was indeed almost badgered into, reviewing. He did not care for the work though he did it conscientiously and well, but it made the financial future decidedly less gloomy.

True to his nature, Tchaikovsky took all this as an omen of a relenting fate and was galvanized into great activity. He turned to *The Oprichnik* again, spent the summer at Kamenka in excellent spirits (writing a ballet *Swan Lake* for his nieces to dance and, going to the other extreme, *A Guide to the Practical Study of Harmony* which Rimsky-Korsakov was soon to regard as his bible) and when he returned to Moscow in autumn returned at last to rooms of his own.

The opera forged ahead, with the inevitable longueurs of dissatisfaction, but was still unfinished when he went off for a round of southern visits, to Nice, Genoa, Venice, and Vienna, with the Begichev boy still struggling unsuccessfully to master his tuberculosis.

There were many wearisome moments, as in the German spa, yet Tchaikovsky's melancholy was not due wholly to dancing attendance on an invalid; he liked Vladimir Shilovsky and did it willingly. What subdued him, as it was always to do, was the realization that none of the undoubted charms of Italy, Austria, and southern France could compete for one moment with the solid virtues of his Russia. Like almost all creative men he had a strong compulsion towards movement; after a few months in Moscow his sources of inspiration seemed to dry up and he was eager to try anything new, the warm sunshine of the Riviera, the sophistication of Vienna, the brightness of Paris, to revive his failing muse, but unlike many great creators he could not escape his destiny. 'I am Russian, Russian, Russian!' he was to cry; and this was so true that he was never to be at ease for more than a week or two outside his own country.

Back again in February of the new year, 1872, he went hard at *The Oprichnik*. By May he had done and the score was sent off to Petersburg to be considered by the Imperial Theatres Committee. He left for Kamenka as soon as the Conservatoire term ended, and found a new arrival there, a baby nephew, Vladimir.

The change from Europe to Moscow and from Moscow to Kamenka had put him in fine fettle; it had been a joy to get back to a Russian city but the joy paled before his rapture when he reached the countryside. Never had his family seen him so lighthearted. Again he ate great meals and went for great walks, played the piano, romped with his nieces, hung over his nephew's cradle and talked animatedly to Aleksandra and her husband. He stopped heavy drinking, partly because the strain of city life, of Rubinstein and reviewing and lecturing, had disappeared, but more because he was ashamed to worry Aleksandra. He could never make up his mind whether she knew of his sexual weakness; in the hope that she did not he said nothing.

This slight cloud apart (for he loathed anything even faintly suggestive of deceit), he loved everything about the long holiday, his family, the people of Kamenka, the Ukraine countryside, and as always this feeling immediately began to express itself in music; he wrote the beginnings of his Second Symphony.

CHAPTER TEN

Second Symphony

1872-4

This summer saw a turn in Tchaikovsky's fortunes. By the time he had finished his round with a visit to the Begichev country house he had sketched out the entire symphony. He came back to Moscow to find his salary increased once more, and this, his reviewing fees and the occasional sales of work which Jurgenson had begun to publish pushed his total income up to the three-thousand-rouble mark. It was not a fortune—about three hundred pounds a year—and he managed to make it seem even less than it was: 'I'm such an ass with money that I'm always in debt.' But he did one wise thing, to move to rooms he liked in place of rooms dictated by the lowest possible rent.

The move had one main purpose, to help him to compose more quickly—the apartment was quieter and roomy—and by the middle of November he was apologizing for a break in his letters because 'I can't think of anything but the symphony'.

By the end of the year it was done and he took it with him to Petersburg where he had been summoned by the Imperial Theatres Committee. After the usual bout of nervousness—he could never accustom himself to perform or conduct in public—he managed to get through *The Oprichnik* sufficiently well to sway the committee in his favour, so the new year of 1873 opened auspiciously with a decision to stage the opera at the Maryinsky the following year.

He stayed as usual with his father and stepmother, and it can be assumed with some confidence that part of their conversations concerned his wish to get married, for his letters to his father dealt

largely with this problem. He was in a dilemma. He wanted to find a
woman as like his stepmother as possible—an intelligent woman who
would make the kind of home for him that Aleksandra had made for
Lyov—but had never met a woman of this sort who attracted him.
He also disliked the idea of asking any woman to take the risk of
marrying a man whose income was small and much of it uncertain—
a man who had not yet managed to make his mark as a composer
even in his own country. He was still regarded in Moscow as a
promising young composer, in Petersburg he was scarcely known at
all. Yet he was nearly thirty-three. So: 'If a man is single his debts
are not of much moment, but if I had to keep a wife and children it
would be a very different matter.'

This kind of argument delivered him into his father's hands. For
many years, ever since in a fit of conscience he had suggested a
musical career for his son, Ilya Petrovich had set his face against it.
He had never hidden his view that Pyotr Ilyich was foolish to throw
up the Civil Service for professional music instead of preserving
music as a pleasant hobby, and to him the six years in Moscow had
proved his point—his son appeared to be as unknown, and as hard
up, at the end of them as at the beginning.

He listened sceptically when Pyotr Ilyich told him in these early
days of 1873 that he had at last written a work which must surely
make his name: 'I think it the best thing I've done.' He had been told
this after every composition and his son's words were thrown away.
Tchaikovsky no doubt believed them—it is a necessary characteristic
of creative men to think their most recent work better than any
other—but must have had uneasy memories, not only of past
rejections by the public but also of his own volte-faces.

He was soon to be vociferously supported, for the week he
arrived in Petersburg he saw much of Balakirev and his disciples and
was persuaded to play some of his symphony at a party held in his
honour at the Rimsky-Korsakov apartment. It is not known how
much he played but he certainly played the last movement and as
certainly swept his audience off its feet. 'They almost tore me to
pieces,' he reported to the family, 'and Madame Korsakova implored
me to arrange the Finale for four hands.' In the event Nadyezhda
Nikolayevna arranged it herself as she had arranged the *Romeo and
Juliet*.

He could not doubt that all present thought they were listening
to one of the most important works composed by a contemporary Russian. Even the critical Stasov, who did not usually favour

works he had not suggested, had nothing but praise for the symphony, and Tchaikovsky was so overcome by this extraordinary event that he ventured to beg a subject from him for another work after the style of *Romeo and Juliet*, on a Shakespearean theme if possible.

The gratified Stasov followed him back to Moscow with a long letter suggesting three subjects—*The Tempest*, *Taras Gulba*, and *Ivanhoe*—and when Tchaikovsky chose the first, gave detailed instructions which the composer accepted without demur.

This meekness owed something to the events of the previous evening, 7 February, when his symphony was played by Rubinstein for the first time with such success that a second performance was demanded 'by general request'. News of the new symphony—the first truly Russian symphony ever written, many claimed—travelled fast to the right quarters in Petersburg, and one month later Napravnik played it there. Again it had a great welcome. And to round off weeks of triumph, the repeat Moscow performance in April saw a spontaneous demonstration of esteem by the packed house. Tchaikovsky was called on to the platform at the end of each movement—the audience refused to stop applauding until he appeared—and at the end of the Finale was given a silver goblet and a laurel wreath.

The public instinct was right, as it so often is, and began a reaction to the old, snobbish prejudice against Russian music; Tchaikovsky had not only made his name known in his own country, he had cleared the way for others to write Russian music and to receive a hearing—not always a fair hearing but at least a hearing.

The Symphony in C Minor was called the 'Little Russian' and the title is apt because three of its four movements owe much of their power and charm to Kamenka folk songs. Although this Second Symphony is played more often today than in the past it is still strangely neglected. It has been Tchaikovsky's fate to be known by a handful of works which crowd the rest out of the concert hall; the omission of the Second Symphony from the regular repertory is a considerable loss to all who love his music; it is not only a splendid work in its own right but exhibits the composer in a sunny mood which it is a delight to share.

A word must be said about the mood in which Tchaikovsky wrote his music. He is often accused of morbidity, of a preoccupation with the dark side of life. It is true that he looked at life straight and that, not being unthinking or unfeeling, he saw it in general as a sombre pilgrimage. That aspect colours a great deal of his music, and as it is the aspect shared by all great and thoughtful men he can scarcely be blamed for expressing it. What he does, being a truthful man as well as an artist, is to show, above the ground-plan of sobriety, the facets of life which make it tolerable—the love of one for another, the beauty in nature, the humour in human contacts, the style and charm of man's work and, above all, the sense of form which the unconquerable human soul imposes on the chaos by which he is surrounded. If a Tchaikovsky work is heard correctly it can give much greater cheer to the listener than the work of an 'optimist'—a word which usually means no more than a man who refuses to think—because it is a heartening as well as moving experience.

The Second Symphony is an almost wholly extrovert work, the result of a summer in the peaceful, unspoilt Russian countryside spent by a man who had recently been abroad. It is his joyful response to reunion with everything he loved, the life of the home, the leisurely bustle of the village, and the calm grandeur of the country scene.

Tchaikovsky speaks of its satisfactory form—for once he is almost satisfied—and certainly the entire symphony is closely knit in the classical manner though built almost entirely on Russian themes. The pleasantly melancholy introduction, in no way sad, rather the mood of a man walking the country at evening, soon gives way to a Ukrainian version of one of the oldest songs in Russia, 'On the Volga'. This Allegro Vivo, which occupies the greater part of the first movement, is brilliantly handled—with constant variety, pace, and vigour. For the second movement, Andante Marziale, Tchaikovsky takes up one of the most fetching remnants of the destroyed *Undine*, the wedding march, and presents it with a masterly use of the woodwinds, always his most successful instruments, and with which he obtains original effects of poetical nostalgia. The Scherzo goes back to folk-song themes tossed about with audacious use of rhythm—a lighthearted movement into which the composer manages, true to his passion for novelty, to introduce the sounds of the balalaika.

The Finale is the cream of the work and compares favourably with anything written by Tchaikovsky. It is based on two themes, one his own, the other heard at Kamenka—but it is in his treatment of the latter that he shows his genius. It is a well-known song called 'The Crane', a fascinating song, which the composer repeats no fewer than eight times. He does not alter the theme, he obtains his variety by constant changes of orchestral colour. It is sheer joy to hear, vigorous, charming, nostalgic; one can never have enough of it, a fact which speaks for itself. With easy mastery Tchaikovsky gives the appearance of spontaneity throughout his repetitions; in fact they are devised with extreme skill. The Balakirev circle had understood at once when they heard this movement that they were listening to a great composer and to their infinite credit the concert audiences of Petersburg and Moscow understood it too.

ii

There were two immediate effects of the success of the Second Symphony. The first, as would be expected, was a rapid rise in Tchaikovsky's spirits and this, to the reader of today who cannot hear the composer keeping Moscow social gatherings in fits of laughter, comes across in his letters. The bulk of the fantastically large number of letters Tchaikovsky wrote can be divided into four distinct categories. There are the personal and family letters in which, in exchange for news of the family doings, he replies with full details of his own life, triumphs and failures, moral and concrete, and accounts of steps he is taking to help the latest of the many lame dogs attached in some way or other (often very tenuously) to the vast Tchaikovsky family group—he was the family conscience incarnate. There are letters devoted almost entirely to music and musicians. There are his begging letters, dozens of them in his early Moscow years, by means of which he comprehensively relieves Jurgenson and his Conservatoire friends, Albrecht, Rubinstein, and Kashkin foremost, of anything from four to fifteen to twenty roubles at a time—some of the letters gay and impudent, some written in true desperation. There are also his bright and humorous letters which range at this time from a note to Jurgenson—'Nikolai Mikhailovich [Kashkin] tells me you are dropping in to see me tonight. Splendid! Three wine glasses filled with vodka, and a piece of pie, will be waiting for you'—to pure nonsense.

In general his humour, in line with the taste of his time, seems infantile to the present-day reader and embarrassing rather than amusing. But there are exceptions. As the twins had discovered with joy in their childhood, he had a penchant for word-twisting. His nonsense letters and poems are often most refreshing and show a man too often forgotten by the reader brought up to think of the name Tchaikovsky as synonymous with gloom and struggle. The following letter, written just after the success of the Second Symphony, is a good example of the genre. In it Tchaikovsky demonstrates the fun to be had by a man who has half learned English and revenges himself on the intractable language by mocking its syntactic absurdities. It is easy to imagine Aleksandra and Modest (then staying at Kamenka) revelling in this letter addressed to them jointly, and it is still very much worth reading.

My good sister and my dear brother! I have know what motsch plesir that you learn the Englisch langage bot you cannot told that I cannot understand. I kan understand wery biutifoll oll what you will and enough bether. My brother! you are one fulischmen, bot you, my dear sister, are one biutiffoll women. I have not times to scrive this letter englisch bot God sawe the Quenn and collection of Britisch autors is one trifles. I can you told that the spanierds wear their hats cocked and I cocked my pistol directly. The King has conferred the order of the Garter on him bot i will cringe to nobody. We always deal with him and We dined on soup and fisch.

Tell me: How did he come by so musch money and Why do you call out? Call un your brother and your sister, call down the servant. I will call for you at six. He assisted me with all his endeavours, i have atoned for my foult and i will ask him to dine. Do not argue withe me. You argue against reason and i abide by what I say: France abounds with fruit and several trees are bliwn down.

My brother, what are you gaping at? My sister, you lies in with your first child.

I are your affectioned brother Pither.

So much for Tchaikovsky's reaction to success. The first practical effect of the welcome given to the new symphony was an invitation from the Imperial Theatres at Moscow to supply incidental music for Ostrovsky's new play *Snyegurochka*. The commission pleased Tchaikovsky in every way; he appreciated the compliment of being asked to collaborate with Russia's greatest dramatist, he needed the three hundred and fifty roubles fee, and the subject suited him precisely. He flew at it and in three weeks had it ready for production in April.

Ostrovsky's lovely play was not to make its name until Rimsky-Korsakov used it for *The Snow Maiden*, one of the most charming operas ever written, but Tchaikovsky's music caught on and was often played as a kind of suite and published as Opus 12. The popularity of the music is not surprising—what is surprising is its disappearance from modern music programmes.

Tchaikovsky had to provide nineteen numbers—dances, solos, and choruses—and for three of them he used fragments of *Undine*. The first was the Prelude, which became the Overture to the new work, transplanted entire. It was not one of his happiest thoughts, but the second and third borrowings were entirely successful. Undine's song 'Little Storm, my Sister', became the first of Lel's three songs and the best, though all are charming. In this first song Tchaikovsky broke new ground by using a piano with the orchestra, a then hair-raising stroke of modernism.

An Allegro for Mixed Choir became the young girls' chorus, a ravishing little theme, and just as attractive is Tchaikovsky's original theme for the flower scene. The carnival music is pure Russian, gay, tender, bright, and the clowns' dance is Russian too but at the opposite extreme and demonstrates the composer's virtuosity. Some critics were hard on this dance music—'noisy and vulgar' was a typical comment—but they missed the unconventional use of instruments, the trumpets in particular, which was to reappear in *Petrushka* and in much of Shostakovich. Tchaikovsky was often to point the way to the future and this little number contains one of his happiest original thoughts.

Having money in his pocket meant a departure from Moscow as soon as term ended, and again he went off to the west, picking up the Jurgensons in Dresden and doing Switzerland, north Italy, and Paris with them. He enjoyed their company (Jurgenson was a forthright, homely, self-made man) and he dutifully and often sincerely admired the sights, the antiquities, the climate, but in the end, and not a far end, his continental ardour collapsed once more. In Switzerland he confided to a diary he had begun to keep, and which is chiefly notable for a record of excellent food and wine taken *en route*: 'My soul yearns for Russia and when I see in my mind's eye its plains, fields, and forests I feel a pang at the heart. Oh my dear country, you are a hundred times lovelier and dearer to me than these majestic mountain ranges famed for their beauty!'

In such a mood—and it became more frequent the longer he stayed away—nothing would quiet him but Russia. By August he was back in Moscow and only paused to collect what money he could rake together, having as usual spent everything, before he was off into the country. Kamenka was too far and too expensive to reach, so he again took up Begichev's permanent invitation to his country estate at Usovo in Tambov Province, only some two hundred miles south-east of the capital.

He had another reason for choosing Usovo; he wanted absolute quiet to work and would get it; the house was larger than Kamenka, there were no children to tempt him from music, and the Begichevs, like so many rich people, were for ever dashing from one place to another in search of some new way of passing the time.

Sure enough, after a few days the family went off, leaving him in the midst of a countryside he loved almost as well as the Ukraine. He at once began work on *The Tempest* which, in the spirit of Balakirev's advice, he had been meditating more than six months.

The work leapt ahead: 'At last I was alone, absolutely alone, in a marvellous steppe country . . .' he was to recall years later. 'I couldn't possibly tell you what great happiness I felt in this solitude. I found myself in a state of exaltation, of uninterrupted ecstasy, of beatitude. During the day I wandered in the woods, in the evening I walked across the steppe, at night I stood by the window listening to the profound silence of the great spaces, a silence broken rarely by a confused noise from far away. Without the least effort and as though borne up by some supernatural power I wrote, almost in spite of myself, the entire first draft of *The Tempest*.'

In December Rubinstein conducted the first performance of the new work. It was hailed as the Second Symphony had been hailed and a repeat performance demanded, and from that time became one of the most popular works of Tchaikovsky.

There are many mysteries in music and *The Tempest* is one of them. It is difficult to understand why an audience which rejected *Romeo and Juliet* should welcome *The Tempest* with open arms. It is as difficult to explain why modern audiences have completely reversed the taste of Tchaikovsky's day so that we hear *Romeo and Juliet* often and *The Tempest* virtually not at all. For the first mystery there seems only one explanation, that *The Tempest* had a printed programme which the composer followed religiously. This seems almost absurd, yet concert audiences like to get their teeth into programme music, to be able to say that they are following every action of the drama set out before them. For the second mystery there seems to be no adequate explanation. Music critics know that certain works of every great composer are preferred to others not less good but they have not been able to explain the unaccountable except by the vagary of public taste.

The Tempest is in one respect a more remarkable work than

Romeo and Juliet because Tchaikovsky obeyed Stasov's detailed instructions to the letter yet managed to write music which sounds perfectly integrated, unforced, spontaneous. Possibly his, for him, long wait before writing the work released him from the sense of writing to order. Possibly again those magical ten days at Usovo wove the spell that he in turn weaves in his score. It is melodious, balanced, and orchestrated with an appearance of consummate ease and richness. If a fault must be found it is perhaps in the storm music. Tchaikovsky plainly did not wish to write this in the first instance but Stasov was adamant, indeed shocked at the thought of *The Tempest* without its storm. The result is a battery of sound that deafens rather than awes. Tchaikovsky was frequently to be attacked by contemporary critics for his penchant for noise. Usually the critics are at fault; here, when they said nothing, one feels that they would have had a case.

iii

With a second successful orchestral work behind him, Tchaikovsky turned back to chamber music and in a few weeks in the new year of 1874—'in one breath' as he was to say—wrote his Second String Quartet. It had a wretched beginning; at a private first performance Anton Rubinstein, visiting Moscow, took his brother's place as honoured guest and returned the compliment by comprehensively damning the quartet which, he declared, he could not understand.

Those who hear this work today will be unable to understand Anton Rubinstein, but Tchaikovsky, still the uncertain student Pyotr Ilyich whenever he came in contact with Anton, feverishly tried to rewrite some of it despite the protests of those who had played it. He might have spared himself the trouble; he could do no more than tinker with some of the parts, leaving the whole very much as it was, and when it had its first public performance in March it was praised by all.

Looking back on this quartet, Tchaikovsky claimed that it was one of the finest things he had written: 'I have never composed anything so easily, so spontaneously.' Opinions about it since his death have varied widely; some think it an advance on his First Quartet, others find it laboured, rather dull, and too long—it is half as long again as the earlier work. This latter opinion is probably due to the

above Anton
Grigoryevich Rubinstein

below Nikolai
Grigoryevich Rubinstein

left Désirée Artôt
below Modest Tchaikovsk
Nikolai Kondratyev, and
Anatoly and Pyotr
Tchaikovsky in 1872

somewhat uninspired Finale; the first three movements have all Tchaikovsky's genius for melody and dexterous use of material and instruments. Nothing can be hidden in a quartet and he rises to the challenge.

Two points about the quartet are worth notice. In the Adagio we can see plainly what disturbed Rubinstein, some extremely advanced dissonances. The entire third movement, an Andante, is moving and as beautifully written as the almost notorious Andante Cantabile of the First Quartet but has remained virtually unknown. It is what is too often labelled typical Tchaikovsky music, sweet and tender and a shade melancholy, but the rumbustious Scherzo is just as typical and demonstrated the composer's innate feeling for rhythm which he handled to the point of audacity. The dissonances are now too ordinary to arouse a moment's surprise—one has to remember hard when the work was written—but the rhythms remain a joy as rhythm by a master always is.

The staging of *The Oprichnik* had been delayed so long that Tchaikovsky embarked on yet another opera, this time taken from Gogol's *Christmas Eve*, but soon after the quartet was played he at last had word from Petersburg that *The Oprichnik* was scheduled for a première in Easter week and that he was wanted for rehearsals.

Partly because of the long delay since he had finished the opera, partly because of his enthusiasm for the new opera, and partly because Napravnik, the chief opera conductor at the Maryinsky, was a tetchy pedant, Tchaikovsky's faith in his work evaporated rapidly. No composer likes his work to be cut and Napravnik insisted on many cuts. Tchaikovsky had not been a week in Petersburg before he began to look gloomily on the prospects of the opera. From despair at the sight and sound of butchery he deteriorated rapidly to dislike of his own music; stupefied with boredom, he regularly walked out of the theatre after the end of the second act.

To add to his embarrassment, everyone he knew (and he had dozens of friends) was determined to make an occasion of the première. The family had taken a box and colleagues and students at the Moscow Conservatoire clamoured for tickets. He tried to discourage them all. He told his best student and most devoted disciple, Sergei Ivanovich Taneyev, for example, 'If you're really thinking of coming up here simply to hear my opera, Seryozha, do think again, I entreat you. It doesn't contain anything out of the way and is not worth rushing up to Petersburg for.'

His appeals were useless, and the Maryinsky was thick with his supporters from Moscow and Petersburg when the opera was finally staged on 24 April. Ilya Petrovich, bearing his seventy-nine years well, was sitting stiffly in his bemedalled uniform in a box beside his 'dumpling', as Pyotr Ilyich fondly called Yelizaveta Mikhailovna, the twins (both small young men) were in attendance and a highly nervous and despondent Tchaikovsky was walking uneasily up and down in the background.

There was not in fact any obvious cause for despondency except for the usual dingy production, but then all Russian operas were shabbily mounted, the Italian opera vogue still persisted and was to be the cause of ferocious complaints by Shalyapin nearly thirty years later. For the rest the opera was well sung, enthusiastically received and Tchaikovsky had to take a bow as early as the end of the second act. And if this was not enough, at an after-performance supper given in his honour by the combined Conservatoire staffs the Director of the Petersburg Conservatoire announced that he had been awarded a prize worth three hundred roubles for the outstanding Russian composer of the year.

It was an amiable weakness with Tchaikovsky that he was off with the old and on with the new, like so many creative men. His darling of the moment was the new opera *Vakula the Smith* and to him *The Oprichnik* was *vieux jeu*. The praise and the prize left him comparatively unmoved. He left Petersburg soon afterwards with relief —he had promised to review a La Scala production of *A Life for the Tsar*—and without waiting for the critics to give tongue.

In the event the opera was praised by his well-wishers (prominently a forgiven Larosh) and damned by others, headed as usual by the vitriolic Kui. The keynote of the latter's notice was the absence of inspiration, and in spite of the fact that the opera was performed more often than most and always with acclamation, Tchaikovsky agreed with him: 'For all its beastliness and obvious animosity, Kui's criticism is basically correct . . . the opera lacks style, action, and inspiration.'

If one is to judge by the number of representations a work is given, the composer was to be proved right. *The Oprichnik* is not heard today except for the occasional Soviet production and is unknown to most musicians in the West. Yet there is much to be said for it. It had, unlike most Tchaikovsky operas, a workable libretto after the play by the well-known novelist Ivan Ivanovich Lazhechnikov, and the plot was congenial to a man absorbed by the ironies of fate: Andrei Morozov, one of Ivan the Terrible's picked band of Oprichniks (a kind of personal bodyguard notorious for their suppression of all human feelings) meets the young Natalya and falls in love; Ivan revenges himself on the girl, Andrei revolts and is executed.

Here we have another version of *Romeo and Juliet* and even more obviously the forerunners of Tatyana and Lenski. Natalya is created with that heart-warming blend, so typical of the composer, of passion and compassion. She stands as model for the modest, artless heroine drawn from life by all the great Russian poets and novelists, and Tchaikovsky's version is full-blooded and absolutely convincing. Her two ariosos express this type of Russian girl with tenderness and understanding. Balancing the heroine and hero (another full-bodied portrait) is the Countess Morozova, Andrei's mother, a symbol for Mother Russia, old, wise, far-seeing, fatalistic. She is given a remarkable monologue in the lydian mode.

Three fine portraits, then, but the outstanding success of the opera is not its principals but the atmosphere surrounding them. The use of the chorus in particular gives the work an unmistakably Russian colour. Tchaikovsky's operas often lack the vigour, the form, and even the melodiousness of his orchestral works and the composer's symphonic dramatic sense often deserts him in opera, but in one respect he can scarcely be faulted; he faithfully sets *The Oprichnik* in Old Russia and keeps it there. He was following Glinka but he improved upon him too. Today we hear only of *Boris Godunov* and *Kovanschina*, which are hailed as masterpieces of originality. Mussorgsky did go further than Tchaikovsky in his abandonment of key signatures and his insistence on a kind of realistic declamation with a vocal line based on the actual inflexions of the words—all after Dargomyzhsky—but in creation of national atmosphere and in truthful re-creation of a past age he was forestalled and sometimes excelled, as this forgotten work demonstrates.

CHAPTER ELEVEN

Piano Concerto
1874-7

At thirty-four Tchaikovsky had begun to make his name in Russia; his Second Symphony, *The Tempest*, his quartets, his songs, and to a certain extent *The Oprichnik*, had established him in general favour. He was by no means considered a 'great' composer but as a very sympathetic one who happened to be a Russian without making an embarrassing parade of it. He could feel reasonably sure of a public hearing for anything he wrote and quite sure that Jurgenson would print it.

So far, so good, but Russia, musically speaking, still lagged far behind the West. *The Oprichnik*, for example, was given single performances in Kiev and Odessa as well as one or two at Moscow and there its possibilities ended. The number of people from whom concert audiences could be drawn was, compared with any western country or the United States, pitifully small and, as has been seen, the hold of Western music was still very strong; Italian opera continued to be socially 'the thing', and the few concert programmes remained ninety per cent foreign.

It was natural, then, to look to the West for fame and fortune, and in this respect Tchaikovsky had not moved one step forward since he began to write music; he was to all intents and purposes unknown. He was not destined to conquer the foreigner by one dramatic flourish but he was on the point of securing a foothold outside his own country, and a few weeks before the première of *The Oprichnik* he met the man who was to make the step possible.

This man was Hans von Bülow. He arrived in Moscow in March

1874 to give a series of recitals. Many of the people who crammed the Bolshoi to hear his first recital no doubt did so to stare at the man whose wife Cosima, daughter of Liszt, had left him for Wagner five years earlier—a European *cause célèbre* made specially piquant by the fact that Von Bülow had studied under both men, the one for the piano, the other for conductorship, and revered them both.

To the musical members of the audience he was known as one of the most renowned opera conductors in the world and one of the finest pianists. To Tchaikovsky his playing and his manner at the keyboard were a revelation, for he was the first of what may be called the restrained virtuosos. Instead of pounding the piano he played it, as Tchaikovsky said, 'with mastery, taste, and a remarkable gift for conveying objectively the spirit and mood of a composition'. In appearance as in manner he was the scholar; the long hair of Liszt and Rubinstein had been discarded and replaced by a Louis Napoleon beard; everything about him bespoke intellect governing feeling.

Unlike many visiting virtuosos from the West, Von Bülow interested himself in local talent; he met Tchaikovsky (they had in common an education in law) and awed the younger man, who was fascinated by his wit and slightly alarmed by his caustic comments. Someone—it was certainly not Pyotr Ilyich and almost certainly Nikolai Rubinstein—showed him a group of pianoforte pieces Tchaikovsky had written a few months earlier. Von Bülow took them away with him on his tour of Russia and by the time he had got to Kharkov was writing home, 'This man Tchaikovsky is very talented; I am working on his Variations with a view to playing them.'

He did play them and, not content with this, singled out Tchaikovsky in an article he wrote about his tour when he got home. He had, of course, picked the one piece of any value from the six published under the one opus number. One could say, of considerable value, because although *Variations on an Original Theme* are rarely played today they are excellent in themselves and indicate plainly that in Tchaikovsky the musical world had found one of its great variation writers, perhaps the greatest. He was not to be an outstanding writer for pianoforte solo but his genius for variations shines out even in this uncongenial medium.

ii

For the moment the brief rapport with Von Bülow seemed to have faded away. Tchaikovsky did not forget, however. For a few months after his return from Italy (a fruitless visit since *A Life for the Tsar* was constantly postponed and he never heard it) he was entirely taken up with one of his most unhappy ideas, the opera after Gogol called *Vakula the Smith*. This formed the subject of a prize contest in honour of Serov (who had died in 1871 before he could begin work on it) which offered one thousand roubles for the best entry and five hundred for the second best.

Tchaikovsky wanted the money—he dreamed always of escape from the Conservatoire—and even more wanted to write the opera he believed he had in him, but he was no businessman and failed entirely to get the prize conditions into his head. The first condition and the most important was that the score should be delivered by August 1875. He misread the date, tore at the opera in a frenzy and triumphantly finished it in August 1874. Having discovered his mistake, he could not endure the thought of his work lying idle a whole year and impulsively wrote to his friend G. P. Kondratyev, the Chief Régisseur of the Maryinsky, asking him to sound Napravnik as to whether the opera could be mounted right away regardless of the prize.

This brought on his head general wrath from the prize judges and he received a sharp and rather suspicious letter from Napravnik, pointing out that he had no rights in the libretto and that such a request was dishonourable. His reply was absolutely typical of the man and banished any remnant of ill-feeling in Petersburg; it was not so much an explanation—'performance of the opera means much more to me than prize money'—as a reproof couched in the terms which made him so difficult to quarrel with: 'Why couldn't you simply have asked Kondratyev to tell me what an ass I'd made of myself instead of imagining unworthy motives that never even entered my head?'

For the next year or more he was to wait with burning impatience for the fate of his opera to be decided and his letters are full of it. Fortunately for everyone he could not do anything about it and was obliged to turn to something else, and so, almost by accident, his first world-famous work came into existence.

The first open news of what he was doing was given in a letter to Anatoly: 'I am at the moment completely absorbed by a pianoforte concerto which I am most anxious shall be played by Rubinstein. It is not going well—very slow progress—but I am sticking to it and manage to hammer passages for the instrument out of my brain.'

The millions who have heard this First Piano Concerto must wonder not only why it came so hard to Tchaikovsky—'I bite my nails to the quick, smoke endless cigarettes and walk up and down the room for hours before an idea comes to me'—but why he did not think of writing a concerto long before. There was no lack of examples; in addition to Beethoven's five, his god Mozart had written at least half a dozen entrancing concertos, Schumann's one and Liszt's two were both well known to him and it seems likely that he must have heard the work of the man who was to become his greatest rival for European popularity, Brahms.

His feeling that he must carry on the work of Glinka literally was chiefly responsible for holding Tchaikovsky back from his right paths. He was not a man to be confined to any one branch of composition and he proved that he could write great works in every genre, but much of the time given to opera must be considered lost. Yet it does not seem that to the end of his life he ever fully realized that one could continue the work of Glinka without writing opera, and that he had in fact continued the master's work in almost all directions so successfully that Russian music had become known and loved all over the world.

What finally set him on the track of the piano concerto was the remembrance of the very effective use of the piano with orchestra in the accompaniment to the first of Lel's songs. And—irony could scarcely go further—he only recalled this to the point of doing anything about it because he found himself at a loss when *Vakula the Smith* was completed a year before time; like nature, he abhorred a vacuum and had to compose something.

In spite of his difficulties with the concerto at the outset he soon found himself very much at home in it, and in the end wrote the whole thing before the end of the year. He had Nikolai Rubinstein in mind all the time and wrote the piano part with a view to his special gifts as pianist. Naturally he dedicated the work to him. As naturally, he kept Rubinstein informed and on Christmas Eve of 1874, just before he, Rubinstein, and N. A. Hubert (one of his fellow students at the Petersburg Conservatoire who had followed him to Moscow as a professor) went off to spend the evening with Albrecht, they arranged that he should play it through to them in one of the class-rooms.

The result of this first run through the concerto has become one of the best-known stories in the history of music. Tchaikovsky was to describe the scene three years later.

I played the first movement. Not one word was said—absolute silence. Do you know the awkward and humiliating feeling one has when offering someone a meal cooked by oneself which he eats without a word? . . . But somehow I restrained myself and played to the end of the concerto. I finished and waited. Still not a word. I got up from the piano. 'Well?' I said. Then a torrent burst from Rubinstein, gentle at first and gathering volume till it exploded in fury. My concerto was worthless and unplayable, the passages so broken, disconnected, and badly written that they were beyond mending. The work was bad, trivial, vulgar. In some parts I had stolen from others. Only one or two pages had any value, the rest must be destroyed or rewritten.

At this point Rubinstein sat down at the piano and demonstrated the unplayability of the score, turning round to Tchaikovsky and Hubert from time to time with a '*That*, for instance,' 'What does *this* mean?', 'How could anyone possibly play such a passage?' and so on until Tchaikovsky went out of the room.

I couldn't have said a word, I was so angry, so shaken. Rubinstein soon followed me and, seeing how upset I was, motioned me into another room. There he said the same things all over again, pointing out the revisions necessary. He added that he would certainly play the concerto if I made the alterations he wanted. I replied 'I shan't alter a note. I shall publish it as it stands.'

It was at this point that Tchaikovsky remembered Von Bülow. He reacted to the double blow—of Rubinstein's inexplicable attitude and the loss of a first performance with Rubinstein as soloist—with a defiant gesture. He scratched out the dedication to his friend and sent the score to Von Bülow with an offer of a dedication if he thought the work worthy of sponsorship.

This act was more timely than Tchaikovsky could have dreamed. All he knew was that Von Bülow had played his Variations nine months earlier and had said some kind things about his work. What he did not know was that Von Bülow had been going into his work more carefully and with most gratifying result. He too had gone to see *A Life for the Tsar* at La Scala and, having greater patience than Tchaikovsky, had stayed in Milan until it was actually staged. Back in Germany, he wrote an article in the *Allgemeine Zeitung* about the music he had heard in Italy. He dealt with *A Life for the Tsar*, then added, 'At the moment we only know of one other Russian who strives and aspires like Glinka and whose works, though they have not yet reached full maturity, promise with certainty that the maturity is not far away. I speak of the young professor of composition at the Moscow Conservatoire—Tchaikovsky. One of his splendid string quartets has already been played with success in many German towns and many other of his works deserve equal recognition—his compositions for pianoforte, for example, his two symphonies and his extremely interesting overture to *Romeo and Juliet* which is both original and extraordinarily melodious.'

Von Bülow ended: 'Because of his many-sidedness this composer is in no danger of being neglected outside his own country as Glinka was.'

He saw what Tchaikovsky did not, that he could become the natural successor to Glinka without following Glinka precisely, that indeed he would succeed where Glinka had failed precisely because of his excursions into other fields than opera. When the score of the Piano Concerto reached him, the German was at once captivated. It was, he declared, the most perfect thing by Tchaikovsky he had seen. 'The ideas are lofty, strong, and original. The details, though profuse, do not obscure the work as a whole and are most interesting. The form is perfect, mature, and redolent of style, that best of styles in which intention and craftsmanship are everywhere concealed.'

He ended by accepting the dedication and by offering to take the concerto with him on an American tour he was to make that autumn. In Boston in October 1875 he played the work as promised.

The Americans have always been noted for their appreciation of the modern. At that time, in 1875, they had no musical tradition of their own and were regarded by most Europeans as, artistically speaking, mere savages—the long and bitter caricature in *Martin Chuzzlewit* faithfully represented the feeling of the Old World towards the New. Yet the Americans already were offering virtuosi the most lucrative tours and their audiences were showing an enthusiasm which outrivalled the blasé Europeans. It was only justice that their freshness of approach should be rewarded by the honour—as it afterwards appeared—of providing the first world performance of what was to become the most popular work of classical music ever known.

The critics had certain reservations, especially with the first movement which, one thought, 'lacked a central idea around which to assemble the host of musical fantasies which make up the breezy and ethereal whole' and singled out, to the amusement of the composer, 'syncopation in the trills, spasmodic interruptions of the subject and thundering octave passages in the Finale'. The audiences had no reservations whatever. Von Bülow's reception was so emotional in Boston that he cabled the good news to Tchaikovsky. When he played the work in New York under Damrosch the next month his reception was even more fervent and he wrote to a friend: 'It was a distinct success and is to be repeated next Saturday. In fact Tchaikovsky has become popular in the New World.'

How popular this work had made him at one blow—for scarcely anyone in America had heard a note of his music before—he understood when Von Bülow sent him press-cuttings: 'Just imagine the capacity these Americans have for musical appreciation—after every performance Von Bülow had to repeat *the entire Finale*,' he told Rimsky-Korsakov, with whom he had begun a correspondence. He added gloomily, 'Such a thing could never happen here.'

His prophecy was proved only too correct when the concerto was played, first in Petersburg on 1 December, then in Moscow two days later with Sergei Taneyev as soloist—only his second appearance on a public concert platform. The work was received enthusiastically by the public but in almost every case was politely damned by the critics. In general they echoed Rubinstein, though more temperately, and Larosh stood for almost all when he summed up: 'It is unrewarding for pianists and has no future.' That this remark was a criticism of the inadequate technique of the pianists of his day and a compliment to an original composer, Larosh did not see—not until the work had become one of the glories of Russia.

Everybody now knows who was right. For the greater part of the past hundred years the Concerto in B flat Minor has been by far the most popular concerto—and the most popular work of any kind—at symphony concerts everywhere. Today it is being played more frequently than ever before. This in spite of repeated attempts by so-called serious critics to decry it, attempts which have virtually never ceased since the work was first presented.

The concerto is a refreshing proof of the fact that in the long run the public knows a good thing and will have it whatever its mentors tell them. The one unfortunate aspect of the concerto's popularity is that it too often rules out performance of works not less worthy, though less obviously so—one thinks in this connexion of Tchaikovsky's splendid Second Piano Concerto.

There is of course a sound reason for this. It is the reason why the Mozart A major Concerto is played far more often than any other of the many great concertos by that master. That is its thematic felicities—in vulgar parlance, the writing of extraordinarily good tunes. One essential attribute of the great composer is the ability to write good tunes and of all composers Tchaikovsky wrote the most; in the B flat Minor Concerto, just as in Mozart's A major Concerto, the tunes in each movement are what are popularly known as winners; there is not one indifferent or ordinary theme in either work.

For the rest, Von Bülow's little analysis can scarcely be bettered. The obvious merits of the work have often been pointed out but it is filled with minor felicities too, such as the little second movement cadenza, a piece of writing for pianoforte at least fifty years ahead of its time, and the witty comments by the woodwinds. In general its enduring popularity stems from its summing-up of the entire romantic movement which in this unromantic age men and women regard nostalgically. It is written throughout with great panache and is a masterly demonstration of the art that conceals art; it is fiery, tender, impassioned, lyrical, and, above all, essentially noble.

iii

In the six months or so which elapsed between the finishing of this concerto and its first performance Tchaikovsky worked almost without a break. He did so partly to take his mind off *Vakula the Smith*, which obsessed him to the point of telling Anatoly, 'If it doesn't change my luck I think I shall go mad. I'm not interested in the prize, I despise it even though the money would not be a bad thing to have, what I want is to get my opera performed.'

As the winner of the prize, and so the performance, would not be known for the best part of a year, something had to be done to keep down his rising anxiety. Work was the answer and he had not long finished the concerto than the answer appeared—or seemed to appear—in a most gratifying commission from the Imperial Opera to write a ballet on the theme of *Swan Lake*. 'I accepted the invitation,' he told Rimsky-Korsakov, 'because I could do with the money but also because I have wanted for a long time to try my hand at this kind of music.'

The reader, who knows what Tchaikovsky did not, will think this a most inadequate statement, particularly when one recalls the little sketch of this very ballet written for his nieces some years earlier, but the flatness of the composer's epistolary style—so often directly opposed to his music—is misleading. What Tchaikovsky wanted was to write the music in the appropriate place so that he could get the right atmosphere.

He had, besides, already determined to write another symphony, and it was this that he got down to the moment he left for Usovo at the end of the Conservatoire term, having finally despatched the score of *Vakula* to Petersburg. Between the completion of the concerto and the beginning of his holiday he had written some notable things—the *Sérénade Mélancolique* for violin and orchestra, a sort of preparation, pleasant but rather thin, for the violin concerto he was soon to compose, and a group of songs, melancholy too, but including the powerful 'Corals'.

By the time he left Usovo late in June the symphony was sketched out, and he began to orchestrate it right away at his next port of call. This was one of his favourite country places, the estate of a wealthy amateur of music, N. D. Kondratyev, at Nizy in Kharkov Province.

He finished the orchestration at his sister's house by the end of July. Nizy was roughly half-way between Usovo and Kamenka, so that Tchaikovsky progressed farther from Moscow as the summer deepened. It was convenient to travel that way but it also expressed his wishes, for he always preferred to end his summer break with Aleksandra.

He did not travel alone. He had with him his 'beloved Dinochka', the nine-year-old daughter of Kondratyev who was so devoted to him that he had not the heart to leave her at Nizy. Besides, she loved Kamenka almost as much as he. She found Aleksandra 'bewitching and with all the charm and fascination of Pyotr Ilyich', and she managed to support his absence or the loss of his sole company (they used to take long walks together at Nizy) just by looking at Aleksandra 'who looked amazingly like him'. Besides, to come to Kamenka after the quiet of her father's house was a never-failing joy; the house was always lively and 'time passed like lightning in this merry circle'.

This time Aleksandra was not at Kamenka (which was owned by the elder Davydov) but at the near-by Verbovka, to which she had moved the better to accommodate her now large family. Here, after

Tchaikovsky had finished orchestrating the symphony, he wrote the Prologue and the first act of *Swan Lake* in two weeks.

The speed of composition tells its own story. At Verbovka were not only Aleksandra and her children and husband but Ilya Petrovich and his wife and Anatoly, and Tchaikovsky was doubly happy, in the heart of the Ukraine and of his family. He was to write a revealing letter to Aleksandra a year later which can be quoted now since it explains his feelings in the summer of 1875 and so explains the sense of effortless felicity in the *Swan Lake* score.

The letter was caused by a sad one from his sister. In her way she was as sensitive as Pyotr Ilyich, and a harsh word from her husband or an unloving one from her children was enough to drive her to the depths of self-abasement.

My darling [he replied] you probably weren't very well when you wrote. The note of heartfelt melancholy in your letter is only too well known to me. With me too there are hours, days, weeks—yes, even months—when everything looks black and I am tormented by the thought that I am forsaken and that none loves me. And why should they? What use am I to anyone? If I vanished from this earth today it would be no great loss to Russian music and no great loss to anyone personally . . . But for *you* to give way to depression, *you* who are indispensable, who make the happiness of us all—this I find incredible. How can you for a moment doubt that everyone who knows you loves and admires you? How could anyone *not* love you? No, there is none in the world more dearly loved. For me to speak of my love for you would be absurd. I love you far above everyone else in the world—you, your family, my brothers and our old father. And I love you all, not because you are my relatives but because you are the best people in the world.

This has the air of an infatuated man even in a country where partiality for one's family was the rule rather than the exception, yet his view of the Tchaikovskys was widely held. Ilya Petrovich was loved wherever he went, Ippolit was a highly popular officer on his ship, Nikolai was respected for his uprightness and good sense, Anatoly was winning golden opinions in his office, and Modest had enormous charm, as his career was to prove. Aleksandra had one of the loveliest characters and natures imaginable; everybody who met her responded instantly to her goodness. Pyotr Ilyich the reader will know for himself. Many witnesses can be produced, including the entire Conservatoire staff, but perhaps one of the best is the young Nadyezhda Kondratyeva. She was to know and love her hero to the day of his death and when grown-up was always included in the after-theatre supper parties and dinners he gave whenever he was in Petersburg. Here she met 'all the most interesting theatre and musical people in the city'. For a young woman fascinated by the arts these artistes must have had a magnetism that the Tchaikovskys, whom she had known most of her life, could not possibly offer. Yet in her account of Tchaikovsky's social life in Petersburg she goes out of her way to add that members of his family were always included in these parties when in town and that she found one and all 'notable for their unusual likeableness'.

To Tchaikovsky this had been gospel from the moment he learned to feel and observe at Votkinsk, and in this mood, surrounded by the people he loved in the country he loved, he wrote the first half of *Swan Lake.*

Back in Moscow that autumn he soon heard that his opera had won the prize and would be produced at some unspecified date. This news virtually coincided with Von Bülow's triumphant cable from Boston, but so little are men able to judge their own work that most of Tchaikovsky's joy was given to the promised presentation of the opera rather than the actual promise of world fame in the American reception of his concerto.

A few weeks later his Third Symphony had its first performance by Nikolai Rubinstein. Tchaikovsky was in Petersburg at the time but heard the symphony when he returned and wrote rather coolly about it to Rimsky-Korsakov. 'I can't see any specially happy ideas in the work but its form is an advance in the right direction. I like the first movement and the Scherzos best.'

The public was mildly enthusiastic, though not to the point of demanding repeat performances, and the critics differed. In the future the work was not destined to hold concert audiences and today it is rarely heard. This severity of judgement is excessive—no work taken seriously by Tchaikovsky should be neglected—but it must be confessed that the Symphony in D Major is a disappointment after the possibilities of its predecessor.

It is curious that Tchaikovsky should feel happy about the form because that is just what worries so many hearers. The work has even been described as a suite masquerading under the name of a symphony—the two Scherzos are a stumbling block to the purist—but this is going too far, and could be regarded as a slur on the suites he was to write. The most serious criticism is that the symphony does not hang together in content and that there is no true progression or development of thought; if there was an idea or a feeling which insisted on expressing itself, it does not emerge clearly. Tchaikovsky's letters, often so explanatory of the music he was writing, do not help here.

The symphony was to be the only one he was to write in a major key and seems to prove that he was happier in the minor, which offers so many opportunities for obtaining dramatic effect. The Introduzione e Allegro is Tchaikovsky almost at his best, a stirring theme handled with superb command of contrapuntal writing. The Alla Tedesca is the first of the Scherzos, placed unusually before the Andante; it is light but charming, reminiscent of the dances made famous in Vienna. The familiar Tchaikovsky emerges fully in the Andante Elegiaco, a nostalgic theme merging into dim suggestions of a ghostly waltz. As an evocation of dream it must rate amongst his more memorable moments. The fourth movement, a true Scherzo, is Tchaikovsky in reverse, the lover of speed and bustle, every instrument employed in a rattling series of good tunes sparklingly orchestrated. In the Finale the composer seems to lose grip. He uses a Polonaise—hence the symphony's title 'The Polish', which was not bestowed by him—but somehow and most exceptionally in him it is treated too intellectually and only succeeds in giving the effect— the last one would expect from such a hand—of dryness.

Almost everyone has been baffled by this work, probably because it moves without apparent connexion from mood to mood. It does not appear to have been sufficiently well thought out or felt—it is notable that Tchaikovsky scarcely says a word about it in his letters. Nevertheless it contains splendid things and the first three movements, possibly the first four, are worthy of regular hearings.

This symphony and the piano concerto were heard in Moscow by a distinguished visitor, Camille Saint-Saëns, who was to conduct and play his own works in the two capitals. He met Tchaikovsky at a reception—the change in the Russian's status at home was shown by the fact that he was one of the first to be introduced to all visitors of moment—and the men took a fancy to each other. The forty-year-old Saint-Saëns, five years older than Tchaikovsky, was the antithesis of the Russian, small, vivacious, amusing in a brittle way, and the tall, strong, unassuming Pyotr Ilyich admired him as usual for all that he himself did not possess and as a famous representative of his mother's nation. He thought at first that Saint-Saëns was beginning a new era in music, combining the elegance and wit of the French with the solidity of the Germans, a superficial judgement owing a great deal to the visitor's charm (he was like another Nikolai Rubinstein) and his formidable technical equipment.

The meetings between them were not notable for anything creative in music; Saint-Saëns understood the originality of *Romeo and Juliet* well enough to propose an entire Tchaikovsky concert in Paris as an excuse to play the work—'Cela l'a posé, cette overture'— but the compliment carried its own criticism of the rest of the composer's output. The notable fact about their brief friendship is the view it provides of a side of Tchaikovsky almost buried beneath the weight of evidence of the serious and painfully sensitive man. This other side was very real, however; it was the Tchaikovsky who fooled about with Nikolai Rubinstein, the Tchaikovsky who larked with his nieces and nephews with such huge enjoyment that they would never let him go, the Tchaikovsky of the village romps. So the story, though so well known, must be repeated: he and Saint-Saëns together wrote a little ballet, *Pygmalion and Galatea*, and danced it themselves on the Conservatoire stage with Rubinstein accompanying—Tchaikovsky as Pygmalion, Saint-Saëns as Galatea.

To meet a Frenchman was quite enough to turn Tchaikovsky's mind westward, and he celebrated the winning of the opera competition by a short trip to Paris that winter. He used the break to see Modest, who had caused him little but trouble ever since he left the Law School and indeed at the school too. Tchaikovsky took his self-imposed responsibilities towards the twins with an earnestness that would surely have caused Aleksandra Andreyevna to raise languid eyebrows. He had not been particularly well repaid but the affection both undoubtedly felt for him seemed reward enough. He agonized often and uselessly. Probably the money he was always sending them—money he certainly could not afford—did more harm than good.

Of the two Anatoly was the steadier. His trouble was a perpetual restlessness; wherever his job took him he always discovered that he wanted to be somewhere else. This meant a letter to Petya asking for help. When young he had a strong feeling against the provinces and his brother was for ever trying to get him out of them. Shortly before the visit to Paris, Anatoly, posted to Kiev three months earlier, demanded that he be removed to one of the capitals. Tchaikovsky at once got to work for him. He shot up to Petersburg for a couple of days—the excuse was Shilovsky, ill and begging a visit. 'I wanted to be incognito but on Nevsky I met Ditlova and though I took to my heels she spotted me and soon everyone knew I was there.

However I didn't go to see anyone except Balakirev, Apukhtin, and Adamov.'

The last visit was as much for Anatoly as for himself—both men being in the legal profession—and he persuaded his old friend to write to Anatoly's chief in Moscow, Motovilov. As soon as he got back to Moscow he followed up the Adamov letter with a personal call—several, in fact, as Motovilov was hard to catch.

When at last tracked down, Motovilov proved more sensible than any of the Tchaikovskys; there was some plain speech which Pyotr Ilyich toned down as best he could: 'He promised not to forget you but added that it wouldn't do you any harm to stay at Kiev for at least a year. . . . I left him with misgivings but don't lose hope, I'll write to Adamov today.'

In this same letter he told Anatoly, not for the first time, 'I have had a very silly letter from Modest', and had no sooner sealed his own letter than he was writing one to Modest. 'I'm told you have done something very dishonourable and nasty. I don't yet know what it is but I know your character well, you are so spineless that you will do absolutely anything to be able to go on the spree and have a good time.' And he added a familiar cry of 'Ah, Modka! I'm seriously worried about you. Have you forgotten already how I spoke to you about your utter lack of purpose, the way you never think of your life? For heaven's sake do consider your future instead of always trying to enjoy yourself.'

Modest, as the reader will gather, was a playboy and not too scrupulous at that. He got into bad company at school and had never got out of it, much to Tchaikovsky's distress, until suddenly, moved by some quirk (which could have been unpaid debts), he took a job as tutor to a deaf-and-dumb boy and went off with him to Lyons to take a course of treatment for deafness.

It was partly to visit Modest—reformed, he hoped—and his charge that Tchaikovsky made his Paris trip. It was a visit made memorable by the birth of a lifelong passion for the work of Bizet—Tchaikovsky went quite mad over *Carmen* which he saw at the Opéra-Comique—and for the beginning of another quartet.

In Moscow again he wrote hard in the intervals between classes and by March the quartet was finished and played five times within the next few weeks. As this indicates, it was immediately appreciated, but Tchaikovsky was not pleased with it and talked gloomily of having written himself out. He was mistaken, as time has proved; this Quartet in E flat Minor is the best of his string quartets.

In one sense the work is a little unbalanced. It was dedicated to the memory of Ferdinand Laub, the violinist for whom Tchaikovsky had written the *Sérénade Mélancolique*, and as a compliment to the dead man the composer threw the onus of every movement on to the first violin. Like so many of his works, the quartet has become famous for one movement, the Andante Funebre, but this partiality of the public does real disservice to the rest of the quartet as well as giving quite the wrong impression of its mood. Though written as an elegy the general tone of the work is serene and even joyful. Not the joy of the thoughtless but of a man beginning to come to terms with himself about the problems of life and death.

The first movement opens and closes as an Andante Sostenuto, a kind of mourning theme, but so free from morbidity as to be undisturbedly beautiful, and is broken by a lyrical Allegro Moderato portraying by strong syncopated rhythms man's refusal to accept death as the end. The Scherzo-Allegretto is marked 'vivo e scherzando' and is one of the most brilliant little movements Tchaikovsky ever wrote for strings, fiery, fanciful, and bubbling over with so many ideas so briefly treated that the listener is as much tantalized as fascinated. This is the Tchaikovsky who danced the ballet with Saint-Saëns, gay, defiant, determined to enjoy life while he had it.

It may be mentioned here that Tchaikovsky was the most meticulous of composers; he gave no excuse for wrong tempi on the part of performers or conductors, going so far as to include metronome markings on his scores. The third and best-known movement of this third quartet is a case in point; it is marked 'Andante funebre e doloroso, ma con moto'. All the weight is given to the first violin which sings the funeral march, a plaintive melody of infinite charm, sad but never hopeless, never sentimental. The Finale, an Allegro, lifts one at once into the village dance-measure so much loved by the composer, brisk, vigorous, full of gaiety and with sparkling tunes. It is not namby-pamby stuff and has offended some critics, just as the Clown's Dance in *Snyegurochka* offended them, as vulgar. It is vulgar in the true meaning of that word; in the phrase of a more discerning critic it has a real 'whiff of village streets'.

The quartet is a model in the writing of an elegiac work; it is not stuffed with dripping sentiment but is manly, thoughtful, positive, keeping a memory alive, not burying it. It is also an object lesson in how to stress the importance and value of the first violin without overloading the part to the point of formlessness. It has always been regarded as Tchaikovsky's best work for string quartet and as proof that he was never content to rest in his tracks.

The quartet done, he turned back to *Swan Lake* and finished it, most suitably deep in the country that Easter. He did not pause, he was in a rage of work, and at once began a symphonic poem on *Francesca da Rimini*. He had toyed with the idea of making an opera on this Dante theme but disliked the libretto when he read it and abruptly abandoned the opera in favour of a symphonic work.

He did not rest until summer when he went abroad again, first to see Modest and his pupil at Lyons and to take the waters at Vichy— without effect, he thought—then to move to Bayreuth for the festival. There he met Wagner and Liszt (whom he found amiable but something of an actor) and groaned his way through *The Ring* in company with Rubinstein, Larosh, and Kui. He was there in the capacity of critic for his Moscow journal as well as a Russian composer who, he was gratified to discover, was not entirely unknown in the West. His report to the journal was a model of fairmindedness, his private opinion was refreshingly blunt. 'After the last chords of the *Götterdämmerung* had ended and we were allowed to go I felt as though I had come out of prison. *The Nibelungen* may be a great work of art—it is possible—but it is certainly a crashing bore; it goes on far too long.'

The music evidently proved altogether too much for Larosh. He had become a heavy drinker but at Bayreuth 'he is drunk from morning to night'. Tchaikovsky's effort to occupy his mind was unsuccessful: 'I threw him together with Kui only to see them quarrel after a couple of hours.'

He went back very happily to Russia feeling that he was breathing a purer air in every sense of the word in the heart of it, Kamenka. And there he unleashed a minor bombshell.

iv

The atmosphere of domestic happiness was too much for him that summer and he announced to Modest an underlined '*I have decided to get married*'.

This sounded tolerably definite but would not cause much of a flutter in the family dove-cot, as he knew, so he added a 'This decision is irrevocable'—as much to nerve himself to the act as to stop family discussions.

In the event it did neither; he was left painfully undecided and the family rose up in protest. Not for the first time, since he had mooted the marriage plan regularly for some years, every time, in fact, he saw at first hand what he was missing by living alone.

Aleksandra, Lyov, Modest, and Anatoly all protested because they foresaw disaster if Pyotr Ilyich married without love, simply to get a home life. Many men could and did marry 'sensibly' and made a success of it, but the sensitive, romantic Tchaikovsky who had adored a highly romantic soprano was not of this type, much though he insisted on his strong commonsense.

The subject was discussed through the summer holiday and beyond it; when he returned to Moscow he was followed by an agitated letter from Aleksandra, to which he answered with a 'Don't worry about my marriage, my angel. It is a long way ahead, certainly not before next year.' He then added, ruining all his attempt at consolation, 'Next month I shall begin to look about me.'

He was to explain this decision in a letter to Modest which has become notorious; the purpose was to stop Moscow gossip. He claimed that he wanted to save his family and friends from the disgrace of having him publicly branded as a homosexual.

There is no doubt that this was his main preoccupation; letter after letter expresses his conviction that all the people he loved might be 'ruined'—he uses this word often—by the connexion with him. His imagination was lively: he visualized his brothers forced to resign their posts, Aleksandra and Lyov socially snubbed and their children's future blemished, and the last years of his father and stepmother blighted. But he was thinking of his music too. If, as seemed only too possible to him, he was hounded out of the Conservatoire how would he get his compositions played? The official view of homosexuality was strict and he was haunted by dread of imprisonment. He owed his immunity to the good and powerful friends he had made. But could even they protect him if the growing rumours threatened the good name of the Conservatoire?

The decision to marry was not sudden: it had been forming in his mind for years, as far back as the understanding with Artôt six years earlier. They had been years of steadily increasing bouts of wretchedness as he realized that what he had once taken so lightly had become an unmanageable force that might bring him and everyone he loved down in shame.

A conclusion of this kind is slow to mature—everything in a man's mind tempts him to ignore or underrate it. Tchaikovsky had good reason to play down his fears. If one judges by the evidence of his early letters he was like many teenagers and young men; his inclinations were bi-sexual. The first open references to his homo-sexuality occur, as expected, in the years immediately following his graduation from the Law School. These references are all carefree, those of a young man sowing his wild oats. At the same time he is flirting often and persistently with the young women of his circle and writing of them with the kind of besotted devotion common to 'bloods' of the day.

Obviously it had never entered his head that the first inclination might destroy the second. If he thought much about the matter—and there is no sign that he did—he plainly assumed, in the style of numberless boys and young men, that this delightful indulgence would prove superfluous and indeed tame in the course of nature—that is, when he had the money to marry, met the right girl, and began to raise a family his homosexual impulse would fade away. Certainly he never dreamed for a moment that he might not enjoy the domestic life he loved with a passion rare even in the purely heterosexual male.

In this he differentiates himself sharply from the true homosexual to whom the thought of sleeping with a woman and begetting child-ren would be a form of nightmare. What he anticipated so light-heartedly in these Petersburg days was not unreasonable; nine out of ten young men who carry schooldays' homosexuality into their late teens and early twenties find the habit dies imperceptibly and painlessly when they fall in love with a girl and marry her.

There is no reason to suppose that Tchaikovsky's sexual life would not have followed this normal pattern. That it did not was due to a stroke of irony, an irony so cruel that he was to be preoccupied for the rest of his life with the workings of fate in human lives. This irony was nothing less than his decision to follow the great love of his youth and take up music professionally.

The decision was a late one—he was twenty-two when he joined the Petersburg Conservatoire—and in practical terms meant that the safe and marriageable income he would soon have reached in the Civil Service was reduced to a pittance barely enough to keep him alive.

The crucial years began when he went to Moscow as professor. He was then twenty-six, very badly paid (marriage was out of the question) and very lonely. In this he differs from the average young man who reacts positively to fresh surroundings and flourishes on his own. Tchaikovsky was ambitious too but with him ambition always came a poor second to affection. He was deeply feeling to a degree few could rival. When he moved to Moscow he lost his best and surest hold on a normal sexual life, his family.

A man of twenty-six in those days was sexually mature, was expected to settle down, and usually wanted to settle down. Tchaikovsky was no exception to the rule; his wish to settle down was even greater than the norm. But this was out of the question, he had not the money, he had not any reasonable prospect of earning enough money for many years, but his sexual desires were strong. Failing marriage, the delightful pastime of Petersburg became a necessity in Moscow. The one or two Petersburg friends with whom he had enjoyed himself were no longer available. The inevitable happened. Love of some kind he had to have. He began to pay for it.

From that moment he was lost. No man will admit that he is lost. For years Tchaikovsky kept up the pretence of normality; he talked about marriage, wrote about it, dreamed of it, longed for it, tried to convince himself that only money and the right woman were lacking and that in time he would have both. He was helped in the illusion by the undeniable fact that for several years his salary in Moscow remained utterly inadequate to support two people, let alone a family, and that he loved women and children and the idea of a home with ever greater fervour. A man who could sit by the side of a woman, as he did afternoon by afternoon, while she suckled her child has little in common with the homosexual as he is commonly known.

But a Tchaikovsky—extraordinarily sensitive, self-analytical, physically fastidious—could not live a secret life which he felt to be reprehensible, weak, and disgusting without extreme reactions. In these first Moscow years his letters begin to reveal his sufferings.

Yet he was not fully committed to homosexuality until the unsuccessful understanding with Artôt when he was twenty-nine. After that he seems not to have abandoned hope so much as relaxed guard. It is from this time that the first of his begging notes dates. All his Moscow friends received them. Not all this money—for he seems never to have been refused—went on those expensive luxuries the twins in Petersburg, old nurses and governesses and the hundred and one small charities he was busy about. Nor was it all absorbed by the alcohol he was drinking increasingly to try to stun his uneasiness and misery. He no longer made a secret of his vice, as it had become, nor did he try to justify it; he confessed freely and often to all these good friends, almost all married and with families; he protested again and again that he wanted nothing better than to be like them.

The protests were genuine. For the tragedy of Tchaikovsky was not that he was a homosexual but that he was a reluctant one. As his ravaged face, his prematurely white hair, agonized letters and deeply introvert music show, the further he got into the toils of homosexuality the more he longed for the normal life that had once seemed so inevitable, for a wife, children, home. Not for him the arguments that what he did was highly civilized and sanctified by the Greeks, that he wanted nothing better. Whatever physical satisfaction he may have had was fleeting and with a dreadful sting in its tail. His attitude after the first years in Moscow was one of almost unrelieved self-disgust, as both letters and diaries bear witness. The most he could find to say in extenuation was that he could not be held responsible for a bodily urge implanted in him by the fate of which he thought so much and so bitterly.

The truth was that he had all the instincts of the bi-sexual but, owing perhaps to his long-enforced celibacy, had lost a vital part of one, the ability or the will (it is difficult to separate them) to consummate marriage. Of course he suspected this some time before the 1875 announcement that he had decided 'irrevocably' to marry but, feeling as he did, he dared not face its full implications. On the contrary he insisted that he needed only the 'habit' of marriage to restore his sexual life to normal.

What he was forced to face as the years went on and his occasional homosexual excursions fastened into a virtually unbreakable desire were the repercussions on his family and friends. How he first came to hear of the growing Moscow rumours is not known. A professor in a college of music is fair game and he had a thousand ways of learning, from anonymous notes to sotto-voce remarks in class, that he was becoming the talk of the town.

This stirred him as nothing else could do. His letters began to reflect the new terror. He no longer borrowed money with a joke but a cry of fear. His loyal Moscow friends began to receive notes such as 'Send me 15 silver roubles for God's sake and save me and my family from certain ruin!'

They paid up uncomplainingly and, it seems, uncritically—they were all very fond of him. Tchaikovsky paid in another fashion. Living from hand to mouth, with exposure and disgrace hanging over one day by day, night by night, would break a far less sensitive man. He made effort after effort to fight the homosexual in him. He always failed; it had grown too strong. Then he loathed himself because of this thing in him he could not conquer, an unclean thing which, unless something were done and done quickly, would kill his dreams of becoming one of Russia's great composers and wreck the happiness and peace of mind of everyone he loved.

And it was at this point, in the summer of 1875, that he announced his irrevocable decision to marry or—for the first time in his life he admitted that marriage might be beyond him—'at least form some public bond with a woman which would silence contemptible creatures whose judgements mean nothing to me but who have the power to hurt those I love'.

v

His compositions went on regardless—which, incidentally, puts his state of mind that summer and autumn in truer perspective—and he worked hard at *Francesca da Rimini*. In the summer, moved by the war between tiny Serbia and the Turkish Empire, he had written *Marche Slave*. It is a jingoistic piece of music, unashamedly emotional, but is extremely well done and still has the power to move even against one's will. *Francesca* is emotional too but the love he gave it was quite another thing from his outburst of slavophilism. He finished it late in October and tried to get it put on right away in Petersburg but failed; it had to wait until the next year and by that time other matters had reduced its importance.

This work has become as popular as *Romeo and Juliet*. The subject is, superficially, similar and is treated just as brilliantly, with an array of unforgettable themes and a barrage of magnificent orchestral sound. In truth, Tchaikovsky here attacked a very different subject. Francesca is no Juliet, she is the languorous lover, the eternal temptress, the *femme fatale*, and remarkably—for his instincts were all towards the Juliet type of woman—he creates her without one false note.

When the music of *Francesca da Rimini* is not martially vigorous it is sultry, sensual, exotic, and at the risk of undue harping on argument it must be said that Tchaikovsky was to offer few better proofs than this symphonic poem that he was not at heart a natural homo-sexual; such a theme and such treatment of such a theme is quite beyond any of that persuasion. But the final thought on *Francesca*, as on so many of his major works, must be of his marvellous orchestra-tion. The word is used advisedly, for he has a supple genius for wielding the orchestra rivalled only perhaps by Rimsky-Korsakov and the then unborn Igor Sravinsky.

Another link with Stravinsky was forged a matter of days after *Francesca* was finished, for on 6 December the long-awaited première of *Vakula the Smith* was given at the Maryinsky and one of the major roles was taken by Stravinsky's father, Fyodor. Neither he nor any-one else in the cast could save this opera. Tchaikovsky had a sense of humour but it was not the kind needed for a comic opera. Throughout the Overture and the first scene he managed to keep up the fun and earned considerable applause. After that it was a tale of mounting disappointment for the audience and it ended with as many jeers as applause at the curtain calls. To complete his chagrin the composer overheard a comment during one of the intervals which summed up the audience's reaction: 'I came here to amuse myself, not to be bored to tears.'

Tchaikovsky's ability to divert every failure to himself—a refreshingly rare trait in creative men—was hard pressed when he had to admit failure once again; unlike his previous operas, in which he had lost faith before they were even staged, he attended the first performance of *Vakula* filled with optimism—a rare sensation aroused by a most unusual event, praise from Kui at the dress re-hearsal.

Later, in his review of the first performance, Kui, who was per-ceptive when he was not being merely catty, put his finger on the fault of all Tchaikovsky operas up to date; the music was symphonic, not operatic, he wrote, and though often beautiful and always noble, did not match the action on stage. Tchaikovsky afterwards agreed with the criticism *in toto*. He did not take the hint, however; before leaving Petersburg he asked Stasov for a libretto for yet another opera, on *Othello*, and at first refused to accept Stasov's reaction, that the subject would not suit him. Later he dropped it, but not opera; he was merely biding his time.

For the moment he demonstrated both courage and his real gift for humour, for in spite of the failure of *Vakula* and of performances of *Romeo and Juliet* in Paris and Vienna, he immediately began work on *Variations on a Rococo Theme*. Nor was that the end of the surprise

—one that he often has in store for the categorist of human behaviour; the work does not bear a single trace of pique or sorrow.

This is the more surprising because the *Rococo Variations* were written for his friend W. K. F. Fitzenhagen, the noted cellist, who played in the Conservatoire quartet, and dedicated to him. It might be thought that of all composers Tchaikovsky would respond emotionally to the obvious characteristics of the cello and that anything he wrote for it would be luscious and sentimental to a degree. That is what we have been taught to think of Tchaikovsky. Instead, he showed the instrument in a new light, as graceful, witty, elegant, and himself as a man with a real sense of humour.

It has often been said that the *Variations* show Tchaikovsky in his most Mozartian light. It could be added, in his French style too and, of course, as a master of the variation form. It is possible to experience this work heavily treated but if one hears, for example, Rostropovich play it under Rozhdestvensky, the full beauty of the composer's wit is brought out and from first bar to last it is a joy—economical, pithy, inventive. It is what is known as a light work, that is to say the composer is not plunging into the profound, merely enjoying himself. If all enjoyed themselves as Tchaikovsky did in the *Rococo Variations*, the world would be a more bearable place to live in.

The year of 1876 ended in comedy. Tolstoy visited Moscow and called on Tchaikovsky. To the composer, as to millions in Russia, Tolstoy was a god, the maker of the greatest novels every written, and a psychologist to be dreaded. The honour of the visit was therefore clouded: 'The great prober of the human heart must obviously possess the power of reading the inmost secrets of mine; I felt sure that neither the smallest weakness nor sin could escape his eye and that it would be useless to try to show him nothing but the best in me.'

In such a mood Pyotr Ilyich braced himself for trouble, which, with his imagination, could end only by a contemptuous Tolstoy turning on his heel after expressing disgust at having come into contact with such a vile creature. He was right in thinking that his visitor had the power to make men tell the truth—everyone who met Tolstoy was agreed that under the scrutiny of those extraordinary eyes dissimulation was useless—but to his immense surprise Tchaikovsky passed muster. Typically, he did not once think that Tolstoy had found him worthy and interesting. No, for him, 'evidently the great analyst of human nature did not consider me a fit subject for dissection but simply decided to chat about music.'

Tolstoy, having satisfied himself at a glance, put the conversation, as always, on the other man's level. In his relief Tchaikovsky rebounded into criticism: 'He seemed to enjoy depreciating Beethoven and even directly questioning his genius. This is an unworthy trait in a great man.'

Tolstoy was not at all disturbed by his companion's agitation at this slight on the god of music. He attended a concert arranged in his honour by Rubinstein at which the Andante Cantabile from Tchaikovsky's First Quartet was played, freely wept during it to the unspeakable emotion of the composer sitting next to him, and, when he left, promised to make a collection of the folk songs of his region which he was sure 'will become wonderful gems in your hands'. And when, a few days later, he duly sent the songs, he added unregenerately, 'For God's sake treat them in the Mozart-Handel style and not in the manner of the Beethoven-Schumann-Berlioz school which strives only after the sensational.'

The comedy reached its height when, mastering his anger, Tchaikovsky dutifully looked through the songs. They were absolutely useless and his letter to Tolstoy informing him of this fact is a masterpiece of tact.

I must tell you frankly that the songs have been taken down by an unskilful hand and that almost all their original beauty has disappeared. The chief mistake is that they have been forced artificially into a regular rhythm. Only the Russian choral dances have a regularly accentuated measure; the legends [Bylini] have nothing in common with the dances. In addition, most of these songs have been written down in the cheerful key of D Major. This is quite out of keeping with the tonality of genuine Russian folk songs which are always in some indefinite key like the old church modes . . . I could not make them into a folk song album because such songs must be taken down exactly as the people sing them. This is highly skilled work which calls for the most delicate musical perception as well as a thorough knowledge of musical history. With the exception of Balakirev—and possibly Prokunin—I know no one who really understands this work.

Having stated the fact, he added, 'But your songs can be used as symphonic material—and very fine material too—which I shall certainly take advantage of.'

vi

Early in 1877 Tchaikovsky began to write his Fourth Symphony. It was intended to deal in a more extensive form than ever before with his preoccupation with the workings of fate. It can be no surprise that Tchaikovsky's belief that he was born under an unlucky star had strengthened; and in truth many a less emotionally introspective man than Pyotr Ilyich might justifiably have considered that fate had been sporting with him with particular malice during the past three years.

At the beginning of 1874 he was poised ready for fame and fortune, well established in his own country and on the point of invading the West. Since that time he had written many works he considered an advance on anything he had done before, but apart from a success in the United States which had not been followed up and one or two minor triumphs in Russia he seemed to have slipped back everywhere. In England he remained little known and even less thought of (the pianoforte concerto had made no mark there), in Paris he had been frigidly received and his music very badly played, and even in Germany where he had a staunch champion in the powerful Von Bülow neither critics nor public, absorbed by Brahms, would take him seriously. In his own country he was in danger of being relegated to the position of the nice second-rater who wrote pleasant but rather ineffective music, a man who could not make the grade. Even critics formerly hostile had begun to treat him leniently and this he well knew to be the last stage of infirmity; when a man like Kui began to talk of his nobility, he could almost write himself off.

This he was not for one moment prepared to do. He often said and wrote the most absurd things—he was past his prime, written out, not far from senile—and believed them in the moment, but the letter posted, the speech made, he was once more the ambitious man conscious of his superiority to most living composers and determined to give his music to the world. Yet there he was in early 1877, nearly thirty-seven years old, the finest living composer in his own country and one of the finest in the world, but who would acknowledge it? He thought of Brahms, idolized in Germany and with a strong foothold in every civilized country, and felt as bitter as he was able.

There was, in short, every reason for a symphony which would try to express his feelings about the inexplicable, incalculable hand of chance, one of the strongest powers in man's life. Tchaikovsky was not one to accept such a phenomenon without trying to resolve it in musical terms. The Fourth Symphony was intended to do that.

It was probably sparked off by the deplorable production of *Swan Lake*. The ballet was staged at the Bolshoi on 4 March—five days before the first performance of *Francesca da Rimini*. The success of the latter was a mockery to Tchaikovsky after the stupendous, the almost unbelievable bungling of *Swan Lake*—a record in mismanagement even for one of the Imperial Theatres. Everything went wrong that could go wrong; the ballet was appallingly badly dressed, the sets were a disgrace, the choreography farcical, the dancing poor, and the rendering of the music—which most of the orchestra had not troubled to learn and the rest could not play—was incredibly inept. To round matters off, the score had been hacked about on the grounds that some of it was too difficult for both dancers and musicians. What poor Tchaikovsky must have suffered as he looked and listened passes comprehension.

Naturally, the ballet was an abject flop. After a few performances it was taken off. *Swan Lake* was not seen again for the best part of twenty years, when the Petipa version swept the world. Tchaikovsky was then in his grave.

It would be absurd in this day and age to comment in detail on Tchaikovsky's score. The one point of interest not always known is that the most famous part of it—the second act *pas de deux*—came straight from *Undine*, probably the happiest piece of borrowing that any composer has ever thought of; it fitted *Swan Lake* like a glove, and the solo violin theme has become immortal.

It is almost impossible now to imagine the kind of ballet music Tchaikovsky had listened to ever since he first came to Petersburg as a boy, the kind of music still being played in the Russian capitals when he wrote *Swan Lake*—and for that matter the kind of ballet music played everywhere and accepted as normal fare in the eighteen-seventies. Occasionally the ballet-goer of today will hear a Minkus *pas de deux*, and that gives some idea of the triviality, the inanity of music considered good enough for ballet. Yet it is only if one can imagine oneself back into that now distant past that it is possible to understand exactly what Tchaikovsky did with *Swan Lake*. For the first time in history he gave ballet music symphonic proportions; he gave it dignity, elegance, and true feeling.

Today the *Swan Lake* music sounds simple and inevitable; it was anything but that in 1877, it was daring to the last degree. As it happened, it was not to be the first of Tchaikovsky's scores publicly to revolutionize ballet (for it demanded and so created great choreography and great dancing); this honour was to fall to *The Sleeping Beauty* thirteen years later.

Thirteen years! That is the measure of the loss that millions of ballet-goers have sustained. For thirteen years after the shambles of the *Swan Lake* production Tchaikovsky wrote no ballet music. But though *Swan Lake* was not to make its mark first, it finally eclipsed every other ballet score, even those by the same hand. To millions in every part of the world today it is the very essence of ballet—the art at its purest and greatest.

In the spring of 1877 nothing of this was even faintly imaginable by the distressed composer. As usual he tried to take much of the blame for the fiasco on to his own shoulders, but his feeling that fate was against him deepened and darkened, and those who examine his life dispassionately must feel that he was severely tested. Something of this was due, of course, to his disposition and to his public standing; every creative man takes his life in his hands every time he offers something to the world. But when all is said, Tchaikovsky seems to have been peculiarly vulnerable to the slings and arrows of fortune, and never was this to be more true than at the time he had now reached, for it was then, early in 1877, that he first properly made the acquaintance of Antonina Ivanovna Milyukova and Nadyezhda Filaretovna von Meck.

CHAPTER TWELVE

Nadyezhda Filaretovna
1877

Antonina Milyukova was the first of these women to come into his life although by the end of 1876 he had forgotten all about her. This was not surprising for he did not think much of his women students:

Although it is a dreary business to have been forced to explain to my young men's classes for eleven consecutive years what a triad consists of, at least I have had the consolation of feeling that I am ramming essential knowledge into them because they intend to take up music as a profession. But the young women's classes! Heavens above! Out of sixty or seventy only five at the most will ever make musicians. The rest come to the Conservatoire to fill in time or from motives which have nothing to do with music. They are not less intelligent or less hard-working than the men, rather the opposite . . . but they all come to grief the moment they are unable to apply a rule mechanically or use it by rote. I often lose patience with them—and my head—and go quite frantic with rage.

As this remark indicates, Tchaikovsky's dislike of lecturing had long since passed the stage of silent resentment and his widespread popularity in class had gone. One of the Conservatoire pupils, A. N. Levitskaya-Amfiteatrova, who was later to create the role of Olga in *Yevgeny Onyegin*, described Tchaikovsky the professor with refreshing frankness: 'He was handsome but very stern and the expression on his face was of almost constant displeasure. When he came into the classroom he looked sombrely at us under eyebrows drawn into a frown and answered the students' greeting with a barely noticeable nod of the head.'

147

The opinion of the classes was divided: 'Some thought he was not only a composer of genius but an ideal teacher. According to these students Pyotr Ilyich always went through their work with great interest and care, correcting mistakes patiently and giving them the most valuable advice. Others were convinced that he neglected them.'

That he could be sharp and severe was demonstrated by a student friend in his harmony class who told Levitskaya-Amfiteatrova indignantly what happened when he came to her desk one day to look at a specimen score she had written out. She had forgotten to add the tails to the demi-semi-quavers and he at once fell into a fury and slashed the page across with a red pencil. 'You'd better try to master the art of making tails before you try to master harmony,' he said coldly, and moved on to the next student.

This story, and his grim manner in class, impressed Levitskaya-Amfiteatrova so unfavourably that she eventually complained to Kashkin. All she got for her pains was a shout of incredulous laughter and a 'Pyotr Ilyich irritable! Why he's the kindest, gentlest, most sympathetic man breathing. He's far too kind, that's his trouble, he pities every poor, unfortunate and oppressed man and woman to the point of absurdity. As for ragged, deserted children, he can't even speak of them without tears!'

She was not reassured; to her Tchaikovsky remained a harsh taskmaster who only interested himself in promising students, and by 1877 this was no doubt true. He had never been able to convince himself that he was a good teacher let alone a born one. He felt trapped for life at the Conservatoire and resented every moment spent away from composition unless he was dealing with a student whom he felt might make his mark in music if carefully trained. His horror of stupidity and laziness had reached a pitch of ferocity that burst on his classes week after week. Hence 'I go quite frantic with rage' and the dismay of students who meant well but had little hope of becoming serious musicians.

But there was a third type of student who was anything but dismayed by these classroom scenes. Tchaikovsky did not understand that his explosions made him even more attractive to those who had joined 'from motives which have nothing to do with music'. It is doubtful whether, of all the hundreds in this category who had passed through his hands, a girl was ever as indifferent to music as Antonina Milyukova. She had one thought in her head—men—and at that particular moment, one man, the lecturer whose furiously glaring blue eyes gave her such a pleasant thrill. She had joined his class at the Conservatoire four years earlier, when she was twenty-four. She had not joined the class to learn harmony; like most of the other young women, she had joined to stare at the handsome professor and to try to engage his attention.

Of this Tchaikovsky had no notion; the numbers in his class were too great for him to individualize every girl and young man; he only became intimate with the most gifted and Antonina was not among these. When he met her for a few moments at the end-of-term parties he remained innocent; she was pretty, with fine eyes and a mass of fair hair, a good figure and a manner which a more experienced man than Pyotr Ilyich would have found difficult to penetrate; she said little and looked much; she was apparently a demure, rather shy and earnest girl deeply interested in music in general and his in particular.

He was mildly attracted. He was accustomed to student crushes, and when this student completed her course towards the end of 1876 and left his classes he forgot her completely.

ii

In the five months before he was to be reminded of her he had gone some way in intimacy with the second woman who was to influence his life so powerfully. Just about the time when Antonina Milyukova left the Conservatoire he was offered and accepted a commission to arrange some orchestral music for violin and pianoforte. The commission came through one of his favourite students, Iosif Iosifovich Kotek, who had just finished his Conservatoire course. This young man had obtained a post as violin tutor in the household of Nadyezhda Filaretovna von Meck, and had raved to her about his god Pyotr Ilyich, what a noble soul he was and what wonderful music he composed.

Tchaikovsky knew a good deal about Nadyezhda Filaretovna. Indeed all Moscow was gossiping about her, for earlier that year her husband—a railway king—had died and left her a great fortune. He had also left her eleven children, ten of whom were alive, and with one still unborn. The talk in Moscow salons was all about what she would do with herself and who would share the money with her—for she was only in her mid-forties, nine years older than Tchaikovsky.

He knew more than the town gossips. Whenever he met Kotek the young man was full of her autocratic manner, her violent changes of moods, her equally violent headaches when the whole household trembled, her journeyings in search of health, her vast retinue of servants, her enormous estate at Brailov in the Ukraine, and above all her passion for music.

Nikolai Rubinstein filled in some of the gaps left by Kotek. He had come to know her fairly well in the past year or so—as Director of the Conservatoire he was the only man unconnected with the household who was allowed to visit her—and made fun of her and her queer ways. If he was to be believed—never a foregone conclusion with him—she was half demented but very much worth cultivating. She had already helped the shaky Conservatoire funds and would almost certainly do more, she never missed a Moscow concert, which she attended incognito. He predicted that she would not marry again but would give her life to music; she was a fair pianist, she surrounded herself with a staff of musicians and would be for ever demanding arrangements for two pianos and violin and piano for which she would pay handsomely.

Rubinstein, it may be assumed with fair confidence, urged Tchaikovsky to accept the commission; Nadyezhda Filaretovna was the kind of patron no Director of a penurious Conservatoire dare offend. He would be anxious to help his friend too; he knew that Pyotr Ilyich, constitutionally unable to say no to a borrower, had at last fallen into the moneylenders' hands, he knew that he could turn out the required arrangement with the greatest of ease; everything seemed to add up to the beginnings of a lucrative period for all.

Tchaikovsky agreed, supplied the arrangement quickly just before the end of the year and received by return a payment which must have made him open his eyes, together with a short but gratifying note. From this note it was clear that the great patroness of music preferred his music to that of all others; she said so no fewer than three times in a few lines, ending, 'I simply ask you to believe as a fact that your music makes my life easier and more endurable.'

Tchaikovsky's reply to this considerable compliment from such a quarter was restrained, a mere formal letter of thanks. There was a short interval of two or three weeks before he heard from her again. In that time the industrious Kotek, who oscillated between his mistress of the Von Meck mansion and his idol of the Conservatoire, had provided more information about this unusual woman. She had vowed, he said, to live for the rest of her life as a recluse. She did not think this period would be very long; she had tubercular symptoms and put down her dreadful headaches and not less dreadful attacks of nerves to the beginning of the end. She was an atheist. She had two photographs of Tchaikovsky prominently displayed in her music room; she talked at length of him and questioned Kotek and Rubinstein closely about him.

This news must have made Tchaikovsky thoughtful. As everyone must have their god an atheist will search for a human god. To worship a human being is to long to possess him; everything he heard about this woman suggested that she was a tyrant; not one person in her house could really be said to call his soul his own.

He was soon tested. In February of the new year, 1877, he was offered and accepted another commission to make an arrangement for piano and violin. He again made it quickly and before the end of the month had received an even more generous payment with a covering letter which virtually forced him into intimacy. 'I should dearly like to tell you fully what I think and feel about you but I don't want to waste your precious time, so let me just say that my feeling for you is spiritual and one of my dearest possessions.'

There was only one answer to this and Tchaikovsky made it. He was a human being and had his fair share of vanity. He could not forget that this woman who had voluntarily offered her admiration was fabulously wealthy and could at one stroke relieve him of all money worries. But apart from the money and the flattery he was touched. Kotek and Rubinstein had both made plain that this Nadyezhda Filaretovna was unhappy. She was lonely in spite of her large family and huge household. She loved music. She appealed to all the kindness in him. In reply the next day he urged her to write to him as she wished, fully: 'Perhaps I know you better than you think.'

He believed what he said. He considered himself a lonely man in Moscow for all the company he kept and was not entirely mistaken. By and large he detested Moscow social life—or, to be exact, he detested himself every time he came back from a soirée chiefly given over to gossip and insincerities. He was not a prodigious letter writer for nothing; he preferred a letter friendship to a drinking bout which was what most friendships in Moscow led to. He was sorry for the rich woman in her mansion in Rozhdestvensky Boulevard and admired the stand she was taking, the stand he had so often talked about, to give up the world for music. He thought she could be right, that he and she had in common the greatest love on earth.

His note opened the floodgates. In the middle of March he received the first of what was to become a unique collection of long and intimate letters. This first one began with a request for a photograph. 'I want to discover in your face the thoughts and feelings which inspired you to write music that transports me into a world of high emotion, of hope, of an unquenchable craving.'

She explained that her ideal man was a musician but that she expected to be able to look up to the man as much as to the musician —she could not divorce the one from the other. She had been searching for this man and thought she had found him after she heard her first Tchaikovsky work, *The Tempest*. 'I couldn't possibly describe the impression it made on me; for days afterwards I was practically out of my mind with excitement.'

Being the business-woman she was, she immediately set about to discover 'what kind of man had created the music that had given me such unparalleled joy. I seized every opportunity to learn more about you, I listened to everything that was said about you, in general and in passing, from those who knew you and from those who only knew about you. . . . I am interested in everything about you, where you are and what you are doing all day and every day. And already I feel from what I have heard, favourable and otherwise, an enormous conviction that we are one in thought and feeling.'

Raptures of this kind were not strange to Tchaikovsky; he had been receiving them, in writing and speech, from men and women students alike, for the greater part of the ten years he had been teaching at the Conservatoire. But Nadyezhda Filaretovna was forty-five, one of the richest women in Russia, famed for her strong business sense, her rigid morals, her unapproachability. And as if she realized that even the composer of emotional music might balk at such an outpouring she hurriedly added that she had lost all her wish to meet him: 'I prefer to think about you, to hear you in your music and to feel it with you.'

As Kotek had said, she was a confirmed hypochondriac. One of her many delusions was that she was dying—she was in fact to outlive Tchaikovsky—and as further evidence that she was not pursuing him, she implored him, 'Don't grudge a woman who is nearing the end of her life, who is almost at the point of death, the chance to feel so divinely alive for a fleeting moment.'

She offered another commission in her own way. 'In your *Oprichnik* there is a theme that drives me distracted. What music! I could give my life for it, I long to die hearing it! Could you please, Pyotr Ilyich, write me a *Marche Funèbre* on this theme? I enclose the score with the passages marked. Do please, I beg, arrange it for four hands.'

He wrote the March and at the end of the month was overwhelmed with thanks:

It is so superb that, as I had hoped, it elevates and transports me into a state of such frenzied happiness that I forget everything bitter and offensive in the world. I couldn't describe the disorder reigning in my head and heart every time I hear it. My nerves are shaken by a thrill, I long to sob, to die, I have visions of another life, not the one all men believe in and wait for but quite another life, inaccessible, indescribable. Life, death, pain, joy all disappear as I wing my way above the earth, my temples beating, my heart palpitating madly, my eyes misted so that I see nothing and hear only that magnificent, enchanting music. I forget the exterior world, I feel only the beauty it has to offer, I dread to waken from the spell. My God! what a great man he is who can give such moments to a fellow spirit!

There was a great deal more—all her letters were lengthy—and all setting the key in which she had determined the correspondence should be written. The very next letter, in the middle of May (each had been away from Moscow in the interval), was a love-letter pure and simple, though cast in a spiritual mould: she confessed to terrible loneliness without a letter from him, she begged him to 'save my sinless musical soul for earthly musical joy' by permitting her to write whenever she felt inclined to 'the pure prophet of my beloved art'. She also sent another commission, this time not an arrangement of music already written but a new composition on a theme she outlined.

At this point Tchaikovsky put his foot down. He showed the strong commonsense to be so wretchedly absent within the next few weeks. What he thought about Nadyezhda Filaretovna must be a matter for conjecture. That he considered her entry into his life as the hand of fate is certain. That he rode her extravagances with ease is probable; he was a Russian and emotional himself. That he was flattered is surely inevitable; men cannot avoid a feeling of pleasure when their work is praised even when they laugh at the terms in which it is praised.

But he was no fool. By this time he knew his correspondent fairly well. He believed that she felt what she said she felt about his music, but must have been uneasy about her wish to worship him. He knew that he could not live up to her portrait of him and had told her so. He was unquestionably uneasy about the form their relationship would take in spite of her protests that she was content to know him by his music and his letters.

But what worried him most of all was the fear of being dominated. He knew her to be a born autocrat. Her love of music was only one side of a complex character; from the moment she left her managing mother to marry Von Meck at the age of seventeen she had ridden roughshod over everyone. The famous railway which had made the Von Meck fortune was her railway in every real sense, for it was she who had forced her husband out of the Civil Service. When she met him he was a government engineer much less well placed than Ilya Petrovich and without even the moderate future of Tchaikovsky's father. As soon as Nadyezhda Filaretovna took over the reins Von Meck struck out on his own and, after years of struggle and sacrifice (mostly on her side, since she continued to bear children regularly in spite of their poverty), her energy and faith were rewarded, the railway was built and her husband became one of Russia's biggest industrialists.

All this Tchaikovsky knew. He knew too that an autocrat in one sphere is an autocrat in all. Nadyezhda Filaretovna might genuinely love music and passionately admire him and his—he did not doubt it—but she remained a woman who must rule. Her household proved it; it was a household of slaves and her lavish payments merely turned their work into gilded slavery.

It was this that made him dig in his heels. His fear was less for himself than for his music. In that house in Moscow she had secured tame piano teachers and now a violin tutor; she was soon to own a complete quartet which would include the young Debussy. These young men were at her beck and call; they had to play for her or with her whenever she felt the mood. Now, in her latest letter, she showed her hand; she wanted a tame composer too, a man who would write music on themes chosen by her, a man who would be in every real sense her property.

He dealt with this subtly and boldly. If their relationship was to survive she had to understand his terms. He proceeded to test her feeling for him and for music. This is what he said. 'Every time I get a letter from you I find money in it. Everyone assumes that an artist is never humiliated by being paid for his work, but in order to write the kind of creative work you are now asking for the artist must be in a certain frame of mind (inspired, as we say) and he can't produce this mood to order. I am not prepared to deny the artist in me for the sake of money. I refuse to give you bad coin for good by using my technical skill.'

Having affirmed his principles, he came to the test. 'But I need those coins very badly all the same! I won't bore you by explaining how a man who ought to be able to live on his income has managed to get into such a state of debt that his life is often poisoned and his ability to work is crippled by worry; all I need say is that I have managed to get myself into serious financial trouble and can't get myself out without help. I have decided to ask you for that help.'

He explained why: 'You are the only person living I am not ashamed to beg money from, because you are kind, generous and wealthy. I want to free myself from the clutches of the money-lenders by placing all the repayments of my debts in the one hand. If you would have the kindness to *lend* me the money to do this I should be intensely grateful. The total is not small—three thousand roubles.'

He outlined the methods by which he intended to repay the loan: by making piano arrangements for her, by sending her a percentage of his monthly salary and of his royalties from operas.

He ended with an appeal which was both skilful and genuine, that she should allow him to dedicate his Fourth Symphony to her. This was the work he wanted to get on with instead of commissions from her and he said so pleasantly but plainly. The compliment was not only flattering but truthful; he wanted to make the dedication; in a symphony intended to illustrate the workings of fate in human lives, what could be more apposite than that it should bear the name of the woman whom fate had sent him at such a moment?

She accepted her defeat in a good spirit. To such a woman, accustomed to rule, only this determined stand was necessary to raise her feeling for Tchaikovsky to the highest level, for she was now forced to feel respect as well as admiration. He had made plain in the nicest possible way that if their intimacy was to grow as both wished she must help him to write the music she professed to love and not hinder it by telling him what she wished him to write. He would not be her tool but he would allow her to be associated with the work he truly wanted to do.

From this moment, in the middle of May 1877, the lines of one of the most civilized friendships ever known were clearly drawn. He had found a champion of immense influence and a woman who felt as he did in the thing dearest to him—his music—and she had found her ideal in a world she hated and despised.

When she replied to him with a surrender and with the three thousand roubles (which she of course said she did not wish to be returned—the sum was nothing to her) Tchaikovsky must have felt that at long last the fates were smiling on him. He was out of debt, he had won a friend in a million and a powerful ally, he could write as he wished free from worry.

All this was true but he had not reckoned on the fate he talked and thought about so much. If it gave with the one hand it took with the other. As he learned within a few days of receiving her letter. For it was then that he received a letter of a very different kind. It was from Antonina Milyukova.

CHAPTER THIRTEEN

Antonina Milyukova
1877

Before dealing with this letter it is necessary to look at the work which, in spite of Nadyezhda Filaretovna and her commissions, Tchaikovsky was continuing in spurts. The Fourth Symphony was only one item; he had begun another opera and this work was soon to provide him with horrifying proof of the macabre caprices of fate.

As usual he considered several subjects before, at a musical party, the then favourite Moscow soprano Lavrovskaya asked him why he did not write on *Yevgeny Onyegin*. He rejected the idea, then, whilst dining that same evening, began to think more favourably of it. He at once went out to buy Pushkin's poems and, astonishingly, had trouble in getting hold of a copy. He finally came across the book, took it home, read the verse novel and was so excited by its possibilities that he did not get a wink of sleep that night. He never thought of sleep, he was hard at work, and by the morning had made a rough sketch of the opera. He went straight off to Shilovsky to beg him to write a libretto.

He told Modest excitedly that he was almost out of his mind with joy at having found such a subject. 'What bliss to be free from boring Pharaohs, incredible Ethiopian princesses, poisoned goblets and all the rest of the lifeless rubbish. What riches of poetry Onyegin possesses! It has faults, I know, it doesn't offer much scope for stage effects or treatment, but the splendour of the poetry, the humanity and simplicity of the subject, expressed in Pushkin's inspired verses, make up for all its shortcomings.'

The humanity and the simplicity—here were the keynotes of a

subject which went straight to Tchaikovsky's heart. The pure and innocent Tatyana fascinated by the roué Onyegin and writing him one of the most moving love-letters ever created—the story continued, but with a genius unknown to him before, a trend of Pyotr Ilyich's mind ever since he had begun to write music. In Tatyana he saw and felt yet another Russian heroine whom he equated as always with Aleksandra. He loved her with a passion. And he hated Onyegin—equated with himself—so fervently that he felt ill when he thought of his rejection of Tatyana, his failure to see in her avowal his one chance to break free from a useless life and win lasting happiness.

To think of Aleksandra as another Tatyana is not difficult, to think of Tchaikovsky as an Onyegin seems impossible. But he managed it. To him, he had all the makings of just such a villain, and by the middle of May he had reached a frenzy of fury at the thought of Onyegin's heartlessness. He had forgotten long since that he was dealing with a story; for him the fantasy did not lie in Pushkin's poem but in the people around him, the professors, the students, the men and women in the streets and restaurants; reality was in the drama, the true, everyday drama he was setting to music. 'I am in love with Tatyana,' he told Modest.

At this point came a letter from Antonina Milyukova.

The letter was devastatingly simple. It said that she had loved him ever since she had first come to the Conservatoire four years earlier. She begged him to come to see her.

Tchaikovsky was no stranger to love-letters or proposals; they were regular fare for the most handsome professor in the Conservatoire and one of Russia's outstanding composers. No doubt these letters caused him some worry, for he was considerate to the point of folly, but he had resisted the temptation to reply; he believed that the kindest thing was to remain silent and let the infatuation die even if his image suffered in the process. But though she could not know it, Antonina's letter was perfectly timed. To a man who was obsessed by fate the coincidence was extraordinary. Tchaikovsky was reading the love-letter of a modern Tatyana to the modern Onyegin. His immediate reacion was that he was being given the chance to prove that he, in Onyegin's place, would act very differently.

He replied to the letter. He said that he did not feel love for her (in truth he could scarcely remember her) and could offer her only friendship. He listed some of his failings in an effort to show that her

ANTONINA MILYUKOVA

love was given to a romantic girl's vision, not a flesh-and-blood man. No doubt he thought that he was acting cautiously; in fact the moment he put pen to paper he had destroyed himself; Antonina was not the kind of woman to let him go if given the slightest encouragement.

As it turned out. She replied promptly and at length. 'I don't expect I shall stay in Moscow but wherever I go I shan't forget you or stop loving you and I have no hope of finding in any other man what I love in you.' She then added a sentence which would have told a more sophisticated man all he wanted to know about her. 'Only last week I had to hear the declaration of a man who has been in love with me ever since I was at school and has been faithful to me for five years.'

To Tchaikovsky this meant only one thing, as she intended him to think, that she was desirable but pure, that she would marry only where she loved. Again the perfect identification with his image of Tatyana, as were the final sentences of her letter: 'I am dying with wretchedness and frustration because although I long so desperately to sit by you and talk to you I'm afraid that at first I shouldn't be able to speak one word. Why bother to list your failings to me—nothing could stop me loving you. My love isn't a passing whim, it's for life.'

Modest and faithful. Apprehensive too, making him feel that her fate was in his hands. For Antonina, fearing that his first letter was intended as the last, had slipped in a pathetic 'Is it possible that you could stop writing to me before I've even seen you? You wouldn't be so cruel.'

This was decisive. No, he would not be so cruel. Onyegin would, he would not. He went to see her.

At the interview he repeated what he had said in his letter, that he was not the hero she imagined but a faulty man, that he had nothing but friendship to offer. Again unknowingly she said the right thing; her reply, banal enough and inevitable, chimed in with the thoughts he had long been having on the subject of marriage. She said she could expect no more than friendship at the moment; love would come if they married.

Now this was precisely the argument he had been using to placate his protesting family over the past two years, ever since he told them that he intended to get married, and unlike Antonina he believed it. That was why, when actually faced with a decision, he ignored all the material advantages of the Von Meck connexion, which must have been beyond his most optimistic imaginings, and acted in a way calculated to put an end to it. There he could see only gratitude and flattered vanity, not a substantial base for a man–woman relationship to rest on.

Nadyezhda Filaretovna was not merely a dominating woman, she was nine years his senior and not attractive—the photograph she had sent him shows a forbidding face notable only for fine eyes. He could not bring himself even to try to see her.

What he did was to go to a woman nine years younger than himself, an attractive woman with considerable sexual charm, a woman who, if her words and manner were to be believed, would rely completely on him, a woman who was not well born or well off, quite the contrary. In short, he behaved just as most normal, red-blooded men would behave; he went for youth, looks, femininity. As for his music, one woman matched the other, for Antonina assured him that she loved his music as she loved him.

One flash of prudence—or what he liked to tell himself was prudence—remained. He asked a friend to find out what kind of reputation the girl had in Moscow. The reply seems to have been unfavourable—no details have come down, nor would one expect them—but could have said little more than that her reputation was suspect because she lived alone and not as was customary with her family. It certainly did not reveal the real truth, that she was far gone in nymphomania, completely unbalanced, and obsessed by delusions of being desired by all men. Had this been the reply to his enquiry even the gallant and unworldly Pyotr Ilyich would have thought better of his impulse.

As it was, he was given little time to ponder what he had been told. Two days later he had another letter from her. She had discovered that he had been out of town the previous day (when he went to consult his friend) and, as a result, 'I didn't leave my room all day, pacing from corner to corner like a mad thing. I could think of nothing but the moment I should see you again. And when I do I don't know how I shall prevent myself from throwing myself into your arms and kissing you. But you have given me no right to do that and you would think me shameless.'

This demanded an explanation. 'Don't, please, think badly of me because I confess what I feel for you. My reputation is good, I can tell you, and I have nothing to hide. When I kiss you it will be the first time I have ever kissed a man.'

She once again dismissed his attempt to show her what he was

really like—'You are only wasting your time'—and ended with a
formidable threat. 'I can't live without you and shall probably kill
myself very soon. But please let me see you once more and kiss you
so that I can carry the memory of that kiss into the next world.'

There it was; the challenge had to be taken up or he had to
surrender. Readers knowing the sequel and the true character of
Antonina will feel that a letter of this kind should have been ignored,
that no decent woman would write it. But Tchaikovsky was then
Onyegin and Antonina was Tatyana, he had long wanted to get
married and probably wished it more than ever then to protect himself from the somewhat alarming warmth of the widow Nadyezhda
Filaretovna, and Antonina was sexually very attractive. Add to these
reasons the most powerful of all, that he was a man of extraordinary
innocence and nobility, never thinking ill of man or woman unless
proof stared him in the face, and his next action becomes almost
inevitable.

He was to explain himself a few weeks later, just before his
marriage, to Nadyezhda Filaretovna. It was a difficult letter to write;
he knew he would hurt her, he feared he would disappoint her, he
thought it probable that he had thrown away the support which
promised to free him from money worries and allow him to write
music unhampered. The letter took him weeks to write yet in the
end it was an honest letter without special pleading and gives a
truthful account of the affair except that, naturally, he did not enlarge on Antonina's youth and charm.

These are the salient points of his letter:

Some time ago I had a letter from a girl I had once known. The letter
told me that she had done me the honour of loving me for a long time past.
The letter was so sincere and so affectionate that I felt bound to break my
rule in such cases and answer it. I was careful however to hold out no
hope that the feeling could be mutual. But I had answered and the result
was that in the end I agreed to go to see her. Why? After thinking it over I
believe that I was destined to go by fate. At the meeting I repeated what I
had said in my letter, that I could only return her love with friendship and
gratitude, but after I had gone away I began to question my actions. If I
did not love her and did not want to encourage her feelings, why had I
gone to see her?

That was the first stage. The second stage was her suicide threat,
which he typically thrust on his own shoulders.

In her next letter she made plain that if I did not continue the acquaintance after writing to her and going to see her I should make her utterly wretched and drive her to make away with herself. I was at once faced with a dreadful decision. I had to marry her or preserve my freedom at the cost of her destruction—I don't exaggerate, she seems to love me to the point of desperation. How could I choose anything but the former? . . . So I went to see her, reiterated that my character was difficult—irritable, temperamental, unsociable—and my means slender, repeated that I did not love her but said that I would be a faithful and devoted friend. I asked her if, knowing all these facts, she would be my wife. She accepted me.

He described Antonina. 'She is twenty-eight and not unattractive. Her reputation is without flaw. She earns her own living so that she can live an independent and free life, but she and her mother love each other. She is poor and has been educated according to her station in life, in the Yelizaveta Institute. She seems to have a very kind nature and to be willing to identify herself with her husband without reservations.'

His final thought was 'My conscience is clear. Heaven knows I have nothing but good will for my future wife. If we are not destined to be happy it will not be through any fault of mine. Though I am marrying without love I could take no other course with honour.'

When he wrote this letter in the middle of July only three days were left before the marriage. Soon after the engagement he had gone to the country for a month to think things over calmly. So little did he understand the woman he was to marry that he actually persuaded himself into a sufficiently placid state of mind to work hard on the opera which had caused all the trouble. By the end of the month, before he came back to Moscow, he had written two-thirds of it.

His letters home—delayed for another reason—were also calm. His father replied joyously, Anatoly took the first train to Moscow.

In Moscow, Nadyezhda Filaretovna had responded gallantly to the shock; she wrote a fine letter, concealing her feelings until the very last. 'Never forget the one whose whole soul is devoted to you.'

Tchaikovsky approached his marriage with this load off his mind; the friendship with Nadyezhda would continue. Anatoly was not so obliging; he insisted on seeing Antonina, was horrified and said so. He tried to stop the marriage. Tchaikovsky would not listen. On 18 July, 1877 he and Antonina were married.

ii

Only when he was in the train to Petersburg that evening on his way to present his bride to Ilya Petrovich did Tchaikovsky begin to come to his senses. He did not understand Antonina any better, but after having to entertain her until the train reached Klin and she fell asleep in her chair he began to realize that she was, as he put it, 'very limited'.

Even this he tried to see as a benefit, that it would prevent her from interfering with his work. This negative consolation did not last long. A glimpse of the truth came to him when at last she slept beside him. It is a glimpse that has come to many newly married men. He had undertaken to live with this stranger for the rest of his life. This frightening thought was followed by 'the conviction that all that is best in me—my music—has been destroyed'.

In these sleepless hours he hated her. During the next few days— they spent a week in Petersburg—his feelings veered wildly. At one point he was declaring that he thought he would love her when he got used to her: 'all she asks is to caress me and look after me'. At another moment these apparently simple wishes had become un- endurable: 'physically she had become thoroughly repulsive to me'.

Three days after the marriage he forgot his plight when he heard that Larosh was on the verge of delirium tremens. He had kept clear of him; Larosh was one of the many Petersburghers—the Aleksan- drinsky Theatre actor Delazari (professionally known as Kon- stantinov) was another—who always thought him good for a few roubles. But as ever he had second thoughts. 'How hard and un- feeling I was when I told you I wouldn't go to Larosh for fear of parting with twenty-five roubles,' he told Anatoly repentantly. 'What selfishness! So I went to him after all and thank goodness I did go. In the first place I found him on the verge of complete ruin and clutching at me like a straw. I want to be that straw for him. I must do everything I can to rescue the poor sinking fellow.'

He was rewarded. 'He came to dinner and spent the whole even- ing with us; he was very nice to my wife and above all he broke up our irksome *tête-à-tête*. However the irksomeness is all on my side; *she* seems perfectly happy and contented. In the evening we all went to the Kamennoostrovsky Theatre, then drank tea and beer (a lot of it) *chez moi*. His presence was a great help.'

His feelings towards Antonina Ivanovna can be gauged by his

immediate reaction when he met old friends unexpectedly. 'In the morning, walking arm in arm with my wife on the Nevsky, I ran into Niks Litke and spoke to him but for some reason couldn't bring myself to tell him that the lady was my wife. On the way to the theatre in the evening I met Konstantinov. I said nothing to him either and managed to escape for once in a while with no more than a loan of five roubles. Money flows like water. I feel that the happiest day of my life will be the first of August.'

August 1st was the day he was due at Kamenka but much water was to run under the bridges before then. Four days later, his last day in Petersburg, he told Anatoly, 'Tolichka, yesterday was the most frightful since 18 July. In the morning it seemed to me that my life was completely smashed and a dreadful attack of despair possessed me. At three o'clock *a great number* of people gathered at our place: N. Rubinstein, his sister Sofya, Malozemova, K. Yu. Davydov, Ivanov, Bessel, Larosh. We all dined together. In the evening we first of all saw N. G. [Rubinstein] off to Moscow, then Malozemova and Sofya to Peterhof.'

The dinner evidently put heart into Tchaikovsky, for he goes on to tell his brother, 'Today the awful crisis has passed. I am recovering. But the crisis was *awful, awful, awful*; if it weren't for my love for you and all the other people I'm intimate with, the thought of whom supported me through *excruciating mental tortures*, it could have ended badly, in illness or even insanity.'

His last thought was typically of the worry he must have caused Anatoly and he assures him: 'I give you my word that there's nothing for you to worry about. I'm recovering completely.' This was unhappily no more than a pious hope which scarcely outlasted the arrival back in Moscow. There they took lodgings before going on to Antonina's mother for a week's stay. They had planned to rent an apartment to come back to but Tchaikovsky found himself virtually without money—his wife was even more spendthrift than himself and in his guilt at not feeling more for her he had splashed money about more than usual since the marriage. Besides, he had relied on her assurance that she owned a forest which was on the point of being sold. The forest was not sold. It may not even have existed for, as he was soon to discover, Antonina was incapable of telling the truth.

Penned in one lodging-house room with her all his optimism vanished. He thought he would go mad. He still saw no further than that she was a silly woman and stupid with it but even this at close

range he found insupportable. He could not write a line of music—
she was for ever leaning over him, heavily scented, in an effort to get
all his attention for herself—and began to drink heavily so that he
could restrain himself from telling or showing her what he was
feeling. He did restrain himself but could think of nothing but an
apartment where he would have his own room to work in. He was
still at moments hopeful that time and habit would give him
strength to live with her contentedly.

He wrote to Nadyezhda Filaretovna and begged a loan to rent an
apartment. His letter was more than honest. He could have blamed
his wife and assured himself of sympathy; instead: 'My wife is not to
blame; she did not ask for marriage.'

Self-reproach could scarcely go further. By the time he had her
reply he had spent the week with Antonina at his mother-in-law's.
He came back from this visit desperate to get away; he felt that he
must have some respite if he were to continue the marriage. He had
not had one moment to himself since they married, and the week out
of Moscow was absolutely agony. For the first time he realized that
Antonina had lied to him. 'I disliked the mother and the entire
family. They have narrow ideas, they express themselves coarsely
and all of them are at daggers drawn.' He began to see why Antonina
had lived by herself in Moscow, but why had she lied about it? 'It
may be unfair but my wife grows more abhorrent to me every hour.'

His wretchedness was increased by news of the sudden death of
Adamov; their friendship had never faltered since the days of school,
and Pyotr Ilyich felt as though the abrupt end to the long tie was a
sign that his own life had changed course and was bound irrevocably
for the philistine surroundings symbolized by the Milyukov family.

Nadyezhda's letter was waiting for him. She lent him the money
willingly. No doubt she could foresee the future if he could not.
She sent the money and her advice, that he should go off for a holiday by himself and think things out.

As she had reckoned, the money freed him. He knew enough of
Antonina by this time to feel sure that she would be happy enough
looking about for an apartment and furnishing it when she found
one that pleased her. As it turned out; she saw him go off in the
second week of August without any regret, promising to have a nice
home ready for him when he came back. They had then spent three
weeks together without a break, two of them in the homes of
relatives.

He intended to take the waters at Yessentuki in the Caucasus but not surprisingly changed his mind at Kiev and went to Verbovka where Aleksandra, Lyov, Modest, and Anatoly were waiting for him. The change was part bliss, part an increase of despair. He was once again with civilized people who did not snarl and bicker, people who loved art, people who lived creatively, people who loved him, whose life was built on truth. The contrast between what he had left and what he had before him was almost too painful to be borne. When the children frisked round him he remembered that Antonina had told him—after the marriage—that she did not like children and did not want them. The tastefulness of the house threw up in horrid relief the dreadful nothingness of the Milyukov home where commonness of behaviour was matched by vulgarity of surroundings.

In the end the influence of Kamenka and its surroundings soothed him back to composition. He continued, not the opera, but the symphony. Perhaps he tried to think of Nadyezhda Filaretovna as he wrote, but the idea behind the work was now appallingly justified. When he began it he had thought of fate's perverse handling of his reputation as a composer; her latest caprice put this long injustice completely in the shade.

Yet finally the musician expelled the man as always, and he was soon absorbed in a novelty which still gives a thrill of pleasure nearly one hundred years later. 'The Scherzo will display a new orchestral effect that I think will be most effective. The strings at first play pizzicato by themselves, in the Trio the woodwinds are given a solo passage followed by the brasses, and towards the end of the movement all three groups converse with one another in brief phrases.'

By the time, in mid-September, Antonina wrote to tell him that she had found and furnished an apartment, the orchestration of the symphony had gone far and he had even orchestrated the first act of the opera, about which he now had the deepest doubts: 'The story is simple, the stage effects are practically nil and the music is without brilliance or grandeur. All the same I feel that when a few chosen people hear my music they may respond to the emotion I felt when I wrote it.'

The Conservatoire term was due to begin, the apartment was ready, he could delay no more. He dragged himself back to Moscow after a final note to Anatoly, who had gone back to work ahead of him, an Anatoly who had not embittered the Kamenka stay with 'I told you so'. 'A man only realizes just how strongly he loves a person when that person is far away. Tolya, I love you enormously!

ANTONINA MILYUKOVA

But oh, how little I love Antonina Ivanovna Tchaikovskaya! With
what colossal indifference does that lady fill me! How little am I
enlivened by the thought of seeing her again!'

He added, 'It is not that she alarms me, she is simply a bore.'

iii

This was bravado or forgetfulness. Up to this time he had discovered in Antonina a common young woman, apparently stupid
and with little regard for the truth. He came back to find a new
Antonina or, correctly, a woman who was beginning to show her
true colours. When she met him at the station on 23 September she
felt a security she had not felt earlier; she had her own apartment,
she was married, her husband was famous. She began to blossom
out.

In public she maintained the façade that had so much impressed
Tchaikovsky. At a dinner to the couple given by Jurgenson she said
little, seeming to wait for her husband's prompting. She had all the
cunning of the near insane and her act of the dependent female took
in every man present.

Tchaikovsky's attitude in his classes successfully misled everyone
too; he made a special effort to be brisk and carefree. In the tiny
apartment matters were different. It was not big enough for him to
escape his wife; she was in the room hour after hour. He tried to
work, it was impossible. Another lie disclosed itself. 'After assuring
me that she had loved me for four years and was a devoted musician,
I found that she didn't know a single note of any of my works . . .
and had not once gone to the concerts of the Musical Society where
she knew that I, whom she had loved for four years, could always be
found!'

This music lover, then, was not interested in music. What did she
want? To talk, the horrified Tchaikovsky discovered. And what
talk! 'Everything she said always led to the same topic, the numberless men who had loved her (she harped on this theme incessantly)
all of them very important, mostly generals, relations of well-known
financial wizards, famous actors or members of the royal family.'

That was the main stream of her conversation—'she is extremely
talkative'—but the subsidiary theme though less mad was even less
bearable. 'All the wickednesses, the baseness, and abominable behaviour of her family were described incessantly and with a fury

167

quite beyond all sense. Most of her venom was directed at her mother.'

So much for the day—a stream of insane and vitriolic commonplaces interrupted by nauseating lovemaking. 'I know now that she never loved me,' he said a few weeks later. But the nights passed beyond description. 'She lavished her caresses on me to the point of satiety.'

All his abomination of the workings of fate returned a hundredfold. Fate's instrument became more and more abhorrent to him each day. The prettiness which had attracted him vanished. He saw beneath it. Antonina's lips, he now realized, were unpleasantly thin, her smile calculating and abnormal, and her affectations—she put on a cultured accent, she used her arms and hands in a bad imitation of the best society—almost drove him out of his mind. 'As soon as I met her again I saw that I could never love her, that the affection born of habit on which I had counted was unattainable. I felt absolute despair and longed for death.'

After a week his feelings had become dangerous. 'My whole being was filled with such hatred of the poor woman that I longed to throttle her.' One particular night—he was to remember it with horror for the rest of his life—'I was within a hair's-breadth of succumbing to that blind, unreasoning, diseased loathing that ends in murder. I was only saved by a miracle.'

To protect her—for he persisted in thinking that all the fault was on his side—he began to go out every evening. He could not go where he was known, to the theatres, well-known restaurants or cafés, because he might be seen and asked why he had not brought his wife. He roamed the streets like one lost—his mind was beginning to cloud—and at last, one night early in October, he could bear the strain no longer. He walked down to the river, waded into it and stood in the bitterly cold water up to his armpits.

Even in this extremity he thought of others. His death must not be accounted suicide, that would unbearably hurt all who loved him and make his wife the subject of hostile gossip. He chose the way of death which could be put down to accident.

He never knew afterwards how long he stood there, praying for death. At last he stumbled out of the water and went home, sure that he had caught a fatal chill. He told the astonished Antonina that he had had a fishing accident, went to bed and prepared for death.

The next morning he was as well as ever; his strong constitution had thrown off even this extraordinary exposure to cold and wet.

There was only one thing left to do if he was not to murder Antonina. He invented a sudden call to Petersburg. On the evening of 6 October he caught the train.

When Anatoly met him at the station he did not recognize him. He got him to a hotel. There he had a kind of fit. He lay unconscious for two days. The doctor, after giving him up, said that he must get away as soon as he was fit to move, go right out of Russia.

The moment Tchaikovsky came out of his coma and had explained everything, Anatoly took the train to Moscow, had a long talk with Nikolai Rubinstein and together with him went to see Antonina.

The meeting was short. They told her that Tchaikovsky could not live with her, that he would keep her with a home and generous allowance wherever she wanted to be. For the moment they suggested that she took a fully paid holiday in Odessa, out of range of Moscow gossip.

She scarcely seemed to take in what they were saying, and her final words indicated that she had been far too much preoccupied to listen. She thrust tea on them and did nothing but stare enraptured at Rubinstein who, to those who liked that kind of looks, appeared smarter and more distinguished with the years. After he had hurriedly swallowed his tea and left, she said to Anatoly in a kind of ecstasy, 'Who would ever have thought that Nikolai Rubinstein would have drunk tea in my house!' If Anatoly had had any doubt of his brother's action it disappeared in that moment. He left her plenty of money to enjoy herself in Odessa, then went back to Pyotr Ilyich.

A few days later he and Tchaikovsky left for Switzerland.

iv

Tchaikovsky's retreat abroad has been quoted by many as yet another proof of his lack of manliness; faced with a woman at close range, they say, he went to pieces.

It is a pity that those who so glibly take away the character of a great man cannot be obliged to spend one night with an Antonina Milyukova—just one night, not the thirty-five spent by Tchaikovsky. No question of sexual relations; all that is necessary is to spend the night in her company; they would hurriedly eat their words. The few who have had the misfortune to do this with a highly developed

nymphomaniac know the experience to be quite dreadful, a shattering revelation of the beastliness to which human beings can descend.
No man of average stolidity has come out of it without a following
period of nightmare. What the extraordinarily sensitive Tchaikovsky suffered during his thirty-five nights and especially the last
fourteen defies the imagination; for weeks afterwards he was like a
man half insane and only kept on the right side of the borderline by
drinking heavily.

His misfortune in becoming the object of Antonina's attentions is
beyond words striking and justifies his preoccupation with fate only
too well. There were tens of thousands of reasonably decent women
in Moscow but he had to receive a letter from one of the very few
who could have done such harm to him at precisely the moment
when circumstances made him least fitted to deal with her advances.
Had he been a worldly man, or a suspicious one or anything but the
trustful creature he was, he might have seen what kind of woman he
was dealing with. He might; but it must be said that he was not
alone; no one who saw Antonina at that time dreamed what she was
really like. The sexually half-mad are cunning as well as stupid. She
misled everyone.

Abnormality will out, however, and before following Tchaikovsky in his struggle to recover it may be salutary to complete an
account of her career. Readers who have never met a woman of her
type and who do not wish to check the statements here with a doctor
may see for themselves how time was to explain the inevitability of
Tchaikovsky's collapse and flight.

One person who could not credit the necessity for her brother's
breakdown was Aleksandra Davydova. She had been against a love-
less marriage but once the marriage was made she felt that her
brother ought to have tried harder to make a success of it. Pure and
normal herself, Aleksandra walked blindly into trouble; she went
down to Odessa and fetched Antonina home.

Her eyes were soon opened. Antonina adopted a new role, of the
deserted wife, and spent much of her time whining about her hard
lot. She did not stop at whining; she wept copiously, day after day
and most of the day. Sympathy only made her weep the more. She
told Aleksandra and Lyov that she had been duped by Pyotr Ilyich,
that he had caught her by a trick.

As she accused him she fell to biting her nails. It was an old habit
of hers, one of the many habits which had sickened the fastidious
Tchaikovsky when he saw it for the first time in that apartment in

Moscow. Antonina did not merely bite the tips of her nails, she bit them to the quick, she bit round the edges until they bled. Drops of blood began to disfigure the Davydov furnishings. Nothing Aleksandra could say would stop the disgusting habit; Antonina merely wept the more violently and bit the harder.

The complaints of the deserted wife did not end at the Verbovka household; she wrote long and largely incoherent letters to Anatoly and to Tchaikovsky. Neither could understand what she wanted except to cause trouble; she showed no great wish to live with Tchaikovsky again.

To try to cheer her, Aleksandra invited guests. She succeeded beyond her wildest hopes; Antonina immediately developed a passion for one of the better looking of the men, flirted madly with him and would afterwards talk of nothing but the manner in which he was pursuing her; it was, she assured Aleksandra, her fate to attract men like flies.

At first Aleksandra had begun to try to convince Pyotr Ilyich that his wife only needed to be educated in a happy and good-mannered family circle—the Kamenka circle—to 'make an excellent companion for life'. She dwelt on the girl's many good qualities and begged her brother to be patient.

As autumn moved into winter her letters changed; she was discovering that she had taken on the impossible. She ended, inevitably, by wondering how Pyotr Ilyich could ever have seen anything in the girl and, only too humanly, blamed him in her heart for this too. By this time she had begun to drop broad hints to Antonina Ivanovna that her stay had lasted long enough. Antonina feigned ignorance; she was doing very nicely where she was. She stayed on. By the end of November the household was in chaos and Aleksandra wrote urgently to Anatoly demanding that he come and remove her visitor.

Tchaikovsky read this and another 'poisonous' letter from Antonina enclosed with it and for the first and last time wrote to his sister a letter which was not wholly loving.

I'm glad she has at last dropped the role of meek sheep which moved you so much. I have replied to her letter and enclose it. *I beg you* to give it to her and read it with her. Then, my angel, please explain to her that I acknowledge my guilt fully. But let her know, too, that I remember everything down to the smallest detail that took place before our wedding and that she ought to remember even better than I how our intimacy began. Obviously she has forgotten everything that really happened and, indulged by you, has persuaded herself that I angled for the marriage and touched her heart by writing amorous letters—in short, that I alone am to blame.

But this is not true. She must share the blame. I can't conceal from you that Antonina Ivanovna's stay with you has wounded me painfully. I'm glad that you have been kind to her but I am far from glad that my history is known now to every inhabitant of Kamenka. How can I ever stay with you again when even Baby will look accusingly at me? How can I look Aleksandra Ivanovna in the face and all the rest of the inhabitants of your big house? Much time will have to pass before I can come to your so dear and so necessary home without unbearable moral and mental torments.

Having said this mildest of reproofs, he immediately tried to qualify it.

For God's sake don't think I am reproaching you! I know that you've done everything out of love for me. I admit I would have been happier if you had confined your meeting with Antonina Ivanovna to Odessa. To be absolutely honest, I had even hoped that my miserable history, in detail at any rate, would never be known at Kamenka, but your angelic heart carried you too far. I'm even glad that you have caressed Antonina Ivanovna though it is painful to me to think that these caresses have been lavished in vain and always to my detriment. But the thing that shames me most horribly is that every hour of every day you have in front of you a perpetual reminder of my wretched situation.

This letter did not fall on deaf ears. Aleksandra was only too ready to forgive. She was not yet to escape the consequences of her quixotic impulse in carrying her sister-in-law back from Odessa; it was not until the end of December that Anatoly—surely the most obliging brother ever known—removed Antonina from Kamenka on his way back from Vienna. He settled her in her Moscow apartment, evading as best he could her persistent attempt to make love to him and set him against Pyotr Ilyich, and paid over the first instalment of his brother's extremely generous allowance.

He left her apparently contented. But a woman who is slowly going mad cannot be contented. The letters to Tchaikovsky continued—a stream of insane complaints mingled with accounts of her triumphs with other men. By the early years of the next decade she had had affair after affair and had borne at least two children to different lovers. Even more embarrassing to Tchaikovsky, she began to borrow money from his friends; she would call at the house of well-known Petersburg and Moscow men, insist on an interview, pour out a long and largely incomprehensible story of her woes at the hands of her husband and demand help as an abandoned wife.

By the end of the decade she was no longer responsible for her actions but the authorities hesitated, possibly because they were naturally sluggish, possibly because Tchaikovsky was then world-famous. Eventually she was put into a Petersburg mental home, where she spent the last twenty years of her life.

But this was not until 1896, three years after Tchaikovsky's death. All the time he was alive she was left free to plague him. As she did. In vain he paid her the allowance regularly, in vain he tried to reason with her. His response to that declaration of love in 1877—a more innocent and well-meaning act could hardly be imagined—was to poison the last sixteen years of his life.

His response to this embarrassment, worry, and public humiliation was in line with every other contact he had with human beings. He loathed the very thought of her and loathed himself even more for every encouragement he had given her. He was therefore all the more careful to treat her with particular generosity. He offered her a divorce though this meant publicly branding himself as an adulterer. She refused, doubtless because she feared that the courts would award her alimony very much less than the allowance he voluntarily made. Later, when she stood self-confessed as a loose woman, he would not take divorce proceedings against her; he insisted on thinking that he had started her on the downward path; every argument his friends put forward, showing plainly that the girl was irreclaimable, had no effect on him. He not only continued to pay her allowance to the day of his death but several times sent her extra after she had written a particularly outrageous letter to him.

One of the most revealing incidents in this long purgatory was to occur in 1886. Antonina Ivanovna that year excelled herself by demanding not only money, sympathy, compassion and tact but that he relieve her of her illegitimate children so that she should be freer to enjoy herself.

Like all the rest of these shattering eruptions into the world he was trying to rebuild, this letter made him ill—'Have been like a madman all day,' was a typical diary entry after an Antonina letter—but when he recovered he wrote a kind reply and enclosed more money than usual in the hope, which must have been rather faint, that the children would benefit from some of it.

Above all, he wrote in his diary, that place of absolute truth as he felt it at the moment of writing: 'I feel very sorry for her in spite of all she's done and all she is. She must be one of the world's biggest misfits but all the same everything has gone wrong for her, poor thing.'

How much this extraordinary generosity was due to pity, how much to guilt, how much to pure humanity must be left to every reader to decide for himself. This much is certain, that not one man in a million would have acted as he did. But then he was a man in a million.

CHAPTER FOURTEEN

Fourth Symphony and *Yevgeny Onyegin*
1877–8

One inevitable result of the tragedy was to swing Tchaikovsky decisively towards Nadyezhda Filaretovna. Any fear that she wanted to marry him had disappeared and there was left only immense gratitude and faith. He opened his mind and heart to her. The result was a series of letters without parallel in musical history and perhaps in any man–woman relationship. They are not letters to be read for pleasure in themselves—neither correspondent was an attractive letter-writer and on her side the key is always too high-pitched—but they help to maintain an optimistic view of human nature.

He needed her faith as much as any man when he was taken away by Anatoly late in October 1877. He needed her good sense even more. He was a nervous wreck; his dreams passed beyond description, his waking hours were tormented by dreadful guilt feelings and the equally dreadful sense that he had wrecked his own and another life.

They went to Switzerland, then to Italy. For all his intense Russianness and his longing to get home when he was abroad, Tchaikovsky felt a natural kinship with the Italians and responded to their out-in-the-open expression of feeling, but that winter Italy could do little for him. He yearned for Aleksandra and Kamenka, 'the one place that is always home to me, that has always been my refuge in trouble and doubt, and that will always remain for me the most loved spot on this earth'. But Kamenka was barred to him; Antonina was still there, hanging on persistently, deaf to every hint.

From Petersburg came a welcome surprise. Apukhtin, now one of

Russia's most famous living poets, had the happy knack of weighing in with a letter just when it was needed. He sent one now. He was on the bellicose side and detested injustice. Tchaikovsky always called to see him when he visited Petersburg and though their correspondence had dwindled he loved him dearly—the more that his other schoolfriend Adamov had gone. Apukhtin demonstrated his feelings by writing forcefully and in lordly disgust of the gossipers. He instructed Pyotr Ilyich in schoolboy style to ignore the 'scum' who had nothing better to do than make a nine days' wonder of the Tchaikovsky marriage: 'Your country is going to be proud of you. . . . Turn your back on these nobodies and ascend the creative heights where you can't see or think of them. From there fling the rabble another *Romeo* or *Tempest* and let the weight of your fame squash them!'

Back in Moscow Rubinstein acted promptly and generously; he granted Tchaikovsky unlimited leave of absence and persuaded the board of the Musical Society to vote a special sum of money as a token of appreciation for his eleven years of work in the Conservatoire.

Anatoly was with him, a tower of strength as they moved restlessly from Switzerland to Italy and back to Austria, but Anatoly, for all his affection and commonsense, had one grave defect as healer of the mentally sick man—he was not musical. Tchaikovsky's recovery was assured by the letters from Nadyezhda Filaretovna; they finally pulled him together and preserved for the world the masterpieces still to come.

It is not possible to know whether she had wished to marry him— as she was to offer him ten thousand roubles to pay for a divorce, the presumption must be that she had. Short of accomplishing this, she won a great victory for herself and every lover of music. The manager, the artist, and the woman in her all had cause for gratification in the next few months, for in that time she won the complete confidence and deep affection of the best-known modern composer in Russia and, as she never doubted, a man who would become famous everywhere. In every sense but the purely physical one she could think of Tchaikovsky as her property, providing always that she did not try to force work on him that he had no wish to do, providing also that she was content to limit her personal demands on him.

Readers often find her letters absurdly over-emotional—she wrote in the emotional climate of the day and was at times definitely unbalanced—and frequently naïve and crude, as when she tries to make Tchaikovsky explain exactly how and why he wrote as he did. She was curious, she was possessive and occasionally forgot that she was dealing with a genius and a human being with his own soul. The time was to come when Tchaikovsky was to rescue the relationship from the impossible strain she wanted to put on it, but she was on balance extraordinarily good for him, and never more so than in those winter months. She restrained herself from reproach and, for a time, almost from questions. The practical woman in her was to the fore and the kind woman, and they combined to rescue him from the pit.

She showed her instinctive wisdom there and then by two actions. She wrote to beg him to accept an annual allowance of six thousand roubles and enclosed the first instalment before he could hesitate. That freed him at one stroke from money worries and allowed him to visualize another longed-for freedom, from lectures at the Conservatoire. She also urged him in letter after letter to get down to composition as the only way back to sanity and health. She refused to hear of inability to write and her faith and strength of character came through the letters and actually set him to work again—this and his feeling, once he accepted the allowance, that he must justify it.

It is true that Tchaikovsky would have come back to music on his own; nothing short of complete mental breakdown would keep him from composition. No one can now say what would have happened to him without the faith and the financial help of the woman he had so recently discarded in favour of Antonina, but it would be less than generous to deny her the credit; he certainly was to regard her for the rest of his days as the main source of his recovery.

ii

He spent almost exactly six months out of Russia—from October 1877 to April 1878—and the proof of the new spirit that was born slowly and agonizingly in him remains today in the major works he wrote during this time; he finished the Fourth Symphony and *Yevgeny Onyegin* and he composed a large part of his Violin Concerto. Early in January 1878, he sent off the completed symphony to Moscow. One month almost to the day, *Yevgeny Onyegin* followed it.

This sounds like the Tchaikovsky of old, pouring out music day after day, even though much of the opera and symphony had been sketched out before he left Russia. In truth he could scarcely bring himself to write a note until the new year opened, he was fighting the horrors.

When Anatoly had to go back to Russia early in December Tchaikovsky was for a time left to himself. Other rescuers were to make the long journey to support him, Modest and Kotek among them—an indication of the love he inspired—but not until he had fought his fight and won it.

His recovery was hindered by a new crisis that once more thrust music into the background. Rubinstein was an impatient man who had not a nerve in his body. He thought that Tchaikovsky was coddling himself and needed shaking out of hypochondria. He suggested that he went to Paris as Chief Delegate of Russian Music at the World Fair just opening there.

The suggestion threw Tchaikovsky into despair, and when Anatoly supported Rubinstein he retired to another line of defence. This was a well-known blessing that was soon to help to give the world many of the paintings of Vincent Van Gogh. Only those despise it who have not known the need of it. Tchaikovsky refers to it in his reply to Anatoly's attempt to persuade him to go to Paris.

If you could see my wretched face and could see me pacing up and down like a madman you would say, stay where you are. I have not told you that since you left I have drunk several glasses of brandy at night. I drink a lot during the day too. I can't do without it. I only feel calm when I have a lot of brandy inside me. I have grown so accustomed to this solitary drinking that the very look of the bottle—which is always by my side— gives me a thrill of joy. I can't write letters until I have had a drink—that shows how ill I still am. If I went to Paris I should be at it from morning to night to cope with the excitement of life there.

Anatoly dropped the subject. Not Rubinstein. Furious at the loss of such an advertisement for Russian music and the Moscow Conservatoire, he angrily accused Tchaikovsky of 'putting it on'.

Tchaikovsky's reply shows why he was so widely beloved. 'Have it your own way—I am *putting it on*. But if I am that is exactly what my illness consists of.' And he added an irresistible 'How often must I tell you that though I loathe being a professor chained to the Conservatoire for life, I can't imagine wanting to be anywhere but in Moscow and with you.' To which he added in his next letter, 'I would gladly give up all the beauties and sunshine of this place to be in my beloved Moscow again.' And to this again, he made a kind of postscript, to Nadyezhda this time. He was moving slowly through northern Italy—Venice, Milan, Florence, Genoa, San Remo—and he felt for Italy what he felt for no other foreign country, as his music testifies. All the same 'I have never met anyone so passionately in love with Mother Russia—especially Great Russia—as I ... I love the Russian people, language, spirit, customs, yes, even the Russian face, with a fervour.'

He enlarged on his objections by way of Albrecht. There was another reason why he would not go to Paris. It is a reason which will be understood by many who know the French and demonstrates what it is too easy to forget with Tchaikovsky and all modest men, that true modesty does not preclude true pride. How, Tchaikovsky asked, could he be expected to explain Russian music to people like the French: 'You know I'm a useless kind of man apart from my music.'

He believed this but there was more to come.

Pride expresses itself in many ways. I show it by refusing to meet people who either don't know my real worth or don't appreciate it. How frightful, for instance, to be forced to stand meekly in front of Saint-Saëns and allow myself to be graciously condescended to when I know in my heart that I stand *as high above him as the Alps*. In Paris my self-respect, which is considerable for all my outward modesty, would be bruised every second of the day by having to mix with celebrities who would all look down on me. To brag to them about my works, to try to persuade them that I am a person of consequence—this kind of thing is quite beyond me.

Rubinstein gave way with a growl—obviously he would have to go himself—and, the question settled as he wanted it, Tchaikovsky felt a good deal better for the sharp fight and began to orchestrate the symphony and opera and discuss them with Nadyezhda and his friends at the Conservatoire who had already seen much of the work in sketch. The first reaction came from Taneyev. Tchaikovsky had enormous faith in this old pupil—Taneyev was fast becoming one of the most erudite musicians Russia had ever known—and felt mingled despair and irritation when told that *Yevgeny Onyegin* would not be effective on the stage.

In true style of every born creative man the composer, who had said the same thing himself a few months earlier, flew to the defence of his child. 'If it really wouldn't be effective then it had better not be staged. I composed the opera because I was moved to express in music everything that seems to me to cry out for expression in

Yevgeny Onyegin. I spit on "effectiveness". What are effects, anyway? If *Aida* is effective I can tell you I wouldn't compose an opera on such a subject if you gave me a fortune. I want to create human beings, not puppets.'

He was to say this in another way a week or so later to Nadyezhda Filaretovna. She was pouring out letters to him as well as money and every letter contained questions as well as encouragement. She wanted to know how the clock ticked—that was the gist of it—and Tchaikovsky, trying conscientiously to satisfy his patroness, had to attempt more than once to describe the indescribable, the creative process in himself. We all know what he said—it has been repeated almost too often—but his reply to a less impossible but more intimate question—Had he ever experienced anything more than platonic love?—has a direct bearing on his defence of *Yevgeny Onyegin.*

His answer to the personal side of the question, which ought never to have been put, was vague. 'Yes and No. If you had asked, Have I ever found complete satisfaction or happiness in love? I should have answered No and again—No.'

He then firmly placed the subject where it should always have been. 'My music is my best answer. If you had asked, Have I ever known the full power and indescribable torment of love? I should have to reply Yes, Yes, Yes! Time after time I have tried to express through my music the intolerable anguish and supreme bliss of love. I must leave it to others to say whether I have succeeded, but this does not affect the validity of my attempt. I don't agree at all with your view that music is incapable of expressing the universal nature of love. On the contrary, I believe that music *alone* can do it.'

In this spirit he continued his defence of *Yevgeny Onyegin* to Taneyev. 'What do I want? you may ask. . . . Above all I want an intimate but dramatic story based on a conflict of circumstance or character which is within the bounds of my imagination and which I feel deeply.'

He showed his good sense by admitting that it would never do at the Maryinsky or any big opera house; he would like to see it put on by the students in the Conservatoire theatre. 'I won't even describe my modest work as an opera but as something like "lyrical scenes".' He ended defiantly, 'If my enthusiasm for *Yevgeny Onyegin* merely underlines or exposes my limitations, my stupidity in not understanding the basic requirements of an opera, I apologize. But this I will say, that my music comes *literally from my inmost being.*'

above Nadyezhda Filaretovna von Meck and her family, about 1875

below Pyotr Ilyich and his wife, Antonina Ivanovna, in 1877 *left* Mily Alexeyevich Balakirev, about 1865

below Nikolai Andreyevich Rimsky-Korsakov

His postscript was an uneasy wonder what Taneyev would think of the symphony: 'I know you are absolutely sincere and I think a great deal of your judgement. But I also fear it.'

He had some reason for alarm. When Taneyev at last told him, early in March, what he thought of the symphony, the letter made hard reading; he disliked it and said so, as was his way, plainly. Curiously enough, Taneyev had completely changed his view of *Yevgeny Onyegin* after playing the full score over time after time. As a sop to this letter mutilating the symphony he said, 'But your opera is without parallel in the world.' And, in reference to one of Tchaikovsky's despairing moments, 'And you talk of giving up composing!'

Tchaikovsky brushed aside his *volte-face* which he would normally have received in high delight. Taneyev's chief complaint about the symphony was that so much of it sounded like ballet music. He was particularly savage about the Scherzo Tchaikovsky was so proud of: 'I can't stand it.' But for that matter, wrote Taneyev, almost every movement reminded him of Moscow's prima ballerina, Sobyesychanskaya—the middle of the Andante, the Trio, and the March in the Finale.

Tchaikovsky sat down and tried to control his fury sufficiently to reply coherently. He succeeded, and his answer stands to this day as a complete disposal of the same stupid objection which some critics still raise.

I can't imagine what your idea of 'ballet music' is nor why you should object to it. Does every melody in a lively dance rhythm seem like 'ballet music' to you? If so I don't understand how you can endure most of Beethoven's symphonies, for melodies of this kind are found on every page. Or do you mean you think the Trio of my Scherzo is like Minkus, Gerber, or Pugni? I can't really believe it is as bad as that.

In any case, why should 'ballet music' be considered a derogatory term? The music of a ballet is not always bad, it can be good—Delibes' *Sylvia*, for instance—and when it is good what does it matter whether Sobye-sychanskaya is dancing to it or not? I can only think you don't like some parts of my symphony *because they remind you of the ballet* and not because they are intrinsically bad.

You may be right, but I really can't see why dance tunes should not be used from time to time in a symphony even when it is with the declared intention of introducing a touch of down-to-earth humour. Let me appeal once more to Beethoven who often used such effects.

He ended his defence of this aspect of his symphony with an

outburst every musician will understand and love him for. 'But how on earth did you manage to find "ballet music" in my Allegro? I have racked my brains but can't think of a single bar that could possibly come under that heading.'

So much for ballet music. Evidently it had not occurred to the serious young Taneyev (though it ought to have done after he had heard *Swan Lake,* which Tchaikovsky was too modest to give as an example) that the very man he was writing to had already lifted ballet music on to the plane of the symphony—the exact opposite of his charge that he had degraded the symphony to the level of dance music.

There remained the other major objection by Taneyev, that the symphony obviously had been written to a programme and that this also degraded a noble form. This leads once more to Nadyezhda Filaretovna and her letters. She, of course, expected to be kept *au fait* with 'our' symphony, as it had become. Particularly, she wanted to know exactly what it meant, what Tchaikovsky had in mind when writing it. He obliged, as he always did. His description of the meaning of the symphony is well known—it is printed in every concert programme when the Fourth Symphony is played—and will not be repeated here. Even to her he prefaced his attempt to provide a literary programme with 'How is it possible to express what one feels when writing an orchestral work since one has sensations for which words have never been invented? Didn't Heine say, music begins where words leave off?'

He did his best for her, however. He was a very personal composer and though he could not properly explain what was in his mind because it was also in his heart, he was almost always moved to composition by a reaction to some manifestation of life. The Fourth Symphony can be said, briefly and inadequately, to express man's struggle with fate throughout his life. The word fate is Tchaikovsky's own; everybody will insert the word which most closely represents his own view of life and its hazards.

Tchaikovsky, then, though he balked at the thought of putting a programme on paper as Balakirev and Stasov did, was not going to deny the existence of a programme; that would be to deny his whole *raison d'être* as artist. So he replied to Taneyev:

I never want to write a symphonic work consisting of meaningless harmonies and modulations and a rhythmical scheme expressing nothing. Of course my symphony is programme music but I couldn't put the programme into words; it would merely sound ridiculous and give you an excuse to laugh. But isn't a programme precisely what one would expect from a symphony, the most lyrical of musical forms? Should it not express everything that words cannot—things that rise in the heart and cry out for expression?

In my innocence I thought the idea behind my symphony was so plain that everyone would grasp it, or at any rate its chief outlines, without the need of a written programme. Please don't think I want to pose as a man of profound emotions and lofty ideas. I don't express any new thought and haven't even tried to. The idea behind my work is basically a reflection of Beethoven's Fifth—not the musical content, naturally, but the central plan.

He allowed himself a friendly dig at the pedant. 'Must I tell you that the Fifth not only had a programme but such an obvious one that everybody agrees about it? The same thing ought to apply to my symphony. If you haven't grasped the programme here, all it proves is that I am no Beethoven—and I shan't dispute that!'

Then came a characteristic display of Tchaikovskian honesty. He began by protesting in high emotion that there was not 'a single bar' in the symphony that he had not felt deeply. He had no sooner written the words than he hurriedly qualified them: 'Yes, there is perhaps one exception, some forced passages and a few laboured and artificial things in the middle section of the first movement.'

Men warmed to him for this kind of thing, and his end to the letter begun in such anger was absolutely typical and helps to explain why Taneyev worshipped him. 'I can see you laughing as you read all this, you sceptic and mocking-bird. In spite of your great love of music it seems you still can't believe that a man can express his inmost feelings in his compositions. You just wait!'

The little battle put him into tremendous form, and for the first time for a year he got down to his work with all the old speed and enthusiasm. He began a Violin Concerto and wrote it *con amore*, as it was to appear when heard, and shot off a warning letter to Jurgenson. 'I hit on the idea by chance, was quite carried away and the sketch is all but done.' He added in the kind of mock fear he knew his publisher loved: 'One way and another a considerable number of works are hanging over your head and I shall need to hire a railway truck to get them all to you. I can imagine your "The devil take you!" when you get them all.'

Jurgenson's fondness for him will be understood by one or two notes from Tchaikovsky at this time. First, he refused the large sum the publisher offered him for *Yevgeny Onyegin* with a 'I shan't take anything unless the opera is done in an opera house and even then nothing like the sum you offer.' As for some translations he had made of a group of German songs at Jurgenson's request, 'I can't take a rouble for them, they're so frightfully bad!' When the 'truck load' finally reached Moscow there came with it a list with all the items priced—a piano sonata he had written in Italy, some songs, a children's album and so on. The total came to nine hundred and ten roubles. 'In round figures, say nine hundred roubles,' said Tchaikovsky's note, 'but as I've written such a lot all at once you can have them for eight hundred.' That Tchaikovsky would never grow rich is clear from these business dealings; that he would never be without good friends is equally clear.

Late in February the Fourth Symphony was given its first performance by Rubinstein in Moscow. Nadyezhda Filaretovna, who was there, sent Tchaikovsky a telegram which gave him the impression that the work had succeeded, and he was rather irritated by a telegram from Rubinstein and his colleagues containing a bare mention of the performance. Mercifully, he did not know the truth for some time. He moved back to Switzerland in April, full of the Violin Concerto. Kotek, who had had much to do with the inception of the concerto, was still with him; he had left Nadyezhda Filaretovna and was supposed long since to be in Berlin studying under Joachim, but simply could not bring himself to leave Pyotr Ilyich until the work was done to everyone's satisfaction.

By the first days of April Tchaikovsky had written and Kotek had played over the first two movements to the rapture of the composer and Modest, who was also with him, but not until Kotek approved the last movement would Tchaikovsky budge. Then, enormously exhilarated, he made for Russia. By the twenty-third of the month he was at Verbovka (the family always spoke of Kamenka, the village, rather than the name of the house they lived in) where he was greeted by a penitent Aleksandra. They had differed for the first and last time.

Only after he had settled happily in this blessed spot did he hear the truth about the Fourth Symphony. It had been received with incomprehension and with little more than the vaguest of comments. Not until that winter of 1878, when the symphony was first played in Petersburg, was its importance to be recognized.

iii

In this day and age, when the Symphony in F Minor has become one of the most popular symphonies in the world, a detailed analysis would be absurd. A case could be made for it as Tchaikovsky's most masterly symphonic work, virtually faultless in construction and with a taut grasp of argument developed with an unobrusive skill throughout, yet it has never had the appeal of its two famous successors. Some people find the opening movement with its insistent Fate theme a little on the grim and gaunt side. For a Tchaikovsky the orchestral colour and thematic material sounds subdued, but this was deliberate. He succeeds in his aim, to present man's dilemma in the world, a very real one as he knew only too well. And who could deny that life is precisely as he illustrates it in this movement, a continuous ebb and flow of fortune? No living person can be sure that he will not be dead the next moment, or rebuffed, or humiliated, or become the victim of one of a thousand accidents unimaginable the moment earlier. This is the picture the composer paints. He sets the scene so that he can follow with his own comment.

But if the first movement is sparing in the charm and colour associated specially with Tchaikovsky, the Scherzo amply makes up for it—its delicate originality delights to this day—and the splendour of the Finale remains breathtaking when conducted by a man who feels the composer's thought and emotion, observes his markings, and can breathe enthusiasm into an orchestra which has rehearsed adequately.

The Fourth Symphony has been hailed as the first great Russian symphony, comparable to anything written in Western Europe. This is less than just to its predecessors but it is true that in the later work Tchaikovsky shows himself for the first time as the complete master of his art. Throughout it is written with superb confidence and drive which communicates itself to every audience.

Some critics have complained that the symphony is an earthly work, that the spiritual is not found in it. They tread difficult ground—who is to decide or agree on a spiritual work as distinct from an earthbound one? In any case they are criticizing a man for not doing what he never intended to do, which is absurd, though critics are for ever basing their criticism on nothing more potent than this. Tchaikovsky was preoccupied by the problem of fate in the lives of men on earth. His Fourth Symphony is his intensely personal answer to it. The rest is up to the listener. One can enjoy it as pure music or one can get strength from its courageous message.

CHAPTER FIFTEEN

First Suite

1878–80

That summer of 1878 saw Tchaikovsky on his way back to something of the state he was in before his marriage. He was never again to be free from regrets—it is a commentary on the fate he thought so much about that he no sooner attained the bliss of comparative affluence than he was tormented by conscience—but at least he was reconciled with Aleksandra, an essential part of a tolerable life for him, and was tackling his work with real determination.

He had another cause for relief too. He had decided to resign his post at the Conservatoire and give the rest of his life to composition. His feelings will be understood by many less exalted people who have come to the end of a long drudgery and face the prospect of doing what they really believe in and think they were born for.

At Kamenka he tidied up his recent compositions, big and small, and completed the Violin Concerto which he had decided to dedicate to Leopold Auer, violin professor at the Petersburg Conservatoire, the man who had asked him to write the *Sérénade Mélancolique*. He played over the opera to the family. All were in tears. He wrote in his notebook, 'If only audiences of the future feel as the composer does about this music!' For once a wish of his was to be granted.

From Kamenka he moved half-way up to Moscow, to a place he was to know well, the great Brailov estate of the Von Mecks. Nadyezhda Filaretovna was not there, of course; the entire vast house was left to him. His comments read rather amusingly today. He was evidently somewhat overwhelmed by the attentions of the staff left behind to look after him. One not unexpected result was a feeling of extreme exhaustion followed by heavy sleep after dinner, and his diagnosis was refreshingly frank; his dreams were often blissful but not much work followed: 'Too often, alas, a pickled gherkin has played a vital role in the highest functions of the human intellect.'

But though stifled by grandeur he revelled in the garden and countryside. He spent hours walking. Working too; he wrote the Scherzo of what was to be one of his most charming light compositions, his First Suite. He planned it in five movements.

Back at Verbovka, he got on with the suite at top speed until he was obliged to return for the last time to the Conservatoire in the autumn. He saw Moscow again with mixed feelings; Antonina was there—he had had the usual incoherent letter from her as well as a gushing one from her mother—and he stood in daily dread of her appearing at the Conservatoire with some cooked-up story for the first person she could persuade to listen. However, the step had to be taken.

How difficult it was to be he did not know until he heard that Rubinstein, appearing at the Trocadéro in Paris during the World's Fair Russian concerts, had conducted and played his own works, including *The Tempest* and the piano concerto, with astonishing success. Never before, Tchaikovsky was told, had Paris audiences shown such enthusiasm. The concerto, in particular, produced scenes of uninhibited rapture and Rubinstein had to repeat it at his last concert.

Being the man he was, Tchaikovsky's gratification was practically submerged by embarrassment. The embarrassment became almost unbearable when, at a dinner in honour of Rubinstein at The Hermitage, the Director made a speech given over mostly to praise of their great composer who had carried the standard of Russian music into the heart of the West—a composer who, he added, they were also honoured to know was one of the pillars of the Conservatoire.

How Tchaikovsky managed to give his resignation to Rubinstein the next morning he never knew. But Rubinstein rose to the occasion as he usually did. Before the talk was ended it was agreed that Taneyev should take the place of Tchaikovsky—a good exchange, the latter thought.

He shot off to Petersburg, light-hearted, but, after a round of dinners with Apuhktin, had the misfortune to attend a revival of *Vakula the Smith*. His reaction was in character. He felt very angry:

'With *myself*. Heavens! What a mass of unforgivable mistakes which no man except me could ever have made!'

This sounded tolerably final, but had no effect whatever on his passion for opera. After he had spent a few more autumn days at Kamenka where he finished sketching out the suite, he went off to Italy—Nadyezhda Filaretovna had taken an apartment for him in Florence—and one of his first acts there was to decide to write an opera on Schiller's *Jungfrau von Orleans*. At Kamenka he had read Zhukovsky's translation, in itself a work of art, and the more he thought about the subject the more he liked it.

He forgot that he had just written the kind of opera that suited him perfectly, he forgot that he had said so, he forgot his contempt for grand opera and his condemnation of his work on *Vakula*; all he could remember was that his first childish poem at Votkinsk had been written on Joan of Arc and that his reading of Zhukovsky brought back all the old love and worship. Not once did he pause to wonder whether his particular genius was able to handle historical subjects in the grand manner or whether Joan of Arc could be treated successfully in this or any other way. He began at once to write the opera.

The truth was that for him Joan of Arc was yet another of the girls who fascinated him by their purity, their innocence and unshakeable moral strength; she was a Tatyana on the grand scale. That was why he could not resist her. He did not consider what followed Joan's belief in a divine mission, her sense of power, her essential ruthlessness. He did not see further than Tatyana because he did not want to.

As usual when writing quickly on a subject close to his heart, he was in the highest spirits, dashed only from time to time when he heard of Antonina's extravagances in Moscow or received one of her insane letters. He was enormously cheered by news of the success of the Fourth Symphony in Petersburg in December, and when he moved to Switzerland at the end of the year so that he could concentrate more strenuously on the opera (Italy attracted him too much and was too lively for hard work) he was soon writing to Jurgenson in a way which, even though the manner sat a little uneasily on him, showed plainly how pleased he was.

To make this letter understandable, it should be said that he wrote his reviews (given up with the professorship) under one pseudonym and his translations of German lyrics for Jurgenson under another.

TCHAIKOVSKY

I don't have to introduce you to three extraordinary people [he writes]. The feeble scribbler N.N., the late music critic B.L. of the *Russkiye Vyedomosti* and the composer and ex-professor Mr. T. An hour ago Mr. T invited the other two gentlemen—who live with him—to the piano where he played the second act of his new opera *The Maid of Orleans*.

Mr. T. who is on the most intimate terms with Mr. N.N. and Mr. B.L., overcame his natural modesty without much trouble and played with great skill and even inspiration. I wish you had seen the enthusiasm of the two gentlemen! To see them strutting about the room, one might have thought they had written the opera.... They tried without success to convince Mr. T that operas can't be tossed out like pancakes. His answer was to bemoan the limitations of a mind and body that couldn't write down in one night all the music tormenting him with the wish to be composed and which might so easily vanish unless captured right away.

This light-heartedness did not survive the later stages of the opera. When he was reading everything he could lay his hands on about Saint Joan he had found the end of her life unendurable even to think about and when he came to sketch out this part of the opera his sufferings were terrible. As was his hatred of the English. He was never to like the English, not even when, later, they were amongst the most enthusiastic followers of his music. This is not surprising; few people outside England do like the English; but in these first days of 1879, Tchaikovsky loathed them for what they had done to Joan of Arc. For a time he could neither bear to go on with the opera nor bear to leave it alone.

In February he went off to Paris—*The Tempest* was to be played by the Colonne Orchestra and he was curious to hear it—after a most affecting leave-taking at the Villa Richelieu at Clarens, as he told Jurgenson: 'The landlady wept, the landlord gave me a preter-naturally long handshake, the maid (a very nice girl) wept too, so what could I do but join in?'

Paris was quite another matter. One did not weep in Paris nor did one agonize about Joan of Arc. In a very few days he had be-come the dandy. He bought a new overcoat and promenaded the streets in his silk hat and with elegantly gloved hand twirling a cane. He did not see many people—he refused to call on Turgenyev (who had been rude about the libretto of *Yevgeny Onyegin*) on the grounds that great men were better known by their works than their com-pany—but 'I feel at home, I feel happy.' He added in a moment of attempted realism, 'The performance of *The Tempest* next Sunday may have something to do with it.' It may have had, but that was not all; Paris enlivened him and by March the whole opera was sketched out and he had turned to the suite (parts of which he had left in Petersburg and which had only just reached him) for a final orchestration.

The Tempest was not well received, as it happened, but he put the whole failure on his own back as usual. 'I still write like a gifted young man. What miserable orchestration!' Once again the French escaped scot-free; he alone was to blame, and though he told Nadyezhda Filaretovna that he remained the misanthrope, this was true only in a limited sense, for in Paris he, like everyone else, preferred to walk the busy streets and drink in the crowded cafés and listen to the buzz of talk even if he took no part in it. Admittedly most of the conversation was nonsense and boastful nonsense at that, but if one was careful not to listen too hard the overall result was stimulation. None need be lonely in Paris and none was unless he shut himself in his room. So Tchaikovsky flourished even in the midst of his would-be misanthropy because Paris overbears the most acute critics.

He was still there in April, working hard, listening hard, and generally loving life, when he heard that *Yevgeny Onyegin* was to have its première at the Maly; the Conservatoire students were to sing the opera as he had wished. He hurried back to Moscow and was just in time to attend the dress rehearsal.

Perhaps the most moving part of the first performance was the unanimous tribute paid by the entire Conservatoire staff and students; they insisted on crowning the composer with a wreath. The performance itself was chiefly notable for the reactions of the supposedly unemotional Taneyev and the flighty Nikolai Rubinstein; Taneyev subsided in tears, Rubinstein could not raise a joke. 'He's really fallen in love with it,' cried Tchaikovsky, scarcely able to believe eyes or ears.

This apart, the opera fell rather flat. There was plenty of applause but, as the composer saw plainly, 'for me rather than for my work'. With the best will in the world the students were not up to it.

However, the evening was not yet over. Anton Rubinstein had been lured down to Moscow for the event and he, rather than the composer, became the guest of honour at the after-performance supper at The Hermitage. Tchaikovsky waited on tenterhooks for his comment during and after the supper. He waited in vain; Rubinstein did not say one word about the opera.

Tchaikovsky was angry. Over the years since he first joined the

Petersburg Conservatoire in 1862 his devotion to Anton Rubinstein
had been subjected to increasing strain: Rubinstein had damned the
First Symphony, damned the Second String Quartet, and freely
criticized in the most wounding terms almost every other Tchaikovsky work he had seen or heard. On top of this he had deterred (one
could almost say forbidden, so great was his reputation) Tchaikovsky's old student friend V. V. Bessel from printing a score.

This last snub hit Tchaikovsky hard:

Isn't it strange [he wrote to Von Bülow, who made a point of sending
good news from the West when he heard it] that of the *two most famous
artists* of our epoch you *who have not known me long* have supported my
music so splendidly and Anton Rubinstein who was my master has not?
That Olympian god has never shown anything but supreme contempt for
my compositions and I can tell you under the seal of the confessional that
I have always felt deeply hurt by this. Apropos of my quartet whose
success you tell me about, may I reveal a small detail which will enable you
to understand *how* great this contempt is? When I suggested to the publisher Bessel of Petersburg that he publish (without any payment to me)
this same quartet that you tell me has found favour in America, he went to
Rubinstein to ask his advice. 'Was the work good enough to be published?'
he asked. 'No,' said my old master decisively. Thereupon Bessel sends me
the most formal and humiliating refusal.

And the great master is still treating my works in the same fashion—
utter contempt. But let me add, Monsieur, that I tell you this only to show
you how great my gratitude is towards you who are neither my master
nor even a compatriot.

There was, then, every reason why Tchaikovsky should consign
Anton Rubinstein to the devil in so far as his ability to judge his
work was concerned, yet such was his habit of reverence from years
past that he could never shake off the wish to win the master's
approval. Once again he thought this triumphant moment had
come; he believed *Yevgeny Onyegin* was his best work to date and
felt that Rubinstein must surely respond to the genuine feeling in
the score.

Rubinstein did nothing of the kind. Obviously he did not like the
opera but he refused to say why, refused even to discuss it. Only
when he had returned to Petersburg did he explain to his wife why
he could not congratulate his old student: 'It has none of the style of
grand opera.'

ii

Anton Rubinstein's objection was to dog the fortunes of *Yevgeny Onyegin* for two years in Russia and many more outside Russia. It must be said that those who hear the opera for the first time must dismiss from their minds every preconceived notion about opera if they are to appreciate it. It is now generally agreed to be Tchaikovsky's operatic masterpiece. One might go further and suggest that he invented a new kind of modern opera, the intimate drama, which must be played on a small stage in a small theatre if it is to have its full effect.

People have often wondered how a symphonist who revels in the broad sweep and large effects goes to the other extreme when he writes opera that suits him. Clearly *Yevgeny Onyegin* could have been written in quite another way. For instance, Prokofiev, who loved it and Tchaikovsky, often expressed his amazement that the composer had omitted some of the more obvious dramatic parts of the story— parts which would have drawn it closer to grand opera.

But when Tchaikovsky brought people on to the stage his instinct was to keep them life-size, as he and his audience would understand them from their own experience. He resisted every temptation to inflate them to the size of gods. The strife and fall of gods is dramatic, as we all know, and the first definition of tragedy limited the participators to those of high estate. Tchaikovsky, who did not lack courage (after an attempt on the Tsar's life at this time he wrote, 'as long as all of us—the people of Russia—are refused a say in the government of our country there is no hope of a happier future'), insisted on presenting from everyday life characters that he knew and could understand. His Tatyana was a Russian girl to be found in every town and village in the land. He had met Lenskis and Onyegins by the score in Petersburg and Moscow. Even the duel in which the wrong man was killed had been justified by the virtual murder of Pushkin by a nobody who lived into his eighties, to say nothing of lesser examples every other day in the capitals.

The music follows the characters. It too is unpretentious, quiet, avoiding bombast and heroics. It takes its cue from the heroine who is in the worldly sense nothing, in the spiritual sense everything. The composer does not strain himself to produce unforgettable themes as he could well have done; he chooses to rely on music precisely suited to character and situation, to a small event happening in remote

Russia to people who might be expected to live and die without raising a flutter outside their little provincial circle.

Lensky's aria, the Letter Song and Onyegin's 'The Power of Love' do not constitute an opera; lesser-known parts of the opera are as unique and as satisfactory. All the Overtures are little works of art and the three main scenes between Tatyana and Onyegin are beautifully contrived; they do not possess one notable theme, they possess something far better, music perfectly attuned to the moment and the people occupying the stage. This is the secret of the opera's success; it does not swerve from truth for one instant—has any opera ever ended on such a note?—and truth, as Tchaikovsky unforgettably demonstrates here, is beauty, as is another ever-present attribute of *Yevgeny Onyegin*, an indefinable but unmistakable charm.

iii

Tchaikovsky did not fret about the cool reception of his opera, chiefly for the old reason that he was too much taken up with its successor *The Maid of Orleans*, the suite and a Second Piano Concerto he was meditating. He was also preoccupied by Antonina. From Moscow he went up to Petersburg as usual to see his father and friends (he never let many months go by without this visit to the old man) but was poorly repaid by the sudden irruption of his wife. She hung about outside his rooms until she found him in, but it was difficult to understand what she wanted except money; she talked incessantly about her love for him and of his for her and of those who wanted to keep them apart. She also threw in for good measure a long and rambling recital of the latest scalps she had added to her belt. Nothing he could say would calm her or stop the flow. She took the money he offered her, however.

In the end she drove him out of the city by taking a room in the house in which he was staying. He went back to Moscow. She followed him and again forced her way into his rooms. The Petersburg scene was repeated. He retreated to Kamenka and she bombarded him with letters.

The significant fact about this revival of persecution was the manner in which he dealt with it. A year earlier it would have driven him abroad, a guilty man struggling with a nervous breakdown. By the early summer of 1879 he had rationalized his guilt feelings and had began to understand that he was dealing with a woman who could not be held responsible for her actions. But to deal with a half-mad woman face to face is a terrifying experience. He was terrified but he kept his head because he was compassionate too. He could not acquit himself from responsibility and did not try—he was never to do that—but he refused to allow her to get between him and his work.

This he demonstrated at Kamenka. He finished *The Maid of Orleans* and quickly polished off the orchestration of the suite. He added a sixth movement, a Divertimento, which he placed second, and very good it was, but the movement which caused something of a sensation in the Davydov house was an Andante. 'Everyone here is mad about it,' he told Jurgenson. 'When I played it with my brother as a piano duet one girl fainted!'

From Kamenka he went on to Brailov. Not to the main mansion, as Nadyezhda Filaretovna was there; she had left open a smaller house at Simaki on the Brailov estate. He went with some misgivings: 'I've grown so used to thinking of Nadyezhda Filaretovna as some sort of remote and invisible godmother that the thought of her so close to me in the flesh is a little disturbing.'

His concern was well founded. She would not at all have cared for being cast in the role of godmother, as she began to show. In Florence she had lived only a short way from him and he had passed her one day in the street. Now, at Simaki, she wanted to send her daughter over to him. He stopped that politely but firmly. Then, in August, she drove through the Simaki grounds and came face to face with him in a wood he was walking through. Both were confused and he was not pleased. He understood, if she did not, that a flesh and blood friendship would never do; it could not stay that way, on her side at any rate, and it would destroy the spiritual basis on which the relationship had to rest if it were to last.

He could not explain this in so many words, but he was soon to make clear enough what he felt—he was driven to it by more obvious signs that she was thinking in terms of a closer tie.

She had already mooted a marriage between one of her sons and one of Aleksandra's daughters so that the Tchaikovsky and Von Meck blood could mingle literally as well as spiritually. He did not dissent—he could scarcely do that—but replied coolly to her request for an opinion as to which Davydov daughter would be most fitted as her daughter-in-law. This cold-blooded marriage-making was not to his taste—his own marriage had exposed it for ever—and he would not give an opinion. For him, the young people must meet and make up their own minds. As, later on, they did.

All this was as nothing to her outburst a few weeks later. It was caused, she said, by the piano transcription of the Fourth Symphony which she had received shortly before she wrote. She had been playing it ever since.

Her letter had little to do with the symphony. After the first sentence she broke out:

I don't expect you could ever understand how jealous I am of you in spite of the fact that we have never even spoken to each other. Let me confess that I am jealous in an unforgivable way, as a woman is jealous of the man she loves. Can you imagine how I felt when you married? I had a dreadful struggle, my heart was all but broken. The thought that you were with that woman was scarcely bearable torture. And that is not all. I must tell you how wicked I was—I was overjoyed when I realized that you were wretched to be with her. . . . I hated her for not making you happy but if she had made you happy I should have hated her a hundred times more. I felt that she had stolen from me what ought to belong to me only, what I have a right to possess for the best of all reasons, that I love you more than anyone else and cherish you more than anything else in the world.

At this point she seems to have realized what she was saying and what Tchaikovsky might think of it. She did not tear up the letter as she could so easily have done; she added a would-be reassuring statement that in spite of her feelings she had no wish to alter the present relationship—a statement she went far to render valueless by another addition which bore a horrifying resemblance to a somewhat similar remark by Antonina more than two years earlier. She said that before her life came to its end she would like to feel sure that nothing was changed, that nobody. . . . She did not finish this sentence, having no need to do so. She then threw in an Antoninan 'But I have no right to say that.'

Tchaikovsky's feelings on receiving this letter are not difficult to imagine. He could no longer believe in Nadyezhda Filaretovna's imminent decease. He knew from Rubinstein, from Kotek, and from another Conservatoire violinist who had taken Kotek's place— V. A. Pakhulsky— that she suffered much physically. He also knew from his own experience that if one tears one's nerves to pieces one will feel physically unwell. But to die was another matter; the way his patroness dashed about Europe in search of cures did not suggest death.

He had to proceed on the assumption—quite correct as it turned out—that she would live as long as he. He was not a stupid man; he knew something of what she must have felt when he wrote to tell her about his engagement to Antonina. But her reply then had been calm, two years had passed and he, familiar with the flowery epistolary style of the day, had been encouraged to think that she really wished their friendship to be on a platonic level. Recently, as has been seen, her attitude had worried him; now she had come out into the open.

About one thing he was definite; he would neither live with her nor, should such a thing ever be possible, would he marry her. He did not even wish to meet her; he felt with reason that any kind of intimacy other than the kind they enjoyed would be fatal to the relationship. Yet he did not wish the relationship to end; the mere thought dismayed him beyond words. He needed her money for himself and his music chiefly, though for others too, but he needed her faith and moral support just as much. He was still unrecognized abroad as an outstanding composer and still had far to go in his own country. Her faith and her money kept him writing and hopeful of eventual triumph; without them he could no longer feel sure of going on. Besides, he was immensely grateful for what she had done for him in the past two years; she had almost literally made a new man of him.

It was up to him to save the relationship. He did so with great skill. She had given him the opportunity to put down everything she had written to the effect of playing his symphony. He took the opportunity. 'I can't bear to think,' he wrote after reaffirming his belief in the dedication of the symphony as truly meant and earned, 'what might have happened if you had not been sent to me by fate. I owe you everything—life, freedom that had seemed out of my grasp, and indeed so much good fortune that I could never have dreamed of it coming my way.'

Then came the crucial sentence; it was no more than a repetition of what he had told her many times, particularly when she had questioned the power of music to convey the feeling of love. 'I read your letter with such gratitude and love that I can only express what I feel by means of music.'

He had said in his own way what he was and was not prepared to do or feel. She submitted, more fearful than he of losing what she had. From that moment there was a change in the balance of power; the relationship, its limits and its scope were henceforth left in his hands to decide. He was never again to receive such a letter from her.

iv

To this tactful and wise Tchaikovsky must be added a demonstration of the businesslike one, forceful and quick. It is a Tchaikovsky little known, thanks chiefly to the modesty which so often falsifies his letters. Here for once the man of affairs comes into the open, due typically to a threat to the wellbeing of someone he loved.

He heard suddenly that Anatoly was likely to lose his job. He took the next train to Petersburg where his brother worked, demanded full particulars and, having got them, made a round of calls on Anatoly's superiors. What Pyotr Ilyich said and how he said it we shall never know but we do know the immediate result; Anatoly was reinstated.

The taste of triumph did not last; he no sooner reached Moscow on his way back to Kamenka than Rubinstein and Jurgenson called. He was having his morning tea but they routed him out and insisted that he come along with them to what was euphemistically called breakfast. By the evening he had drunk more than was good for him. 'Oh Moscow!' he wrote to Anatoly the next morning. 'One has scarcely set foot in it before one begins drinking. At five o'clock I had to go along to the Jurgensons' where it all began over again. This Moscow tippling is more abhorrent to me than I can tell you.'

As he was writing to a brother who deplored drinking in any shape or form, and specially his own fondness for it, his excess of regret may be suspect. Nevertheless he was sick of what went with the drink in Conservatoire company—gossip and not much but gossip. After a few more weeks at Kamenka, where he began his Second Piano Concerto, he developed 'an intense Italian craze'. That is to say, he longed for blue Italian skies and hot sun and longed too for the wine on which men did not become fuddled but merely more amusing.

By November he was in Paris *en route* for Rome. 'I'm so happy!' he cried as always when he first left Russia.

The stay in Paris was elongated. Nadyezhda Filaretovna was there busily bribing Colonne to play the Fourth Symphony. She was determined to make Pyotr Ilyich world-famous and was prepared to buy fame for him if he could get it no other way.

He deprecated the whole business; you could lead a horse to the water but you could not make him drink. And even if the horse did drink, what pleasure was there in bought success? His pride was wounded. But he had just checked his patroness in one direction and had temporarily to allow her latitude in another; he washed his hands of the whole affair and kept away from Colonne. But he was determined that this should be the first and last excursion of hers into the world of concert and theatre management. There were times when the business-woman in her offended him deeply. This was one of them. When she next brought up the subject, as he knew she would, he insisted that no more payments should be made. Either his music was good enough to force people to play it or it was not. He stood on this and she was obliged to give up.

Colonne and the symphony did not keep him in Paris; he stayed on because of the new piano concerto; it was going splendidly and he was not moving until it was done. The moment the sketch was completed, in the middle of December, he went off to Rome.

Soon afterwards the First Suite had its first performance in Moscow. The success—as it was—was soured for the composer by hearing from Jurgenson that Rubinstein said the music was impossible to play (though he had done so) because the writing for some of the parts was too difficult.

Tchaikovsky flew into a rage. 'If he is right I had better give up writing music.'

When Taneyev tried to pour oil on the waters he merely let himself in for another storm from Rome. Defending Rubinstein, he particularized: some of the woodwind writing, he explained, especially for the oboe, was unplayable; Tchaikovsky had not allowed enough time for the instrumentalist to take breath.

Tchaikovsky denied the imputation comprehensively and hit back. 'I can see plainly that Rubinstein was in a bad mood and took it out on my suite. For ten years I taught instrumentation at the Conservatoire—not very well, admittedly, but without exactly disgracing myself—and now, two years later, I have to endure remarks which should be confined to backward students! Let's get this thing straight; either I have never known how to write for an orchestra or Rubinstein's criticism is on a par with his remarks about my piano concerto. In 1875 he said it was impossible to play but by 1878 he had found it perfectly possible!'

This was a cruel cut—Rubinstein had become one of the concerto's most ardent advocates and was playing it brilliantly. But Tchaikovsky, who did not bear malice, soon found a likelier explanation than ill-humour in Rubinstein when he heard that the leading oboeist had complained. All the same, what was Rubinstein doing, listening to the growlings of a lazy man? Tchaikovsky knew him, a German who was more preoccupied with flirtations than with his instrument. 'So the high notes I have written will spoil the beautiful shape of my German friend's lips, will they!' he wrote in high sarcasm. 'So his kisses won't be quite so emphatic or luscious! All right. But this tragedy won't stop me from writing high notes that every oboeist can play!'

The fuss blew over and the supposedly impossible writing—of which every advanced composer has been accused in his time—has long since been proved eminently playable. The suite was to be immediately popular everywhere it was played and one of the many mysteries of music is its complete disappearance from the concert repertory. It is never heard now and no gramophone recording is available.

The suite is not and was not supposed to be great music. It is very pleasing music written with superlative skill and many a concert programme would be the happier and the more popular if it opened or closed with this work. One notable feature is the use of the woodwinds. Tchaikovsky never failed in this department of an orchestra and in this First Suite, written in one of his sunniest moods, the writing for woodwinds is wholly delightful. Four of the six movements open with woodwinds—the Introduction and Fugue (a fine pastiche, this) opens with the bassoon, the Divertimento with the clarinet, the Intermezzo with flute and bassoon, and the final Gavotte with bassoon, clarinet, oboe, and flute each echoing the same catchy phrase in turn against a string background.

But the triumph of the work is unquestionably the little Marche Miniature. There are only 124 bars in this tiny movement but all are magical. They also point ahead. Just as the first movement of the First Symphony points unmistakably to the Transformation music of *The Nutcracker*, so this suite—and specially the Marche Miniature —point clearly to the first act of the same ballet.

Within a few months this suite was to be played and praised by a much greater musician than Rubinstein—none other than the young Debussy. Nadyezhda Filaretovna engaged the eighteen-year-old boy during the summer vacation of the Paris Conservatoire. He was to play four-hand arrangements with her. When he did, she was critical; he wasn't, she thought, much of a pianist—'there is no comparison between French and Russian pianists, ours are so much better in technique and as musicians'—but she allowed him an astonishing gift as sight-reader.

He was soon exercising this gift on the suite, which they played together, and, said the gratified Nadyezhda Filaretovna, in doing so disclosed another virtue: 'He likes your music. Massenet teaches him theory, so naturally Massenet is a hero of his, but after we had played your suite he was so pleased with the Fugue that he volunteered, "I've never come across anything so beautiful in all modern fugues; even Monsieur Massenet could not have written it."'

The composer's mind was soon and unhappily taken off this fine little work; from Petersburg and Kamenka came bad news early in the new year of 1880; Ilya Petrovich was ill at the one place, Aleksandra at the other. Tchaikovsky prepared to go back to Petersburg but before he could move he had a telegram announcing his father's death.

Those who pursue the well-worn spectre of the Œdipus complex have lost no time in pointing out that the death of Ilya Petrovich did not cause Tchaikovsky the grief he had felt when he lost his mother. This is a typical example of wishful thinking. No one knows what Pyotr Ilyich felt—grief is not measurable—and those who say they do are talking nonsense. Moreover, Aleksandra Andreyevna was forty-one when she died, her husband eighty-five! Forty-one was young even in those days, eighty-five a great age. What Tchaikovsky said when he had the news was: 'What an angelic old soul he was! It is a bitter grief to me that I shan't see him again.' He meant exactly what he said.

Part Four

Fame

CHAPTER SIXTEEN

Serenade for Strings and Violin Concerto
1880-1

Ilya Petrovich did not live to see his son a famous man. He had heard him applauded in the Maryinsky and the Petersburg concert halls. He had also read the newspapers afterwards and had watched Pyotr Ilyich growing more and more despondent and looking older every time he saw him; already—he was not quite forty—there was grey on the head which was coming to look so much like his own, hair brushed back stiffly from the forehead. It seems most probable that Ilya Petrovich died with his original opinion unchanged, that his son would have lived more happily as a very talented amateur. Had he read the letter from Apukhtin two years earlier he would surely have felt himself justified, for after twelve years as a professional musician and with all the lustre and help of a Conservatoire post and powerful friends, his son could only draw from the poet a 'Your country is going to be proud of you.' He might well wonder whether this was not merely poetic licence.

Yet had he lived another few months he would have seen his son's and Apukhtin's faith justified, for the year 1880 was to be notable for the beginnings of world fame—fame to a degree that no other Russian before or since has enjoyed.

The opening of the year gave little sign of what was so soon to come. Nadyezhda Filaretovna could splash her money about but the recipient was only obliged to fulfil the letter of the law, as Colonne demonstrated. He played the Fourth Symphony; how he played it was another matter. It was a comparative failure. There were mitigating circumstances. The French were to prove one of the stubbornest nuts to crack—regular and enthusiastically received performances of Tchaikovsky in Paris have only recently been known—but by 1880 they were at least aware of him as a possible force in modern music. The triumph of his First Piano Concerto during the World Fair had done him a power of good; his name was known though his music was not often played, and comments on the Fourth Symphony if cool were respectful. Besides, he was succeeding in Paris with other works; both the Third Quartet and the *Sérénade Mélancolique* were praised rapturously, the latter far beyond its merits.

Elsewhere this year his music went from triumph to triumph. The First Suite was given a wonderful reception in Petersburg, then in New York under Damrosch. The Concerto in B flat Minor was at last welcomed by the Germans—it was played three times within a few weeks—as well as making its mark in Budapest, and in New York it scored a renewed ovation with Rummel at the piano.

This was not fame but a hint of it was in the air and when he returned to Russia in March he found in the capitals that subtle but unmistakable change of climate when a man begins to advance from purely national to international notice. In Petersburg he was in such demand at dinners and soirées given by musical and social celebrities that he panted to be away into the country; he never had a moment to himself and, feeling that this widespread notice might well have been given some years earlier when, for one thing, his father would have been alive and would have revelled in it much more than he, his comments were unflattering to those who suddenly discovered that it was the thing to patronize the local boy who had made good.

Even a performance of his Second Quartet, with Auer playing first violin, after which he was presented with a wreath amidst scenes of enormous enthusiasm—even this could not rouse him. It had all come rather late. He stayed on for one purpose only, to try to see that *The Maid of Orleans* was given a fair hearing by the Imperial Theatres committee. His disgust with the creatures who had sensed correctly (as they almost always do) the prevailing wind of change was natural enough, but his assumption that their praise was nauseatingly worthless was going too far; that the Petersburg musicians and aristocrats could be right for the wrong reason seems never to have occurred to him, so obsessed was he by this latest opera.

At last he escaped to Moscow, dead tired and rather cynical, only to find that one of his most persistent new admirers, the Grand-Duke

Konstantin Nikolayevich, had followed him and wanted to repeat the banquet he had given in his honour in Petersburg. Tchaikovsky hurriedly made his excuses and fled to Kamenka.

There he found Aleksandra still unwell and Lyov waiting to take her to Carlsbad for treatment. Leaving Pyotr Ilyich in charge of the children, they went off soon after he arrived. He was not in the best shape for dealing with the children's demands on his time—they were all growing up fast and very lively with it—but he kept them in some sort of order and himself in good physical trim and managed to get down to some work too. Before he broke the Kamenka stay with a few weeks at Brailov and Simaki as usual he had finished orchestrating the piano concerto and a *Capriccio Italien* he had written very quickly in Rome.

At Brailov he did more work, getting the *Maid of Orleans* ready for the printer, and went for more great walks. At Simaki too he was for ever out of doors when the weather allowed and his passion for Russia expressed itself, not in music this time, but in an uninhibited and full-hearted cry of thanks. He was walking through a field of millet when suddenly the beauty of the country came over him with such a rush of feeling that he fell on his knees and thanked God for the joy he felt. 'Everywhere beauty and space!' he wrote in his notebook that night. 'What moments life holds! Thanks to them one can forget all the rest.'

Back at Kamenka he had more news of the latest acquisition to the Von Meck musical staff, the young cellist Danilchenko fresh from the Moscow Conservatoire, and of the boy Nadyezhda Filaretovna insisted on calling Bussy. She sent a photograph of him—Tchaikovsky thought he looked very much like Anton Rubinstein when young—and asked whether he might take back to Paris (his vacation was almost up) a copy of the *Maid of Orleans* score. Tchaikovsky agreed readily and sent the score but by the time she received it Nadyezhda Filaretovna had changed her mind; she had remembered the French magpies.

Debussy went off without the score. 'I was afraid,' she explained to Pyotr Ilyich, 'that those thieving French composers, Massenet, Delibes and the rest of them, would steal whole handfuls of your opera and play them to Parisian audiences as their own.' She hastened to forestall an incredulous objection—she thought she knew the French better than her correspondent and tended to look on the uncharitable side—with a 'They have already stolen from you, Pyotr Ilyich, believe me. For instance only the other day when we were playing the four-hand arrangement of your First Symphony I noticed passages I had heard in Paris, *not* under your name.'

Tchaikovsky was hard at work again—Kamenka had an extraordinarily good effect on him—on two very different compositions, *1812* and Serenade for Strings. He wrote *1812* with his tongue in his cheek—Rubinstein had been plaguing him to write something suitable for the Moscow Exposition of Industrial Art in 1882—and it is not mentioned in high critical quarters. It is difficult not to laugh at the bombast—'it will be very noisy,' he warned Nadyezhda Filaretovna—yet it is also difficult to deny that it is effective. Tchaikovsky was a consummate workman—a real professional musician who knew his job from A to Z—and this piece precisely filled the need; it roused patriotic fervour, it was dramatic and it did not go on too long.

The Serenade for Strings was a very different matter. When he had finished it early in November he told Jurgenson, 'I am violently in love with this work and can't wait for it to be played.'

He had to wait quite a while but scarcely had time to notice it, for the moment he left Kamenka he was caught up in a veritable barrage of first performances of works written earlier. A man's own country rarely hails him as great until the outside world shows signs of doing so, and this was precisely what was happening in Russia in the beginning of the eighteen eighties. The musical section of high society in Petersburg had already given him a foretaste of the kind of public life he must expect; now came a rush of Moscow performances, as if there could not be enough Tchaikovsky music played.

Apart from chamber concerts—his songs and quartets were becoming firm favourites—the first orchestral work to be heard that winter was the *Capriccio Italien*; it was played several times in both capitals and public and critics alike (Kui excepted, as usual) received it rapturously. Too rapturously perhaps; it is popular music and was not intended to be anything else. To complain, as Kui did, that its brilliance was all on the surface was to mistake the composer's aim, as critics so often do. Tchaikovsky had no wish to write a profound work but to give his own personal impression of Italy in music, and the impression was deliberately of Carnival in Rome, using the tunes he had heard sung in the streets. A superficial impression, possibly, of an event which, based on religious feeling, is absolutely true of the Italian people at this time. The work has held its popularity for almost one hundred years and is likely to hold it, for, given the restricted aim, it is brilliantly worked out, tuneful, varied, and economical.

At the Bolshoi there was a revival of *Oprichnik*—applauded more because the composer had suddenly caught public favour than for its real merits—and at the other extreme came a Musical Society performance of a Liturgy he had written some months previously, a work which produced vast applause and that sure sign of virtue, violent opposition from the Church.

A few weeks later, after Tchaikovsky had spent a thanksgiving Christmas and the New Year of 1881 with the Kamenka family and an Aleksandra somewhat recovered, *Yevgeny Onyegin* was given its first Bolshoi performance with a professional cast. This time it gradually won its way with the public who, not for the first time, proved themselves more malleable than the critics. To accept this chamber opera—especially in the vast Bolshoi—when one has been accustomed to a diet of grand opera is not easy. It took some time for the audiences to adapt themselves to the change but they made the effort. While the critics were still harping on the old objections of lack of large-scale dramatic effects, quietness of the music matching undistinguished happenings on stage, the people were obstinately coming back for more. They would not let the opera die and from that moment its fate was certain; unlike previous operas by the same composer, *Yevgeny Onyegin* was to go from strength to strength as the years passed.

Three weeks later his Second Symphony had its first performance in its revised form—he had rewritten some of the first movement and tightened up the rest—and went down with a bang. One has the impression that anything he wrote then would have been acclaimed; Moscow had become Tchaikovsky-conscious at last, realizing that this undemonstrative composer possessed all the dynamism of the Russian spirit and would change world opinion about a supposed backward country.

The quiet and popular ex-professor did not hear the ovations; he was in Petersburg showing quite another Tchaikovsky to the producers of *The Maid of Orleans*.

ii

Tchaikovsky's use of his new status in Russia was typical of the man. We have seen what he thought of the adulation; when it did not bore it sickened him, with himself and the flatterers. Now he saw the practical side and sized it.

As his scores demonstrate, he was a punctilious writer of music. He left nothing to chance; he knew just what he wanted and explained it in the clearest possible manner. In performances of chamber works and occasionally in the symphonic works he had had his way; that is to say, he often managed to impress on the members of quartets and on Nikolai Rubinstein as conductor that his markings were meant to be followed and that if they were not his music was not being played, only a travesty of it. But in opera he had had to stand aside and watch and hear his work mutilated. He had no power to influence the bureaucratic conductors, producers, and the dozens of hangers-on of the state opera houses, including a non-musical government representative who would cut and change the score and libretto at will. Shalyapin was to rage against these back-stage Napoleons many years later. What Tchaikovsky must have suffered during earlier rehearsals in the Imperial Theatres beggars the imagination.

Now, in February 1881, he went up to Petersburg determined to use his sudden rise to fame to some purpose. As he did, to the general amazement of all the theatre people. They knew him well, as they thought, by this time, and rated him a mild and easygoing man. They now discovered during rehearsals a meticulous tyrant insistent that his work should be produced and played and sung as he had imagined it during composition and who was prepared to keep singers, producer, conductor, and orchestra in the theatre all night if he did not get his way.

Napravnik's chief assistant, O. O. Palyechek, was to put everybody's astonishment into words: 'He attended all the rehearsals and had something to say about everything that went on. He literally cavilled at every phrase that was played or sung. . . . Assisted by Napravnik and me, he worked out every move on stage with the singers, every note they sang, every gesture they made. He insisted that we study the character of the music as he had written it before allowing it to be played and sung. . . . And I must admit that his directions were so very much to the point that it would be true to say that he alone was the real producer of the opera.'

To this Palyechek adds a plaintive: 'Although I know that everyone thinks of him as simply a mild, good man, at such times he was extremely severe.'

In this instance it is sad to have to report that all his trouble was wasted. He attended the first performance at the Maryinsky before leaving for his usual winter in Italy and, not for the first time, was deceived by the applause in the theatre as he had long since deceived himself about the opera: 'I believe it will make my name as an opera composer,' he had told Modest.

The near future was to show that the applause was almost wholly a tribute to him and his work in general rather than for the opera on stage. He had not reached Rome before a reading of newspapers warned him that the critics to a man were likely to condemn the opera.

As it turned out. They tore it to shreds. And for once one can say, justly. Tchaikovsky's taste, which was not impeccable, had failed him badly. He presented Joan of Arc as a Russian girl whose spirituality did not prevent a hopeless love for an imaginary Lionel of Burgundy and gave them a love duet as one of the central pieces of the opera. His historical sense was not equal to the challenge; he surrounded Saint Joan with a chorus which was in essence nothing more than a crowd of Russian peasants.

But then, as has often been said, Joan of Arc is not a fit subject for an opera stage; like Fauré's Requiem in a concert hall, it is out of place. Having chosen to present her in an opera Tchaikovsky was no doubt obliged to follow the conventions but could not hope to succeed. He made bad worse by reacting violently to criticisms that he was incapable of writing grand opera—this in spite of his many asseverations that he had no wish to attempt it. It is true that he chose for his grand opera a real person and not a puppet but his treatment of the work is painfully reminiscent of Meyerbeer.

At times he wrote good music, as the critics acknowledge, but the action on stage made nonsense of it. Only twice did he manage to create a Joan of Arc in which one could believe, once when she makes her farewell to her birthplace—a very moving aria—and again in the second act when, in an inspired solo, she invokes the blessing of God and his angels. These apart—and they are still sung —the opera is best forgotten.

iii

He was prevented from overmuch brooding on this latest operatic disaster by two events, the one intermingling with the other. So soon does fame spread even in a country which scarcely knew his work that his new reputation had preceded him. He had no sooner arrived in Rome than he discovered that the days of anonymity were over; the society hostesses made a dead set at this latest lion. He found himself in a Roman version of the Petersburg of his last two visits and rapidly tired of it.

He was, besides, worried about Nikolai Rubinstein and the chatter at dinners and soirées seemed indecent as well as silly. For the last few months his old Director had been troubled by severe stomach pains. In spite of everything Tchaikovsky and every other friend could say he would not see a doctor nor would he give up his usual gargantuan meals washed down by the usual wine and brandy.

A few days after Tchaikovsky left Russia Rubinstein felt so ill that he was forced to see a doctor. The doctor sent him off immediately to Paris for treatment accompanied by his close friends, the Tretyakovs. They had got no further than Vilna when news came that the Tsar had been assassinated. As Governor of Moscow, Tretyakov had to return, but his wife and Nikolai went on to Paris.

Tchaikovsky did not know of the hurried journey to Paris; he knew only that this old friend was seriously ill and would do nothing about it. He feared his obstinacy. Rome quickly became unendurable and he went down to Naples hoping to forget his uneasiness in the work he could never get time for in the capital. He had scarcely put pen to paper before he heard of the assassination of Aleksandr II, which made him long to be home, and, before he could do anything about it, that Rubinstein was in Paris and dangerously ill with tuberculosis of the stomach.

He forgot all about Russia and the Tsar and got ready to go to Paris. He had not reached the train before a second telegram told him that Rubinstein was dead. He had died a death absolutely in character; on his last morning he demanded a plate of oysters followed by an ice and would accept no refusals. He died a few hours later.

In the train Tchaikovsky spent long hours of wretchedness. He describes what he felt and at once sets himself apart from the ordinary man. The difference between the great man and the ordinary one lies not so much in what they think as that the one says what he thinks and the other does not. Tchaikovsky in the Rome–Paris express provides the perfect example. His thoughts during the journey were given less to sorrow at the loss of an old friend and companion than to sheer horror at the thought of seeing Rubinstein's dead body.

This is one of the commonest of fears and is shared by most

above Tchaikovsky is greeted by local notables on the way to Tiflis in 1886

below Tchaikovsky's home at Klin

From the score of *The Nutcracker*, part of Act I

people but not one in a thousand would ever have the moral courage to say so. Tchaikovsky frankly confesses it. 'I was afraid I would break down under the shock.' His journey was one long struggle 'to try to brace myself to conquer such shameful cowardice'.

All his fears were unnecessary; Rubinstein's body was already lying in the Russian church by the time he arrived. Anton was there, so too at the Paris funeral service were Turgenyev, Lalo, Pauline Viardot, and Massenet.

Tchaikovsky would not go back to Moscow with the funeral party for a strange reason, that Anton showed relief rather than grief; it seems that the long hero-worship, twenty years of it, had finally expired. Anton's attitude at The Hermitage had been deeply wounding, not for the first time, and his attitude towards his dead brother —which Tchaikovsky must surely have misread—settled the matter.

A few days later Tchaikovsky followed the party to Moscow. The choice of a new Director had to be made and he must have suspected that his name would be raised; he had already been offered the Directorship at Kiev and had refused.

Sure enough, he was unanimously begged to take the post. He refused and recommended Taneyev. His refusal was courageous because he had recently heard that the Von Meck fortune had suffered serious losses and had begged Nadyezhda Filaretovna to stop paying him an allowance; he was free from fear of poverty, he told her, and could always go back to the Conservatoire if the need arose.

She would not listen; Brailov might have to go (she did in fact sell it) but she had plenty left and in any case, heavily underlined: 'I absolutely refuse to abandon my right to look after you.'

He did not protest further. He could do with the allowance. Although his income was going up steadily—the sales of songs and piano pieces in particular had grown substantially—his outgoings kept pace with it. Unlike most men who begin to flourish his generosity increased with his income; the fact that he had been poor and might well be poor again had no effect whatever; he helped every genuine hard-luck case brought to his notice—his begging post had become enormous—and many ungenuine ones. He had begun his charity at home with the lame duck Modest. He made him a handsome allowance that left him free to write, with the result that he had a play due to be staged in Petersburg shortly and was soon to be in demand, heaven knows why, as a librettist.

Although quite a few completed works were hanging fire—the Violin Concerto was waiting on Auer, the Second Piano Concerto was awaiting a suitable soloist, and the Serenade for Strings was waiting on Napravnik—Tchaikovsky returned to Russia anxious to write more. That more was an opera—obviously he would never learn his limitations—and again he made a mistake at the outset by choosing what was for him an impossible subject. In Petersburg before going to Kamenka for the summer he was told by K. Y. Davydov the cellist, one of his professors at the Petersburg Conservatoire who had become Director, about a Pushkin libretto that had never been used—with some reason, it turned out. But when Tchaikovsky sent for the libretto, by V. P. Burenin on *Poltava*, he thought he could make a good thing of it with a few judicious alterations. He made the alterations—as has been seen, he rather fancied himself as librettist—and by the autumn, before leaving for another Italian winter, he had renamed it *Maʒepa* and had sketched out quite a bit. He was tremendously enthusiastic about it; if he never learned, he never grew up either, which is refreshing even when it leads to trouble.

In October the Serenade for Strings had its first performance in Petersburg. It was immediately hailed by public and critics as a splendid work. Anton Rubinstein, breaking a long silence, said that it was the best thing his old student had done; he meant perhaps the only tolerable thing. The Moscow première of the Serenade some months later confirmed the success of what has become one of Tchaikovsky's best-known and best-liked works. The most popular movement, the Waltz, has suffered the fate of so many of Tchaikovsky's delightful themes and is so much overplayed as to make it difficult for a modern listener to evaluate. The other three movements are more substantial and show the composer at his brilliant best; as a lesson in writing for strings they have rarely been surpassed. If any doubt existed that Tchaikovsky was a master of his craft it was finally dispelled when the Serenade was first played.

Less than two months later, when Tchaikovsky was settled in Rome for the winter, the Violin Concerto was played at last. For the second time he had to scratch out a dedication. Auer, he discovered, not content with declining the dedication after three years, had been trumpeting the legend of the unplayability of the violin part to all and sundry. Two possible substitutes, Sauret and Kotek, had withdrawn after listening to him. A third, Adolf Brodsky, could not face the difficulties for more than two years, then saw the possibilities if he could brush up his technique. With more gumption than the others he proceeded from words to deeds, learned the solo part and was all on fire to play it. He persuaded Hans Richter to put it on in Vienna early in December of 1881.

The reaction of the Vienna audience is difficult to credit today when the technique of violin playing has advanced enormously; the concert hall was pandemonium, a battle between the modernists and traditionalists. The critics parted company in much the same way, some hurling abuse at the 'brutality' of the work and its insensitive handling of the solo instrument, others welcoming the composer's original use of the violin. In fact Tchaikovsky had the absorbing idea of using the kind of violin playing he had heard with Rubinstein at the gypsy encampments outside Moscow within the framework of one of the most classical orchestral scores he was ever to write.

Nowadays, when the technical feats of violinists have ceased to amaze, the form of the concerto is perhaps its greatest virtue. The violin writing is difficult even by present-day standards—the double stopping, the glissandi, the trills, the hair-raising leaps are formidable by any standard and the Cossack Dance in the Finale tests every soloist—but as Tchaikovsky felt instinctively, the excitement and joy of this superb work must stand or fall by the mingling of classical and barbaric, of form and freedom. The themes are too familiar now to comment on; one and all are Tchaikovsky at his best and what more could one say?

As for the manner in which he introduced these themes, one is still overcome by admiration after innumerable hearings. Consider, for instance, the first movement of the concerto. It opens with what could be called a broadcloth introduction. Out of this rises the principal theme but so gradually and so inevitably that one is scarcely aware what is happening until the theme is all about one, radiant and glowing. It is Tchaikovsky magic.

It is instructive to note that the errant Auer, who was to become a renowned teacher of the violin, recanted and spent his later days urging the work on all his pupils. This is perhaps the best tribute ever paid to a rejected work. Tchaikovsky was not to write a second violin concerto. This is understandable; he was an artist; the merits of the one he did write could scarcely be repeated, could certainly not be excelled.

CHAPTER SEVENTEEN

Trio and Second Suite

1882–4

Tchaikovsky had been thinking a great deal about Nikolai Rubinstein. He was possibly suffering from conscience—he spent much of his life in this state—about his immediate reactions to his old friend's death. These were, that he would have felt his death much more if it had taken place some years earlier. This was the truth; he and Rubinstein had gradually drifted apart since giving up their joint apartment. Rubinstein's private life had gone from bad to worse in these years and Tchaikovsky neither would nor could keep pace with him. Rubinstein's rejection of the piano concerto had left a wound—it was heartlessly done—and his later championship of it was almost cancelled out by his criticisms of the Fourth Symphony.

These were some of the reasons which drove the men apart. Yet there were many other reasons for Tchaikovsky to feel grateful and affectionate; with very rare exceptions Rubinstein had championed him for all his Moscow years and had played his work as conductor and pianist with understanding and generosity. He was, besides, for all his silly side, a thoroughly nice man.

Tchaikovsky's wave of conscience together with the effect of time—we all miss the dead much more after the first shock—finally and inevitably expressed itself in music. The surprise was the form the music took. He decided early in 1882 to write a piano trio in memory of Rubinstein. It is true that the inclusion of a piano was essential in a work in memory of a pianist. It is also true that Nadyezhda Filaretovna had asked him some time before to write such a trio. But he had replied firmly that he did not care for this combination of timbres. Yet before the old year was out he was at work on a trio of this kind that was to prove one of his most satisfactory compositions.

The work was broken into by a marriage in the family. Vera Lvovna, Aleksandra's daughter, had already married a Rimsky-Korsakov and by doing so (though her husband was only a distant relative of the composer) had drawn Tchaikovsky still closer to the man he most admired in the Balakirev circle. Now Anatoly was to marry, and Pyotr Ilyich greeted the news of the engagement with a recommendation that his brother should read *Anna Karenina* and especially the descriptions of Levin's love for Kitty; he had just reread them with ecstasy. With sorrow too. 'How I long for a woman's caresses!' he cried.

The marriage ceremony, in Moscow that April, struck him as it does many others, as a tiresome bore. Some envy may have come into it, as it also does with others; the oncoming of fame had made him lonelier, for he could no longer distinguish good friends from false. When he wrote 'None but the Lonely Heart' he wrote it from the heart, that is why it has an undying appeal, and the domestic happiness of others made him sad. This was perhaps why Konstantin Stanislavsky, a distant relative of Anatoly's wife, found the composer 'nervous' in society. The men were to meet often—the Moscow Art Theatre was a dream of the future but both were ardent admirers of the Maly Theatre productions and actors and Stanislavsky became a director of the Moscow Musical Society—but the younger man rarely saw the composer in the light of a social adept; unlike most witnesses he was impressed more by Tchaikovsky's unusual modesty than by his man-of-the-world manner.

Tchaikovsky went off sombrely to Kamenka that May and to work on his trio and his new opera. He was not in Moscow when Anton Rubinstein opened the musical side of the Exhibition of Industrial Art with a concert in which the chief item was a first performance of the new Second Piano Concerto. Taneyev played the solo part.

The generous applause then seems to have set the style for the reception of this work ever since, that is, applause for the pianist for mastering a fantastically difficult part, and applause for the composer more because he is loved than for that particular example of his genius. Astonishment has frequently been registered that this Concerto in G Major has failed to establish itself in the concert repertory and one can only echo this astonishment. Criticisms of the form are beside the point; a composer has a perfect right to write a concerto in which the piano is as much accompanist as solo instrument, the only point of moment is whether he has done it successfully and no one has seriously doubted this in Tchaikovsky.

The concerto is almost as rich in typically Tchaikovskian themes as anything he wrote, it is both grand and continuously effective. The construction is better than the construction of the First Concerto and if the mood behind the work is more detached than usual with this composer, if the work is more of a showpiece than an expression of deep feeling, one can scarcely complain. Critic after critic has inveighed against the Tchaikovsky who 'wears his heart on his sleeve'—a curious complaint, this—but most of them are equally annoyed when the composer steps outside his work. This does not make sense.

Music-loving men and women are happily untroubled by these extra-musical considerations and the concerto would become a firm favourite with them if only they were allowed to hear it frequently. That has never yet happened. A criticism could be made of the Andante; it is a little slight and a little sentimental, though the lush melody is difficult to resist. But the first movement is as magnificent a piece of writing as Tchaikovsky or any other man was to produce (it reminds one of Mozart's great C Major Concerto) and the Finale is a real joy.

This Finale is the surprise of the work. It reveals a Tchaikovsky everyone must love, a witty man and a master of original rhythms. Apart from his Clown's Dance in *Snegourochka* (which was more humour than wit) nothing remotely like this movement had been written before this concerto and nothing remotely like it was to be written for many years. It was almost half a century ahead of its time. Stravinsky was the first to take advantage of what it taught, Prokofiev improved on him (listen to the first movement of his Fifth Concerto) and the cycle was finished by Shostakovich. The Finale of the latter's Concerto for Piano and Trumpet is a logical and inevitable result of Tchaikovsky's lead.

ii

Tchaikovsky's growing stature as the leading Russian composer of the day became more marked as 1882 wore on. The musical part of the Moscow Exhibition was completely dominated by his works and culminated in an all-Tchaikovsky night when the Violin Concerto had its first Russian performance. Abroad, the concerto roused immense enthusiasm in London—it was the first Tchaikovsky composition to take a firm hold there—Prague staged *The Maid of Orleans* (watched by Aleksandra on her way back from another visit to Carlsbad) and this first performance of a Tchaikovsky opera outside his own country was sufficiently successful to bring about a revival a few months later. In New York his works were becoming well known and his music selling fast. He was winning disciples abroad as well as at home where Arensky was begging to be allowed to use the libretto of *Voivode*; Brodsky and Hans Richter added themselves to Von Bülow as converts and in Prague the young Anton Dvŏrák, like the young Vincent D'Indy in Paris, was an enthusiastic admirer of *Yevgeny Onyegin*.

But perhaps the surest sign of his supremacy as a contemporary composer came out of the blue from the still half-barbaric Votkinsk. It was a long letter to her dear Petya from his one-time and first piano teacher, Maria Markovna Palchikova. She had married but was no nearer to flourishing than when he had known her more than thirty years earlier. She begged for money.

He sent the money, more than she asked. He said that he owed a lot to her. At first sight this appears no more than sentimentality since he in fact taught her as much as she taught him. But that was not the point; his memory was good—indeed, he largely lived in the past of those happy days the more the present fame disappointed him—and he remembered not so' much the girl who could never struggle through a piece unaided as the humble champion of hard-pressed music when the all-conquering Fanny was bent on making a writer of him.

The result of all this notice was, unhappily, an extension of the kind of life Pyotr Ilyich could not endure and by August he was crying 'Life in Moscow and Petersburg is becoming impossible for me. I shall have to stay in the country or go abroad. Why this is, God only knows—the strain of it is driving me half mad. Perhaps in some better world I shall be told why I can never spend one hour in either capital without horrible suffering.'

Like many other men he felt impelled to struggle after fame but when the first signs of it appeared the gratification was almost always outweighed by boredom and worse. He could no longer enter a room in Moscow without being besieged by people. He became tired and cynical. He knew that most of these people were merely running with the hounds and that they would be equally fulsome with the next sensation to turn up. Not necessarily a musical one either; he suspected that they would be just as intrigued if a champion ice skater or trapeze artist suddenly made his appearance in the city.

He also despised himself. His natural kindness forbade the snub. Afterwards he berated himself for feebleness and for a more serious fault, of actually enjoying praise from those whom he knew in his heart were completely false.

Finally and inevitably his gloomy view of the lionhunters made him suspect almost everyone, even the sincere—it was the old story of the rich unable to trust a single profession of friendship or love— and this made him think unkindly even of people such as the Rimsky-Korsakovs. He wrote bitterly of them turning a fond face to him in Moscow and saying and writing nasty things in Petersburg. This was nonsense—he was confusing them with Kui—and he was eventually to recognize it; he was then specially irritated with Rimsky-Korsakov for writing *The Snow Maiden* but was to be among the first to appreciate the lovely opera when he heard it.

This was later. At the moment he yearned for the country whenever he was obliged to be in town (which was increasingly often) and when he got back to Kamenka gave a deep sigh of relief: 'How marvellous to be oneself again instead of being forced to play a different part a thousand times a day. How insincere social life is— and how senseless!'

In October his Trio had its first performance in Moscow. The public response was warm, the critics were cool, but Taneyev's reaction pleased the composer immensely: 'It is a glorious work. I have been studying it six hours a day for more than three weeks!'

The public won, as usual, and Taneyev has been justified to the hilt; this long work—it is the size of a full symphony—has since become one of the most admired pieces of chamber music in the world. It is curious that Tchaikovsky should have been repelled by the thought of using pianoforte with violin and cello for he blends them as if he had been writing for this combination all his life; despite its enormous length the Trio holds the listener throughout.

The construction is unusual for an elegiac work; the composer devotes the whole of the massive central movement to an evocation of Rubinstein. It is a musical impression of the life of Nikolai and, one could say, of any artist, of his struggles, failures, successes, and the composer creates it by means of eleven variations on a simple but memorable theme. Here he illustrates the career of a man who was both a musical educationalist (symbolized by a skilful Fugue) and an outstanding pianist (symbolized by a Mazurka written and played with great verve) and finally a man who had to face death.

Tchaikovsky understood Rubinstein's love of life—he too did not want to die—and since the death of his friend he had been examining his heart closely. In his letters to Nadyezhda Filaretovna, who stoutly denied the possibility of another life, he wavered; his intellect told him that it was impossible, that she was right, something else told him that she was wrong: 'There *may* be another life,' he was to tell Anatoly (he was discussing the subject widely). 'My heart rebels against the idea of complete annihilation and my instinct is repelled by it. They both compel me to believe that another life does exist.'

In the final variation of the 'Rubinstein' theme he transfers the argument to music; it is a moving and convincing picture of man coming to grips with this final problem and accepting death. It was certainly true of Rubinstein; he died as gaily as he had lived.

The first movement of the Trio can be said to represent Tchaikovsky facing fate and conquering it on behalf of a man who was taken out of life at forty-five and in the prime of his career and talents. He does so by two warring themes, the first sombre, the second almost gay, both fascinating examples of the writer of supremely lyrical melodies. The richness of the writing set a new standard in chamber music; listening, it is difficult to believe that there are only three instruments, the scale and sound suggests a chamber orchestra. The only other man to give such an impression —Brahms—had not yet met Tchaikovsky.

The Finale also presents two themes in opposition but in a totally different manner; it is altogether lighter until the end of the movement when a splendid funeral march, solemn but never joyless, brings the work to a close.

iii

By January of the new year, 1883, he was off on his winter travels again, *Mazepa* still unfinished. This time he did not go to Italy direct but to Paris where once again he was enchanted and loath to leave. He saw Bernhardt in *Fedora* and thought her an 'arch genius', he saw De Musset, he listened night after night to *Figaro* at the

Opéra-Comique and marvelled at its magic. He worked hard, too, at *Mazepa* and at two commissioned compositions in connexion with the forthcoming coronation of the new Tsar, Aleksandr III. One of these, the Cantata *Moscow*, was much more than a routine job that Russia's most famous composer could not avoid, and it is difficult to understand why it is now never sung.

He enjoyed Paris as usual and felt the better for it, but his bump of perception did not leave him despite the power of the charm. One day he went into the Russian church where Rubinstein's body had lain two years earlier. He had been overcome by one of his violent longings for his country and estimated correctly that, short of taking the train, he could only recapture the feeling of Russia there. He enjoyed the by now unfamiliar service and he disenjoyed it and said so, putting his finger precisely on one of the strange idiosyncrasies of human nature and, especially at that time, his own reaction to fame. 'I felt rather moved when I held the wax taper and kneaded the little pellets of wax after each gospel, then I began to feel impatient—I wanted the service to end—and when it did end I felt miserable because it was over!'

On a larger scale, or at least a more concrete one, he had a good example of the peculiarities of his hosts. While he was in Paris the news of Wagner's death was received. Drinking punch at a café—the winter and spring were bitterly cold—Tchaikovsky read the newspapers and listened to the flood of talk caustically. All of a sudden Wagner had become the rage, every orchestra competing with its Wagner programme. Men could talk of nothing but his greatness. Pyotr Ilyich could remember, if the French could not, the time when Wagner's operas were howled down and the critics excelled themselves in vituperation. Though he was no great admirer of the composer—he had recently seen and described *Tristan and Isolde* as 'an endless void, without life or movement'—he could see in him the fate of all artists. He could with particular clarity see the French and art: 'Curious people, the French. One has to die to catch their attention.'

He might criticize his hosts but on his way back to Russia that summer—he had worked so hard that Italy was never reached—he stayed a night or two in Berlin and this put Paris in perspective; it was a capital city, not a provincial outpost, he said.

He did not leave Paris until he had finished the score of *Mazepa* but he continued to tinker with it in the country all summer. He heard that the opera would be performed both in Moscow and

Petersburg the next year—an exceptional honour, the one city vying with the other for the honour of first performance—but by this time he had begun to weary of the subject. He was more interested in a new suite—the second—which he was writing at a great rate, and by the end of the year he had finished it and a rewriting or, to be exact, a trimming of his First Symphony.

The battle for first performance was won by the Bolshoi, and in the middle of February 1884, a few weeks after a Davydov girl had married a Von Meck boy as Nadyezhda Filaretovna wished, *Mazepa* had its Moscow première. Four days later it was produced at the Maryinsky. The opera was greeted warmly in Moscow, coldly in Petersburg, and this difference fairly indicates how much of the applause was due to the work and how much to the composer—Tchaikovsky was present at the Bolshoi but absent from the Maryinsky.

By this time he could fill a theatre or concert hall if audiences knew they could bring him on to the platform after the work was played; the sight of him roused tremendous enthusiasm. Fame concretely only reaches its climax when people can worship a creator in person. That was why Tchaikovsky's fame abroad was still confined to composers, musicians, musical coteries and their social hangers-on. His reputation as Russia's leading composer had become, for many Russians, little more important than his reputation for kindness and good-humour. Besides, he was a man worth seeing, the beautiful fast-greying head poised on a perfectly proportioned body. His carriage was a joy—he walked and moved, as he held himself, with natural grace—and his modesty endeared him to everyone just as the habitually sad expression on his face tugged at the heart.

Conductors were in despair when he refused to attend an opening night but could not move him if his mind was made up. He knew by this time what a hold he had on the public affection but refused to trade on it. He still loathed publicity and personal appearances, he still had to force himself on to a platform though years of experience had taught him how to conceal nervousness. But he did as little of it as possible. So after the Bolshoi first night he left for Paris.

Some time before, keeping Nadyezhda Filaretovna *au fait* with his doings as usual, he had written, 'So far I haven't managed to work up the enthusiasm I felt for *Onyegin*. The score advances gradually but I must confess that the characters haven't really caught my imagination.' These were ominous words and *Mazepa* bore them out; to the very end he felt it to be more a task than a necessity and the music sounds like it; the only suggestion of inspiration comes in the mad song of Marie, the rest is so much conventional melodrama. Even the orchestral writing seems to have become stereotyped, as if the composer cannot believe in his characters or their situation.

All this was pointed out by the critics; respectful now because they were dealing with a great man. Disappointment was the keynote of their notices and it was understandable. Yet no one asked why Tchaikovsky continued to write operas.

He heard the truth in Paris. He was despondent but not over-whelmed—he must have been getting used to this kind of thing—and had in any case a swift consolation. The Second Suite had been unreservedly welcomed in Moscow and plans were already afoot for repeat performances.

It is to be feared that the composer found this consolation fairly thin; he was rarely to judge his own work correctly and his passion for the theatre was too strong to be shifted. Yet the difference between the pasteboard drama of *Mazepa* and the cheerful charm of the Second Suite might well have struck anyone, even the man who had written both. The opera was competently written—he could scarcely be other than competent by this time—but the suite was much more, a charming example of his genius for handling an orchestra. The variety of the five movements, the economy, the fascinating rhythms and the delightful themes make the work a rare pleasure from the first Jeu de Sons to the final Danse Baroque.

Tchaikovsky probably thought less of the suite as a whole than of his splendidly humorous use of four accordions in the third movement, the Scherzo Burlesque. It lives up to the description. This was the first time accordions had been included in a classical work and he had great fun with them; they are only used for a total of some sixty bars but most effectively. Also included in the orchestra was a tambourine and harp with very telling use of glissandi by the latter in the fourth movement Rêves d'enfant by a devotee of the instrument.

The suite was described on the score by the composer as *Suite caractéristique*. Like everything he wrote that had to do with music the title was exact. This is characteristic Tchaikovsky but a side of him all too little heard. He had enjoyed writing the work as he enjoyed writing the First Suite—the mood was as identical as the place he had written them in—and the enjoyment and the high spirits come through to the listener with a thrill of pleasure and surprise.

It is a great pity that so few people are allowed today to share the pleasure. The Second Suite is played little if at all more often than its predecessor and concert audiences are the losers for it. That it is beautifully constructed goes without saying, that it is all great and tuneful fun cannot be said too often. Regular performances of the first two suites would make a serious dent in the stubbornly prevailing impression of Tchaikovsky as the melancholy Slav.

CHAPTER EIGHTEEN

A Home of His Own
1884–5

Tchaikovsky's next year was an eventful one—one in which he was to change his mode of life drastically. But that was far from all; in the period ending in April 1885 he was to be decorated by the Tsar, to write his popular Third Suite and strange *Concert Fantasy* and the opening pages of yet another opera, to find a country home for himself, to re-establish relations with Balakirev and his group, and to begin the *Manfred* Symphony.

The decoration by the Tsar—the Order of St. Vladimir of the Fourth Class—for which he had to return from Paris in the spring of 1884 was a confirmation of his position as Russia's great contemporary composer. But it was more than that. Aleksandr III did not decorate him just because public demand insisted on it (the public being, of course, the aristocracy and influential musicians); he really liked his music and proved it in the most arduous way, by sitting through the entire performance of *Mazepa*. This would have been a rare enough sign of condescension by a Tsar whatever the work (etiquette and inclination usually resulted in members of the royal family coming into their box when an opera was half-way through or leaving it before it ended) but the incident was all the more remarkable because the composer was not in the theatre—he was on his way to Paris.

Nor was this the end of the Tsar's obvious interest; he sat through and congratulated the composer on *Yevgeny Onyegin*, which was having a long run in Petersburg. He returned more than once to it, an unprecedented honour. Most remarkable of all in the political climate of the day, he told Tchaikovsky that he would be permitted to write an opera on Pugachev, the Cossack rebel Pyotr Ilyich's great-grandfather had fought against. This was a quite staggering compliment. One might think that such an opera could only be the means of increasing whatever patriotic fervour was still left in Russia but the usual court and government mind did not work that way; the mere suggestion that a man could rise against his Tsar was considered highly unwise, not to say treasonable.

Tchaikovsky did not in fact write the opera. He took up a subject which Modest, rashly it could be thought, claimed as his suggestion. This was to be *The Enchantress*.

But first came the Third Suite and the *Concert Fantasy*, both written at Kamenka in the summer of 1884 and both played for the first time early in 1885.

The suite arrived first; it was performed in both capitals in January. In Petersburg it had the benefit of a world-famous conductor, none other than Von Bülow on a triumphant return visit to Russia as conductor and soloist. His admiration for Tchaikovsky's music knew few bounds and he made the very most of the suite. Everyone, public and critics, hailed it as one of the best things Tchaikovsky had written. The Moscow première a few days later lacked the sparkle of the northern city's effort, possibly because Von Bülow had changed roles and was playing the First Piano Concerto in the same programme, which rather stole the thunder. Nevertheless, the suite was praised.

This suite has become too popular to discuss at length. Whether it is a substantial improvement on its two predecessors is questionable; there is some reason for thinking that chance alone has led to its elevation as Tchaikovsky's most successful composition in this genre. This is not to say that the suite is anything but excellent throughout; it has splendid themes, variety of mood and treatment, and the advantage of ending with a long and substantial movement that everyone has found memorable. This Theme and Variations is often played apart from the rest of the suite with much success (Tchaikovsky began the practice on his first concert tour) and it could be claimed with some reason that even he never excelled this example of the variation form. The suite in general is rather less joyous than its predecessors though it gives a similar impression of spontaneity in the writing. Like them it is light classical music at its best, varied, melodious and perhaps above all finished—the rich scoring is beyond praise.

There have been several splendid orchestrators in the past century—Borodin and Rimsky-Korsakov, Stravinsky and Shostakovich come naturally to mind—but Tchaikovsky's special and unrivalled gift was his ability to score superbly for every instrument, by itself, when blended with other instruments and again when used with full orchestra. The Third Suite offers a near-faultless example of this extraordinary talent.

The *Concert Fantasy* which Taneyev played for the first time in Moscow in March 1885 is a curious work. It puzzled the critics then and has puzzled them ever since. It began as a Third Piano Concerto, then, the composer's inventiveness for once giving out, dwindled to this queer hotchpotch, formless and leaving one with the feeling that Tchaikovsky had decided to display his gift for dazzling pianoforte writing. The solo part is not merely arduous to such a degree that few pianists can get through it without exhaustion but is fantastically difficult. It could be called bravura stretched to the point of excess. Yet when every criticism has been made the work has undoubted charm and one must regret, when regular public performance of pianoforte concertos is limited to so few works, that the *Concert Fantasy* is not given an occasional airing. The themes are not Tchaikovsky at his best—that is to say they are, for him, a little ordinary and even sentimental—but they have wide appeal and the work as a whole has moments of real grandeur.

ii

The difficulty he had in writing this work and his inability to extend it to concerto form was not without significance. A fluent and highly skilled writer like Tchaikovsky does not dry up for nothing. There were two special reasons for the fact that the world intruded on him with particular vehemence at this time. The lesser reason—though Tchaikovsky would not have described it so then—was the serious illness of Kotek. The young man had contracted tuberculosis and was about to go to Davos for treatment. As Tchaikovsky well knew—these were the days when the disease was regarded as virtually incurable—the move to Davos was almost equivalent to a death-warrant.

Kotek could not be said to have behaved well to the composer—his withdrawal from the Violin Concerto was cowardly to say the least—but Tchaikovsky typically remembered only the good things:

Kotek enthusiastically praising him to Nadyezhda Filaretovna, Kotek practising the concerto at Clarens hour by hour, day after day. Also typically, he was to hurry to Davos that winter of 1884 and to leave instructions that all expenses in connexion with the illness were to be charged to him. Kotek in fact died in the first days of 1885 but in the previous summer Tchaikovsky felt worried about him and this was sufficient to cloud his usually fertile musical imagination.

Yet this was the lesser by far of the troubles of that summer and the work he did then, troubles which even show through the would-be high spirits of the Third Suite. The second reason was a sad one; after nineteen years of bliss at Kamenka the place was losing its charm for him and so its power to draw good work from him. In most of those years a great deal of his best work was initiated, written, or completed at Kamenka or inspired by its domestic peace, its fascinating rural surroundings. By the summer of 1884 the magic had largely gone.

There were many explanations. First the most painful was the change in Aleksandra. Her health fluctuated; the now regular trips abroad to take the waters did her good but could not cure her. She was ill and was not to recover. To Pyotr Ilyich she was a shadow of herself when there and when she was not the thought of her unwell distressed him beyond measure. In those melancholy days he learned the truth that when one loves no scenery on earth can compete with feeling for a human being. The beauties of Kamenka might not have existed so little did he see in them.

If Aleksandra was often absent during his summer months at Kamenka, others were only too much present. The children had grown up. They brought their friends home and the house was stuffed with boys and girls turning the place upside down. Tchaikovsky was one of those men who love small children much more than the hearty types they so often turn into, and however glad he may have been to see the young people enjoying themselves, the racket they made effectually prevented him from concentrating for any length of time on composition; either they insisted on having his company or they made such a din that he had to walk out to the village in despair.

Then there were the usual hangers-on. Every large Russian house had them, as readers of Russian literature will know. At Votkinsk there were cousin Lydya and aunt Lisa, at Alapayevsk cousin Anastasia, and at Verbovka in 1884 Tchaikovsky found Lyov's mother and her daughter Vera Vasilyevna. Time had changed them; they were far from the cheerful and loving people of Petersburg and Hapsal days. The mother, Aleksandra Ivanova Davydova, was going blind and depended on company, the daughter had married unhappily and was for ever hinting to Pyotr Ilyich that she could have been happy if he had only married her; her half-melancholy, half-flirtatious references to the love they had for one another in past years and the suggestion that she still felt as before drove him almost distracted. Mother and daughter were obviously there for life in the Russian way; neither Aleksandra nor Lyov would have dreamt of asking them to leave.

There was one ray of sunshine in this gloomy summer and one only. During a walk he went deep into a wood a few miles from Kamenka. In the centre of the wood he came across a forester's cottage. The man was pleased to see him—passers-by were rare—and asked him in. He met the wife and her child, a girl of four. He and the little girl took to each other at once and every day after that until he had to leave Tchaikovsky walked to the forester's cottage to see her, talk to her and play with her. They became great friends. 'I love her dearly,' he wrote.

Had she lived he might not have had the heart to give up Verbovka as his summer retreat but to his fury she died that winter of diphtheria. He was furious as well as frantic with grief because, as he said, her life had been thrown away like the lives of thousands of children every year. 'She need not have died if our people would take the most elementary precautions.'

After that everything pointed to an end to Kamenka as a home— the only home he had ever known since he took the professorship at Moscow in 1866, nearly twenty years earlier. His apartments in Moscow were never more for him than perching places for they provided none of the essentials to home life for him, a woman or children or, failing them, country surroundings. Essentials to good composition too; and as in the last resort his music always had the final say, he took the plunge; in February 1885 he rented a furnished house at Maidanovo.

With this move he began an association with the Klin district which was to last for the rest of his life. Maidanovo was a village on the outskirts of Klin and Klin, for Tchaikovsky, had two great advantages, it was surrounded by fertile and beautiful country and it was on the main railway and road between Moscow and Petersburg; from it he could reach Moscow fairly soon and was at the same time within reasonable striking distance of the northern capital. Before his life here is described, what was virtually a birthday note in his diary (actually made on 6 May 1884) must be printed. The reader will have seen the kind of life lived by Pyotr Ilyich and will draw his own conclusions. How little Tchaikovsky saw himself as he was is illustrated here. 'I shall very soon be forty-four,' he writes. 'What I have been through in those years and—without any false modesty— how little I have accomplished! I have not written a single perfect composition. I have written nothing worthy to stand as a model for others to follow. At this age I am still searching and still vacillating. I read nothing and I know nothing.' He adds, 'I don't want to be young again. Once is enough!'

iii

Readers of biography have often asked for a description of the simple, everyday actions of the principal figure, things they can understand better than the work he does and which help to bring a great man alive. Surrounded by trees, Maidanovo was beautifully situated in a large park bordering a river and Tchaikovsky took his walks through the flower garden, then struck into the wood or sauntered by the river bank according to his mood.

His first walk was usually made as soon as he had got out of bed and dressed, which he did every morning at seven-thirty to the minute. At half past eight he breakfasted—usually taking no more than several cups of strong tea with lemon—went for another walk, then settled back in a chair and, helped by many cigarettes, read any book he fancied, or studied—in the summer months of 1885 he was trying hard to learn English which he could read after a fashion but not speak. After an hour or so of this he took a third walk and came back to compose. He broke off to lunch at midday, a substantial meal washed down with much wine. More composition followed until five or six o'clock when he walked again and came back to the evening meal. After this he worked once more, helped by stronger drink than wine—brandy or vodka most commonly—until late at night. A final walk, and bed well after midnight.

This was his unvarying routine when alone. Often he had guests, picked ones. Modest, the Jurgensons, Kashkin (sometimes with his wife and daughter), Taneyev, Albrecht and Hubert—these were the regulars. Occasionally he would invite a famous soprano or tenor who was to sing in one of his operas, the producer, the conductor, or one of his Petersburg friends down in Moscow for a few days. But whoever was there the rule remained absolute, that if he felt in the mood he was to be left alone to work until evening.

He had a curious way of indicating his wishes. If he wanted to work through the day he would not speak during breakfast. If he felt unlike composition that day he would invite his guest to walk with him after breakfast and would talk freely and entertainingly. That was a sign that he would spend much of the day catching up with his vast correspondence and dealing with the many begging letters he received. If he did feel like composition no one saw him except at meals until the period after the evening meal. He was then at his guests' disposal.

As a host he was a great favourite, generous, undemanding, tactful, unfussy, and a fine and amusing conversationalist. Modest, Jurgenson, Kashkin and his wife all commented later on these lively evenings and the good talk everyone enjoyed. They do not seem to have cared so much for the food; Tchaikovsky relied absolutely on the choice of his manservant Aleksei. Nor did they admire the furnishings, also the work of Aleksei, but Tchaikovsky seems never to have questioned his taste; all he had eyes for were his piano and desk and the pictures of other composers and the family spread liberally over the walls.

The liveliness of the Maidanovo evenings, like the speed of the evening work when Tchaikovsky was composing, owed a great deal to the drink taken. The Russians have always been heavy drinkers, partly because the severity of the climate demands it, and Tchaikovsky could drink most of his guests under the table if so inclined. He was not so inclined, he was no Rubinstein, but when the company was all male it was generally understood that some stiff drinking would be the order of the day at Maidanovo and the conversation flourished accordingly.

Tchaikovsky was one of the most open-eyed drinkers; he knew just what he was doing and could be worth hearing on the subject of teetotallers. Gone was the old sense of weakness and sin; he needed the drink and blessed the day he first came across it, and if he met a critic he would point to the work that drink had made possible. When he read cranks he made gentle fun of them, as he did of one of Tolstoy's many extreme followers who had founded a Tolstoyan colony and, describing the life lived there, wrote an article in which he condemned the 'poison' of alcohol. Tchaikovsky read the article and protested humorously in his diary that he could not live without such poison. Of course it could be abused, like everything else in life, but that was a far cry from the Tolstoyan 'boasting that he has never known the pleasures of vodka or any other alcoholic drink'. He asks mildly, 'Isn't it unjust and a little arrogant to judge other people by oneself and to forbid them everything one doesn't happen to like? How about me, for example? Every evening I drink "more than is good for me" as such a man would say. But I can't live any other way.'

He did not want, or think that he ought, to live any other way, what was more, and continues his note with 'Anyway, is this man right? When I drink I feel absolutely wonderful, especially at first when gently tipsy, and my brain functions a good deal better than it does when I abstain from the "poison"!' And he dealt with the usual accusation, that drinking ruined a man's constitution, with 'If my health has declined, I haven't noticed it, nor has anyone else. For the rest, *Quid licet Jovi, non licet bovi.*'

His life proved the truth of his claim that, if anything, alcohol preserves a man; he was never to know serious illness except the sort that comes from the highly sensitive nervous system he was born with, and up to a few days before his death he remained strong and healthy.

iv

These convivial Maidanovo evenings revealed only one aspect of Tchaikovsky—the man-of-the-world aspect, the good talker and excellent host. Another side of him is shown by the childlike man who gravitated naturally towards children for his chief pleasure and had a genius for getting on terms with them. One reason for his restlessness at Kamenka recently had been the growth of the children he had loved so much in their early years; to him the movement into teens and twenties was mostly sad; he remembered his own childhood days with as great a pang of regret as he thought of his youth and young manhood with a shudder.

When the Kashkins came to Maidanovo their young daughter usually came with them. In the first Maidanovo year she was thirteen but her love for Tchaikovsky had begun with her first memories of him, when she was six. That evening her mother and father had a number of people in to play cards and Sofya Nikolayevna was allowed to stay up and help to carry round refreshments.

To make the story comprehensible it should be said that one of the Kashkins' frequent visitors was the actor and Conservatoire professor of dramatic art, I. V. Samarin, a rather vain man who had the habit of claiming the attention of a roomful by suddenly breaking out of normal conversation into a stentorian monologue taken from his latest play; it was a habit that could be effective or boring. In the present case it was frightening.

When the cardplayers were ready for refreshment on this particular evening Sofya's *nyanya* carried round a trayful of glasses of tea and Sofya carefully followed with a bowl of sugar. When she came to the table where Samarin, N. S. Zverev, and Tchaikovsky were sitting, the actor, seeing a chance to shine, abruptly addressed a 'thunderous monologue' straight at the child.

'Understanding nothing,' says Sofya, 'I was struck dumb and quite lost my head. I couldn't move because Samarin kept one hand on the sugar basin and when I tried to detach it from him he said loudly, "Wait, wait. Stay where you are. I'm going to have more sugar. Besides, I like little messengers."'

He did not help himself to more sugar but launched himself again into the monologue at the top of his voice. Sofya was terrified. And at this point Tchaikovsky, seeing what she felt, came to the rescue; he gave her the bowl of sugar and stopped the declamation in midstream with a few sharp words.

'To this day,' recalls Sofya Nikolayevna, 'I remember how grateful I felt. I can't remember what he looked like then; all I felt was a general impression of a friendly man, a man with whom you feel you can be simple and at ease although you also feel that he is not really simple but special—but what his specialness is you don't know.'

This extremely pertinent account of child reaction was followed by another incident about a year later. 'I ran out of the nursery and saw Tchaikovsky coming out of the ante-room. I was very glad to see him but for a moment or two I couldn't say anything because I had just noticed how grey his hair was.'

Tchaikovsky understood immediately that she was embarrassed, walked up to her and with a 'May I kiss you?' bent down and kissed her on the top of her head. 'I'm awfully fond of kissing children on their hair!' he explained in a boyish fashion which at once put Sofya at her ease.

He knew that she had begun to have pianoforte lessons from Zverev and asked how she was getting on and whether she would like to play for him. They went into the music room where she proudly went through her scales. 'And do you play anything of mine?' he asked afterwards.

'Now by this time,' says Sofya, 'I knew that he was a composer and very celebrated—in fact in my eyes he had a kind of halo—but for all that I wanted to show off, so with great pride I played an old-fashioned 'French Song' from his *Children's Album*. He said it was very good and my day was made.'

From that time onwards she loved him dearly and waited impatiently for him to come to her parents' apartment to play cards or hear or talk music, theatre, or books. She had divined as children do that he loved children and persuaded herself that he loved her best. Looking back when she had grown up, she understood what a rare thing his manner with children was: 'He treated them particularly nicely and kindly. Like my father he seemed to know that grown-ups must not talk to children in a special way, talking down to them, but simply, as if they were grown-up too. He always did this, that's why I and other children were so happy to be with him; he felt one of us.'

By Maidanovo days, when the Kashkins came up for a weekend, Sofya was more observant. She noticed, for instance, that Tchaikovsky could never go out for a walk without being hailed by groups of the village children. 'They had discovered the times he went out and, as he always gave them something, sweets or a small coin, they used to lie in wait for him.'

One day he and Kashkin went out for one of their usual country walks when Tchaikovsky felt in his pockets and, grimacing, said that he had forgotten to bring anything for the children. Not wanting to disappoint them, he told Kashkin to continue by the usual footpath; he would make a detour and meet him in the forest they were making for. But when the children saw Kashkin alone 'they at once guessed Pyotr Ilyich's ruse, rushed off and rounded him up in great triumph. And in the end my father heard Tchaikovsky running towards him, crying, "Nikolai Dmitrievich, lend me a coin or two, will you?"'

Tchaikovsky, it may be added, was not content to spoil the village children, much though he liked to see their faces light up when he came into sight. He thought further: why were they always free to catch him during his walks? He asked the local priest who told him that there was no school and no money for one. Tchaikovsky forthwith provided the money and guaranteed it in the future, and the school was opened early in 1886. And though Tchaikovsky was not to stay at Maidanovo all the rest of his life he never forgot the children or their school; each year his grant arrived to the day.

One last word about the daily life at Maidanovo. If Tchaikovsky had any doubts about the growth of his fame, they were unpleasantly dispelled by the crowds of tourists who found their way to the village seeking autographs, wishing to show him their work, to beg or simply stare. With them he dealt firmly. He got Aleksei to paint and fix to the entrance gate a notice: 'Pyotr Ilyich Tchaikovsky. Receives Mondays and Thursdays, 3 to 5. Otherwise not at home. Please do not ring or knock.'

The first work he did in this first home of his own was to revise an old opera, *Vakula the Smith*. Unlike most of his operatic works, which he usually came to dislike, he had rarely wavered in his opinion of its merits. He did see plenty of scope for revision, however, and believing correctly that with his present-day reputation he could almost dictate presentation of a work, he got down to the rewriting, including a change of title. It now became *Cherevichki*, the Russian name for the boots worn by the women in Kamenka.

After this revision, which he made with great speed, he turned with a certain reluctance to *Manfred*. This symphony had been in his mind for two years, ever since Balakirev had suggested it to him. When he went up to Petersburg about the staging of *Cherevichki* he seized the chance to have a word with Balakirev about the symphony. Much had happened to Balakirev and his group since the days when he had recommended *Romeo and Juliet* and praised *The Tempest* and First Symphony and we must go back some years to understand what Tchaikovsky found when he called on him.

CHAPTER NINETEEN

Balakirev and the *Manfred* Symphony
1885–6

The new history of Balakirev had best begin in 1867, a few weeks before he came down to Moscow to hear Berlioz and met Pyotr Ilyich for the first time. He had just had a spectacular triumph in Petersburg, having been appointed conductor of the Russian Musical Society concerts in place of his great enemy Anton Rubinstein. When he returned to Petersburg after talking with Tchaikovsky he soon took another forward step, being appointed Director of the Free School of Music in place of Lomakin.

In the next eighteen months he did a great deal to popularize advanced Russian music and the more adventurous works of western composers. He made plenty of enemies and one of particular power, the Grand-Duchess Yelena Pavlovna. She saw him oust Rubinstein, her special protégé, with anger and determined to get rid of him.

As she did. Balakirev put no store on charm or tact; indeed he often went to the other extreme, setting people by the ears for what appeared no better reason than contrariness; he always said exactly what he thought and usually very pungently. He would not fawn or even be moderately pleasant to wealthy or high-born patrons who did not care for music. He might have paid court to the Grand-Duchess, who was interested in music of a kind, and won her over to his way of thinking—even she might have found it hard to resist his immense conviction and physical mesmerism—but he would not. He ignored her and all who sympathized with her.

In Petersburg in the eighteen-sixties one could not offend anyone close to the throne and hope to survive. By May 1869, he had been forced to resign the conductorship.

These events were followed with high feeling in Moscow where, thanks largely to Tchaikovsky's advocacy, Balakirev's reputation actually stood higher than in his own city. The forced resignation infuriated Tchaikovsky and he worked on Nikolai Rubinstein to the point that the Director offered Balakirev a professorship at the Moscow Conservatoire.

Balakirev refused with a modesty that charmed and surprised everyone in the Conservatoire; he was not fitted for such a post, he said, because his technical background was faulty.

He could not be persuaded to change his mind so Tchaikovsky, whose temperament demanded action of some sort, risked his own future by printing an article in a Moscow journal praising Balakirev and openly criticizing the moves that had led to his resignation.

The article did not change the situation, it merely relieved Pyotr Ilyich's feelings, but it led to much for himself. Somehow he escaped official rebuke—which might have extended to his own dismissal— and he won the gratitude and respect of Balakirev, already well disposed. That summer Balakirev's father was ill at Klin, and after his death his son stayed in Moscow until the late autumn. It was then that he suggested *Romeo and Juliet*—a practical and historic repayment of debt.

For the next year or so the two men saw a fair amount of each other and corresponded largely about *Romeo and Juliet*, but towards the end of 1870 Balakirev began to fade out of Petersburg musical life and Tchaikovsky lost touch with him. The Free School Concerts which Balakirev had taken up did not pay their way and he was forced to take a menial job in the goods department of the Warsaw Railway in Petersburg. Three-quarters of the way through the 1871–2 season the concerts collapsed—people refused to support them—and he lost his Directorship. This blow was followed by the loss of the railway job, and for the next four or five years he withdrew from all public life. He went through a spiritual crisis from which he emerged as fiery a believer as he had formerly been a scathing sceptic. He kept himself alive by taking a few pupils. Nobody in his old group saw him; Tchaikovsky did not hear from him.

The death of the Grand-Duchess saw the beginnings of a more liberal-minded phase; everybody in Petersburg who knew anything about music was well aware that Russian music could not afford the loss of such a man. Glinka's sister, Lyudmila Shestakova, helped him begin his climb back into public life. She alone had refused to accept his withdrawal from music and under her influence he began to compose again and to take up the long-planned editing of Glinka's scores.

When Aleksandr II was assassinated in March 1881 the last obstacle to Balakirev's reinstatement disappeared. Once more the Muscovites tried to tempt him to their Conservatoire; after Tchaikovsky refused the Directorship it was offered to Balakirev. He stuck to his plea of insufficient technical knowledge but at once accepted the direction of the Free School and the conductorship of the concerts when it was offered later that year. He finished his *Tamara* about which he had written to Tchaikovsky many years earlier—it was first performed in March 1883—just one month after receiving the official benediction of an appointment as Director of the Imperial Court Chapel.

It was a few months before this appointment that Tchaikovsky heard from him again after a break of nearly ten years. He had not been without information all this time but the information did not come from an unbiased quarter. He kept up with the Rimsky-Korsakovs and Rimsky-Korsakov was already in the early stages of the resentment that was later completely to distort his view of Balakirev, that his teaching had deprived him of thorough technical training.

Unhappily Tchaikovsky did not at all understand the noble character of Borodin any more than he understood the extraordinary merits of the Borodin Second Symphony when it was played in Moscow in the same programme as his *Capriccio Italien*. Instead of Borodin's kindly and concerned comments on Balakirev, therefore, he had the rather waspish ones of the Rimsky-Korsakovs. He took them with a grain of salt—as will be seen, he disliked gossip—but he was forced to agree with Rimsky-Korsakov that Balakirev had done him harm as well as immense good and this, with his hatred of interference, may have prevented him from trying to come to the rescue of his old hero.

But if he had any reservations about Balakirev by the time he received his letter of November 1882 they did not survive a reading. All the old magic came back because the vigorous letter was in character; it proposed a work which, in the writer's view, only Tchaikovsky could compose and a work which ought to be written for moral as well as musical reasons.

The suggestion was a symphony based on Byron's *Manfred*. Balakirev obviously had the Symphonie Fantastique in mind and had first asked Berlioz if he would write the new symphony. This was far back in 1867 when the master visited Russia at the suggestion of Stasov and Balakirev. Berlioz had refused; he was too old, he said. Now, fifteen years later, Balakirev reverted to the idea after a hearing of *Francesca da Rimini*; that convinced him, he told Tchaikovsky, that he was the only man who could take the place of Berlioz. He added a typical 'providing you take great pains, subject your work to stringent self-criticism, let your imagination run freely and above all, don't hurry'.

He enclosed a detailed programme for the symphony with a final 'The subject is not only very profound but in line with present-day feelings since all modern man's troubles stem from the fact that he has no idea how to preserve his ideals—they rot away and leave nothing but bitterness in the soul. And that explains all the spiritual sufferings of our age.'

Tchaikovsky took the adjuration 'don't hurry' in quite a different sense from that intended by Balakirev; he was not anxious to go back to the kind of plan beloved by the Balakirev circle and particularly not in a symphony. He had not written a note of it when, late in 1884, he went up to Petersburg and had a long talk with Balakirev. He found the master irresistible as ever for all his moods and left him committed to the work.

ii

He found that youth had succumbed to the old fascination; in the few years since his return to normal musical life Balakirev had attracted a new generation of Russian modernists, all of whom worshipped him. Musorgsy was dead and Rimsky-Korsakov disapproving but Kui was there still and Borodin. To Tchaikovsky, however, the newcomers were the real live-wires of this Balakirev evening and one of them he knew very well.

This one was an ex-pupil of his at the Conservatoire, Sergei Mikhailovich Lyapunov. He had joined Balakirev as assistant at the Court Chapel and was to be the sole faithful disciple after his master's death. With Lyapunov in Balakirev's rooms Tchaikovsky found a number of extremely bright and enthusiastic young men. He knew only one of them slightly; he was Anatoly Konstantinovich

Lyadov, slightly senior to the others, a fine pianist and promising composer. Lyadov had just gone back to the Petersburg Conservatoire, where he had studied under Rimsky-Korsakov, as professor in harmony and composition. Together with Lyapunov and Balakirev he had been given a grant by the Imperial Geographical Society to collect and score folk songs in several districts. One of these districts, Tchaikovsky now heard with great interest, was the province in which he had been born.

The other unusually gifted young man present that evening, like the rest of the crowd except the few elders, was unknown to Tchaikovsky, yet was to become one of his most devoted admirers. This was Aleksander Konstantinovich Glazunov. Tchaikovsky had heard about the feats of this prodigy who had written his First Symphony, First Quartet and Pianoforte Suite at the age of sixteen, all so highly thought of that the extraordinary sight had been seen in Petersburg of the music of a Balakirev and Rimsky-Korsakov disciple (inspired by the first and taught by the second) being played by Anton Rubinstein at a concert of the Musical Society. When Tchaikovsky met Glazunov at the Balakirev gathering the boy was nineteen, his symphony had just had its first foreign performance, and all musical people in the city were prophesying the most brilliant future for him.

One would never have guessed this from Glazunov's attitude when Tchaikovsky entered the room, nor would one have thought that any of the young men there were anything but overgrown schoolboys. Glazunov explains: 'Although the Balakirev circle was no longer as isolated or exclusive as it had been before my time, Tchaikovsky did not belong to it and that at once raised a barrier in our minds. Balakirev used to hold him up to us as an example of fine writing but was critical of his deficiencies. We esteemed *Romeo and Juliet, The Tempest, Francesca*, and the Finale of the Second Symphony; the rest of his work we either did not know well or it did not fit in with our tenets.'

For all this, the news that Tchaikovsky was to brave the temple of modernism had caused a considerable flutter. 'We young members discussed the visit very seriously. How should we treat this outsider who was not a member of our group? We decided to be very reserved with him. The result was a certain stiffness in the atmosphere when Tchaikovsky arrived. It did not last long. We were all staggered by his dignity, his refinement, and well-bred self-command that we thought of as exclusively European. We began to breathe freely and when he spoke the atmosphere of reserve—you could call it disapproval—melted away because he obviously felt no constraint whatever. We younger ones said nothing, partly because we were overcome by admiration at the way he spoke about music, partly for fear of putting ourselves forward. *Manfred* was talked about, I remember, and at one point Lyapunov and I each played our works.'

It may be that Balakirev sensed that Tchaikovsky was stealing the evening and his disciples' admiration; he was a proud and touchy man. At any rate he decided to introduce a controversial note—for, as Glazunov puts it, 'in spite of his genuine cordiality and generous hospitality he loved to make caustic and derisive remarks calculated to offend one or more of his guests'.

He decided to strike home: 'He began to describe in sharp and uncomplimentary terms a Moscow musician and his wife, knowing them to be friends of his guest of honour.'

For a moment all the disciples felt uncomfortable and Glazunov had the impression that the evening was on the verge of collapse, 'but Tchaikovsky quickly and playfully took up the remark; he showed no sign of offence, but merely asked, did Balakirev know them, had he met them?'

'To this Balakirev returned an evasive answer—everybody spoke about them, it was common property, etc., etc. Tchaikovsky made only one comment and made it in the friendliest manner: Hearsay, he said mildly, was a dangerous stick to lean on.'

The reproof and the way in which it was made, allowing of no quarrel or even argument, settled Balakirev: 'his eyes shifted about nervously and he made no more attacks that evening.'

All the young men were tremendously impressed and, soon after Tchaikovsky left, Glazunov, Lyadov, and Lyapunov went off to a tavern to talk over their visitor. Lyadov summed up the evening by saying that it had been a rare honour to meet such a great composer but what they all talked about until the early hours was the enormous charm of Tchaikovsky's personality, his tact, and his moral courage. Never before had they seen the hallowed Balakirev bearded in his own den and worsted without a single harsh word or lifted voice. From that moment Tchaikovsky and his music had doughty champions in the Balakirev circle.

iii

What the young disciples did not know and could scarcely have guessed was that for all his sangfroid and dislike of gossip Tchaikovsky had come under the spell again in spite of everything Balakirev could do to ruin the effect of his own strong personality and genuine wish to glorify Russian music. Within a few months, by April 1855, he had settled into Maidanovo and down to *Manfred*. After that he never seriously turned away from the symphony he had delayed so long. There were times when he felt that it would wear him out and at one point he complained rather curiously that he would become a Manfred if he went on with it much longer. When the work became too arduous and he felt downright ill—the symphony was drawing out to a fantastic length to include all Balakirev's instructions—he turned for a day or two to his new opera *The Enchantress* with enormous relief. He found it beautifully easy to write. This ease was significant too, though he was not aware of it. Occasionally he put in an hour or two on yet another future opus, a sextet, but for most of the spring and summer and the greater part of the autumn he laboured on *Manfred*.

Early in October it was done and six months later played for the first time in Moscow. It was received with a certain bewilderment that has lasted to this day. Kui, strangely enough, was its most enthusiastic supporter, a new role for him and a lonely one on this occasion. The great length of the work places a severe strain on everybody, orchestra and audience alike, and it is difficult to think that the programme is sufficient to carry such a burden.

It is surprising that Balakirev, who first thought of Tchaikovsky as the obvious composer because he had just heard a performance of *Francesca*, did not follow this thought to its logical conclusion. Why he suggested a symphony after listening to a symphonic poem is a mystery; it would seem that he was influenced by purely literary considerations.

At first Tchaikovsky announced almost automatically that this was his finest composition to date. He had forgotten all his weariness of the previous summer with Manfred and his doings, a Manfred he was afraid he would turn into if he went on long enough. That this remark indicated clearly that he was tackling the wrong subject did not dawn for a long time although it was no doubt symptomatic that he refused to allow Jurgenson to pay him for the printed score; it would be lucky if it was played once in a decade, he said. Eventually

—in 1889—he turned right round and damned everything but the first movement. He described the work as repulsive, the second and third movements as trivial, and the last as impossible. He said it must be made into a symphonic poem.

This is a pretty comprehensive writing-off. He was too severe. The last movement with its pseudo-church music does seem to be beyond the pale—it is certainly an attempt to hit below the belt—but with this admittedly considerable exception there is much to admire. The Manfred theme is altogether fine—a large and noble theme treated in every conceivable manner throughout the symphony but used at its most impressive in the opening movement. One has glimpses of Byron's hero—there are moments of real feeling—and the almost complete oblivion that has fallen on the symphony cannot be justified; we are not so rich in symphonic wealth as all that. A success it can never be; Tchaikovsky was no Manfred; but the splendours are there and the public ought to be allowed the chance of relishing them from time to time.

CHAPTER TWENTY

Composer-Conductor

1886–7

Two weeks after the *Manfred* first performance Tchaikovsky set off for his most romantic and, though he could not know it, one of his most triumphant vacations. He was bound for Tiflis, now Tbilisi, a place which to a Muscovite was synonymous with the ends of the earth.

Anatoly had been posted to Tiflis. That was the origin of the journey. It does not seem that Anatoly had any thought of trying to persuade his famous brother to risk the dangerous roads and appallingly dirty hotels between Russia proper and its outlying Trans-Caucasian province. The initiative seems to have come from a local musician, Mikhail Mikhailovich Ippolitov-Ivanov, the conductor of the Tiflis Symphony Orchestra and the genial inspiration behind the flourishing arts movement there.

As soon as Ippolitov-Ivanov heard that a Tchaikovsky had come to the town he got in touch with him, persuaded him to join the board of the local musical society, and, later, begged him to use his influence to get the great composer there.

The two men put their heads together. What, short of an Anatoly in trouble, could they put forward as a convincing reason for his brother to make the journey? As Anatoly was flourishing and had a loving wife and child with him this excuse would not hold water even with the unsuspecting Pyotr Ilyich. Anatoly finally produced the answer as Ippolitov-Ivanov recalled long afterwards: 'He said that his brother loved the country with a passion and that he might be induced to come down to us if he suspected how beautiful our Caucasian countryside was.'

Thereafter a barrage of propaganda went out to Maidanovo about the semi-oriental beauties of Tiflis and its surroundings, of the magnificence of the Caucasus mountains which one crossed *en route*, of the fine city, the hospitable people, the great strides they were making in music and the greater still if a certain famous man would only appear to convert the waverers.

By the beginning of April 1886 Tchaikovsky had succumbed— he was fast growing into an inveterate traveller though he preferred to travel in comfort—and before the end of the month he was there after a journey which had taken in a visit to Ippolit on his ship at Taganrog, nights of fearsome discomfort at bug-ridden inns and days corkscrewing alarmingly up and down fabulously romantic mountain passes.

Like almost everybody who gets himself to Tiflis he found the journey handsomely repaid and shared the usual surprise that the city was so beautiful and so up to date with its theatre, opera house, and concert hall in which the latest plays and operas and symphonic works were performed, including his own. The countryside was all the conspirators had claimed and the climate divine.

The biggest and most joyful surprise, apart from seeing Anatoly and his family again, was the obvious determination of every musical person, not in Tiflis alone but in the entire vast province, to show appreciation of the visit of a great man. If Tchaikovsky doubted whether his fame extended farther than Moscow and Petersburg he was soon and unforgettably undeceived.

He had met Ippolitov-Ivanov once before, at the house of K. Y. Davydov, and now became very much attached to the enthusiastic young champion of Caucasian music who was also, as he demonstrated, a very good conductor. His feeling was reciprocated to the point of idolatry and the two men became almost inseparable. The gratified Tchaikovsky (he could never quite bring himself to take anything for granted) was escorted into the country, through the city and to every play, concert, and opera. He loved every moment of it. These wonderful people even had their own drink, and very potent it was.

The climax of his stay came on the first day of May when a gala performance of his work was given at the Opera House. Never in his life had he seen or heard such enthusiasm. Ippolitov-Ivanov had thought of everything, even of finding out by devious means what his favourite flower was. This flower did not grow in the Tiflis area, so Ippolitov-Ivanov sent to Kutasi, some three hundred miles away. He ordered an entire railway carriage to be filled with them.

When the composer entered the theatre he was simply staggered by the look and scent of it.

Spring that year [said Ippolitov-Ivanov] had been marvellous and the wealth of flowers was almost unbelievable—in particular, of Pyotr Ilyich's beloved lilies of the valley. So the theatre was decorated with greenery and an assortment of flowers and the box set apart for our dear guest and his relations was filled with lilies of the valley—Tchaikovsky was seated in an absolute bower of them.

Sharp at eight o'clock [Ippolitov-Ivanov continues], Pyotr Ilyich, his brother Anatoly Ilyich and his wife and daughter entered the theatre in which the whole of musical Tiflis had been waiting in impatient expectation for the best part of an hour. Everybody rose to their feet, and choir, chorus, soloists and audience burst out with 'Glory to our dear and honoured guest' which we took, with suitably altered words, from the first act of *Mazepa*, 'Praise to our great genius!'

Before the performance began musical teachers from Tiflis and every other large town within a radius of several hundred miles presented Tchaikovsky with a portrait of himself surrounded with a silver wreath, and a long line of city notables and leaders of local institutions followed with their own presentations, chiefly wreaths and costly silver gifts. After the performance the Musical Society arranged a vast banquet at which hundreds of people filled tables stretched the length of the great hall of the civic centre building. Addresses and toasts lasted into the small hours.

The guest of honour did not get back to Anatoly's house until close on dawn. 'Never have I known anything remotely like this before!' he wrote to Modest. 'The cheering seemed unending.'

He sailed a few days later from Batum for Italy but had to change his plans. Naples was cut off by cholera and the ship went on to Marseilles. Pyotr Ilyich proceeded to Paris and to another experience he was not to forget.

In Paris he was made much of for the first time, meeting Delibes, Lalo, and Fauré (whom he particularly liked) and being dined and fêted by all the musical leaders of the day. But what thrilled him was not these signs of fame but an evening he spent at the house of Pauline Viardot. He had always felt a sentimental regard for her, because she had taught Artôt and he listened patiently to a long recital of her relationship with the dead Turgenyev. He was re-warded beyond his wildest dreams when Viardot finally produced the autograph score of *Don Giovanni* and left him to pore over it by himself. He was still fingering it reverently two hours later. 'I felt as though I had spoken to Mozart and had shaken him by the hand,' he said afterwards, and those who know the magic of autograph scores by the great masters will understand exactly how he felt.

He was back at Maidanovo in time to enjoy the summer—he had become a keen, if haphazard gardener—and to exclaim in his note-book, 'I'm at my best when I'm alone with trees and flowers and books.' To which, being an honest man with a sense of purpose that no garden could entirely lull, he added, 'But God! How short life is and how much I still have to do!'

ii

By the beginning of the next year, 1887, this thought had driven him to what, given his temperament, can be described as little less than an act of heroism, or rather a succession of them. He decided that if he was to make his work known as he wanted it to be known throughout Russia and the West he must conduct it himself. He had listened to many, many performances under other conductors. He had praised often but still more often had writhed with anger at the travesty of his music that was dragged out of orchestra or singers. To this there was only one answer and after struggles that can scarcely be overestimated he made up his mind to conquer what he called 'the contemptible coward' in himself. He took lessons in conducting and, after surviving several rehearsals, took charge of the first performance of *Cherevichki* at the Bolshoi on the last day of January.

His conducting proved a greater success than the revived and recast opera (it had been greatly improved but his sense of humour had not changed for the better) and in spite of a sudden shock before the second performance when he heard that his eldest niece Tatyana had died of heart failure at a masked ball he carried on though feeling like death himself.

The experience did nothing to free him from the terrors of public appearances but he stuck to his guns and agreed to conduct an all-Tchaikovsky concert at Petersburg in March. His uncertain confi-dence was nearly shattered when he noticed Balakirev (whose conducting he particularly admired) sitting in the stalls at the final rehearsal, but somehow he got through the evening and on the first night won praise from everyone, even the critics—Kui was to say of his next opera that the conducting was a great deal better than the work.

He did not allow this new and forced interest to get in the way of composition; by May he had at last finished the orchestration of *The Enchantress*, had sketched out the beginnings of a new suite and made notes for the sextet that had been in his mind for more than a year. All this before, unable to resist Tiflis, he set off to go there by water, the inns of the previous year having effectively put him off the land route. He sailed down the Volga and across the Caspian without a hitch and spent nearly a month in Tiflis hearing music and watching plays and driving and walking out into the country so different from the trees and woods and rivers and villas of Maidanovo.

If he was not quite so happy there the second time it had nothing to do with the town or the country or the amazingly hospitable people but to the workings of his conscience. His old friend and champion, N. D. Kondratyev, who had placed Nizy at his disposal so often, was seriously ill and had been sent as a final resort to take the waters at Aix-la-Chapelle.

Tchaikovsky dreaded sick beds and invalids who could scarcely be recognized for the men they used to be. So do most of us. But unlike most of us he went just the same, making the long and tiring journey from Tiflis. He was at Aix-la-Chapelle by the end of July. It was obvious to him at once that Kondratyev was dying and that his death would be slow. He stayed on for six weeks, until his old friend no longer knew him.

What he felt during these six weeks is within the imagination of us all. What he wrote about it shows, as with his openly confessed fear of seeing Rubinstein's body, that he stood head and shoulders above ordinary men. He said: 'I sit in my hotel filled with thoughts that cause me extreme disquiet. Life is going by and nearing its end and I still don't understand it. What is more, far from trying to understand it I shirk all thoughts about another life and try to run away from them by thinking of something else. How can I be right? Is this the way to live? Look for instance at my behaviour now. Everybody is admiring the way I *sacrifice* myself by staying here but there is no question of sacrifice—I am leading a life of ease, stuffing myself with food and doing nothing but spend my money on luxuries although I know that other people need this money for necessities. What gross egotism! I don't act towards my neighbour as I ought.'

The final effort to be absolutely honest came with a diary note about his reactions to the dying man. 'I haven't felt *pity* once all day, only *horror* and a longing to be home.'

He was home by September after going to see Kondratyev's wife. Six weeks later he was continuing the fight to overcome his fears of conducting by taking on an even more formidable task—the first performance of *The Enchantress* at the Maryinsky. In spite of the usual rehearsal and first night attacks of nerves he looked calm enough when he stepped on to the rostrum and his conducting was praised by everyone.

This was about all that was praised. Once again a Tchaikovsky opera had failed convincingly. The libretto of *The Enchantress* is so stupid, even by operatic standards, that one is baffled to know why Tchaikovsky ever gave it a second thought. However, as we know, the most incredible stories can make great opera. *The Enchantress* did not and the blame for this must rest fairly and squarely on the composer. He had said again and again that he must be able to put himself into the place of his operatic characters if he were to write living music for them. How, one wonders, did he ever imagine that he could put himself into the place of a young widow who keeps an inn and fascinates in turn a prince and his son to such a degree that the princess poisons her and the prince murders his son and goes mad with remorse?

No doubt artists exist who could have performed the feat but not Tchaikovsky, and his attempt to write an opera on this and similar types of librettos merely shows how little he knew himself. In truth his imagination was a limited one and when he said that he must imagine himself into his characters he really meant that he must actually have met people who could stand as models—either that or could feel himself in the role, as he did with Onyegin.

When he failed completely to do this, as in *The Enchantress*, the characters become wooden and unbelievable and, worse, his music becomes flat. He was accused of failing to write music that created dramatic situations. The accusation was as true in *The Enchantress* as it would have been untrue in his symphonies or the two operas in which he felt completely at home.

He was not given long to brood about this new failure—treated, it should be said, with considerable gentleness by critics and public. The public simply stopped coming to the theatre, the critics preferred to look ahead to the future of this great composer who had merely taken a wrong turning. They even forebore to say another wrong turning. Towards the end of November he had a concert to conduct and a second première, this time in Moscow. The concert was an all-Tchaikovsky one, the novelty the Fourth Suite.

The concert was a roaring success and his spirits leaped. He felt, he said, that he had never conducted so well and that the audience knew it. They would not let him go. Even his experience at Tiflis paled before the Moscow cheers: 'I've never known such enthusiasm nor have I ever had such a triumph.'

At this distance from the concert it is not possible to know what the cheers were chiefly aimed at beyond Tchaikovsky himself; obviously the applause was deafening for every item—*Francesca*, the *Concert Fantasy*, songs, *1812*, excerpts from *The Enchantress* as well as the new suite. *1812* was certainly a winner at the end of the programme, but as one movement of the new suite had to be played twice it must be assumed that this work caught the public imagination.

Nearly one hundred years later, when it is no longer possible to watch this extremely handsome and graceful man conduct his work, the reaction to the suite has become more critical. It was called *Mozartiana* and is now not often played. This neglect is not without reason. Tchaikovsky truly loved Mozart and his own work often possesses a Mozartian grace, elegance, and wit. But when, as in the Fourth Suite, he actually uses Mozart's themes or what he chooses to regard as Mozartian themes the limitations of hero-worship at once become apparent. It may seem harsh to say that any orchestral work of Tchaikovsky is dull but that is the impression left by this suite; dull and even trivial in the sense that one has the feeling of the composer lashing himself up over very little. The previous three suites made no claim to depth but they had charm and they were Tchaikovsky in light and happy mood. In the last work he was to write of this kind only the lightness is left.

No considerations of this kind harried the composer at the end of 1887. He was to have second thoughts about this new work—he almost always did—but he was chiefly triumphant in quite another direction. He had won the fight to prove that he could conduct his own work—that was the real source of his pleasure. It was a moral victory and a practical one too. These efforts over the past twelve months to make a conductor of himself had a secondary purpose, to fit himself for a European concert tour. A few days before the end of the year he left for Germany, the first stage of his first tour.

CHAPTER TWENTY-ONE

European Tour and Fifth Symphony
1887–9

One concert tour is very much like another. The orchestras are good, bad, or indifferent, the public and critical reaction likewise. Meetings with local musicians form an inevitable part of the routine as do the dinners in the visitor's honour with the appropriate speeches. It is all very exhausting and, after a time, very boring. Tchaikovsky's tours during the next five years were to follow the pattern—they varied only when he visited the United States, still considered far away and which Russians had yet to conquer.

The first tour, however, is important and even vital. Especially for a man coming from a country which most people in the West continued to regard as barbaric. When Tchaikovsky left for Berlin he was embarking on a course that only the Germanic virtuoso Rubinstein had taken before him. Glinka's attempts to popularize his own work had been few and had failed. Tchaikovsky was trying to blaze a new trail as composer-conductor of genuine Russian music.

Readers of this book will perhaps have difficulty in seeing Pyotr Ilyich in the role of adventurer, and may wonder how a man who hated publicity and loved the country and all that the country implies ever managed to get himself on to the Berlin train late in December 1887.

The answer to this, as to so much in his life, is his love of music. He thought nothing of himself, he thought a great deal of his music. He regarded his music as his *raison d'être* for living. Without it he would have considered himself as one of life's most dismal failures. Whether he was just to himself or not we can decide for ourselves but the impulse to launch himself into a tour of this magnitude, involving weeks of living in the limelight and no private life whatever—everything he hated—is clear. Of course he enjoyed applause at the moment of receiving it as everyone does but this played little part in his venture. What he set out to do was to show Europe some of his work as he knew it ought to be played. He thought that the world would be the better for his music and had come reluctantly to the conclusion that he alone could, or would, interpret this music so that Europeans were given a fair chance of deciding whether it was good or not.

This first tour lasted three months. He conducted concerts of his own works in Leipzig, Hamburg, Berlin, Prague, Paris, and London. He did not have one failure. In London he came into contact with the insular arrogance so many foreign artists have had to endure; no one met him after a terrible journey across a rough Channel and far from being fêted he was left entirely to himself and to the mercies of the Russian Embassy. But if the musical organizers did not know their manners the English musical public atoned for the boorishness as they have so often had to do. They took to his music and made their feelings plain. Even the critics were kind though they pointed out with some justice that the composer might have treated them to some of his larger works—he conducted only the Serenade for Strings and the last movement of the Third Suite. He did not meet English composers because there were none.

In the London concert hall, as everywhere else on the tour, he had half won the fight before he ever lifted his baton. By this time, early in 1888, his hair and beard had turned completely white. It may be doubted whether a more romantic figure had ever ascended the conductor's podium, and the people who filled the hall were not only mesmerized by him but astounded that such grace and dignity could come out of a country which they thought of dimly as populated by bears, bottles of vodka, and muzhiks swathed in furs and driving troikas along snowy roads, when they were not too drunk to drive, that is. That a Russian could wear evening dress with more elegance than an Englishman had not occurred to them. Hence the shock. And to do them credit, pleasurable shock. And when this distinguished man played music which went straight to English hearts the battle was completely won. Never was England to lose its passion for the music of Tchaikovsky. And it may be added, never again was Tchaikovsky to be suffered to land there without a greeting which probably sickened him by its obsequiousness as much as the neglect of 1888 had done. But the people rose to him and his music. That he remembered.

Before London came Paris. There he was fêted to the point of satiety, by his own embassy, by all the leading composers and leaders of musical society—not at all the same thing—and by *émigré* Russians of every description. He was called on by Fauré, Gounod, Massenet, and Viardot amongst others. He gave two concerts at the Châtelet and conducted the Colonne at a private festival. He never had a moment to himself. He was the toast and talk of the town.

He might have been excused for thinking that he had gained a considerable triumph. Yet it was not so. All was gallic froth. When it came to the performances all was not so well. He had great difficulty in inducing the orchestra to follow his beat and not gallop off on its own, the audience cheered in the wrong places and the critics launched with much satisfaction one of those smart half-truths beloved of journalists. They had been reading Kui's recent book on music in Russia, appropriated great gulps of it and came out with a judgement supposedly all their own, that Tchaikovsky was not one of the true heirs of Glinka such as Kui, Borodin, and Rimsky-Korsakov, he was a Germanized Russian. Then, having seen him off in the train to London with enormous enthusiasm they promptly forgot all about him and his music and turned to the next sensation.

Kui's judgement has long since been put into perspective—the Balakirev circle was influenced knowingly by Liszt and Schumann just as much if not more than the early Tchaikovsky—but in 1888 the Paris critics annoyed Tchaikovsky. That is, when he was not laughing, for he had not long left a Germany in which the critics were complaining that he was a trifle too French.

In the eyes of the Parisian journalists he was a Russian version of Brahms and it was as well for the composure of Pyotr Ilyich, tired and sickened by meaningless adulation, that he had already met Brahms. His attitude to Brahms for the past few years had been less than generous and not typical of his usual reactions to other men's music. In many letters to Nadyezhda Filaretovna he attacked his contemporary quite savagely. The gist of his criticism of the man who was leading him in European popularity was that his work showed more intellect than feeling. No doubt he thought so but it was a superficial judgement nevertheless. It is difficult not to wonder whether his harsh words on Brahms were not due in some part to the fact that the German, who was not a theatre man like Pyotr

Ilyich, had had the sense not to try to write opera. Plain envy could have entered into it too, for Brahms was not only accepted by his own country much more quickly than Tchaikovsky by his but had made Tchaikovsky's struggle to get his work played in Germany much more difficult. It may even have occurred to him that he and Brahms were not as unalike as he could have wished.

Then, on the first day of 1888, the day after he had arrived in Leipzig on the opening of his tour, he found Brahms waiting to greet him in the house of the plucky soloist in his Violin Concerto, his young colleague at the Moscow Conservatoire who had moved to the Conservatoire at Leipzig. Bodsky introduced the men and Tchaikovsky's instinctive hostility began to wane. He found that Brahms was not at all the kind of man he had been picturing all these years. Instead of a dried-up and vanity-ridden intellectual he found 'a handsome man, rather short and stout . . . and very friendly'. When they sat down to a meal he discovered that Brahms liked a drink just as much as he did, that he was in fact quite a heavy drinker. This soothed him still further.

The course of their acquaintance was not without humour in the spectacle of Tchaikovsky fighting a losing battle with prejudice. After they had spent many hours together he noted, 'He tries really hard to be kind to me but we never become intimate because we don't fundamentally care for each other.'

The next day Brahms had become 'very pleasant and not nearly as vain as I expected'. Later again, he studied Brahms's head and found it fascinating: 'The soft contour with its pleasant curves, the longish grizzled hair, kind grey eyes and thick beard going white all re-minded me of the pure Russian type so often found in our priests.' This thought was hard to resist in a city where the fiercely Russian Pyotr Ilyich found himself surrounded by excessively Saxon faces. In the end Brahms, who must have worked quite hard with his visitor, won a 'He has a simple manner without a trace of vanity, a nice sense of humour and altogether left me with a very pleasant impression.'

The acceptance of Brahms (with certain reservations) was made a long business by the superior fascination of Grieg, who called at Brodsky's house to welcome Tchaikovsky just after they had all sat down. Tchaikovsky watched him walk into the room 'very short, middle-aged with a most fragile appearance, one shoulder higher than the other, fair hair brushed back, fair beard and moustache slight and almost boyish'.

Although Grieg was neither handsome nor immediately striking to look at, Tchaikovsky was at once won over by his manner: 'Unusually charming, and his small blue eyes, rather like the eyes of a child, fascinated me with their charm and candour.'

Their friendship progressed like lightning—'he has completely won my heart'—and Grieg's wife was soon included. Tchaikovsky found them both 'extraordinarily sympathetic and appealing'. They spent much of the time together at the dinners and concerts (Tchaikovsky not only had to conduct his own works but to listen to the work of other men) that seemed almost without end. Brodsky was a tower of strength, as was Alexander Siloti, an old Tchaikovsky student who had become professor in his turn as well as one of the most noted young Russian pianists of the day.

The musical fraternity of Leipzig generally wined and dined and praised their guest to the point of exhaustion and the reception of the First Suite, which he conducted, and a performance of the Trio and First Quartet which he listened to sitting between Grieg and his wife were greeted with respect and even enthusiasm. This from a town considering itself the fountain-head of music and reluctant to admit the serious existence of any music other than German, was a tribute Tchaikovsky appreciated with a smile. His buoyant spirit was somewhat crushed by earnest Germans. That no doubt is why he took so quickly to Grieg and could have hugged Siloti and Brodsky for their Russianness.

The next German port of call was Hamburg, and there, for all the warm greeting he was given, he succeeded less than in any other city of his tour. He had plenty of applause but the *pièce de résistance* of his concert, the Piano Concerto in B flat Minor which he threw in for good measure, was not played to the critics' satisfaction.

Learning his lesson, Tchaikovsky persuaded Siloti to play the solo part at his Berlin concert. The concerto, and indeed every Tchaikovsky work in the programme, which included *Romeo and Juliet*, was received rapturously and he went off to Prague believing that he had established himself in Germany as a considerable composer. It could not be said that he was enamoured of the Germans. He respected their devotion to music as much as he deplored its four-square beat. Their formality went against the grain with a man who liked to be open and free. Russians do not mix well with Germans, they never have and presumably never will, but the compliment even of being taken seriously was too rare for him to reject. He had undertaken the tour and had to accept patronage as well as triumphs.

Prague could not have been more different. 'I never dreamed how much the Czechs love the Russians and hate the Germans,' he told Nadyezhda Filaretovna. From the moment of arriving he was caught up in a world of what, through dazed senses, seemed to him not far from adoration—not for him alone but as a representative of Slav culture in, musically speaking, a German world. Dvorak piloted him through a mass of delegations, receptions, dinners, and tours of the romantic city and its surrounding country. He heard concerts and operas and he conducted two all-Tchaikovsky concerts, Siloti again playing the solo in the First Concerto, which were received with such rapture that the composer-conductor was almost overwhelmed.

Not quite overwhelmed, however; the experience of the German part of the tour stood him in good stead; he not only kept his head to such effect on the podium that the orchestra played admirably, but managed to pick up enough Czech to reply to speeches of honour. He did not even complain of surfeit of visitors, banquets, and speeches or shortage of sleep. He was far too excited and gratified. He at last knew what happiness was, he said, and felt that all his very real terrors had been nobly repaid. He was finally cheered off to Paris in a flower-filled carriage of the train, a touch reminding him of those other friendly and generous people at Tiflis.

It was to Tiflis that he went for the third time at the end of the tour and nothing could have better illustrated his feeling for the Georgians and their beautiful capital than this; after covering thousands of miles in three months he chose to travel thousands more in anything but comfort to see Tiflis again and be with Anatoly, his wife and child, and Ippolitov-Ivanov.

But the real glory of the tour for him has not yet been mentioned. He came away from it knowing that he had made his mark as composer and conductor in most of the important musical centres of Western Europe and hoping that his music would be played there more often and listened to with greater attention. He was right; he had broken the ice; the Tchaikovsky furore had been set in motion and was never again to be arrested. Yet he thought much less of this at that moment than of an encounter in Berlin. Almost as soon as he had set foot in the city he met Artôt. The meeting was quite by chance. She was fifty-three but still singing unforgettably, she had grown fat but he saw only the old charm. They spoke and the twenty years since they had met rolled away. 'I was inexpressibly glad to see her and we were friends again at once.'

He had to leave for Leipzig but they planned another meeting. When he came back a month later she gave a dinner for him. She was with her husband and happy and Tchaikovsky rejoiced in it. He realized that she could appear elderly, stout, even absurd to those who did not know her. To him 'she is as fascinating as ever'. It was the rare perfect ending to an impossible romance and he knew it.

ii

By May he was at home again. Not the same home. Maidanovo was becoming too popular and he moved a few miles to another, quieter village outside Klin. This was Frolovskoye. It was less developed than Maidanovo, where the wealthy people of Klin had begun to build villas for themselves, and was still surrounded by the woods Tchaikovsky loved. The house Aleksei had taken for him was only a one-story affair but Tchaikovsky had never worried much about luxury, what he wanted was a snatch of true Russian country to look at and walk in and this he had.

He had also in front of the little terrace outside the house a pond in the middle of which rose a hump of earth he proudly called an island. The garden had been neglected and he threw himself into its restoration with the abandon of a man who had had more than enough of travelling, conducting, applause, and overeating. 'I have won a certain amount of fame,' he told Jurgenson, 'but I ask myself again and again what is it all for? Is it worth while? My answer is, a quiet life without fame is infinitely preferable.'

In that spirit he managed to turn himself for a few weeks into gardener, walker, and observer of the Russian scene he loved so much. He thought of little but the seeds he had planted—would they come up and when—and planned for the moment when the garden was gay with flowers. He may not have been a skilful gardener but he was certainly an ardent one; he never could do anything by halves and he did not now; having sown the seeds he used to lie awake wondering whether the night frosts, still heavy there, would kill off the seedlings and what he could do about it. In his intense way he was happy.

Of course it could not last. He excused himself by telling Nadyezhda, 'I am desperately anxious to prove to myself and others that I'm not yet written out.' In fact he simply wanted to write music and by the end of May was hard at work on a symphony and a symphonic poem and was meditating an opera.

He worked fast, not at all like a man who had written himself out; by the end of August he had finished the Fifth Symphony, by the end of October he had written *Hamlet* as well as celebrating his meetings in Berlin with a group of songs—Six French Songs—dedicated to Artôt.

He conducted the first performance of the symphony in Petersburg towards the end of November and followed it a week later with a repeat performance and the première of *Hamlet*. He repeated the symphony for a third time in Prague a few days afterwards as well as conducting *Yevgeny Onyegin*. He then trailed dolefully back to Frolovskoye convinced that he was a failure.

This belief was not unconnected with two deaths, both of which hit him hard, the one of Hubert, the other of Aleksandra's second daughter Vera, the girl who had married a Rimsky-Korsakov. His niece had been young, happy and apparently healthy; Hubert, one of his best friends at the Conservatoire, was younger than he and apparently set for a brilliant academic career—he had succeeded Rubinstein as Director until his illness. Once again he was faced with the incalculable, the fearful strokes of fate. And this plunged him into deeper gloom for in his last two works he had tried once again to grapple with the problem of fate—now, he felt, most inadequately.

His depression had been given weight by the reception at the concerts—receptions which, for him, must be considered almost lukewarm. One critic went so far as to say that Shakespeare could not be expressed in music. Few people will agree today. Tchaikovsky had written *Hamlet*, or had agreed to write it, which is not quite the same thing, as a kind of bargain with Lucien Guitry whom he had met in Petersburg some time before. The bargain was, if he would write incidental music to *Hamlet*, Guitry would play the role.

What actually happened could have been foreseen; when he got down to the work Tchaikovsky was inspired by the character of Hamlet as he had been by Romeo and Juliet. Hamlet too was a figure of fate, no one more so, a man with every apparent advantage in the world yet destined to die young and, one must think, unnecessarily. The final score was not incidental music (he had to write this later) but a symphonic poem, a triumph of characterization and condensation.

In twenty minutes Tchaikovsky carries his hearers through the cogent events of the long drama, giving one vivid impression after another of the characters and their interaction on each other. The score is intensely dramatic, fast moving, and filled with telling themes, and one must ask again why, like *The Tempest*, this brilliant evocation of a great poet's masterpiece is virtually never heard whilst *Romeo and Juliet* is overplayed. Had not the score been used for a ballet the probability is that the music might have remained unplayed in western Europe for the past quarter-century. The mental processes of concert planners are beyond comprehension; *Hamlet* possesses everything concert audiences demand, good tunes, romance, drama and superlative use of the orchestra (woodwinds especially), so that the mere sight of it at work is a rare delight.

It is unnecessary to commend the Fifth Symphony; it has become too popular in so far as it has kept the three early symphonies out of the repertory and shares with the Fourth and Sixth the reputation of being one of the most-played symphonies in the world. Yet in 1888 only one man seems to have grasped its merits to the full. This was Taneyev who was 'enraptured'. Tchaikovsky declared in those unhappy December weeks at Frolovskoye that it was a failure, insincere, and, excelling himself in self-depreciation, 'repellent'.

The only people to dislike the work today are a handful of musicologists. They think it vulgar. Everybody else, knowing that vulgarity is an essential part of life, that it is indeed a very obvious expression of life, are content to accept what a master gives them and to feel with him. More than any other of Tchaikovsky's symphonies the Fifth demands feeling and accurate interpretation. It does not often get it. If one is fortunate enough to hear it conducted by, say, Roshdestvensky, then Tchaikovsky's intentions and his mastery become apparent and the most frequently criticized parts of the symphony—the waltz and the last movement with its possibility of barrel-organ effect—come into focus as the composer imagined them, parts of an integral and majestic whole. The much belaboured Finale, for instance, contains a master-stroke in the change from E minor to E major following the pensive clarinet statement of the motto theme.

This particular example is given because it illustrates Tchaikovsky's programme so well. Like the preceding symphony, the Fifth deals wholly with man's reaction to fate or, as Tchaikovsky sometimes preferred to describe it, to the decrees of providence. Where it differs from the previous symphony is that the argument is lifted on to a higher plane. Tchaikovsky has moved from earth to the spiritual and for the first time he poses the question, should one not resign oneself to fate and choose the way of faith? There are the inevitable rebellions which he had known only too well, but in the end he tends to accept the consolations of faith and even sees men as happy because of it.

The contrast between the two fates, or their presentation, in the two symphonies, is fascinating. In the Fourth the Fate theme is earthy and militant as if the composer visualizes an implacable enemy in the form, say, of a Greek god. In the Fifth the majestic Fate theme has been elevated far above earth and man is seen, not as fighting a force which thinks in his own terms, of revenge, hate, spite, but a wholly spiritual power who subjects him to checks and agonies for the betterment of his soul.

It is possible to hear this and every other important musical work with a pleasure and an emotion which has, consciously at least, nothing to do with the composer's programme. The Fifth Symphony is splendid music, grand and dignified, and its form expresses the content more satisfactorily than in any other of Tchaikovsky's large works for orchestra. But the final thought must be, as with so many of this composer's works, a thought transcending the obvious pleasures of tunefulness, superb orchestration, and passionate self-questioning; it is from first note to last noble. Never querulous, never playing to the gallery, it exposes the soul of a man which all must feel the better for knowing.

Some musicologists have written as though 'the poor, tortured soul of Pyotr Ilyich'—to quote one of them—had no concern with others, as though his own private battle was fought out in his music simply because he was a weakling prone to unhealthy fancies. Nothing could be farther from the truth. What he tries to resolve in his three Fate symphonies is a universal problem. Every man and woman is a potential victim of fate and will remain so through life. Many shirk the problem as Tchaikovsky tried to shirk it in the Aix-la-Chapelle hotel after sitting by Kondratyev's death-bed but sooner or later it catches up with one and all. And never was the problem more acute or more in need of solution than today when organized religion has lost so much ground. Tchaikovsky would have been the last man to claim that he could provide an answer; what he has done is to present the problem of all in a framework which allows every listener, if he so wishes, to reflect. Most people will no doubt wish simply to enjoy the music; those further concerned may find, if nothing more, a sense of kinship with a noble and rightly troubled mind.

He had little time to agonize about the reception of the symphony and *Hamlet*; he had waiting for him at Frolovskoye a subject after his heart and as far removed from self-communings about fate as could be imagined. This was nothing less than a commission from the Imperial Theatres at Petersburg to write a ballet on a libretto after Perrault's fairy-tale *The Sleeping Beauty*.

Unlike the unhappy *Swan Lake*, *The Sleeping Beauty* was to have the benefit of choreography by one of the greatest masters, Petipa. At once Tchaikovsky felt immense confidence; he was not only asked to write ballet music on a subject which he thought one of the most poetical in the world, he had a detailed description by Petipa of the action as it should be danced and mimed. It is not every composer who can work closely with a choreographer, reading his mind and feeling the steps with him, but Petipa was an artist in a thousand and Tchaikovsky rose to his instructions with genius.

He was anything but free to concentrate his attention on this congenial subject unhindered, he was much too good and easygoing a host for that. In these winter weeks he had the usual crowd of visitors at Frolovskoye plus his devoted Siloti and two old friends, Larosh (reclaimed and grateful) and the architect-musicologist A. A. Klimenko. He also had to fill an enforced engagement to conduct at Petersburg, and was often seduced from work by his garden, which he still tended in furious bursts, and always by his walks through the woods.

All the guests reported that they had never known their host in better form; they rallied him about his pessimistic views of the Fifth Symphony and his hero-worship of Mozart, they argued furiously about Tolstoy—whether the disappearance of the novelist was a disaster or not—and about the merits of Dostoyevsky and Tchekhov. Tchaikovsky had just been reading Tchekhov with high excitement and was one of the first to see that he was reading the early work of one of the great literary giants of Russia.

In spite of all these pleasant distractions he was so much in love with the ballet that he had sketched out the first four scenes by the time he had to go to Petersburg again at the end of January 1889. There he saw how a master choreographer worked; at rehearsals he and Petipa discovered that they thought as one man. The score scarcely needed any alteration. When it did, Petipa had only to act out his requirements and Tchaikovsky altered the music on the spot.

There were no disagreements; it was a case of mutual admiration and fellow feeling.

Had he been free he would surely have stayed in Petersburg and finished the ballet there and then. But he was not free. In spite of his genuine hatred of concert tours he had agreed to make another one and early in February he took the train for Berlin.

CHAPTER TWENTY-TWO

The Sleeping Beauty
1889-91

For the four years left to him Tchaikovsky's life was to form a pattern as regular as he could make it. With one exception he went off for a foreign tour as conductor-composer in the early months of each year, followed this with a visit to his family or friends, settled in his own home for a summer of composing, and spent a large part of autumn and early winter trying to satisfy the demands of his own country.

The pattern was broken into increasingly because not Moscow and Petersburg only but all the provincial capitals began to pester him to conduct his works or to help local composers to a good debut by introducing their latest composition. If any kind of celebration was afoot—and it sometimes seemed to him that the Russians did little but celebrate or commemorate something or other—he was always expected to be there to give the occasion the finishing touch and counted himself lucky if he was not asked to compose a piece as well.

It was an exhausting life and he was for ever complaining of it but he could not give it up. Few men have been able to resist the lure of fame and he was not one of them. On the whole he disenjoyed himself pretty comprehensively during these almost incessant public appearances. He worked himself into a state of agitation before each concert, being constitutionally unable to believe that he could get through it without disaster. He always did but he remained a stern self-critic. In a sense he was right; he was not a very good conductor. What saved him time after time was his feeling for his work and his practically pathological sense of duty to audience and orchestra.

The second European tour, in the early months of 1889, followed the lines of the first. The broadened itinerary was much the same—Cologne, Frankfurt, and Dresden took the place of Prague—as were his agitation and boredom and gratification; the gratification was greater, that was all. He took with him some of his more substantial works this time—the Fourth and Fifth Symphonies—and these had the effect of convincing many musicians that he was not only a good but an important composer. In general his concerts were very much more successful than in the previous year, particularly in Berlin, Cologne, and London, and the English musical public confirmed a passion for Tchaikovsky that has lasted to this day.

By the time he left London for Marseilles in April he could feel that he had established himself as a European composer of moment and that all the countries he had visited would be eager to see him back. But what gave him more pleasure than all the tumultuous applause of the past three months put together was another kind of appreciation—the recollection of the first week in Berlin before the tour really got under way. He spent that week with Artôt and her husband. He and she were inseparable and went to all the theatres and concerts and operas together. 'I do love her,' he wrote home; and surely this was one of the nicest loves on record, for he loved to see her happiness with her husband and got his own happiness simply from being with her, looking and listening.

After this the tour was bound to be something of an anticlimax to a man who always put the affections first and it was as well that he scarcely had a moment to himself and that, being very human, he thoroughly enjoyed the storms of applause even though he told himself that he had not earned them.

The curious love-hate relationship with Brahms was resumed at Hamburg where Brahms stayed on to hear Tchaikovsky rehearse the Fifth Symphony. He told him afterwards that he liked all but the Finale which he did not like in any sense whatever. He said this in the nicest possible way and Tchaikovsky, also in the nicest possible way, confessed that there was much in the work of his fellow composer that he also could not like—or perhaps understand. They parted on excellent terms but, on Tchaikovsky's side at least, rather hopelessly; he was never to understand why he could not relax with this obviously excellent man.

At Hamburg too he made one of his pithiest comments. After the concert he was entertained by all the musicians of the city. It was a thoroughly Germanic evening with much hearty laughter and a lot of beer. The comment of the guest of honour was brief and to the point: 'German humour! Pleasant people, though.'

From Marseilles he sailed off for Batum and Tiflis—his fourth visit in successive years—and there Ippolitov-Ivanov organized a forty-ninth birthday dinner for him as well as playing many of his works at a gala concert.

Tchaikovsky left at the end of May with particular regret, not only to leave such a wonderful city and country and people but because he was bound for a most uncongenial task. Towards the end of the year Anton Rubinstein was celebrating the fiftieth anniversary of his first appearance as concert pianist and Tchaikovsky as the reigning Russian composer was expected to play a prominent part. He was in fact expected to conduct concerts of Rubinstein's works and this was what was causing him such pain. He still admired his old Director for what he had done for Russian musicians, he admired him for founding the Conservatoire and Musical Society, he even admired him with reservations as a pianist, but he regarded him as composer with considerable distaste.

He had expressed this distaste in his diary with unusual bitterness three years earlier when he forced himself to play through Rubinstein's much-acclaimed opera *Nero*. 'Idiotic fool!' he scribbled in a fury one day, leaping up from the piano. 'And insolent too! By God, when I go through this score my soul writhes in anger. I only play this vile composition because it makes me feel that I can't be too bad. At least I am sincere. I think *my* writing is rotten, do I! But I've only to look at this insipid rubbish and I cheer up. And it has actually been treated as a serious contribution to our music!'

His opinion had hardened in the three years since he wrote this yet he was to be obliged not merely to hear the master's compositions but to rehearse and conduct them and look as though he liked them. He could not possibly withdraw. Aleksandr III refused to acknowledge the existence of the anniversary because Rubinstein was a Jew, Balakirev because, as he said briefly, 'the man has done nothing but harm to Russian music', but these public slights only had the effect of clamping the unhappy Tchaikovsky to his duty. He went off to Petersburg in a very bad temper and was in such a state after a preliminary interview with a 'gracious' Rubinstein that only one remedy was left him. He joined the men who were writing the kind of Russian music he loved, Rimsky-Korsakov, Glazunov, and Lyadov, and sat in a restaurant with them drinking steadily. By the time they were ejected at two o'clock the next morning he was feeling much better and went off to Frolovskoye and *The Sleeping Beauty* almost resigned to the November celebrations.

By the early days of June he had written a complete sketch for the long ballet. Never in his life had he written with such a sense of felicity. The whole thing had taken only a total of forty days. The orchestration was another matter; not until the end of August had he finished it and then only after days of such intensive work that he wondered at times whether his brain would not burst.

He had a curious ally in the writing of this marvellous score, a little girl. Small children always fascinated him as Kashkin's daughter felt immediately she met him. He had had an absolute passion for the young Vladimir Davydov and his love for the forester's daughter at Kamenka had completely absorbed him for the whole of one summer. Now he found another tiny child and found her at just the right moment.

Thereby hangs a story which throws more light on Pyotr Ilyich. This girl was the daughter of Lyegoshin and Lyegoshin was the manservant of Kondratyev. During the first stages of Kondratyev's fatal illness Lyegoshin used to come over to Tchaikovsky's house with news of his master. Tchaikovsky admired him tremendously. 'What a splendid personality he has!' he wrote in his diary, and with him this thought led inevitably to another. 'Good God! And people are capable of looking down on such a man because he is a servant! Men are equal whatever their position in society and Lyegoshin is a wonderful proof of it. I don't know any man with a purer or nobler soul.'

When Kondratyev died Lyegoshin was left without a position and Tchaikovsky at once performed one of his many unheralded kindnesses; he got him work near his house and made sure that he and his family did not want.

He was handsomely repaid when Lyegoshin's little daughter came into his world. She fascinated him; he saw her every day. She used to 'help' him with the garden; she was just about on a par with him as gardener. They were very happy together. And her prattle of princes and fairies and beautiful princesses and magic castles in the midst of deep forests kept his imagination clear and sweet for the writing of *The Sleeping Beauty*. Nor did the influence of the child end there, for the germ of another ballet was planted in his mind then; the entrancing portrait of Clara in *The Nutcracker* was to owe much to that kindness to Lyegoshin.

By the time the ballet was done the Rubinstein celebrations could no longer be avoided. Tchaikovsky had so many commitments in both capitals—charity concerts and demanded concerts of his own works, the ballet to discuss with Petipa and an unavoidable contribution to the celebrations, the writing of a cantata in honour of the great man in addition to conducting—that he took an apartment in Moscow until the end of the year.

He did not enjoy these months but there were compensations—a few drinking evenings with his growing band of young admirers, the exquisite pleasure of working with a man like Petipa who knew exactly what he wanted and could actually make him wish to cut and alter a score, and a meeting with Tchekhov.

Tchekhov was not thirty and still churning out short stories in order to keep his shiftless family. His fame was still to come, so he was overwhelmed by the news, which soon reached him, that the great Tchaikovsky was recommending all his friends to read him and prophesying a wonderful future for him. He decided to express his thanks in the only way possible, by dedicating his latest volume of stories to him.

Tchaikovsky heard of the intention. He called on the writer to thank him for the honour, a typical touch from this great man to a virtually unknown one. Tchekhov was nervous—a state of mind in such a level-headed man that gives a good indication of Tchaikovsky's status—but they soon got on very well together. Tchekhov said how much he loved *Yevgeny Onyegin* and Tchaikovsky, always on the look-out for a new librettist, had no difficulty in persuading the writer to think seriously of it. They even decided tentatively on a subject, the *Béla* of Lermontov, and when the dedication appeared it was signed 'from a librettist of the future'.

The anniversary rites advanced remorselessly and at last Tchaikovsky was buried in them, a solid procession of concerts, banquets, and speeches ending with two all-Rubinstein programmes on successive nights, the unhappy Pyotr Ilyich conducting both concerts. As a final blow came the last item on the last programme, Rubinstein's fantastic *Tower of Babel* in which he set out to rival Berlioz with augmented orchestra and a choir numbering several hundreds. A martyrdom, Tchaikovsky told Nadyezhda Filaretovna.

There was no possible retirement to the quiet of Frolovskoye, he was booked for concerts and ballet rehearsals to the end of the year and beyond it. He abandoned all thought of the now usual European tour and began to long for a country he had not seen for several years; he decided to winter in Italy.

He did not get away as soon as he had hoped; *The Sleeping Beauty* dress rehearsal was delayed and did not take place in the Maryinsky until the middle of January of the new year, 1890. The occasion was one of the most magnificent in the recent history of Petersburg, no expense spared, the Tsar in his box, the nobles in their stalls and boxes in glittering uniforms, the women thick with jewels, the talk all of the fortune the production had cost. The moment should have been historic, the culmination of the composer's career. In fact it almost missed fire. The Tsar summoned Tchaikovsky to the royal box with an infuriatingly inadequate 'very nice'. The audience applauded dutifully, following the Tsar's handclaps, but were plainly all at sea.

No one can wonder, for this Petersburg audience was hearing and watching a revolution in ballet. If *Swan Lake* is the essence of poetry in ballet, *The Sleeping Beauty* is the essence of grandeur. Nobody before or since had heard a score of such proportions devoted to ballet. Never before had such choreography and such dancing been known, the one art affecting the other. After *The Sleeping Beauty*, ballet could never again sink to its old humdrum and tinselly form with public approval, for the curious fact emerged that the Maryinsky public which had greeted the new ballet with such half-heartedness found itself dissatisfied with its normal ballet fare ever afterwards.

Everybody interested in ballet and many beside has heard or seen *The Sleeping Beauty* danced and played in its entirety, in extracts or in the suite made from it. There is no need to try to gild the lily. Tchaikovsky had approached the work as he approached his symphonies, seriously and imaginatively; the result was a score of great length in which majesty and poetry interchange with dazzling effect. He understood perfectly how to create courtly music, fairy music, the music of youth and of love. As music in itself it is sumptuous, grand, with one noble and ravishing theme after another. As music for dancing it is almost without rival, expressing and often demanding in sound precisely the movements of the dancer. Tchaikovsky had of course been a devotee of the ballet and theatre since his youth; he had watched ballet after ballet in Petersburg in the 'sixties with the eye of a musician. Even so this faultless collaboration with Petipa still arouses astonishment. At one stroke—in forty days of work—he had created a masterpiece by any musical standard, he had provided ballet dancers with a new standard of music to interpret, had inspired a great choreographer to write his finest work and had lifted ballet as a whole to the level of great art.

ii

He had not wintered in Italy for eight years. That gives some indication of the change fame had brought; he had never had time to spare from winter concerts and operas since writing the Trio in Florence in 1882. He would have had no time in 1890 if he had not refused every offer to conduct his work in Europe that season, tempting though the offers were. As it was, he could return to Florence at last with the comfortable feeling that his two European tours had done everything he had hoped and more.

It is doubtful whether he ever made up his mind which city he liked best, Florence or Rome, but this time—it was to be his last glimpse of Italy—he chose Florence, probably because he would be less bothered there by society hostesses chasing the great Russian and by composers of every kind soliciting favours. He wanted a rest.

His idea of a rest was not everybody's; he at once began to write an opera. Perhaps a composer could scarcely spend months in Italy without thinking of opera but Tchaikovsky did not need much urging. He had been thinking about this opera for the past two years —on the whole not very favourably—yet in the end it had its way and the world lost an opportunity of seeing what Tchekhov would have made of an opera libretto. The opera Tchaikovsky now took up had been suggested by Modest before the meeting with Tchekhov and Modest now settled the matter by writing a libretto without waiting for his brother to make up his mind.

The story was taken from Pushkin's *Queen of Spades*. Modest's libretto was anything but perfect—even the fond Pyotr Ilyich demanded liberal cuts—but it did what he had hoped and got the composer to work. When Tchaikovsky had the libretto before him he began to see the subject's possibilities. After a few days he was quite converted and wrote the score at a great pace. By the time he moved to Rome for a week or two in April he had sketched the whole thing out and in Rome he orchestrated half the score.

He returned to Russia in a state of high excitement and finished the entire opera at Frolovskoye by the beginning of June. Everything had gone without a hitch and once more, forgetting all that had happened in the past, he announced that he had 'unquestionably written my masterpiece'. The music was so suggestive of the action, he said, that the scene between Herman and the Countess terrified him when he played it over. Kashkin and Jurgenson, coming up for a few days, were equally taken with the score when they heard it.

Between spells of enthusiastic gardening he at last got to work on the Sextet which had been bobbing up and down in his mind for years. He called it *Souvenir of Florence* and by July had completed the draft. This too pleased him, specially the Fugue which ends it, and he hastened to tell Nadyezhda Filaretovna about it 'for I know how much you love chamber music . . . and can quite easily arrange to have the Sextet well played in your own home'. He characteristically began to think more of it than the opera and, to round matters off, to rebuke himself for pride. But nothing could quell his optimism; he had once more thrust down the spectre of a composer who merely repeats himself.

In high good humour he left for Tiflis in August, travelling by way of Kamenka. He always made a point of spending a week or two there each summer but this visit of 1890 soon damped his spirits. Everything, he thought, had changed. The deaths of the two elder girls and the absence of the third, Anna, who had married into the Von Meck family, had thrown the household into gloom; Aleksandra obviously was not well; both she and Lyov looked much older and their efforts to welcome Pyotr Ilyich with the usual brightness were even more painful than the sight of them sad and silent. The house had gone to the other extreme from the noisy place Tchaikovsky had escaped from years earlier, it was not quiet but dead. Even the village seemed to the sensitive Pyotr Ilyich to have taken its cue from the great house; it had lost all its charm and looked ugly and sordid.

He was glad to be away—he could not rouse his sister—and by the time he reached Tiflis in September had regained enough cheerfulness to respond to the usual warm welcome from everyone. He had grown very fond of his sister-in-law, he loved their little daughter, he admired the way Anatoly was making a good thing of his career, and he found a stimulating musical companion in Ippolitov-Ivanov.

He quickly slipped into the half-oriental life of the city—this was his fifth visit—and threw himself into an orgy of music, conducting his own work and listening to concerts and opera, talking about it and planning what he should write next. He was happy and optimistic, reacting as always to kindness and affection from others. And it was in the midst of this happy period, on 4 October, that he received his last letter from Nadyezhda Filaretovna.

iii

For some time her letters had been growing shorter and more infrequent. More gloomy too. They had troubled Tchaikovsky because much was going wrong in the Von Meck household. Her eldest son, the apple of her eye, was dying slowly, wasting away and showing alarming signs of his mind being affected. Nadyezhda Filaretovna's bouts of prostration with splitting headaches had become longer—she often went to bed for days at a time—she had difficulty in throwing off the colds she was for ever catching, she had what appeared to be a perpetual cough, and her eyesight was beginning to fail. Finally, a slight paralysis of the right arm almost brought an end to her personal correspondence. She still dictated business letters to one or another of her family but when she wanted to write to Tchaikovsky she had to support her right arm with her left in order to guide her hand over the paper.

All this explained the change in her letters and Tchaikovsky had often grieved that beyond writing fully and affectionately he could not help the woman who had done so much for him. But one change there was not; her letters, brief and wider-spaced though they had become, were still as they had been throughout the past twelve years, affectionate, still hotly possessive, still intensely interested in everything he did and wrote. He was worried for her, he was not hurt for himself; as far as he (or anyone else who reads the letters) could judge the relationship remained as it had always been.

The letter he received at Tiflis on 4 October was not like this; it was not like any letter he had ever had from her. It was short and final. It said that she had lost all her money and could no longer make him an allowance. It ended, 'Do not forget me; think of me sometimes.'

He did not at all grasp the meaning of this last sentence. He was terribly shocked but his thought was all for her as his reply, written immediately, clearly showed. He begged her not to worry about him; he could do very well without her allowance. What worried him was the thought of her, used to wealth for so many years, being forced to live without it: 'I simply can't find the words to tell you how sorry I am for you and how fearful.'

Not until he had made plain that all his fears were for her did he speak of the last words of her letter and then he misinterpreted them. Being what he was he could not possibly have taken them in any other sense.

They hurt me a little [he wrote], but I can't believe you really meant them. Could you really think that I am only able to think of you as long as I am spending your money! How could I possibly forget, even for one moment, all you have done for me and all I owe you? I don't exaggerate when I say that without your friendship and sympathy I should have gone mad and died. You saved me. . . . No, me dear friend, you can be quite sure that I shall remember you and bless you as long as I have a breath left in my body. And now that you have no wealth left to share with me I am glad to think that I can freely demonstrate all the fond and limitless gratitude I feel for you.

He told her that he did not expect her to be able to write for some time but he looked to Pakhulsky, now her son-in-law, to give him more details and to relieve his anxiety if he could.

No letter had arrived from Pakhulsky by the time Pyotr Ilyich left Tiflis for Moscow at the beginning of November. When he arrived in the capital the first thing he heard was that the Von Meck fortune was intact.

Even then, at the height of the fresh shock, he failed to see that her final sentence had been a farewell. He wrote at once to Pakhulsky. Pakhulsky replied after some weeks with the politeness he had always shown but was absolutely noncommittal about his mother-in-law. The bewildered Pyotr Ilyich wrote again and again. In due course Pakhulsky sent him a friendly letter but avoided all discussion of Nadyezhda Filaretovna who, he said, was ill. His attitude was that all was as usual except that she was too tired to write.

By this time, in spring of the next year, Tchaikovsky was due to go off on a long tour. He wrote again just before leaving. He was mystified, hurt, astonished, but still could not believe that any human being could cut off an intimacy such as theirs so brutally and without giving any reason except a lie that he was bound to discover.

When he returned from his tour in early summer he found another letter from Pakhulsky waiting for him. It was as negative and uncommunicative as the others. Tchaikovsky, angry now yet still unable to credit such behaviour, made a final effort; he sent him a letter which he begged him to show to Nadyezhda Filaretovna.

I have just had your letter [he wrote]. You tell me that Mme. Nadyezhda Filaretovna is so ill and weak and in such a state of nerves that she can't write to me as she used to. Well, I would not wish for anything in the world to do or say anything that would increase her sufferings. It is not the fact that she does not write to me that hurts and worries and I am bound to say offends me. No, it is the fact that she seems to have lost every scrap of interest in me. It would be quite simple, if she wished to hear about me, to hear through you and Julia Karlovna but she obviously has not once asked either of you to discover how I am or anything about me and my work.

As you know I have tried to get in touch with N.F. through you but every letter you have written me has politely rebuffed my efforts to preserve, even if only for a short time, some semblance of our former relationship.

You must know that N.F. wrote to me last September to say that she was ruined and could not help me any longer with money. You must surely have read my reply? It was obvious that my pre-eminent wish was that my relationship with N.F. should not be changed just because she was not able to support me financially. Incredibly this does not seem possible. Evidently N.F. has lost all her feeling for me. When this idea entered my head I did not write to her again. In other words, for some extraordinary reason the fact that she no longer sent me money had to be the sign for our intimacy to end. This thought is frightfully humiliating for me and I am suffering unbearable worry and agony of mind when I think how I accepted her pension all these years.

At this point the incredulity returned and he tried once more to fight his way out of the nightmare.

When I was in the country last autumn I read all N.F.'s letters over again and whilst I read I thought that the feeling shown in them could not be affected by illness, by worry or by money troubles. But her feelings have altered nevertheless. It may be that because I never met N.F. I put her on a pedestal. I couldn't imagine treachery from the kind of other-worldly person I imagined her to be. I could sooner imagine the earth giving way under my feet than N.F.'s feeling towards me changing. Yet this is just what has happened, and my faith in mankind, my hope for the world has turned to dust and ashes, my peace of mind has been shattered and the last hope of any happiness I may have been intended by fate to enjoy has disappeared.

Pakhulsky returned the letter Tchaikovsky had asked him to hand to Nadyezhda Filaretovna; he could not show it to her, he said; she was too ill in mind and body. He assured Tchaikovsky that she loved her old friends as before; what seemed like coldness was only the result of her condition; she was very ill.

iv

At this point Tchaikovsky abandoned Paknulsky, though not his hope of discovering why he had been so scurvily treated. Presumably he destroyed the letter he had asked Pakhulsky to hand to Nadyezhda Filaretovna and we are unlikely to know exactly what he wrote though the general purport is not difficult to imagine.

He remained mystified as most of us are to this day. Many explanations have been put forward. None of them seems adequate. What would at first sight appear to be the obvious answer—that Nadyezhda Filaretovna had suddenly discovered his abnormality and cut him off—is unlikely to be the correct one. Several of Tchaikovsky's letters to her make his homosexuality quite plain without saying it in so many words. She was, besides, very well informed about everything to do with the musical circles in Moscow and could not have avoided hearing what everybody knew.

Others have suggested that her conscience pricked her unbearably when her son became seriously ill and that she put this down to her feeling for Tchaikovsky; had she looked after him instead of devoting most of her thought to Tchaikovsky and his music, he might have lived to carry on her work. This surmise is given some confirmation by Aleksandra's daughter Anna Lvovna who had married into the Von Meck family. 'Her sorest trial,' she said, 'was the disease of her eldest, her beloved son. He died before her eyes after a protracted and agonizing illness and it seemed to her . . . that her friendship with Pyotr Ilyich had taken her thoughts away from her family and home and that perhaps she was even guilty of the horrible death of her gifted son. "I must atone for my sin," she said. She went back to her Faith, began to pray once more and asked me to order prayers for her in church. Such a frame of mind naturally affected the correspondence with Pyotr Ilyich; she did not feel it to be such a vital necessity as formerly.'

Again it has been thought that Pakhulsky had been intriguing against Tchaikovsky ever since he succeeded in marrying Julia von Meck, fearing that Nadyezhda Filaretovna might will the bulk of her fortune away to the composer. The only evidence of this again comes from Anna Lvovna: 'Why Uncle did not give his letter to

275

Nadyezhda Filaretovna to me or to my husband I can't understand.' The interesting point about this is the implication—which was a fact —that although all the Von Meck family lived together Pakhulsky did not tell Anna Lvovna or her husband about his correspondence with Tchaikovsky. It must be added that Anna Lvovna says she thinks Pakhulsky acted 'very correctly' in returning the letter—why, she does not explain.

Others suggest that when Nadyezhda Filaretovna at last gave up hope of a marriage, when Tchaikovsky refused to divorce Antonina, she began to turn against him and finally cut him off.

Yet again, it has been thought that when Tchaikovsky finally won the fame she had been trying to secure for him all these years, she reacted violently to the very success she had fought for, believing that the last excuse for his dependence on her had disappeared and that she had lost him. And it is certainly true of possessive natures that they cannot in the end endure sharing their possessions.

A final suggestion comes from Anna Lvovna. It must be said that by 1890 this girl had identified herself completely with the Von Meck family she had married into and was obviously under the spell of her strong-minded mother-in-law like everyone else in the house. 'The changes in Pyotr Ilyich's life,' she says, 'did not at first affect his relations with my mother-in-law but little by little towards the end of the 'eighties he began to need her support less and less and did not rely as much as formerly on constant exchange of thoughts with her. In consequence she sometimes began to suspect that his letters to her were written with an effort and that a feeling of reserve was creeping into them.'

This solution (one of many attempted by Tchaikovsky's niece) though unlikely to explain the break may well explain what helped to lead up to it. By the end of the 'eighties Tchaikovsky was in such demand that his correspondence on all sides was necessarily slackening. As Nadyezhda Filaretovna was unable to write as often as in the old days he may have seized the excuse to write less frequently. Her imagination and her intense pride would have done the rest. The tone of his letters, like the tone of hers, however, remained constant; he had never felt for her as she felt for him but his sense of gratitude and of co-feeling in music was as strong as ever.

Perhaps the only two suggestions that have not been made are that she came to suspect him of an incestuous love for Aleksandra or that she invented her own explanation of the 'sin' he used to accuse himself of so strenuously.

However, the truth would seem likely to rest in the simple fact that she was no longer responsible for all her actions. She had always been unbalanced—her manner of life after the death of her husband was far from normal—and in the past few years she had become very much more so. 'She began to feel extremely ill,' says Anna Lvovna, 'and her dreadful headaches prostrated her for days. She became very lifeless . . . tubercular development in her lungs gained ground and by 1889–90 she was also suffering from a serious nervous disease which deeply perturbed us all. The tuberculosis she feared for so long was to kill her three years later.'

Tuberculosis, as is common knowledge, has the most extraordinary effect on the sufferer. Many readers will know from their own experience how a sick person will suddenly show an unreasoning dislike of some harmless visitor, turn away from him and refuse to speak. In tubercular cases these abrupt and senseless likes and dislikes are magnified to the point of insanity—they move from love to hate in moments and for no observable or analysable reason whatever.

Tchaikovsky still had no knowledge of Nadyezhda Filaretovna's true condition; for twelve years he had read accounts of the violent headaches and nerve storms and had inevitably become largely accustomed to them. He would think, as we would all do, that if she was really as ill as she thought she would have been forced to bed and to a doctor long since. Tuberculosis deceives many; it takes its time.

The truth will never be known. Nadyezhda Filaretovna kept her own counsel in everything. Not until the last year of her life and the last few months of Tchaikovsky's did she speak, and then only because the question was put plainly to her. This explanation will be given in its place. It may not convince many readers, and the probable truth would still seem to rest in her illness. When it is remembered what this disease does to the most normal of people, it can be imagined what it could do to a woman already unbalanced and with a son who died showing definite signs of insanity. And when one comes to think of it, was the last note of this extraordinary friendship any more remarkable than its first? Reading again her opening letters to Tchaikovsky, do they not indicate an emotional and probably abrupt end to the relationship—as abrupt and emotional as its beginning?

CHAPTER TWENTY-THREE

The Queen of Spades and American Tour

1890–2

Artists are at once more and less fortunate than the ordinary run of men and women. Tchaikovsky now experienced the fortunate side. In the autumn of 1890 he was a man struck to the heart by what seemed a wholly unmerited snub to his pride and his feelings—and one must admit that he was extraordinarily unfortunate to have had intimate dealings with two unbalanced women. But he was also a composer determined to write music as well as a famous man committed to one engagement after another. However much he might have liked to brood on the insult and the hurt he literally could not do it—neither the world nor his good genius would permit it.

At this time he had three items on his plate none of which could be ignored. The first was the première of *The Queen of Spades*, the second a new ballet, the third a visit to the United States. It cannot be said that he faced any one of them gladly—the wound was fresh and was never to be completely healed—but he faced them and, when the moment came, thought of them only.

The Queen of Spades was presented at the Maryinsky on 19 December. Tchaikovsky was well served by the singers (he had been to see some of them months earlier to make sure that they were really enthusiastic about their roles) and by Napravnik as conductor, and there was never the slightest doubt that at long last he had written an opera which would command something of the affection given to *Yevgeny Onyegin*, an opera that would not follow the rest on to the scrap-heap. The public and critical response was almost unanimous and Tchaikovsky left the opera house believing that his work was safe for posterity.

His confidence has been proved correct. *The Queen of Spades* is not so good an opera as *Yevgeny Onyegin* nor so well suited to the composer's genius but it will always return to the repetory from time to time because it has what his failed operas had not, a genuine dramatic situation treated genuinely and dramatically in musical terms and a group of believable characters differentiated skilfully and truthfully.

Tchaikovsky was no doubt fortunate to begin with a superb story by a master of story-telling. All the same, he rose to it. He could understand these people, they were sufficiently close to his time and class to be recreated without difficulty. In general the characters are all musically well observed and with Herman he went further than a character in the round, he really managed to infuse into the music for him something of the psychological subtlety imagined by Pushkin. The music for the fourth act which had so alarmed him when he played it over still grips audiences; it is permissible melodrama extremely well handled, economical and telling.

For those who have not heard this opera it might perhaps be well to say that it is the type of work which needs several hearings if its full impact is to be felt. Unlike so many popular operas in the repertory it does not rely on great and immediately appealing arias. The entire work possesses only two striking arias, Herman's 'Three Cards!' and Lisa's 'It is almost midnight', and they are scarcely of the whistleable variety. At first this paucity of great melodies strikes many listeners as disappointing and even flat. Those who persevere with it discover something better than the obvious attraction of popular tunes, a sterling honesty of purpose throughout and a score which grows on one with each performance. The score is never brilliant, it is also never cheap. It is effective because it is truly felt.

A few days after the first night, followed by a party to mark the twenty-fifth anniversary of his entry into the Petersburg Conservatoire, Tchaikovsky went off to Kiev on the way to spend the new year at Kamenka. It was a sign of the times that he found *The Queen of Spades* already mounted in the opera house at Kiev and was able to watch and hear it relaxedly. That put him in a good mood for Kamenka—this second view of the opera confirmed his faith in it—and to his enormous pleasure he found that the cloud of the summer had lifted. Aleksandra was much more like her old self and if she was happy he was happy too, it was as simple as that.

Knowing the future, one wonders whether Aleksandra had an instinct that she would never see this dearly loved brother again. She had the brilliance often seen in those who have reconciled themselves to death. Such a thought was beyond Pyotr Ilyich; a world without Aleksandra was unimaginable to him. He saw only that, though frail, she seemed to have taken a new hold on life, deciding to devote herself to the children still left. He rejoiced. Looking back, he could never recall a happier New Year than this one of 1891 and he blessed the premonition which had led him to spend it at Kamenka.

The hint of old and happy times at once reflected itself in his work. He wanted to write another ballet—the success of *The Sleeping Beauty* had encouraged Petipa and Vsevolozhsky, the opera-house director, to beg for more—and with Lyegoshin's daughter in mind he thought of *The Nutcracker* from one of Hoffmann's tales. For a similar reason the success of *The Queen of Spades* made him anxious to write another opera. He read in spurts in the library at Kamenka which had already provided him with such useful material and came across Zvantsev's translation of Hertz's *King René's Daughter*, which had been inspired by Hans Andersen, liked it and put Modest to work on a libretto.

Engagements in Moscow and Petersburg drove him away at last. He wondered for the thousandth time why on earth he submitted to the treadmill of public life but he went just the same; he was at least cheered to have seen Kamenka in its true colours.

He was so much in demand as conductor, as encourager of the young talent for ever waiting on the doorstep of his hotel, and as guest of honour—as at the Guitry *Hamlet* with his incidental music at the Mikhailovsky that February, and at Arensky's first opera the previous month—that he did not get back to Frolovskoye and his new ballet score until a week or two before he was due to leave for the United States. It was to be his last stay at Frolovskoye. The builders were cutting down the woods he loved and he told Aleksei to find another home for him whilst he was away.

He managed in these few days at home to sketch out sufficient of the ballet music to show to Petipa before leaving for Berlin and Paris in the middle of the month. Petipa reacted like the great and practical artist he was; he gave the composer exact details of the music he needed. He specified the precise number of bars and the kind of emotion they must convey for each section. This could be taken as an insult or a compliment, a very considerable one. The touchy Tchaikovsky accepted the directions without a word; he had absolute faith in the choreographer and did not feel any loss of face. It has sometimes been said that he would write to order only for Balakirev. His response to Petipa is even more astonishing for a man of his pride and fame. Armed with the master's instructions—they were no less—he set off for his most arduous tour. He intended, he said, to spend his many spare moments in completing the ballet.

In Paris he conducted an all-Tchaikovsky concert played by the Colonne orchestra. It was received with cries of delight and many encores which he took as an omen of good. He had still two weeks before his ship sailed and once again he became the centre of attention until, tiring of perpetual soirées and of his hosts' bright fulsomeness, he decided to leave the mob and spend a few quiet days by himself. He went down river to Rouen, half-intending to be quit of Paris altogether, to move down to Le Havre from Rouen when his sailing date arrived.

There was another reason for this abrupt change of plan. As usual he was feeling homesick and reproached Modest—who had come to Paris to see him off—for not feeling likewise. To his horror Modest, who had a gift for being all things to all men, had fallen for the Paris charm and was busy aping the fashionable young Parisians in clothes, speech, and manner of life. There was a quarrel.

He had barely settled into his Rouen hotel and into a more equable mood than he was joined by Modest. His brother had come to break very bad news—soon after Pyotr Ilyich left Paris a telegram arrived to say that Aleksandra had died suddenly at Kamenka—but the moment he saw the contented face he knew that he could not tell him the truth, that he must not ruin the American tour. As Tchaikovsky was amazed to see him and as he had to leave for Kamenka the next day, Modest had a bright idea for explaining both events; he said that Pyotr Ilyich had been quite right to reprimand him for forgetting Russia and aping the French; he had taken the reproof so much to heart that he intended to go straight back where he belonged.

Tchaikovsky, incapable of suspecting such a ruse, accepted the explanation without a tremor of suspicion and Modest had to face as best he could an evening of joyousness. He left triumphant, however, and sure that Pyotr Ilyich would reach New York before hearing the news. As he might have done but for a singular chance.

First, he discovered, as we all do, that a provincial French town, however old and beautiful, is very death to spend more than the odd day or two in. Second, he remembered that he ought to say good-bye to two friends of his in Paris, the pianists Sophie Menter, an Austrian, and V. Sapelnikov, a Russian who had been the soloist in his Second Piano Concerto at the Colonne concert.

So at the last moment he hurried back to Paris. The moment was long enough for him, an avid reader of Russian newspapers when out of Russia, to drop into a reading room in the Passage de l'Opéra. There he picked up the *Novoye Vremya*. Still homesick, he read every line of it, even to the obituaries on the last page. There he saw an account of his sister's death.

His first impulse was to rush back to Kamenka. The ship was due to sail the next morning and he spent a dreadful night with his friends. They urged him to carry out the tour; he would be too late to attend the funeral and would disappoint thousands of American admirers for nothing. At last he saw the sense of what they said. The next morning, utterly wretched, he sailed for New York.

ii

It says much for American tact and genuine hospitality that this memorable visit did not collapse before it had properly begun. Tchaikovsky, hating every mile that took him farther from Russia at such a time, arrived on 25 April in a black mood, thinking only how soon he could sail back again. He had come to take part in the festivities to mark the opening of what is now the Carnegie Hall and thought he could leave within a week or two.

Two days later he was reconciled to an extension of the visit by conducting concerts at Philadelphia and Baltimore. He could never resist true kindness and admiration and he found both in New York to a degree that astounded him. He was greeted with heartening warmth by Damrosch and the orchestra he was to conduct, given a luxurious suite in one of Broadway's finest hotels, he was dined by Carnegie, by Damrosch, the Francis Hydes, the Morris Renos in state and in private, taken on tours of the city (the skyscrapers amazed him), taken to Niagara Falls, to Long Island where he spent a night in Ferdinand Mayer's overwhelming summer house, taken to supper at Delmonicos, invited into the opera-house boxes of all New York's great men, and discovered with a likeable amazement,

'I am ten times as famous here as in Europe!' He was not left one minute to think or brood. When he was supposedly resting in his hotel he was besieged by callers, famous and not so famous, anxious to talk with Russia's great composer, to get his autograph, his photograph, to invite him out. His post was enormous. Punctiliously he saw everyone and answered every letter. He was dead tired at the end of each day but undeniably stirred. He could neither write the ballet score nor feel homesick, there simply was no time for it.

To say that he enjoyed himself would be to go too far; life was a constant battle between exhaustion and flattery. He often had to thank his steady head—the champagne flowed freely—and he suffered agonies during a three-and-a-half-hour dinner at which smoking was not permitted, but by and large he came to admire his hosts who laid themselves out so thoroughly to show him that he was a much-honoured guest. He went off to his concerts apprehensive but proud.

Musically, he was immediately struck by the playing of the Symphony Society Orchestra he was to conduct. This gave him confidence and all his contributions to the festival went off triumphantly. At the first, on 5 May, he found himself facing a vast audience of close on six thousand when he came on to the platform of the new hall. He had chosen to conduct his *Coronation March* written for Aleksandr III's accession ceremonies—an unpretentious piece of workmanship which went down well. Three days later, on his fifty-first birthday, he conducted the Third Suite and the next day the B flat Minor Piano Concerto. He was very moved by his reception: 'I was recalled time after time, handkerchiefs were waved, there were shouts and cheers. . . . I've never known such scenes even in Russia. . . . The Americans had plainly taken me to their hearts.' He added typically, 'But what touched me most of all was the orchestra's reaction'—for the men he had conducted were on their feet tapping their instruments and truly offering homage.

At Baltimore the incessant round of hospitality continued, including a visit to the piano works of Knabe, a successful repeat of the concerto as well as a splendid performance of the Serenade for Strings inserted in place of the suite (the orchestra was short of strings) but Washington pleased him more. Here he could be with Russians again in the Embassy and the Metropolitan Club where he was guest of honour. At the Embassy the Trio was played before an Ambassador specially returned for the occasion and all the city diplomats.

Philadelphia's Academy of Music was packed to the doors for his concert and he left glowing reports behind him as he went back to New York and the final days of his tour. He went back tired but game and, surprisingly, very glad to be back. His provincial excursion—if one dare use that term of such illustrious cities—somehow lacked the glamour of New York. It tired him to death, this glamour, but was undeniably exciting. After all he was only fifty-one, not 'well into the sixties' as one unfortunate journalist had described him to his considerable annoyance, and the homage of the greatest city of a great nation went to his heart.

After a few more hectic days he boarded his ship on 21 May, worn out but contented. He was loaded with gifts, dazed by the music and talk he had heard, his hand ached from the signing of autographs, his head buzzed with the champagne he had drunk. But it was a good ending and he sailed off urged to return and intending to do so—only an unhappy misunderstanding of a cable was, in fact, to prevent it. Apart from the manners, or lack of them, of some journalists who, to his astonishment, were more concerned by a man's appearance than by the worth of his music, he looked back to what seemed a whirlwind tour as the final justification of all his efforts to fit himself to conduct his own music. In the United States, as in Western Europe, he was a made man and his music was liked and understood.

By the beginning of June he was in Petersburg and thankful. Looking back, he thought of the round of parties and dinners and interviews with absolute horror, as he always did, and could not comprehend how he had got through it all. What remained in his mind as entirely pleasurable was the attitude of the American people. He contrasted their open-handed and open-hearted welcome with the self-satisfied approval of the Germans on earlier tours, the insincerity of the French, the crudity of the English, and he felt warmly towards this new nation that had taken his music to its heart without reservation. He placed the Americans in his mind with the people of Tiflis, of Prague, people who have never learned the false gospel which confuses nationalism with art.

His happiness to be in Russia again did not live long. Waiting for him was Pakhulsky's final letter and the end of the hopes of a reconciliation with Nadyezhda Filaretovna. Waiting too was irritating news from Aleksei. His manservant, more luxury-loving than he, never liked the bungalow life of Frolovskoye and always regretted the comfort of Maidanovo, and there he transferred the household as soon as Tchaikovsky's back was turned. Tchaikovsky hated suburban life and its endless petty curiosity. He loathed to see trees cut down to make way for yet another rich man's vulgar chalet. Now he was to be plunged into suburbia. He was not pleased and went off in sober mood.

The mood exploded on the platform of Klin station a few days later. Tchaikovsky is usually portrayed as a man almost too amiable for this world. The portrait is a truthful one but naturally enough is not the whole truth. He could be roused by many things, by students who made a mock of the subject they were supposed to be studying, by government interference with the arts and now by a manservant who repaid years of kindness and generosity with an act he knew his master would not approve.

The proverb, he who touches pitch will be defiled, is as true as the day it was written. These contacts with human stupidity and greed did nothing but soil Tchaikovsky's mind and made him for the moment a travesty of his kind and just self. He could even forget his manners. And as ever his anger fell on the wrong person.

It so happened that one of the passengers in the train approaching Klin on this particular day was the singer Aleksandra Valerganovna Panayeva-Kartsova, another pupil of Viardot. Panasha, as he usually called her, was married to a distant cousin of Tchaikovsky. He greatly admired her voice and appearance—'she is the *personification* of my ideal Tatyana'—and was always glad to see her. He was still hoping to persuade her to play the role.

In Moscow she was joined in her railway compartment by Modest and he spent the two hours to Klin telling her about his brother's triumphs in America. 'He had a fantastic success,' he said—he always tended to exaggerate—'and the Americans simply worship him.'

Underneath his chatter she surmised a certain uneasiness and at last it came out: 'Petya is expecting me to stay with him for a while and hear the full story of his tour but I'm having to disappoint him, I've very urgent business at Petersburg and must go straight on there.'

She thought this a little strange; Modest had never had urgent business in his life and might have been expected to spare a day or two for the brother who had been keeping him for years. However, she thought no more of it until the train stopped at Klin and Modest got out. She too got out soon afterwards—her little girl asked for a glass of milk—and saw on the platform a group including

Tchaikovsky, Modest, Larosh, and the actor Delazari. She had not realized that Tchaikovsky would actually be at Klin station to greet Modest—he had a carriage outside to take them back to Maidanovo—but, seeing him there, felt that she must speak to him.

As she walked towards him she could see that he was looking angry and resentful and that Modest's face wore an abashed expression. Evidently he had broken the news.

It was not perhaps the best moment to speak but she had begun to walk towards them and could not go back without causing offence. She went up to Tchaikovsky with hand flung out: 'My dear Pyotr Ilyich, I congratulate you warmly!' she cried.

He stared at her. 'Congratulate me? What for?' he demanded in an irritated voice.

'For your triumphant tour of America, of course.'

He looked with angry irony at Modest and shrugged his shoulders petulantly. 'Congratulate! I've just had a fine kind of congratulation, I can tell you!'

He turned to the rest of his group, gesturing largely, and cried, 'I meet with nothing but annoyances and she congratulates me!'

Everyone turned and looked at her reproachfully.

She became angry and burst out, '*Si vous le prenez sur ce ton-là...*! Goodbye!' With that she twisted on her heel and walked off quickly.

She soon heard someone running after her, then the panting voice of Pyotr Ilyich, 'Aleksandra Valeryanovna... Tatochka... Panasha ... wait, do wait! Don't be angry.'

She walked all the quicker and shouted over her shoulder, 'No, no! While you're in that kind of mood I don't want to talk to you.'

And with that she reached her compartment, got in and slammed the door.

iii

That is another side of a great man. If he is really great it is a side that never shows itself for long. So it was with Tchaikovsky; having sighed over Maidanovo, its depleted woods and growing cluster of villas, he got down to work. By July he had finished the sketch of *The Nutcracker*. He went straight on to the one-act opera *Yolanta* and completed the draft by the middle of September and, as three months of composition left him unappeased, took up a symphonic poem on *Voivode* he had begun in Tiflis the previous year, orchestrated it and soon afterwards heard it played for the first time in Moscow. Siloti had blossomed out as conductor and it was he who directed the symphonic poem in a programme including works by Grieg and Glazunov.

For once Tchaikovsky reacted promptly. The audience cheered *Voivode* 'passionately'. His response was to tear up the score. He understood that a mature man cannot go back to youthful ideas and escape the ludicrous. He was not prepared to be laughed at by posterity for the sake of cheap cheers in the present.

Back he went somewhat ruffled to Maidanovo and *Yolanta*. He broke off work once more to visit Anatoly in his new post at Reval close to the Hapsal of happy memories, then returned to finish the opera just before the end of the year.

He ended it in something of a rush; he was booked to conduct two all-Tchaikovsky concerts in Kiev before beginning another short European tour. By the middle of January 1892 he was breaking fresh ground in Warsaw and earning more 'passionate ovations'.

From Warsaw he moved to Hamburg to conduct *Yevgeny Onyegin* and there provided another example of his conscientious approach to music. When he understood that the translated libretto would confuse his directions to the singers he refused to conduct. He had already heard a possible substitute with admiration the previous evening, insisted that he take his place and listened to his rendering of *Yevgeny Onyegin* in delight. The conductor was the young Gustav Mahler.

That was the whole of the tour—he had decided never again to spend many weeks away from Russia—and after a few days in Paris he was at Maidanovo by the middle of February making a suite out of his *Nutcracker* score. The suite, so well known to present-day concert audiences, was given its first performance under the composer's baton in Petersburg in March and was immediately hailed as a little masterpiece.

There is good reason for seeing this suite as a disaster. Tchaikovsky's taste seems to have deserted him—either that, or, working too hurriedly, he took the easy road. In the event almost all the best music in the ballet was left out of the suite. Those who hear the suite and have not heard the full ballet score think, reasonably enough, that they have heard the essence of the ballet. Never was there a greater error; this rather cheap selection does the ballet score great harm.

An amusing story attaches to this suite. Ever searching for

novelty, Tchaikovsky wanted an instrument that would convey the fragility and other-worldliness of the fairies. He was led to the answer by his work the previous autumn on the symphonic poem *Voivode*. That was a failure but it reminded him that he had used the celesta in the old opera of many years before. The opera had failed and the use of the instrument had passed without notice. He now saw that its exquisite purity of tone would precisely create his conception of the Sugar Plum Fairy and set about with great stealth to have one brought from Paris where they were made. A more generous man than Pyotr Ilyich has rarely existed but when it came to the use of rare or unknown instruments in a symphony orchestra he became the miser in person. He swore everyone concerned to secrecy and lived in perpetual dread that some other composer—he chiefly feared Rimsky-Korsakov and Glazunov—would manage to hear the celesta, appreciate the unique effects obtainable with it, and use it before he did.

Enormously cheered by getting in first he made a symbolic gesture to his old Law School. Thirty-three years had passed since he graduated from it and went into the Finance Ministry with the hopeless feeling that his chance of taking up music had slipped away for ever. He left the school to become a government clerk, he returned in 1892 as Russia's outstanding composer, but one would never have guessed it from his manner when he conducted the school orchestra that spring in excerpts from his own works. The manner and the lesson of the thirty-three years was not lost on one student at least. This was a boy named A. B. Khessin. He vowed there and then to follow in Tchaikovsky's footsteps.

Whilst in Petersburg Tchaikovsky received good news. His complaints about Maidanovo—the crowds peering into the garden on the offchance of seeing him, the bell for ever ringing, the impossibility of taking a walk without running into autograph hunters —had at last melted the stern heart of Aleksei. Possibly Aleksei had grown tired of answering the bell that Tchaikovsky was tired of hearing. At any event he looked about and in the middle of May proudly showed his master into a new home on the outskirts of Klin.

CHAPTER TWENTY-FOUR

Sixth Symphony
1892-3

Aleksei had been feeling for some time that his master was not living in the style befitting a great man and for this last home he did Pyotr Ilyich proud. He was helped in his search for a worthy house for Russia's famous composer by Taneyev's brother, who owned a large estate just outside the town. The garden of the house into which Tchaikovsky settled in May 1892 was bordered on two sides by this estate which ensured him almost complete privacy as well as a sympathetic neighbour who would not sell his land for development.

Some readers will have seen the Klin house which has long been the Tchaikovsky Museum. It is a handsome and substantial building in the fashion of that day, the ground floor brick, the upper floor wood, with a long veranda in front and a pedimented centrepiece. The rooms are spacious, with high ceilings; the size of the music room can be gauged from the fact that between Tchaikovsky's grand pianoforte, which was placed dead centre, and the walls on every side is a space nearly twice the length of the instrument. At right angles to the main window—a double window as everywhere in Russia—he put the long desk on which he did all his composition and behind this again, with its back to the wall, was a couch some seven feet long on which he used to rest between spells of work. Above the couch hung his most prized group of portraits and photographs of his family, specially loved friends, relatives, and musicians. In the centre of this group was a large head and shoulder portrait of Mozart.

Although Tchaikovsky was a man of his period—and Alexei even more so—to the extent of filling the house with knicknacks, it was absolutely devoid of what is now regarded as essential comfort. There was not an easy chair in the place and his bedroom was monastic. He did all his work and all his playing—and he was often at the piano by the hour, day after day—on hard, upright wooden chairs.

In Tchaikovsky's time the garden was large and heavily wooded, with many flower-beds to the front and sides of the house, and though he was only just on the outskirts of Klin, on the Frolovskoye road, he had the impression of being miles from anywhere. He could not see another house and from some parts of the garden he could obtain the view he most loved, of the flat, apparently illimitable spaces he thought of as Russia at her most characteristic. He was free to walk in the Taneyev woods whenever he pleased.

His difficulty, like that of all famous men, was to make time to compose; the longer he lived the more he was in demand. This partly explains why, having celebrated the entry into his new home by beginning a new symphony, he did not get very far with it. There was another reason too; he was not happy with it. The old dread of having written himself out loomed again and he stopped work abruptly and made a quick series of visits—to see Artôt in Berlin and to spend a few days in Paris and Vichy.

Back again, he found himself bogged down by requests from the capitals that he conduct, open festivals, and take part in the direction of the Moscow Musical Society and Conservatoire. He had still to finish the orchestration of *Yolanta* and *The Nutcracker* and by the time he had done this, in September, he had to go off yet again, to Vienna to fulfil a promised concert engagement. In fact he did not fulfil it—the orchestra was so bad that he refused to conduct—and it gives the measure of his standing in Europe that he could take such a high line and be thought all the more of. He was learning, a little late, that ruthlessness pays. He never did learn it, in fact, he was far too nice, but he made the occasional gesture and was always surprised to find how readily it was accepted.

From the end of October he was up and down between Klin and Petersburg supervising rehearsals of new works, and although he managed to slip in one or two spells of home life before the premières began in December the new symphony still hung fire.

His opening engagement—after seeing a Modest play fail—was the first public performance of his Sextet. This work, scored for two violins, two violas, cello, and double bass, had been written specially for Nadyezhda Filaretovna before the break. She had complained that her health did not permit her to get to as many concerts as in earlier years and Tchaikovsky tried to give her at one and the same time a chamber work she could easily arrange to be played in her house and which would give the illusion of a work for small orchestra.

The Sextet was an immediate success in Petersburg and again in Moscow a few days later. It has gradually fallen into disuse but more possibly because of the difficulty of getting the necessary performers together than of any fault in the work itself. It deserves to be played regularly; it is not great music but is very pleasant and extremely cleverly constructed. It is above all suffused with an atmosphere not often associated with this composer, of a calm geniality. One could almost call it an old man's music, serene and resigned. The mood, which is found in other compositions of this final period, has in fact nothing to do with age—he was only fifty when he wrote the Sextet —but a great deal to do with his feeling that he had at last justified his life by his music. To this extent his fame had done nothing but good and in its quiet and unpretentious way the Sextet brings this out most charmingly.

Two days after this Petersburg première came the dress rehearsal of the joint bill of *The Nutcracker* and *Yolanta* in the presence of the Tsar and the nobility. But before this is dealt with it might be as well to look at a small sideline of Tchaikovsky's life which helps to remind one that he remained the kind man in the heat of greatness. It might be forgiven him if, in the midst of a rush of rehearsals of important first performances, of dinners and of talks with the disciples of the Balakirev group, he postponed every interview with importunate people of no standing. In fact he would never do this. His answering of every letter written to him in New York is a pointer to his behaviour in Petersburg eight months later.

The young student Khessin who had watched Tchaikovsky's visit to his old Law School just after the American tour could never afterwards keep his mind on his studies. One day two students, V. Napravnik, son of the conductor, and Sanya Litke, a distant nephew of Tchaikovsky, came across Khessin in one of the lecture rooms after classes had finished. He seemed to be studying something very earnestly. They walked over to him and looked over his shoulder. Instead of the lecture notes they expected to see they saw the scores of *Manfred* and *Kamarinskaya*. They rallied him—

'I thought you were in the Law School to study law'—then left him.

Two weeks later they came up to him with an announcement that took his breath away: 'Pyotr Ilyich will see you in his room at the Grand Hotel at eleven o'clock on 12 December.'

The wretched Khessin scrabbled through the music he had written in spare moments. All of it, he decided, was unfit to show to the great man—'salon trash', he called it. Hurriedly he got to work on a violin and piano sonata, cutting down his law classes to two a week. He persuaded R. Fidelman, pupil of Auer at the Conservatoire, to play the work with him but the music refused to do his bidding: 'I was so agitated that all the themes whined away in the minor and I was in absolute despair.'

By the 12th he had 'cooked up' the first three movements and feverishly rehearsed them with Fidelman. They did not sound too bad and off they went to the hotel well before eleven o'clock. There he found young Napravnik and Litke and all four went up together into Tchaikovsky's room. 'He seemed in the best of humours. He kissed Volodya and Sanya and affably held out his hand to me. I was struck dumb. I could not say a word. I saw his face light up with an extraordinarily kind smile and affectionately taking me by the hand he guided me into a chair.'

It was then that Tchaikovsky showed why he was so much loved. He could see at a glance that young Khessin was in such a state of nerves that he would not be able to play a note of his work. He no doubt suspected that if he did play it it would be worthless—ninety-nine out of a hundred of the young men he saw had no talent. But he decided as always to give the boy a chance; he began to talk with the kind of ease he had shown during that noteworthy Balakirev evening, asking questions, telling stories, until Khessin began to feel at home. Then he said, 'I hear you have composed a sonata specially for me to hear? That is a great compliment. May I hear it?'

They played the work. Tchaikovsky thanked them and walked up and down the room for a few minutes. Khessin, enraptured by his bright eyes, soft voice, expressive use of his hands, and by the elegance with which he wore his suit, waited with little hope.

'Well,' said Tchaikovsky at last, 'I left the law for music, too.'

SIXTH SYMPHONY

ii

Aleksandr III was delighted with *Yolanta* and *The Nutcracker* and told the composer so at the end of an evening which rivalled the glories of *The Sleeping Beauty* première, with the finest singers in Russia taking the chief roles. The audience was very appreciative too, both at the dress rehearsal and at the first performance. The critics were not so kind. *Yolanta* has disappeared from the stage except in Russia, *The Nutcracker* is seen occasionally though performances of the full ballet are comparatively rare outside Russia. The *Nutcracker* music is famous in the West more by way of the misleading suite than by the complete work.

Yolanta is a curious opera. In some respects it could be described as the best opera Tchaikovsky ever wrote. Musicologists have had difficulty in faulting it in construction or in the fittingness of the music. All is smooth and deft, a supreme example of sophisticated writing by a man who obviously has the art of composition at his fingertips. But the whole thing is a little too suave, too much like an exhibition of opera making. It has enormous charm and leaves the impression that the characterization has been smothered in it.

There are, of course, difficulties in the way of a one-act opera reaching the stage. It is a pity that *Yolanta* cannot be heard occasionally for it can give nothing but pleasure even if the pleasure has the atmosphere of a dream world. Tchaikovsky might well protest that the story demands just such an atmosphere. The answer to this must be left to the individual opera-goer.

The Nutcracker is another matter. Tchaikovsky never surpassed this score in his ballet music. What has told heavily against his third great ballet is the last act. This is no more than a series of divertissements for which the composer had to provide music possessing no relation to what had gone before. He did his work well despite a cry of 'How the devil do you expect me to write music to express a kingdom of lollipops!' and in one of the many items of this final act, the grand *pas de deux*, he wrote what is probably the greatest *pas de deux* music ever known—constructed with the simplicity of genius from a descending major scale—but by and large the act falls to pieces and the music with it.

The last act of *The Sleeping Beauty* is also given over to divertissements which were the curse of ballet in days when leading dancers expected the opportunity to show their paces before admirers and earn curtain calls. The *Sleeping Beauty* last act is just saved by

293

sufficient links with the ballet story—the march of the courtiers, the *pas de deux* of Aurora and the Prince and the presence of King, Queen, and, to wind it up, the fairies. In *The Nutcracker* there is scarcely a pretence of continuing the story.

This is the more lamentable because the opening act is one of the most lively and honest ever devised in ballet—a first-rate story—and Tchaikovsky's handling of the music for children and toys shows a genius for characterization; he loves children but sees their humorous side and does not blink at their unpleasantness. This is a slice of real life expressed with a nice musical irony.

The transformation music is in its very different mood perhaps the most poetical he had ever written. Both here and in the snow-flakes scene he reverts to and improves on the undeservedly neglected music in the first movement of his First Symphony. This is the Russia he knows and loves, and every note, every chord builds up the romantic world of a kingdom of snow. If this entrancing scene could have been followed by a fitting conclusion to the story, which should not be beyond the wit of man, *The Nutcracker* would now be as world-wide a favourite as *The Sleeping Beauty* and *Swan Lake*.

iii

Tchaikovsky was roused from disappointment at the tame reception of his work by a message from the past which dissolved his regrets immediately. One month earlier he had been honoured in France; he was elected an Associate Member of the Academy. The news was read down in the little Alsatian town of Montbéliard and a letter of congratulation reached him. It was from Fanny Durbach.

He read it with amazement; he had somehow thought that she could no longer be alive. 'I felt as though I had been told that my mother had risen from the dead, that the past forty-three years were nothing but a dream and that I had wakened and found myself back in my little upstairs room at Votkinsk.'

He replied at once: was there anything he could do for her?

She replied that the best gift he could make her and the only one she wanted was to come to see her.

On the first day of the new year, 1893, he was there 'in a quiet street in this little town which itself is so quiet that it might be one of our Russian "district" towns'.

Fanny opened the door. It was the house she and her sister had been born in and which they still owned—a tiny place with two rooms on each of the three floors. 'I knew her at once,' he told Nikolai, moved to write one of his rare letters to this brother. 'She is seventy but does not look it. She has altered amazingly little, her hair has not gone very grey, she has the old high colour we knew and her eyes are still warm and brown. She greeted me as though we had only been parted for a year or so, joyfully and tenderly but very simply too.'

They went upstairs and talked of the past. She had kept all his old copybooks and all the letters from him and his mother after she had left the family. He fingered them, read them and the past rose up so strongly 'that it seemed as if the very air I was breathing had the old Votkinsk smell; I could distinctly hear my mother's voice'.

He spent the whole of that day and the next with her. At his hotel he discovered that she and her sister, who had also been a governess in Russia, were still teaching locally and were known and loved by the whole town. As he spoke and listened to her and looked at her he could understand why. 'It soon became clear to me why we were all so fond of her. She is a remarkably clever and sympathetic woman. She breathes kindness and integrity.'

At last he had to go—he had a concert to conduct in Brussels—but promised to come back the next time he visited France. There was to be no next time.

Brussels and Odessa took up the next month—triumphs each of them—and he did not settle down again in Klin until the middle of February. He began work at once on a new symphony. He had torn up the score of the earlier one: 'nothing but meaningless sound patterns,' he explained. The new symphony had a programme but he did not intend to divulge it: 'let those discover it who can.'

He set to at a great rate. In four days he had written the first movement and he could see quite clearly how the rest of the symphony would develop. It was the first time he had had such a comprehensive view of a large work.

He was very much excited. 'Much of the work will be new in its form. For instance the Finale won't be a great allegro but an adagio of considerable proportions. You simply can't imagine how happy I am to feel that I am not finished yet as a composer.'

If he had been left free to write on he would have had the whole thing done in a matter of weeks, he was in a ferment of inspiration, but he was again forced to conduct in Moscow. When he was there a young Conservatoire graduate, Sergei Rakhmaninov, presented him with one of his first works, a set of five pieces for piano.

He was no stranger to this form of flattery; Glazunov, Lyadov, and Arensky, to mention only three of the better-known disciples, had begged him to accept autograph scores as a sign of their admiration, Glazunov more than once, Rakhmaninov too. He accepted this latest tribute because he liked all he heard of Rakhmaninov from Taneyev, his old theory professor, and thought the piano pieces promising.

He gave his followers good value for their admiration, from arranging a special first private performance of the Sextet for Lyadov and Glazunov and their friends to the provision of helpful introductions to publishers and concert directors. Above all, he said what he thought, that was one reason why young composers liked him. He did not merely take these offerings as no more than his due, he gave good advice in turn. A notable example was a prophetic letter to Glazunov some time earlier. He had been looking through the latest Glazunov composition sent to him and said, 'I often think of you. In some ways you puzzle me. You have genius, that is obvious, but something in you prevents you from broadening the scope of it.'

This was good criticism if Glazunov could have acted on it successfully and Tchaikovsky now showed with the latest disciple what a practical as well as lovable mentor he could be. In May he again left Klin and his symphony for Moscow because Rakhmaninov had told him that his first opera *Aleko* was to be produced at the Bolshoi. He did not simply come for the first performance but for a rehearsal. He walked into the theatre, sat himself down by Rakhmaninov, listened for a while, then whispered, 'Aren't they taking it a bit too slowly?'

Rakhmaninov admitted that he thought they were. He added, apologetically, that he could not bring himself to interfere with the conductor whose reputation was so much greater than his own.

'But that's absurd,' said Tchaikovsky. His own youthful deprecatory manner rose up before him. Another Pyotr Ilyich! He got up, walked to the orchestra pit and spoke to the conductor. The tempo was immediately changed.

Nor was this the whole of his kindness to this young man. After he had heard the opera, which he thought charming, he said to Rakhmaninov, 'Wouldn't it be a good idea if we put on our operas together—yours and *Yolanta*?' Both were short operas and would just about fill an evening.

The plan never came to anything—Tchaikovsky died before he could arrange it—but Rakhmaninov remembered the gesture to the end of his life and, what was just as extraordinary from a composer of Tchaikovsky's eminence, the manner in which it was made, as if both men were equals and the younger one would be conferring a favour if he agreed.

iv

After another short stay at Klin Tchaikovsky had to go off again with the new symphony still unfinished, this time to England where he had been offered the honorary degree of Doctor of Music at Cambridge University. He broke his journey at Petersburg to attend a party at the Rimsky-Korsakovs and was asked by his host, supported by Lyadov and Glazunov, if he would conduct the Musical Society concerts that winter. He accepted.

The invitation to conduct the orchestra made famous by Rubinstein and Balakirev must have delighted him; certainly it set the seal on his lifelong refusal to take sides; at long last the revolutionaries had accepted him as a nationalist composer in the best sense of the word. He had never given way to the years of pressure to tie himself to a group and had abstained from controversy; his music had done the arguing and at last had won a bloodless victory.

By the end of May he was in London for an honour he could not rate in the same category. It is a little difficult to know why he accepted the invitation from a country which he had described as 'only just made tolerable by Shakespeare and Dickens'. The explanation seems to be the hope of meeting Grieg again, for the Norwegian was one of the group of eminent European musicians to receive a doctorate. In fact he was too unwell to attend and Tchaikovsky had to make do with Saint-Saëns and Boito; Max Bruch he did not like at all.

Nor did he like London, appalled by its dirt and tastelessness, though the sheer volume of traffic and the sense of a great business city impressed him. He conducted the London Philharmonic in the Fourth Symphony and was gratified to find the audience forgetting their famed English reticence to such an extent that Saint-Saëns, following with one of his works, played to a hall rather drained of enthusiasm.

This triumph was repeated at the mixed concert by the University

297

Musical Society; *Francesca*, conducted by Tchaikovsky, had an uproarious welcome which threw into the shade the reception given to the music of Bruch, Boito, Grieg, and the rest.

The day after the awarding of the doctorates, 13 June, Tchaikovsky thankfully departed for Paris and Moscow, taking in a visit to Sophie Menter in Vienna *en route*. He came back to Klin and to news of the loss of more old friends, particularly of Albrecht, his colleague at the Conservatoire from his arrival there nearly thirty years earlier.

Modest, like everyone who has followed him, comments on Tchaikovsky's calm acceptance of these deaths which a few years before would have thrown him into a long fit of melancholy. The reason for this change of attitude is unquestionably the symphony which he took up the moment he reached home—the symphony and all that it stood for. This third attempt to provide an answer to the problem of the workings of fate in men's lives, above all of fate's final stroke—death—was significantly free from the struggles attending the composition of the two earlier symphonies. With this Sixth Symphony he never hesitated; the whole work took only twelve days to sketch out and not much more than twice that time to orchestrate. It was a remarkable feat which made nonsense of his complaints that he was beginning to lose his facility; the score shows no sign of effort.

This summer at Klin was one of his most productive for he not only finished the Sixth Symphony before the end of August but went far to complete a Third Piano Concerto. The history of this concerto is instructive. Like all composers Tchaikovsky was thrifty. He disliked wasting material. He soon regretted having torn up the beginnings of the previous symphony. He had done so because it was impersonal music, wholly extrovert and for that reason unsuitable for a symphony. He thought of a symphony as essentially an expression of the writer's feelings, of his philosophy of life; lacking that, he had no wish to go on with it, to make, as he said, 'meaningless harmonies and modulations and a rhythmical scheme expressive of nothing'.

However, these formed music of a kind that also had a place in the world, particularly when written by a composer whose very handling of a theme was a delight to hear and, for the musicologist, to analyse. The main theme he had used for the abortive symphony might have meant nothing to him personally but as a theme it was highly attractive and, as usual, skilfully worked out.

In this summer of 1893 he realized that the material might be used as the opening movement of a piano concerto which did not demand the introvert mood of a symphony. He remembered what he had written and at once began to reconstruct it from memory in concerto form. He finished the first movement and orchestrated it and sketched out a slow movement and Finale before he had to break off to conduct at Petersburg and Hamburg.

As he did not live to finish this work its future career had best be dealt with here. After his death Taneyev orchestrated the slow movement and the Finale. The completed concerto was often played and has been heard outside Russia several times. Taneyev unhappily was not a Tchaikovsky and the movements he orchestrated are a sad falling away from the first.

Recently another Russian musicologist, Semyon Bogatyrev, has reverted to Tchaikovsky's original idea and has reconstructed the entire work—to which he added a Scherzo from a piano piece of 1893—and put it out as Tchaikovsky's Seventh Symphony. This work has also been played in the West.

It must be said that this devotion to the composer is labour thrown away. Tchaikovsky decided that the work would not make a satisfactory symphony. How right he is Bogatyrev has now demonstrated and it may be hoped that this piece of mistaken idolatry, perpetrated only by defying Tchaikovsky's wishes, may now be forgotten. The first movement of the concerto as Tchaikovsky wrote it is sometimes played alone. It is very well worth playing and should be kept in the repertoire. Anything Tchaikovsky had to say about the use of pianoforte and orchestra is far too valuable and attractive to be lost.

While he was at work on it in the midst of a summer of gardening, entertaining, and composing he received his last letter from Fanny. His last command too; once a governess always a governess and Fanny's reaction to their reunion after the first joy had subsided was in character—she set him a task. Taking up where she had left off forty-five years earlier her instinct to bend the intensely romantic to the service of the intensely practical got to work on her young Petya. He had not turned out to be the great literary genius she had fondly hoped; that was a pity, but to be a great composer was an honour too and a responsibility. Seeing him again she saw Russia again and this, to the undying pedagogue in her, was merely the starting-point for a new educational scheme.

'I never saw such beautiful sunsets as in Russia,' she wrote, 'when the sky was covered with amazingly bright colours. I particularly liked the calm, mild evenings at the end of summer. The canoes of the men fishing rocked on the lake when they cast their lines. The water was smooth and like a mirror in which the dying sun was reflected. I shall never forget these evenings and the view from the balcony. From there too we heard tender, sad songs sung by the peasants and they alone disturbed the silence of those wonderful nights. Do you remember them? You ought to, for neither you nor any other of the children ever wanted to go to bed on such evenings.'

Then came the task. He knew the method well and must have smiled as he read, for this was the Fanny of old, approaching the horse she intended to ride, a tempting piece of sugar in her hand. 'If you do remember those songs at Votkinsk, set them to music. Then you will bring your Russia to those who cannot be there to enjoy them. Pushkin, that noble poet of yours, used to say that he wanted his poems to be known and loved wherever Russian was spoken, down to the meanest peasant's hut. Splendid aspiration! But yours can and should be greater still, for the language in which you speak is universal.'

To Fanny in Montbéliard he remained her pupil at the age of fifty-three and to any children lucky enough to live near the Klin house he remained an ageless playmate, devising the kind of games that had thrilled the twins forty years earlier. Fanny was not mistaken nor were his child friends of Klin; on occasion he was nothing but a child—or, since that can sound condescending, he had preserved a childlike heart. An incident this summer provides a refreshing sidelight on the great man who had so recently marched solemnly and impressively in his red and white robes at Cambridge, the essence of dignity and manly beauty, the world-famous composer who was so soon to give mankind yet another imperishable masterpiece.

Like so many Russians, he was a madly keen collector of mushrooms and could indulge his passion freely at Klin; the woods and fields around his house were filled with them. However, as anyone will know who has taken to the sport, there are mushroom collectors and mushroom collectors; some have the eye for it, others have not. Tchaikovsky was of the latter persuasion, Kashkin of the former.

Kashkin came over for the weekend during the summer and Tchaikovsky at once—he could never believe that his bad luck would last—insisted that they go out mushrooming. When they reached the wood in which the best kind grew (they called them the white ones as distinct from the dark) Kashkin spotted them first as usual, gathering them at times from under Tchaikovsky's very nose.

Tchaikovsky stood this for a time in silence, then looked from his friend's half-filled basket of white mushrooms to his own measly collection of dark ones and burst out irritably, 'Let's split up. You'll only pinch my mushrooms again if we stay together.'

Kashkin agreed and each went to different parts of the wood. For once Tchaikovsky was in luck; after walking some way he stumbled on a colony of white mushrooms, a colony so thick that even he could not miss them. He stared at the treasure for a moment, speechless before the sight of such riches. When the truth dawned he 'let out a fearful yell'.

It was a cry of triumph but to Kashkin, out of sight, it sounded like a cry for help. He hurried through the trees in the direction of the cries—for they were still going on. When he discovered Tchaikovsky at last he saw him standing in the midst of his colony of mushrooms like one possessed, crowing with joy.

Tchaikovsky heard Kashkin's footsteps cracking the twigs. He looked back, his face changed and so did his cry; from a yell of triumph it turned to a scream of fear. He waved one hand violently at him. 'They're mine!' he shouted. 'All mine!' As Kashkin still continued to walk towards the horde Tchaikovsky suddenly threw himself headlong into the heart of the colony. He lay there spread-eagled, his wide-stretched arms covering as many of the precious mushrooms as possible. 'Don't you dare come nearer, Nikolai!' he shouted, his face red and excited. 'They're mine, d'you hear! *I* found them. You aren't going to pinch these. Don't you dare move! Go away, go right away!'

v

In September, with the symphony ready for its first performance in Petersburg, Tchaikovsky went off to see Anatoly in the country at Mikhailovskoe. He loved it and took the train for Hamburg with reluctance. He stayed there only long enough to conduct *Yolanta* successfully, then went back to Klin to try to tidy up the piano concerto. Two more old friends had died—Apukhtin in Petersburg, Zverev in Moscow—and in the middle of October he travelled down to Moscow with his visitors of the moment (the house was rarely free from them) to attend the memorial service for his old colleague who had been professor of pianoforte at the Conservatoire.

At a gathering of still-living friends next day they talked about

L   301

the dead man as survivors usually do and about their own chances of survival. Kashkin decided to keep the subject light and turned to Tchaikovsky with a 'You'll outlive us all, Petya.' He believed it, he said afterwards; he had never seen his friend look so calm and strong. Tchaikovsky smiled and said he thought it unlikely but admitted that he couldn't remember feeling so well or so contented.

This contentment could have come wholly from his feeling that in the new symphony he had at last expressed himself adequately on the subject which had haunted him all his adult life. But there was another possible reason why his friends found him in such excellent form; he heard that Anna Lvovna was in Moscow and went to see her.

He had met his niece for tea at the new Von Meck house in Prechistensky Avenue a few months earlier, when she was on her way to Wiesbaden with Nadyezhda Filaretovna in a final attempt to arrest the rapid spread of her mother-in-law's tuberculosis, and had begged her to try to find out the cause of the break. Anna Lvovna was astounded by the feeling he displayed—'I only knew then how deeply he had taken the rupture to heart'—which gives some idea of the secrecy of life in the Von Meck household.

At that first meeting she promised to do her best. At the second meeting, in October 1893, she had just come back from Wiesbaden. The cure had failed—the disease had already reached the throat—but she had persuaded Nadyezhda Filaretovna to break her long silence at last; in painful whispers—she could scarcely speak—she told her daughter-in-law: 'I knew I was no longer necessary to him, that I could no longer give him anything he wanted. Our correspondence was still a joy to me but I didn't feel I had any right to please myself alone if it had become a burden to him. It is true I refused to give him any further material assistance but could that really have been important to him? If he didn't understand why I had done it and he still felt that I was necessary to him, why didn't he write again?'

What Tchaikovsky thought of this explanation we shall never know. To an outsider it might seem inadequate and even misleading; his instant reply to Nadyezhda Filaretovna's curt note, both the speed and the contents of it, put him firmly in the right, and he had made clear that he would write to Pakhulsky in full only to save her the trouble of replying at such a painful time—for she had led him to believe that she was financially ruined. How any woman could resist replying at once to such a demonstration of sympathy is difficult to understand.

But Tchaikovsky was not an outsider and he was not calculating. He probably thought with immense relief that everything had been the result of the kind of misunderstanding that can happen between correspondents, each waiting for the other to write. This would not lessen the sadness of the break, would probably accentuate it. The one positive thing his niece's explanation did for him was to wipe out the supposed insult of Nadyezhda's final note and reduce it to the tactless action of a sick but still fond woman.

'I did not have time to speak to him fully,' said Anna Lvovna afterwards, 'but I should like to believe that the little I did say was partly the cause of the particularly brilliant mood of his last days, a mood noticed by everyone who met him.'

As against this theory we have Modest's report that in his final hours the unconscious Pyotr Ilyich several times murmured Nadyezhda Filaretovna's name in tones of deep reproach. Modest's report is suspect—he disliked the connexion and was furious at the way his brother had been treated—but even if it were true the two statements are not necessarily incompatible: Tchaikovsky had suffered deeply, and as we know by our own dreams these scars never disappear from the unconscious. Certainly Tchaikovsky's cheerfulness and confidence were marked by all at that gathering of old friends in Moscow the day after Zverev's funeral, and by that time he had seen and spoken to Anna Lvovna.

That night he took the train to Petersburg for the last time—none of them was to see him again—but before he does so it might be as well to take a final look at the Tchaikovsky who was never too busy with his own work or prospects to spare time for others. For months he had thought of little but this new symphony into which he had put all the concentrated wisdom of the years, musical wisdom and moral wisdom too. He was excited by the prospect of conducting it for the first time. Yet when the young Rakhmaninov called on him with a new suite for two pianos in his hands and begged to be allowed to dedicate it to him if he thought well of it, Pyotr Ilyich at once sat down and played it with him. He did more; liking the work, he insisted that Taneyev must hear it.

An appointment was made and at the fixed time they met in Taneyev's music room and played the work over again together. When they had done Tchaikovsky got up and gestured to Taneyev and—Rakhmaninov is telling the story—'said with that kind and attractive smile of his, "Isn't it good? And that's not all. Young Seryozha here has written a concerto this summer, and six songs *and The Rock* as well as this Suite."' He laughed again with a grimace. 'And I think *I* work hard! And all I've done is to write one symphony!'

That is Tchaikovsky, the Tchaikovsky of the mushrooms, the Tchaikovsky who a few days later, on 28 October, ascended the podium at the first concert of the season given by the Musical Society at Petersburg, elegant, assured, handsomer than ever, and, if his facial expression is allowed as evidence, a man at last at peace with himself.

The audience gave far more of their applause to a performance of the B flat Minor concerto that evening than to the première of the Sixth Symphony. This is understandable; the mood and construction of the work demanded a degree of reflection that no contemporary audience could possibly give to a single performance. The Finale alone, that movement of supreme genius, was so original that musicians were to ponder it for years to come. It cannot be repeated, it is unique and sums up the composer's thought and feelings with such beauty and sincerity that one has the sense that there is no more for him to say.

Tchaikovsky perhaps felt this. It is noteworthy that the indifferent reception of the work did not disturb him. He saw that audience and critics were puzzled and understood that they must be puzzled. He trusted to time. 'I have never felt so proud of anything I've written.'

Tchaikovsky was an artist. So too was the fate of which he had thought and written so much. He had composed his requiem and fate acted for the last time. Five days after the concert, on 2 November, he was not at breakfast. Modest looked into his room; he was unwell, he said. He got up nevertheless and paid a promised call on Napravnik. He was feeling no better when he came back but laughed at Modest's suggestion that he call a doctor. At lunch he felt thirsty and before he could be stopped he had filled and drunk a tumblerful of unboiled water.

When Glazunov looked in during the afternoon Tchaikovsky still felt ill but brushed aside every attempt of the alarmed young man to take it seriously.

That evening Modest fetched a doctor without telling Pyotr Ilyich. The doctor at once called in his brother, the famous Leo Bertenson. They diagnosed cholera. Tchaikovsky whispered to Modest, 'This is death.'

He spent a night of agonizing pain. Of courage too, for he refused to be nursed and sent everyone to their beds. The next morning, Friday, he seemed to have recovered and, like his mother so many years ago, thought he had got the better of the disease. By the early hours of Saturday morning the cramps had come back so piercingly that he gave up hope. He told the doctors to go and attend to the living: 'I shan't get better,' he said.

The group about the bedside grew larger on Sunday; his brother Nikolai was there, Aleksei had hurried up from Klin. Tchaikovsky did not recognize them.

The final remedy, the hot bath, was tried.

Early the next morning, 6 November, he died peacefully.

CATALOGUE OF WORKS

(restricted to opus numbers except when work is discussed in text)

ORCHESTRAL WORKS

TITLE	COMPOSED	FIRST PERFORMED	OPUS	
Overture to *The Storm*	1864		76	(posthumous)
Symphony No. 1 in G Minor 'Winter Daydreams'	1866 (revised 1874)	Moscow 1868	13	
Festival Overture on Danish National Anthem	1866		15	
Symphonic Poem *Fatum*	1868	Moscow 1869	77	(posthumous)
Fantasy Overture *Romeo and Juliet*	1869 (revised 1870, 1880)	Moscow 1870		
Symphony No. 2 in C Minor	1872 (revised 1879)	Moscow 1873	17	
Fantasy Overture *The Tempest*	1873	Moscow 1873	18	
Symphony No. 3 in D Major	1875	Moscow 1875	29	
Marche Slave	1876	Moscow 1876	31	
Fantasy *Francesca da Rimini*	1876	Moscow 1877	32	
Symphony No. 4 in F Minor	1877	Moscow 1878	36	
Suite No. 1 in D Minor	1878–9	Moscow 1879	43	
Capriccio Italien	1880	Moscow 1880	45	
Overture *1812*	1880	Moscow 1882	49	
Coronation March	1883	Moscow 1883		
Suite No. 2 in C Major	1883	Moscow 1884	53	
Suite No. 3 in G Major	1884	St. Petersburg 1885	55	
Manfred Symphony	1884–5	Moscow 1886	58	
Suite No. 4 'Mozartiana'	1887	Moscow 1887	61	

307

ORCHESTRAL WORKS—continued

TITLE	COMPOSED	FIRST PERFORMED	OPUS
Symphony No. 5 in E Minor	1888	St. Petersburg 1888	64
Fantasy Overture *Hamlet*	1888	St. Petersburg 1888	67a
Symphonic Poem *Voïvode*	1890–1	Moscow 1891	78
Nutcracker Ballet Suite	1892	St. Petersburg 1892	71a
Symphony No. 6 in B Minor	1893	St. Petersburg 1893	74

BALLETS

Swan Lake	1875–6	Moscow 1877	20
The Sleeping Beauty	1888–9	St. Petersburg 1890	66
The Nutcracker (*Casse Noisette*)	1891–2	St. Petersburg 1892	71

INCIDENTAL MUSIC

Snyegurochka	1873	Moscow 1873	12
Hamlet	1891	St. Petersburg 1891	67b

STRING ORCHESTRA

Serenade for Strings in C Major	1880	Moscow 1882	48

SOLO INSTRUMENTS WITH ORCHESTRA

Concerto No. 1 in B flat Minor for pianoforte	1874–5	Boston 1875	23
Sérénade Mélancolique for violin	1875	Moscow 1876	26

SOLO INSTRUMENTS WITH ORCHESTRA—*continued*

TITLE	COMPOSED	FIRST PERFORMED	OPUS
Variations on a Rococo Theme for cello	1876	Moscow 1877	33
Valse-Scherzo for violin	1877	Paris 1878	34
Concerto in D Major for violin	1877–8	Vienna 1881	35
Concerto No. 2 in G Major for pianoforte	1879–80	Moscow 1882	44
Concert Fantasy for pianoforte	1884	Moscow 1885	56
Pezzo capriccioso for cello	1887	Moscow 1889	62
Concerto in E flat Major for pianoforte (first movement only)	1893	St. Petersburg 1895	75 (posthumous)
Concerto in E flat Major for pianoforte (Andante and Finale with Taneyev's orchestration)	1893 (sketch)	St. Petersburg 1896	79 (posthumous)

CHAMBER MUSIC

TITLE	COMPOSED	FIRST PERFORMED	OPUS
String Quartet No. 1 in D Major	1871	Moscow 1871	11
String Quartet No. 2 in F Major	1874	Moscow 1874	22
String Quartet No. 3 in E flat Minor	1876	Moscow 1876	30
Trio for violin, pianoforte and cello in A Minor	1881–2	Moscow 1882	50
String Sextet in D Minor	1887–92	St. Petersburg 1892	70

VIOLIN AND PIANOFORTE

TITLE	COMPOSED	FIRST PERFORMED	OPUS
Souvenir d'un lieu cher	1878		42

PIANOFORTE

TITLE	COMPOSED	FIRST PERFORMED	OPUS
Sonata in C sharp Minor	1865		80 (posthumous)
Scherzo à la russe and Impromptu in E flat Minor	1867		1
Souvenir de Hapsal	1867		2
Valse-caprice in D Major	1868		4
Romance in F Minor	1868		5
Valse-scherzo in A Major	1870		7
Capriccio in G flat Major	1870		8
Three Pieces	1870		8
Nocturne and Humoresque	1871		10
Six Pieces	1873		19
Six pieces on a single theme	1873		21
The Seasons: Twelve Pieces	1875–6		37b
Twelve Pieces of Moderate Difficulty	1876–8		40
Sonata in G Major	1878		37
Children's Album: 24 easy pieces	1878		39
Six Pieces	1882		51
Dumka	1886		59
Eighteen Pieces	1893		72

OPERAS

TITLE	COMPOSED	PRODUCED	OPUS
Voivode	1867–8	Moscow 1869	3
Undine	1869		
Oprichnik	1870–2	St. Petersburg 1874	
Vakula the Smith	1874	St. Petersburg 1876	14

310

OPERAS—continued

TITLE	COMPOSED	PRODUCED	OPUS
Cherevichki (revision of Vakula the Smith)	1885	Moscow 1887	
Yevgeny Onyegin	1877–8	Moscow 1879	24
The Maid of Orleans	1878–9	St. Petersburg 1881	
Mazepa	1881–3	Moscow 1884	
The Sorceress	1885–7	St. Petersburg 1887	
The Queen of Spades	1890	St. Petersburg 1890	68
Yolanta	1891	St. Petersburg 1892	69

CHORAL WORKS

	COMPOSED		OPUS
Cantata *Ode to Joy* for four solo voices, chorus and orchestra	1865		
Cantata for the opening of the Moscow Polytechnic Exhibitions for tenor, chorus and orchestra	1872		
Coronation Cantata *Moscow* for mezzo-soprano, baritone, chorus and orchestra	1883		
Greetings to Anton Rubinstein Cantata for unaccompanied mixed chorus	1889		

CHURCH MUSIC

	COMPOSED		OPUS
Liturgy of St. John Chrysostom for four-part mixed chorus	1878		41
Vesper Mass: Eighteen harmonized liturgical songs for mixed chorus	1881–2		52

SONGS

TITLE	COMPOSED	DEDICATION	OPUS
Six Songs	1869	Various	6
Six Songs	1872	Various	16
Six Songs	1875	Various	25
Six Songs	1875	Princess R. A. Tsertelevaya	27
Six Songs	1875	Various	28
Six Songs	1878	A. I. Tchaikovsky	38
Seven Songs	1880	A. V. Panayeva	47
Sixteen Songs for Children	1881–3	—	54
Six Songs	1884	Various	57
Twelve Songs	1886	—	60
Six Songs	1887	—	63
Six French Songs	1888	Désirée Artôt-Padilla	65
Six Songs	1893	N. N. Figner	73

VOCAL DUET

| Six Duets | 1880 | T. L. Davydova | 46 |

Bibliography

NOTE. In view of the enormous Tchaikovsky bibliography the following list has been confined to primary sources in Russian with the addition of a few general titles which have been found helpful. Most of the manuscript material referred to in this book (autograph manuscripts and copies of lost originals) will be found in the:

Archives of the Tchaikovsky Museum, Klin
Philharmonic Museum, Leningrad
State Public Library, Leningrad
Conservatory Library, Leningrad
Conservatory Library, Moscow
Central State Archives of Literature and Art
Glinka Central Museum of Musical Culture
State Historical Archives of the Leningrad District
Library of Congress, Washington

LETTERS, ARTICLES, DIARIES AND REMINISCENCES, PRINTED AND UNPRINTED

Perepiska M. A. Balakireva s P. I. Chaikovskim (*Correspondence of M. A. Balakirev with P. I. Tchaikovsky*). St. Petersburg, 1912.

Perepiska Chaikovskogo s Besselem (*Correspondence of Tchaikovsky with Bessel*). Moscow, 1923.

Perepiska s P. I. Jurgensonom (*Correspondence with P. I. Jurgenson*). Ed. V. A. Zhdanov and N. T. Zhegin. Moscow n.d.

Perepiska s N. F. fon Mekk (*Correspondence with N. F. von Meck*). Ed. V. A. Zhdanov and N. T. Zhegin. 3 vols. Moscow, 1934–6.

Perepiska P. I. Chaikovskogo i E. F. Napravnik, 1872–93 (*Correspondence of P. I. Tchaikovsky and E. F. Napravnik, 1872–93*). Moscow n.d.

Pisma P. I. Chaikovskogo i S. I. Taneyeva (*Letters of P. I. Tchaikovsky and S. I. Taneyev*) ed. M. I. Tchaikovsky. Petrograd, 1916.

Ostrovsky i russkie kompozitory: pisma (*Ostrovsky and Russian*

Composers: Letters) ed. E. M. Kolosova and V. Filippov Moscow–Leningrad, 1937.

P. I. Chaikovsky. Pisma k rodnym (*P. I. Tchaikovsky. Letters to Relatives*) ed. V. A. Zhdanov. Moscow, 1940.

P. I. Chaikovsky. Pisma k blizkim (P. I. Tchaikovsky. *Letters to Intimates*). Moscow, 1955.

Dnyevniki P. I. Chaikovskogo 1873–91 (*Diaries of P. I. Tchaikovsky. 1873–91*) ed. I. I. Tchaikovsky. Moscow, 1923 (Eng. trans. New York 1945).

Literaturnie proizvedenia i perepiska (*Literary Works and Correspondence*). Vols 1–8. Moscow, 1944–65 (Vols 9–10 not yet published).

Rukovodstvo k prakticheskomu izucheniu harmonii: uchebnik sostavlenny professorom moskovskoi konservatorii P. Chaikovskim (*Guide to the Practical Study of Harmony:* a manual compiled by the professor of the Moscow Conservatoire, P. Tchaikovsky). Moscow, 1871.

Proshloe russkoi muzyki: materyali i issledovania (*A History of Russian Music*) by B. V. Asafyev. Petrograd, 1920.

Vospominania i pisma (*Recollections and Letters*) Ed. Igor Glebov (B. V. Asafyev). Leningrad, 1924.

50 lyet russkoi muzyki v moikh vospominaniakh (*My Recollections of 50 Years of Russian Music*) by M. M. Ippolitov-Ivanov. Moscow, 1934.

Iz moikh vospominany o P. I. Chaikovsky (*Recollections of P. I. Tchaikovsky*) by V. V. Bessel. Imperial Theatres Yearbook, 1896–7.

Muzykalnie felyetoni i zametki Petra Ilicha Chaikovskogo, s prilozheniem portreta, avtobiograficheskogo opisania puteshestvia zagranitsu v 1888 godu i predislovia G. A. Larosha (*Musical articles and notes of Pyotr Ilyich Tchaikovsky, including a portrait, an autobiographical account of his tour abroad in 1888 and a foreword by H. A. Laroche*). Moscow, 1898.

Iz moikh vospominany o P. I. Chaikovskom (*Recollections of P. I. Tchaikovsky)* by H. A. Larosh. *Syeverny Vyestnik*, 1893, 1894.

Na pamyat o P. I. Chaikovskom (*In memory of P. I. Tchaikovsky*) by H. A. Larosh and N. D. Kashkin. Moscow, 1894.

Sobranie muzykalno-kriticheskix statei (*Collected Musico-critical Articles*) by H. A. Larosh. Moscow, 1922.

BIBLIOGRAPHY

Vospominania o P. I. Chaikovskom (*Recollections of P. I. Tchaikovsky*) by N. D. Kashkin. Moscow, 1896, 1954.

Vospominania o P. I. Chaikovskom (Recollections of P. I. Tchaikovsky) by K. N. de Lazari (Konstantinov). *Rossia*, 1900.

Moi vospominania o P. I. Chaikovskom (*My recollections of P. I. Tchaikovsky*) by I. A. Klimenko. Ryazan, 1908.

Lyetopis moei muzykalnoi zhizni (*Annals of my musical life*) by N. A. Rimsky-Korsakov. 3rd and 4th edns., ed. A. N. Rimsky-Korsakov Moscow–Leningrad 1928, 1932. Reprinted in *Complete Works*, Moscow, 1955. (Eng. trans. 3rd edn. New York 1942).

'P. I. Chaikovsky kak dirizhor' ('P. I. Tchaikovsky as conductor') by I. P. Pryanishnikov. *Russkaya muzyykalnaya gazeta*, Petrograd, 1918.

'P. I. Chaikovsky v roli muzykalnogo kritika' ('P. I. Tchaikovsky as music critic') by G. Timofeyev. *Russkaya muzkalnaya gazeta*, St. Petersburg, 1899.

'Moyo znakomstvo c Chaikovskim' ('My friendship with Tchaikovsky') from *Letters, Articles, and Recollections* by A. K. Glazunov. Moscow, 1958.

'Vstrecha c Chaikovskim' ('A meeting with Tchaikovsky') from *My Recollections* by A. B. Khessin, Moscow, 1960.

'Zavyet khudozhnika' ('An Artist's Advice') by I. E. Grabar. *Ogonyok*, 1940.

'Vospominania o P. I. Chaikovskom' ('Recollections of P. I. Tchaikovsky') from *Letters and recollections* by V. P. Pogozhev, ed. Igor Glebov. Leningrad, 1924.

'Iz vospominany ob avtore Pikovoi damy' ('My recollections of the composer of *The Queen of Spades*') by N. N. Vilde. *Teatralnaya gazeta*, Moscow, 1915.

'Iz konservatorskikh vospominany 1871–79' ('My Conservatoire recollections 1871–9' by R. V. Genika. *Russkaya muzykalnaya gazeta*, Moscow, 1916.

Chaikovsky na Ukraine (Tchaikovsky in the Ukraine) by A. V. Khimichenko. *Mistetstvo*, 1940.

'Vospominania o P. I. Chaikovskom' ('Recollections of P. I. Tchaikovsky') by Bemol (pseudonym, author not established). *Novoe vremya*, 1893.

'Pamyatnie vstrechi' ('Memorable Meetings') by L. P. Steinberg. *Komsomolskaya pravda*, 1940.

'Iz vospominany artista-muzykanta' ('Recollections of an Artist-musician') by I. V. Lipaev. *Russkaya starina*, 1896.

'Moi vospominania o velikom kompozitore' ('My Recollections of a great Composer') by S. I. Levin. *Bolshevistskoe znamya,*Odessa, 1940.

'Vystuplenia P. I. Chaikovskogo v Parizhe' ('Tchaikovsky's Performances in Paris') by D. A. Chernomordikov. *Sovyetskaya muzyka,* 1940.

'Iz moikh vospominany o P. I. Chaikovskom' ('My recollections of P. I. Tchaikovsky') by V. V. Yastrebtsev. *Russkaya muzykalnaya gazeta,* 1899.

'Moi vospominania o Chaikovskom' ('My recollections of Tchaikovsky') by V. E. Napravnik. *Sovyetskaya muzyka,* 1949.

'Posledny dyen P. I. Chaikovskogo v Klinu' ('Tchaikovsky's last day at Klin') by Y. I. Poplavsky. *Artist,* 1894.

'Klochki zhizni c beregov Nevy, 25 oktyabr' ('Glimpses of life on the banks of the Neva, 25 October') by Skitalyets (S. G. Petrov). *Ranneye,* 1913.

'Vospominania opernoi artistki' ('Recollections of an opera artist') by E. K. Pavlovskaya. MS. Tchaikovsky Museum.

'Vospominania' ('Recollections') and 'Vospominania o vstrechakh c Chaikovskim v Tiflise' ('Recollections of my Meetings with Tchaikovsky at Tiflis') by A. N. Amfiteatrova-Levitskaya. MSS. Tchaikovsky and Glinka Museums.

'O moikh vstrechakh c P. I. Chaikovskim' ('My Meetings with Tchaikovsky') by L. V. Nikolaev. MS. Glinka Museum.

'Vospominania o prebyvanii Chaikovskogo v Taganroge i Odesse' ('Recollections of Tchaikovsky at Taganrog and Odessa') by I. I. Tchaikovsky. MS. Tchaikovsky Museum.

'Kontserty P. I. Chaikovskogo v Kharkove—po lichnym vospominaniam' ('P. I. Tchaikovsky's concerts at Kharkov—personal recollections') by I. E. Bukinik 1943. MS. Tchaikovsky Museum.

'Meetings with Tchaikovsky in America and England by Walter U. Damrosch', 1946. With a photograph of letter from Tchaikovsky to Damrosch. MS. Tchaikovsky Museum.

'O Chaikovskom—vospominania svoi i chuzhie' ('Recollections of Tchaikovsky by Myself and Others') by S. N. Neuberg-Kashkina, 1959. MS. Tchaikovsky Museum.

'Vospominania o P. I. Chaikovskom' ('Recollections of P. I. Tchaikovsky) from *Chetyre pyatykh vyeka* (*Four-fifths of a Century*) by A. I. Bryullova 1929. MS. Glinka Museum.

'Vospominania o P. I. Chaikovskom' ('Recollections of P. I.

Tchaikovsky') by N. N. Kondratyeva, 1940. MS. Tchaikovsky Museum.

'Iz moikh vospominany o P. I. Chaikovskom' ('My recollections of P. I. Tchaikovsky'). Talk given at Moscow State Conservatoire 11 May 1940 by A. L. Meck-Davydova. MS. Tchaikovsky Museum.

'Moi vstrechi c P. I. Chaikovskim' ('My Meetings with P. I. Tchaikovsky') by Y. M. Yurev. MS. Tchaikovsky Museum. Part published in *Zapiski* (*Memoirs*). Leningrad–Moscow, 1948.

'Souvenirs de P. I. Tchaikovski' by Fanny Durbach, 1895. MS. Tchaikovsky Museum.

'Avtobiograficheskie zametki M. I. Chaikovskogo' ('Autobiographical Notes by M. I. Tchaikovsky'). MS. Tchaikovsky Museum.

'Letters from Fanny Durbach to P. I. and M. I. Tchaikovsky and from A. A., P. I. and M. I. Tchaikovsky and A. V. Popova to Fanny Durbach'. Tchaikovsky Museum.

Extracts from letters and articles in: *Vospominania o P. I. Chaikovskom* (*Recollections of P. I. Tchaikovsky*) ed. V. V. Protopopov. Moscow, 1962, and in the Annual Reports of the Tchaikovsky Museum.

'Dni i gody P. I. Chaikovskogo: lyetopis zhizni i tvorchestva' ('Days and Years of P. I. Tchaikovsky: Annals of his Life and Work') ed. V. Yakovlev. Moscow-Leningrad, 1940.

GENERAL TITLES

Correspondence between M. A. Balakirev and N. A. Rimsky-Korsakov. *Musical Contemporary*, St. Petersburg 1915–16, 1916–17.

Correspondence between M. A. Balakirev and V. V. Stasov. Moscow, 1935.

'Correspondence between N. A. Rimsky-Korsakov and V. V. Stasov' *Russian Thought*, St Petersburg, 1910.

A. P. Borodin's *Letters*. Ed. S. A. Dyanin. 3 vols. Moscow, 1928, 1936, 1949.

V. V. Stasov *A. P. Borodin: Life, Letters and Musical Articles*. St. Petersburg, 1889.

V. V. Stasov. Pisma k rodnym (*V. V. Stasov. Letters to Relatives*). Moscow, 1958.

S. A. Dyanin. *Borodin*. Moscow, 1962 (Eng. trans. 1963).

V. V. Stasov. *Collected Works*. 4 vols. St. Petersburg, 1894, 1905.

BIBLIOGRAPHY

V. V. Stasov. *The 25th Anniversary of the Free Music School.* St. Petersburg, 1887.

V. Karenin. *Vladimir Stasov.* 2 vols. Leningrad, 1926.

C. Kui, *Musico-critical Articales.* 4 vols. St. Petersburg, 1892–5.

D. Lobanov. *Serov and His Contemporaries.* St. Petersburg, 1889.

V. S. Serova. *Alexander Nikolayevich Serov.* St. Petersburg, 1914.

A. S. Dargomyzhky. *Autobiography, Letters and Reminiscences of my Contemporaries,* Leningrad, 1922.

N. F. Findeisen. *Dargomyzhky.* Moscow, 1904.

N. N. Rimskaya-Korsakova. 'My Reminiscences of A. S. Dargomyzhsky' *Russian Tatler,* 1913.

A. N. Rimsky-Korsakov. *N. A. Rimsky-Korsakov: Life and Creative Work.* 2 vols. Moscow, 1933–5.

A. Famintsyn. 'The Recitals of Hans von Bulow'. *Musical Leaflet.* St. Petersburg, 1873–4.

G. Fedorova. *A. K. Glazunov.* Moscow and Leningrad, 1947.

N. D. Kashkin. *A History of Russian Music.* Moscow, 1908.

S. A. Dyanin. *Balakirev.* Moscow, 1958.

S. V. Rakhmaninov. *Pisma.* Moscow, 1955.

O. von Riesemann. *Rachmaninoff's Recollections.* London, 1934.

F. Shalyapin. *Ma Vie.* Paris, 1932.

K. S. (Alekseyev) Stanislavsky. *My Life in Art.* New York, 1930.

Rosa Newmarch. *The Russian Opera.* London, 1913.

M. Cooper. *Russian Opera.* London, 1952.

Michel R. Hofmann. *Un Siècle d'Opéra Russe.* Paris, 1946.

Tchaikovsky: A Symposium. Ed. Gerald Abraham. London, 1946.

BIOGRAPHIES

Modest Tchaikovsky. *Life and Letters of Pyotr Ilyich Tchaikovsky* 3 vols. Moscow, 1900–2 (Eng. trans. abridged by Rosa Newmarch, London, 1906).

Rosa Newmarch. *Tchaikovsky: His Life and Works.* London, 1900. (Revised edn. 1907).

M. D. Calvocoressi and Gerald Abraham. *Masters of Russian Music.* London, 1936.

H. Weinstock. *Tchaikovsky.* London 1946.

Index

INDEX

INDEX

Tchaikovsky, Anatoly (brother), 72, 73, 76, 118, 136, 166, 301; birth of, 24–5; devotion to T, 34, 39; career, 94, 132–3, 198, 287; T's letters to, 98, 122–3, 127, 163, 164, 166–7, 198, 221; and T's marriage, 162, 169, 171, 172; travels with T, 169, 175–6, 178; marries, 217; in Tiflis, 245–6, 247, 257, 271

Tchaikovsky, Fyodor Afanasyevich (great-grandfather), 3–4, 5

Tchaikovsky, Ilya Petrovich (father), 11, 24, 31, 40–1, 85, 88, 89, 103, 108–9, 118, 129, 194, 206; appearance and character, 4–5, 6, 9; posted to Votkinsk, 5–6; slow promotion, 5; social gifts, 6, 21, 38, 40, 42; marriages, 6; children, 6, 7–10; moves to Moscow, 20; search for work in Petersburg, 30; new home, 38–9; Director of Institute of Technology, 42, 44; suggests T take up music seriously, 44, 109; resigns post, 61; third marriage, 66; death, 201, 205

Tchaikovsky, Ippolyt ('Polya') Ilyich (brother), 9, 11, 20, 24, 41, 246; naval career, 41, 42, 94, 129

Tchaikovsky, Modest (brother), 4, 5, 11, 34, 73, 88, 91, 94, 118, 129, 135, 136, 166, 178, 184, 231, 232, 281, 285–6, 290; his biography of T, 4, 32–3, 39, 44, 105, 298, 303; birth of, 24–5; affection for T, 34, 39; T's letters to, 113, 133, 157, 158, 211, 247; escapades, 132, 133; as librettist, 213, 270, 280; and T's death, 304–5

Tchaikovsky, Nikolai Ilyich (brother), 7, 9, 11, 13, 15, 17, 40, 41, 42, 129, 295; at school, 22, 23, 31; at School of Mining, 23, 25, 29; cannot see T as 'another Glinka', 56; philistinism, 78; at T's deathbed, 305

Tchaikovsky, Pyotr Fyodorovich (grandfather), 4

Tchaikovsky, Pyotr Ilyich: family background, 3–7; birth, 7; relationship with sister, 7–8, 9, 34, 42–3, 46–7, 171–2, 187, 279–80; love of mother, 8, 18, 25–6, 32–4; early love of music, 8–9, 14–16, 18, 19; his kindness, 9, 223, 291–2, 296–7; appearance at age of eight, 10; writes song for mother, 12; childhood, 12–26; Fanny Durbach's influence on, 13–18, 19; sensitivity, 13–14, 19; music lessons, 16–17, 22–3, 24; literary efforts, 17–18, 36–7; effect of loss of Fanny, 18, 20; half-sister's grudging care of, 21–2, 23–4; at boarding school, 22; matriculates, 25; last evening with mother, 25–6; at Law School, 27–32, 35–8, 42; effect of Vakar child's death, 29; entranced by *Don Giovanni*, 29–30, 31; pursues musical interests, 31–2, 37–8, 39–40; effect of mother's death, 32–4; question of homosexuality, 32, 33; writes first waltz, 34; edits school magazine, 36–7; his school friends, 36–8, 43; in school choir, 38; his gift with children, 39–40, 44, 233–6; his piano lessons from Kundinger, 41; clerk in Ministry of Justice, 42–9, 53; a dandy, 42–4; European tour, 44–5; considers music as career, 44, 45, 46–7; capacity for work, 46, 62; study under Zaremba, 47–8; enters Conservatoire, 53, 55, 60–1; enthusiasm for Glinka, 55, 56, 57; bohemianism, 61–2; worship of Anton Rubinstein, 63, 70; meets Larosh, 63–4; his begging letters, 64–5, 102, 112; writes score for *Storm* overture, 65–6; welcomes stepmother, 66; significance of

327

INDEX

Tchaikovsky, (works): *continued*

Symphony, Sixth ('Pathetic'), 260; writing of, 290, 295, 298; première, 301, 303, 304

'Symphony, Seventh' (reconstructed concerto), 299

Tempest, The, Fantasy Overture, 115–16, 120, 152, 188, 190, 191, 236, 241, 260

Trio in A Major, 105, 216–17, 220–1, 256, 283

Undine (opera), 93, 114, 145

Vakula the Smith (opera), 127, 128, 188, 189; writing of, 118, 122, 123; wins prize, 130; failure, 141; revised as *Cherevichki*, 236

Variations on a Rococo Theme, 141–2

Variations on an Original Theme, 121, 124

Violin Concerto, 128, 213, 228, 255; writing of, 177, 183, 184, 187; first played in Vienna, 214–15; first Russian performance, 219

Voivode (opera), 76, 77, 86, 87, 88, 89, 99–100, 219; dances from, 76, 77, 78, 83; failure of, 90–2; use of celesta in, 92

Voivode (symphonic poem), 286–7

'Winter Daydreams'—*see* Symphony, First

Yevgeny Onyegin (opera), 147, 184, 190, 219, 223, 259, 268, 278, 279, 287; writing of, 157–8, 177, 179; Taneyev considers ineffective, 179–81; première, 191; Rubinstein and, 191–2, 193; analysis of, 193–4; first Bolshoi performance, 209; Tsar's interest in, 226

Yolanta (opera), 286, 287, 288, 290, 291, 293, 296, 301

Tchaikovsky, Pyotr Petrovich (uncle), 38

Tchekhov, Anton, 262, 268, 270

Tiflis, 245–8, 249, 257, 266, 271–3, 286

Tolstoy, Leo, 105, 142–3

Tower of Babel (Rubinstein), 268

transformation music, 80, 200, 294

Tristan and Isolde (Wagner), 222

Turgenyev, Ivan, 88, 105, 190, 213, 248

Ukraine, 66–7, 107, 111

Usovo, 115, 120

Vakar, Modest Alekseyevich, 25–6, 27, 28, 29–30

Venice, 106, 179

Verbovka, 128–9, 166, 184, 188, 229–30

Verdi, Giuseppe, 39, 40

Viardot, Pauline, 88, 213, 247–8, 254

Vichy, 135, 290

Vienna, 106, 141, 215, 290, 298

Voivode (Ostrovsky), 76

Von Meck, Julia Karlovna, 274, 275

Von Meck, Nadyezhda Filaretovna, 146, 147, 165, 166, 187, 189, 216, 291; T accepts commissions from, 149, 150, 151, 153, 157; history and character, 149–51, 152, 154, 160, 176–7, 272, 277; increasing interest in T, 150–6; correspondence, 150, 152–3, 154–5, 175, 176–7, 179, 180, 182, 191, 207–8, 213, 221, 223, 254, 257, 258, 268, 271, 272–4; terms of relationship, 154–6, 159–60; her loans, 155, 156, 165; T tells her of marriage, 161–2, 197; helps him to recovery, 175, 176–7; makes him allowance, 177, 213; and Fourth Symphony, 196, 197, 198–9, 205; seeks closer tie, 195–7; T saves relationship, 197; and Debussy, 200–1; breaks off relationship, 272–7, 284, 302–3

INDEX

I

F
A